The Anatomy of ashion

The Anatomy of Fashion
Dressing the Body from the Renaissance to Today

Susan J. Vincent

Oxford • New York

English edition
First published in 2009 by
Berg
Editorial offices:
First Floor, Angel Court, 81 St Clements Street, Oxford OX4 1AW, UK
175 Fifth Avenue, New York, NY 10010, USA

Berg is the imprint of Oxford International Publishers Ltd.

Library of Congress Cataloging-in-Publication Data

Vincent, Susan J.
The anatomy of fashion : dressing the body from the
renaissance to today / Susan J. Vincent. — English ed.
p. cm.
Includes bibliographical references and index.
ISBN-13: 978-1-84520-764-9 (pbk.)
ISBN-10: 1-84520-764-5 (pbk.)
ISBN-13: 978-1-84520-763-2 (cloth)
ISBN-10: 1-84520-763-7 (cloth)
1. Fashion design—History.   2. Body image—History.
3. Body, Human—Social aspects.   I. Title.
TT507.V57 2009
746.9'2—dc22
2009033056

British Library Cataloguing-in-Publication Data

A catalogue record for this book is available from the British Library.

ISBN 978 1 84520 763 2 (Cloth)
978 1 84520 764 9 (Paper)

Typeset by Apex CoVantage, LLC, Madison, WI, USA
Printed in Great Britain by the MPG Books Group, Bodmin and King's Lynn

www.bergpublishers.com

For Al—quite simply, impossible without you
and
For Tom—the most creative and energetic writer
I know
With love and thanks

CONTENTS

ILLUSTRATIONS

ABBREVIATIONS

Diary	Samuel Pepys, *The Diary of Samuel Pepys,* ed. Robert Latham and William Matthews, 11 vols (London: G. Bell) 1970–83
GM	*The Gentleman's Magazine*
LM	*The Lady's Magazine*
SRP	*Stuart Royal Proclamations,* i: *Royal Proclamations of King James I, 1603–1625,* ed. James Larkin and Paul Hughes (Oxford: Oxford University Press, 1973)
TRP	*Tudor Royal Proclamations*, ed. Paul Hughes and James Larkin, 3 vols (New Haven: Yale University Press, 1969)

PROLOGUE: APPROACHING THE PAST

One Sunday an unnamed gentleman made his way along the aisle, looking for an empty pew. The church was a fashionable one, and the congregation were all smartly dressed. It was the nineteenth century, somewhere around its middle years; the men were correct and dark figured, the ladies rustled and swayed at their sides, their brilliant skirts blooming like huge exotic flowers. For this was the age of the iridescent aniline dye, and the vast crinoline skirt that billowed and floated above its steel cage structure. Nodding here and there to an acquaintance, our gentleman settled himself comfortably. His hat, which he had removed at the door, he placed carefully on the ground beside the pew. Then he gazed about the church for a moment, glanced down at his prayer book, and looked up once more. Imagine his consternation on finding his hat had suddenly vanished; a consternation that only increased when his neighbour leaned towards him and whispered, 'The lady yonder has taken it away.' Looking quickly to where his neighbour indicated, the gentleman saw a young woman in the height of fashion and the immensity of her crinoline, sweeping her way up the aisle to her usual pew. 'What! That lady taken my hat? Impossible!' The obliging neighbour was about to recount what he had witnessed, when a pause in the lady's progress made all explanation unnecessary. Arriving at her pew, she shook the expanse of her skirt and began the careful movements required to manage it through the small space so that she could sit down. The hat, captured by the crinoline as it had passed, emerged from underneath the skirt and lay battered at her feet. Blushing furiously she entered the pew and buried her embarrassment in her prayer book. Accompanied by amused glances and titters, the equally discomforted owner of the hat made the long journey up the aisle to retrieve his sadly battered property.

This story is based on the recollections of Lady Dorothy Nevill (1826–1913). A collector of pictures, porcelain, and of people—an eclectic mix that gathered enthusiastically at her salons—Lady Dorothy also had a fondness for anecdotes.[1] In this one she specifies neither the date nor the actors' identity. We do not know where it occurred, or how she came to learn of it. Indeed, it may not even have happened. In a sense, though, none of this matters. It is a story about dress and behaviour, and even if not literally true—though I suspect it is—it shows us some of the assumptions, possibilities, connections and structures of its time. First of all, we have the church: the polite venue of fashionable display; the site where people dressed to magnify not only the Lord, but also themselves. Then there are the gendered rules that so distinctly governed what was done with hats. For women, polite behaviour in church meant keeping their bonnets on; for men, showing respect meant taking their hats off. After that come issues of bodily engagement with space. In hooped skirts, women occupied a great deal of their surroundings. Vividly coloured and vast—the circumference of a crinoline might measure over three metres—women's garments had an insistent presence. Beside them, in clothes distinguished by sobriety of cut and excellence of tailoring, men's claim on space and sight was far more muted. Then what about the crinoline and the hat that figure so centrally in the story? Would the affair have been as embarrassing if other garments were substituted, say, a cloak and a pair of gloves? Is there something about the association of the hat to the head that means the garment so often manages notions of dignity and politeness? Are there connotations here, however slight, of him having his head up her skirt?

Taking a step back from the gaffe at the heart of this narrative, let us consider less obvious connections. We might follow the development of synthetic dyes and their effects on the clothing industry, as well as their impact on visual experience. One French visitor was quite frankly appalled at the English 'want of taste' in this respect. He found the colours 'outrageously crude', 'badly matched' and 'excessively numerous', each unfortunate choice loudly 'swearing at the others'.[2] Aniline dyes had an impact, too, on notions of public health and responsible manufacturing, as it was found that when wet, small amounts of arsenic leached out of magenta-coloured fabric, and other colours were linked with skin complaints.[3] Or perhaps we could consider the renewed popularity of silk, which dyed well and displayed sheen and lustre. After the ubiquity of cotton fabrics earlier in the century, this gave a boost to a flagging industry and eased the lives of the workers and families who clustered in communities devoted to the production of this beautiful textile.[4] Then we might think about the technically innovative steel crinoline and its triumph over cane, whalebone, india rubber, or even inflatable alternatives.[5] There is a technological history waiting to be revealed by a trail of patent numbers and hopeful inventions. Then what of the workers involved in the production of such fashions? This undated Sunday service certainly took place against the backdrop of growing Victorian awareness of the human costs of capitalism. The exploitation of women and children was particularly rife in the clothing trades, and Lady Nevill, politically active and informed, would certainly have been aware of this.[6]

These are just a few ways of approaching this simple story, just some of the reflections it might trigger or areas of investigation it might suggest. It is typical of information that might be utilized in a cultural history of dress insofar as it is both far-reaching—potentially touching on many, many issues—and also profoundly limited, being but a snatch, a mere scrap, of the recollected past. Clothes are everywhere in history, but comments on them tend to be piecemeal and fleeting. As with any historical investigation, commentary needs to be carefully scrutinized for bias, or underlying beliefs. The view of reality held by the diverse texts and images we might call on varies greatly. Satire dwells on extremity and the ridiculous, while personal experience, as narrated through letters, diaries and memoirs, might tell us nothing beyond an individual's eccentricities. Disapproval usually hides a particular moral agenda; manuals of etiquette and behaviour offer a theoretical and ideal standard that might reflect cultural preoccupations more than actual conduct; and paintings, of course, employ their own idealizing techniques and motifs. And any given comment used in evidence might be freighted with not one, but a number of purposes or assumptions. Each of these offers a view of the past that is partial, incomplete and possibly misleading.

Of course, this is so obvious as to barely need stating. Evidence is always approached with a judicious caution over its 'truth' value. Or perhaps not. There is something about fashion that makes many scholars suspend, if not their disbelief, then their critical edge. Sources are not infrequently accepted at face value, with little reflection on either their context or credibility. Instead, modern research latches on to extremity and the atypical, and with a fascination sets about unearthing grubby tendencies and disgusting predilections. It is difficult not to feel that the academic tone at these times is both ghoulish and disapproving. There is, indeed, an interesting resonance here between modern scholarship and contemporary satire and moral discourse. Modern commentary also makes a speciality of sliding in belittling descriptors, slipping them under the readers' gaze unnoticed amidst more measured discussion. Fashions get labelled as 'ridiculous', 'absurd', 'unhealthy', 'uncomfortable': judgements that say more about our values than what the wearers of these garments necessarily felt.[7]

Perhaps this is because fashions from the past can seem strange and odd—so much so that it can be hard to take the wearers seriously. In contrast to the art, music and literature of our cultural heritage, the clothing renders its wearers somehow less intelligent, less rational, less sexy, less like us. Historical dress marks alterity, and it is this otherness that I primarily hope this book will address. I want to examine historical fashion and try to understand it in its own terms and within the context of its own chronological moment. I want to retrieve the normality behind such things as powdered wigs, hooped skirts and the flamboyant codpiece. This book aims, therefore, to bring the unfamiliar closer, to diminish the distance between the past and us. Simultaneously, however, I also hope that this book will push at the present, edging it further away so that we can scrutinize a bit more effectively what it is that we do. By placing ourselves into a historical view, we can contextualize and critique our own habits of dress. Doing so will help us appreciate the contingent nature of our beliefs and aesthetics, and may reveal a little of the strangeness that lies at the heart of our normality.

The discussion in these pages is neither chronological nor complete. This is not a survey but rather, if you like, a series of snapshots, or perhaps invitations to view. The focus is up close, revealing one body part at a time. By screening out the rest, the work of dress—as it shapes, celebrates or perhaps disregards our different physical 'bits'—becomes clear. Every generation is born to this same anatomical legacy; how they then fashion it with clothing is, in miniature, the story of culture. At different times over the centuries, our response to the challenge of appearance has been visually exciting, sometimes disturbing, complex and, above all, creative. Fashion has also been—will always be—playful, insubordinate, uncontrollable. It is never serious, though it may be important; it is empty of absolute meaning, though it may contain messages.[8]

We will never be able to answer satisfactorily the why of fashion: why did Victorian women adopt crinolines? Why did Elizabethans favour ruffs? Why did wigs hold, or for that matter lose, ascendancy? In a sense, why is not even a meaningful question to ask; or at the very least, not a helpful one. Certainly, changing fashions are connected with wider cultural imperatives. The effect of specific social conditions is to make certain styles not just unwearable, but literally unthinkable. The aesthetic expressed by the clothing of the 1920s and 1930s, for instance, could never have found form in an earlier era, for it rests upon a raft of beliefs and technologies specific to its time. 'However, while fashions are coherent with their social conditions, there is no necessary relationship between these conditions and the particularity of fashionable forms. Indeed, the origin of these forms lies in such a tangled conflation of cultural context and individual agency as to be irretrievable. Almost inevitably, therefore, trying to answer the why of dress gives a prescriptive and static response that ties it to accounts of class, gender, aesthetics or technology, and leaves out the experiences and understandings of those long-lost wearers who embodied the fashion in the first place. Instead, 'dress needs to be understood as a situated practice that is the result of complex social forces and individual negotiations in daily life'.[9] What we can do then—as with our story of the crinoline and the hat—is mine the garments on the body for meanings that wearers and viewers might have ascribed to them, for the feelings they may have promoted, and the resonances and connections that they might suggest. Above all, our explanations must not be reductive. Our analysis needs to aspire to the proliferation and playfulness of fashion itself.

1   HEAD AND NECK

DIGNITY AND WIGS

1663. Two years after Charles II's triumphant return as the English monarch, the unspeakable horror of the plague yet two years in the future with the Great Fire to come after that, and Samuel Pepys was facing a personal dilemma. He wanted to try wearing a wig, but lacked the resolution to cut off his hair. While two years earlier he had been very particular about how it was trimmed, 'finding that the length of it doth become me very much', by May 1663 he was experiencing such difficulty keeping it clean that he began to consider a wig instead. However, despite trying on two or three at Jervase the barber's, he remained undecided. His havering carried on through the summer months of June, July and August, until finally at the end of this month he borrowed a wig from Jervase to try at home. Unfortunately he returned it still with his mind not made up, still with 'no great desire or resolution yet to wear one. And so I put it off for a while.' His indecision continued for a further two months until in October, having settled with his wife that the advancement of his career depended on 'better garbe ... and other things modish, and a perruque', he finally determined to buy one. However, it was not for a further five days, having visited Jervase and been much displeased with a wig there 'of greazy and old woman's haire', that he at last himself visited 'one or two Periwegg shops'. He settled on having 'one very handsomely made'. In the event he ordered two. Perhaps, as with modern opticians, a second, cheaply priced 'spare' was an inducement; or perhaps he ordered the wig that cost £3 for best, and a 40 shilling one for more ordinary use. This was part of the relatively high expenditure on his clothing that month of £55, the result of his plan to dress more sharply to cut more of a figure in the world. In Pepys's words, 'I hope I shall with more comfort labour to get more, and with better successe then when, for want of clothes, I was forced to sneak like a beggar'—surely the seventeenth-century equivalent of our heartfelt, if exaggerated complaint, 'I had nothing to wear.'

On 2 November, just the day before Chapman, the maker, delivered the wig, Pepys overheard a bit of chat at Whitehall that must have greatly encouraged him. While walking in the long gallery 'I heard the Duke [of York] say that he was going to wear a perriwigg' and, what is more, 'they say the King also will'.[1] Undoubtedly reassured by this, the following day when Chapman arrived, 'without more ado'—though it is hard to imagine that he could have taken any longer—'I went up and there he cut off my haire'. Pepys immediately put on his new wig and, after showing it to the maids, went straight to the coffee house. Rather to his annoyance, his colleague Sir William Penn went on and on about it—in Pepys's words he 'observed mightily and discoursed much'—yet Pepys assumed Sir William would soon get used to it. He was perfectly right, for the next day his diary entry states that at the office 'no great matter made of my periwig, as I was afeared there would'. However, it was still with some trepidation, or perhaps self-consciousness, that he finally made his appearance at church on Sunday, 8 November. 'I found that my coming in a perriwigg did not prove so strange to the world as I was afeared it would, for I thought that all the church would presently [immediately] have cast their eye all upon me—but I found no such thing.'[2] Over six months after he had first started to revolve the matter in his diary, Pepys had finally achieved the faultless and self-effacing correctness that is the mark of being in fashion.[3]

Pepys did not regret his slow, but finally decisive, transformation. It is true that two years later, planning to wear his own hair once more, he grew it long; but it came to nothing. 'I find the convenience of Perrywiggs is so great, that I have cut of all short again, and will keep to periwigs.'[4] This is not to say that wig wearing was entirely straightforward. For a start, wigs required care and maintenance, such as combing, cleaning, setting and mending, and Pepys records visiting the barber for this purpose.[5] He also notes buying a case for his periwig at the trunk makers.[6] Further trouble arose in July 1664 when, unsurprisingly, he was annoyed at having to have a new wig, presumably made of lousy hair, cleansed of its nits; as it turned out, a perennial problem with Jervase's merchandise.[7] While this sounds repellent to us, parenthetically we must remember that dealing with regular infestations of head lice is today a routine problem for most parents of primary-school-aged children. A cursory glance at the shelves of any pharmacy reveals an array of products developed to kill these ever more resistant parasites, yet leave their young human hosts unharmed. For Pepys though, after nearly five years of keeping 'my perriwigs in good order', he hit on the happy notion of paying his barber a flat fee of 20 shillings a year to do it for him, so 'I am like to go very spruce, more then I used to do'.[8] Unfortunately, the problem of a wig's provenance, encountered in the form of Jervase's nit-infested wares, was to become considerably more acute. In a diary entry of September 1665 Pepys noted first wearing a particular wig, which although purchased some time earlier, he had dared not put on for fear it was infected by the plague. 'And it is a wonder', he mused, 'what will be the fashion after the plague is done as to periwigs, for nobody will dare to buy any haire for fear of the infection—that it had been cut off of the heads of people dead of the plague.'[9] Pepys's unease at the chilling intimacy of this fashion brings into focus the ambivalent nature of the wig. It is owned by the wearer, yet its hair belongs to someone else. It is an item of dress, yet it is also a body part. The hair is natural, yet it is crafted into a garment of artifice.[10] In a negotiation that adds further shading to this complexity, when Chapman first cut off Pepys's hair to fit his wig, the wig maker took the hair away with him 'to make up another of'. Intriguingly, whether Chapman was to make a wig for Pepys with Pepys's own hair, or for another customer, we do not know. Nor do we know whether Chapman paid Pepys for it, or whether Pepys gained a discount on the cost of his wig by, in effect, trading in his own hair for somebody else's.[11]

The traffic in human hair was, of course, an inevitable consequence of the fashion for wigs, although cheap ones could always be made of inferior substitutes like horsehair or wool. In 1747, R. Campbell noted that 'hair merchants' were the principal tradesmen with whom wig makers dealt, and that they sourced their hair from both England and abroad.[12] In 1782, hairdresser James Stewart commented that 'Hair makes a very considerable article in commerce', saying that it sold for between 5 shillings and £5 per ounce, depending on the quality. He also explained that its tubes may retain part of the humours of the body on which it grew, which is why all hair from abroad was required by the government to be quarantined 'for fear of its bringing the plague, or any other terrible disease'.[13] Over fifty years later, around 1836, a Brighton hairdresser offered the young Georgiana Sitwell £20 for her long fair hair, which fell in curls to below her waist.[14] Hair such as hers, cut from the head of a healthy virgin, was the most desirable of commodities. Intriguingly, the recent fashion for extensions has meant that the provenance of hair and the conditions of its trade have again become something of an issue. As one celebrity magazine notes of the particular extensions favoured by some fashionistas (costing £1,500 for a full head), they come from 'the only extensions company to source, manufacture and process their own hair, making them 100 per cent traceable and far more ethical than many other brands'.[15]

The story of Pepys's gradual change, as by degrees he learnt to think of wearing a wig as desirable, appropriate and normal, occurs at the very beginning of the period in England during which the wig was fashionable. Although known before, they were usually worn to disguise grey or thinning hair, as, most famously, by Elizabeth I.[16] It was not until the Restoration court of the 1660s brought from France the idea of wigs as fashionable that the thing really took off. Nor was it a short-lived phenomenon. For about a hundred years the wig was ubiquitous, appearing on nearly every fashionable head. Although in 1765 the wig makers petitioned George III to grant them relief 'in consideration of their distressed condition occasioned by so many people wearing their own hair', the wig continued to exercise its remarkably tenacious influence.[17] Thus, while it was perfectly acceptable for a gentleman to wear his own hair, others were equally at liberty to prefer a wig, or even a combination of the two. Moreover, the looks achieved by these variations on dressing the head were, if not identical, then extremely similar; and certainly, in viewing contemporary pictures and portraits, it is not always possible to tell hair grown by the wearer from hair that he had purchased.

Gradually, however, over the latter part of the century the status of the wig declined, though it continued to be worn by more conservative gentlemen and remained a requirement of the legal, medical and clerical professions. Lady Dorothy Nevill, looking back from an Edwardian vantage point, remembered that in her childhood 'there were still men living who had not abandoned the eighteenth-century fashion of wearing a wig', and that 'some old-fashioned people' continued to wear them as late as the 1830s.[18] The habit persisted even longer amongst the higher clergy. In a letter to her daughter, Lady Sarah Lyttelton (1787–1870) described the christening of Victoria's second son, Prince Alfred, who was born 6 August 1844. Just after the ceremony his elder brother—the future Edward VII, then nearly three—after getting no answer from two or three other adults, went up to the Archbishop and said, 'What is that you have got upon your head?' The Archbishop, to the amusement of those within earshot, stooped down to the little boy and replied gently, 'It is called a wig.'[19] A debate over the last instance of clerical wig wearing was conducted in the pages of *The Times* in 1925. The consensus of personal recollection, supported by pictorial evidence, was that Archbishop Sumner wore a wig for formal occasions, at least until 1862 when photographed at the opening ceremony of that year's International Exhibition.[20] The discarding of wigs by those in positions of respect, although unproblematic to us, was not universally approved: 'For many years, indeed, people of the old school considered this innovation a most undignified change.'[21] As these recollections show, what we commonly think of as a particularly peculiar and pointless habit of dress actually lasted for nearly two hundred years. Indeed, wig wearing has never entirely gone away, its practice by lawyers and judges today being the ossified and vestigial remains of late-seventeenth- and eighteenth-century fashionability.

This fashionability was a very clearly gendered one. Wigs were male garments, and offered men choices of role and persona. The largest wigs, familiar from Restoration and early-seventeenth-century portraits, were known as full-bottomed (see cover image). Queue wigs had long hair at the back arranged in various ways: for example, the tye wig held the hair with a bow; the pigtail bound the long queue with ribbon; in the bag wig, as the name suggests, the hair was contained in a black silk bag. Lady Mary Coke (1726–1811), the redoubtable and long-lived youngest daughter of the Duke of Argyll, described an impoverished gentlewoman who 'gets what money She can by making bags for Mens' hair'. The woman, so Lady Mary wrote in her journal, was applying to her for 'the Money to pay for some silk'. In his memoirs, servant John Macdonald (b. 1741) mentions a silk bag shop in Old Bond Street in 1768, also saying, incidentally, that this was where Lawrence Sterne was taken ill, dying a short time later.[22] The 'snug bob, or natty scratch'[23] were informal wigs, the Ramillies had military pretensions, and the Campaign had three tails to it. Each variety had a name and a connotation, a good deal of which is lost on modern viewers but was rich in significance to contemporaries (Figures 1 and 32). 'All conditions of men were distinguished by the cut of the wig', or so wrote James Stewart, author of the eighteenth-century hairdressing treatise *Plocacosmos*.[24] J.T. Smith (1766–1833) described Mr Caleb Whitefoord, a man about town with literary and artistic connections, as one 'who never ventured abroad but with a full determination to be noticed', and whose flamboyance blossomed in his Garrick wig, with five curls on each side.[25] Playwright Richard Cumberland (1732–1811) reminisced about the rather larger-than-life statesman George Bubb Dodington:

> [H]is bulk and corpulency gave full display to a vast expanse and profusion of brocade and embroidery, and this, when set off with an enormous tye-perriwig and deep laced ruffles, gave the picture of an ancient courtier in his gala habit ... nevertheless it must

Figure 1 'Wigs', etching published by Matthew Darly, 1773, © Trustees of the British Museum. Fourteen caricature heads, each wearing a different type of wig. These include the pigtail queue (top row, middle); the bag wig (middle row, far left); the full-bottomed (middle row, third from left); the campaign wig (middle row, far right); and the bob (bottom row, far left).

be confessed this style, though out of date, was not out of character, but harmonized so well with the person of the wearer, that I remember when he made his first speech in the House of Peers as Lord Melcombe [created 1761], all the flashes of his wit, all the studied phrases and well-turned periods of his rhetoric lost their effect simply because the orator had laid aside his magisterial tye, and put on a modern bag wig, which was as much out of costume upon the broad expanse of his shoulders, as a cue [queue] would have been upon the robes of the Lord Chief Justice.[26]

Thus there were wigs 'to suit the several offices and stations of life'.[27] Pepys may have had something like this in mind when shopping at a periwig maker's shop in 1667: 'there bought me two periwigs, mighty fine; endeed, too fine I thought for me; but he persuaded me'.[28] Satire, however, makes clear that others had no such qualms. A typical example is a burlesque poem called, simply enough, *The wig*.[29] Published in 1765—the same year the wig makers, alarmed at their falling trade, petitioned the king—it ridicules, and seeks to expose, bishops, the clergy, doctors, judges and attorneys. The poem says that wigs confer a spurious authority on these figures and misleadingly imply the wearer is both honest and skilful. The author insists that the 'vast tow'ring ornament of hair' thus enables these professions to make money at their clients' cost—dressing becomes a kind of confidence trick, with the wig as the chief prop.

The descriptors in this poem—'sage', 'grave', 'solemn' and 'formal'—leave no doubt as to the wig's principal meaning for contemporaries. It was the sartorial symbol of masculine authority; or to borrow from writer and reformer Hannah More (1745–1833), we get 'a wise-looking man in great wig'.[30] Charles II, we are told, adopted a full-bottomed wig 'to give him a more majestic physiognomy, and procure him respect'. Physicians dressed in large tye wigs 'to give them an air of gravity and importance'.[31] However, as both *The wig* and More's comment show, this meaning was simultaneously endorsed and refused. It was accepted both that wigs signalled dignity and status *and* that for any individual this might be an empty signal. The semiotics of the wig were an open secret, the echoes of which still sound in the mildly contemptuous term *bigwig*, whose origins the *Oxford English Dictionary* dates to 1731, right slap in the middle of the wig's ascendancy. Most noteworthy from our point of view though, is the lack of negative comment about the garment itself. Wearers might be satirized (the right wig on the wrong head), or extremity (the wrong wig on the wrong head), but seldom the idea itself. During the heyday of wigs, any strangeness in a man cutting off his own hair so that he could wear that cut from another's head just didn't get seen. Wig wearing was so normal, so accepted by the holders of cultural authority, as to be beyond critique. Even that most caustic of publications *The Spectator,* with its self-imposed mission to flay the ridiculous and uphold rational decorum, failed to register the wig as a satirical target. Compared with the many pages devoted to women's dress, Addison and Steele's comments, although tongue-in-cheek, were positively benign: 'I have indeed my self observed that my Banker ever bows lowest to me when I wear my full-bottom'd Wig' (Figure 2).[32]

It might be that this garment escaped censure because of its masculine ownership. This is not to say false hair was never worn by women; as we shall see, it was an essential part of many elaborate coiffures. However, full wigs were worn by women only to redress some deficiency, making good what nature, age or illness had denied them. Satire made wig-wearing women grotesque; real life found them unfortunate or amusing. Thus it was that the appearance of Lady Compton, an elderly acquaintance of Mary Coke's, became something of a long-running joke. 'I wish Lady Margaret Compton wou'd wear a better Wig', wrote Mary Coke in 1768. 'I never saw such a one, excepting upon a stick to frighten away the birds.' The following year she continued, 'Lady Marg^t Compton was the first that went away, & the rest of us very uncharitably laugh'd a good deal at her periwig, which was worse that day then usual. She is a worthy Woman & I esteem her, but why She will wear such a cruel bad Wig, when better are to be had, I cannot imagine.' The year after saw an improvement—'Ly Margaret Compton came in with a new well powder'd perriwig; I hope She'll keep it for next winter'—however, neither improvement nor wig stood the test of time. Comfortably gossiping four years later with Princess Amelia (1711–86), the second daughter of George II, Lady Mary observed that Lady Margaret had been robbed three times. Known for her blunt outspokenness, Amelia replied that she wished Lady Compton

Figure 2 'Joseph Addison', mezzotint by John Smith after Sir Godfrey Kneller, 1700–19(?), © Trustees of the British Museum. Addison (1672–1719) wears a full-bottomed wig rising into two horns on either side of a centre parting. This style was fashionable from the 1660s into the early years of the eighteenth century, and was thereafter reserved for more ceremonial or formal use.

The R! Hon.ble Joseph Addison Esq.
one of his Majesty's Secretaryis of State.

'had pulled off her wig & dash'd it in the highwayman's face'. Mary agreed, for 'it indeed seems fitter for that purpose then any other, for it is worse then ever'.[33]

The dignity and gravitas ascribed to a man in a wig probably had something to do with its physical size and weight, and how the head supporting it moved slowly and with deliberation. In addition, wigs were costly, particularly the larger and more elaborate styles.[34] A big, heavy and expensive fashion, then, is almost certain to carry connotations of authority. As a garment in which status, expense and portability met together, it is not surprising to find that wigs were stolen. We are told that Mary Nollekens (1742/3–1817; wife of the eighteenth-century sculptor, Joseph) used to relate that 'gentlemen were continually annoyed, and frequently robbed of their wigs in the open street and in mid-day'. She described the method as follows:

> A man dressed like a baker, bending beneath a large loaded bread-basket, which he had hoisted upon his shoulders, waited until the first gentleman wearing a costly wig was about to turn the corner of a street in a crowded thoroughfare; and then, just as an accomplice ran forcibly against him, a boy concealed in the baker's basket, knocked off the gentleman's gold-laced hat, and instantly snatched his wig. Whilst the gentleman was stooping to pick up his hat, the fictitious baker made off, with his dexterous assistant, till he came to the first convenient turning, where he released the boy, who walked away

with his booty neatly folded up in a schoolboy's satchel, which he threw carelessly over his shoulder, as if going to school.[35]

Although cited by subsequent scholars, the frequency of this method, or even its likelihood, seems a little dubious.[36] Contemporary newspapers, however, can give us a more reliable sense of more typical wig theft. Mr Corbett, a coach maker, 'was knocked down and robbed of his Hat and wig by two Foot pads in clifford-street, Burlington Gardens'.[37] Two unnamed men 'suffer'd in the same manner at the back of Islington'. Footpads, 'not content with their Money, strip'd one of them of a new Suit of Cloaths, carried off the Hat and Wig of the other, and stabb'd one of them in the Leg for attempting to follow them'.[38] James Boswell, the diarist (1740–95), reported having his stolen while sharing a room at an inn in the Lake District.[39] Equally illustrative of the wig's financial value, but much more public spirited, is an advertisement placed in 1721: 'Fo[u]nd on the 27th of May last, being Whitson Eve, at Highwood-Hill in Hendon Parish, a Perriwig; if the Person that owns it will come to Charles Shuckburgh, Grocer, at the White Hart and Sugar Loaf against Cheapside Conduit, and describe the Sort of Wig, and the Maker, and pay the Charge of the Advertisement, shall have the Wig.'[40]

Partly, no doubt, because they did represent a considerable investment, owners generally took care to maintain a wig's appearance. Pepys took his to be cleaned and mended as required, before arranging with his barber for regular maintenance to keep them 'spruce'. Most commonly, wigs needed to be reset, weather and wear having caused the curls and buckle (from the French *boucle*, 'curl, lock') to drop. In selling a wig, the maker thus anticipated a continuing relationship with the wearer, as the latter returned repeatedly to have his purchase cleaned, combed and curled. This 'regenerative potential' enabled the wig's full value to unfold over time.[41] Customers were not bound to return, however. Peruke makers always hoped to glean new trade by maintaining wigs bought elsewhere. The following advertisement, probably printed in London in 1725, illustrates the kinds of services and the competitive marketplace generated by the demand for wigs:

At the BLUE PERUKE in *Red-Lion-street, White-Chappel,* liveth THO. BARKER, Peruke maker, who maketh all Sorts of new Work, well and fashionable, at very low Prices.

AND He having obtained the greatest Art that ever yet was found out for sweating of Wigs, tho' never so much out of Curl, by which means he causes them to hold a lasting Curl, as well as when first made: He also brings the Hair, if never so high coloured, to a fine pale Colour, which no one can do except himself. He having done many, to the Satisfaction of all the Gentlemen that have try'd his great Performances, they advised him to publish this Advertisement for the good of all Gentlemen. His Days of sweating are *Tuesdays* and *Fridays,* and he sends them home the next Day. His prices are Two Shillings and Six Pence for each Bob, and Three Shillings and Six Pence for a Tye, and Three Shillings a Pig-Tail. Any Gentleman that are at a Distance from him, if they please to write a Penny-Post Letter, he will send for their Wig or Wigs.

If any other propose this, they are Pretenders.[42]

If having to maintain a wig was something of a chore, it was quicker and easier for the wearer than having to sit while his own hair was combed, powdered and dressed. This, then, might partly account for Pepys experiencing wigs as so greatly 'convenient'. The garment was simply taken off, sent to be cleaned and reset, and another worn in its place. As a hairdressing manual of 1770 put it, echoing Pepys, 'some prefer them ... for convenience, as they can be dress'd ready to put on, and save that time they would be obliged to spend in having their natural hair dress'd'.[43] Wigs were also removed for sleeping, an advantage not enjoyed either by men with their own hair or women, who, before retiring, might have to contend with their elaborately dressed heads. Furthermore, a wig wearer with his own hair shaved or cut short had no difficulty in keeping himself clean— something that Pepys, at the start of this chapter, had found irksome. But the wig's benefits extended beyond time management and hygiene. While being worn, a wig kept out the cold. For us, it is perhaps less easy to appreciate the value of being warm. Our homes, workplaces and spaces of leisure are all well heated, as is our transport between them. We have umbrellas—whose adoption in England some memoirists record with real thankfulness[44]—and waterproof fabrics. Most fundamentally, and we will return to this later, we have a different understanding of ill health and physical vulnerability. For us, cold is a temporary discomfort. For much of the past, cold was a danger. This was why Pepys wrote about his 'great Cold', which 'I did lately get with leaving off my periwigg'.[45] Over a hundred years later in 1787, when wigs were rather more staid and rather less fashionable, the convenience of warmth was apparently the sole reason motivating Mr Papendiek's decision to wear one. He and his wife held positions at the court of George III. In her memoirs, Charlotte (1765–1839) explained that 'Mr. Papendiek had long threatened to wear a wig, as his head was bald at the top, and he complained of the cold, and now, in spite of all my remonstrances, he was determined, and did carry his threat into execution.' The young Charlotte, no admirer of perukes, complained that he 'looked older, his fine forehead was hidden, and his beauty greatly diminished by this horrid wig. I said it even lessened my love for him.' Mr Papendiek, however, was inexorable, and comfort triumphed over spousal preference. Although she continued 'long to grieve at it', Charlotte could nevertheless enjoy the funnier side to her husband's wig wearing. Unused to the sensation, for two or three mornings running Mr Papendiek, 'not feeling the cold as before, he forgot his hat at starting'. He had to step back for it, Charlotte wrote, 'to the amusement of us all'.[46] What were felt to be these physical advantages of wig wearing outlasted the garment's significations of fashion or status. Georgiana Sitwell, born in 1824, remembered the parish church of her childhood: 'The old clerk wore a yellow Welsh wig in winter to keep his head warm.'[47]

Worn on the right head, the wig thus managed a range of related notions: propriety, gravitas, control, manliness, wisdom, reason. Warm, convenient and facilitating personal hygiene into the bargain, it becomes easier to appreciate why the fashion for wigs lasted so long. It is also easier to understand an anecdote recounted by the writer and journalist John Taylor (1752–1832). Sometime in the early 1780s Taylor went to a mental institution to see the once-successful actor and theatre manager Samuel Reddish. Taylor described the painful alteration in Reddish's state, and explained that his insanity had developed 'soon after an unlucky occurrence at Covent Garden'. He had come to grief while in the part of Hamlet and performing the fencing scene; the actor playing Laertes had 'made so clumsy a lunge, that he struck off the bagwig of Hamlet, and exposed his bald pate to the laughter of the audience'. The mortification, Taylor continued, made so strong an impression on Reddish's mind that not only did he never return to the stage, he finally ended his days in the York Ayslum.[48] At the heart of this brief, tragi-comic story lies the significance of a man appearing in a public space without his wig. To be without it indicated extremity, eccentricity or perhaps even madness; to lose it unwillingly was to lose face and lie open to derision and contempt.

These two aspects—extremity and derision—appear repeatedly in the sources, in varying shades of emotional colour and sometimes intertwining. From the wronged wife who threw her straying husband's wig in the fire; through Boswell, whose stolen wig made him 'an object of laughter'; to the doctor's emergency visit to the Papendieks in 'no wig, slippers, and dressing gown', the wig's absence constituted a departure from the polite and rational public code.[49] The memoirs of Sophia Baddeley, Margaret Leeson and Ann Sheldon provide us with particularly vivid illustrations of this. These three women were all on the edge of society. Independent, both socially and sexually, they all at some point survived financially by selling sex, and all claimed a voice in the public sphere—two by publishing autobiographies with which they entertained and outraged the polite world, the third with her career on the stage.[50] Perhaps their position on the outside, the very opposite to that occupied by the authoritative male wig wearer, made them more ready to ridicule this garment gone awry. There is certainly a gleeful tone in their retelling of their stories. The first comes from Ann Sheldon, who describes teasing a lover, a Dutch merchant whose particularity about his appearance she clearly could not resist sending up. When 'drinking tea at a public place, and in company with several other persons', Ann took off his wig and threw it, 'in all the pride of bag and buckle, into a tub of water'. He was so offended with her that he left immediately, and she never saw him again. While Ann's 'mad-cap fit' lost her a source of income, she seems not to have been overly repentant.[51] In Margaret Leeson's (1727–97) memoirs, the affront is carried a stage further. In July 1791 she and a party of other courtesans, or 'first-rate impures', took a summer excursion out of the city. At a tavern they met with a party of men in the printing trade, one of whom made 'amorous advances'. Margaret's escort took exception to this and, in the course of a scuffle, pulled off the other's wig, a brown bob. He threw it to another of the party, Fanny Beresford, who 'instantly went aside' and pee'd in it. Having filled the wig 'with the briny produce of her luscious fountain', Fanny returned it to Margaret's escort, who unknowingly thrust it into his breeches pocket. Finding 'his privities' wet and chilled, in a rage he threw the wig into a stream where it was carried off, never to be recovered by its unfortunate owner. Rather, 'he was obliged to return to town with an handkerchief tied about his bald pericranium, to the no small diversion of the company'.[52]

The story from actress and singer Sophia Baddeley's biography (1745?–86) shows us the wig's absence in extremis. Sophia had the tale from her lover, Lord Melbourne. As he told it, he had just bought Holland House in Piccadilly for £16,000. The steward who was to receive the payment waited on Lord Melbourne, and being given the bank notes 'he put them in his pocket-book', which he then lay on the table while he signed a receipt. The unlucky steward then went, leaving the pocketbook behind. He had other business elsewhere that day, and did not notice that his pocketbook—and the £16,000 payment it contained—was missing until undressing for bed. Understandably 'in a fit of distraction at his loss', he immediately retraced his steps, visiting every place he had been that day. In his haste and 'frantic wildness', however, 'he forgot his wig, and came without it'. Going first to Lord Melbourne's he pushed his way upstairs to where Lady Melbourne was sitting. 'Alarmed at seeing a strange man entering her room *bare-headed,* at that time of night, for it was near twelve, she screamed.' Of course, Lord Melbourne came and returned the pocketbook to the steward, whose joy, as the text says, 'may be better conceived than described'.[53]

POLITE HAIR

Running in tandem with the fashion for wigs was a fashion for elaborate hair. Much of the technology for styling the two was identical; indeed, wearers whose own hair was insufficiently long or thick to sustain particular arrangements wore additional hair of various specialized sorts. There were top pieces for the crown, borders for the front, curls, neck braids, and chignons or lengths at the back; all of which we now call hairpieces and extensions. This complex presentation of the head was practised by both men and women. The aesthetic thus made little distinction between the status of the hair or the gender of the wearer. Male, female, real, false—it didn't much matter. What was of importance was the level of craft, refinement and skilled intervention. The aim was not to look 'natural', but styled. Just as an individual's intellect, manners and taste were improved by training and education, eighteenth-century hair was similarly improved. In effect, hair participated in civilized society; dressed hair was 'polite' hair.[54]

This aesthetic reached its apogee in women's hairstyles of the 1770s—the big hair era, when coiffures were very tall, extremely elaborate and frequently ornamented with feathers, flowers or pearls.[55] As a commentator in *The Gentleman's Magazine* remarked, 'such bushes of hair as the ladies bore upon their heads in the last and present year (1773)! bushes so enormous, that they seemed to require the tonsure of a gardener's sheers, instead of scissars, to reduce them to tolerable dimensions!'[56] Big hair provided a rich vein for visual satire in particular, and it was mined to the full, the cartoonists' imagination rioting with the absurdity of sausage curls as telescopes, hairdressers perched atop ladders and pyramids of hair adorned with a cornucopia of produce, and even gardeners to tend it (Figures 3 and 22).[57] Print after print appeared of fashionable ladies dwarfed by the vast, towering edifice of their hair.

Big hair also attracted unfavourable comment from less extreme channels. '[N]othing can be conceived so absurd, extravagant, and fantastical, as the present mode of dressing the

Figure 3 'The Flower Garden', etching published by Matthew Darly, 1777, © Trustees of
the British Museum. A satire on big hair. On
top of the lady's enormous headdress is a
hedged garden accessed by a gate or stile.
A gardener with a rake (right) stands ready
to tend the formal beds. In true eighteenth-
century style, a circular temple lies at the top
of the garden (left) with a statue of Mercury
on its roof. The whole of the headdress is
draped with trailing flowers.

head', wrote Hannah More to her sister in 1775, finding it, she claimed, even as disfiguring
as smallpox. The next year, she continued, 'Again I am annoyed by the foolish absurdity of
the present mode of dress. Some ladies carry on their heads a large quantity of fruit, and yet
they would despise a poor useful member of society, who carried it there for the purpose of
selling it for bread.' The following year found her more humorous, but equally damning: 'I
protest I hardly do them justice, when I pronounce that they had, amongst them, on their
heads, an acre and a half of shrubbery, besides slopes, grass-plats, tulip-beds, clumps of
peonies, kitchen-gardens, and green-houses.'[58] More's acerbic commentary, however, was
far from being impartial. As a moral reformer she was opposed to an excess that she judged
in ethical terms. When likening big hair to smallpox, she actually preferred the ravages of
the disease. Smallpox may, she wrote, 'be greater in its consequences', but the disfigurement of fashionable hair 'is more corrupt in its cause'.[59]

Poet Samuel Rogers (1763–1855) recollected that in his youth, the ladies' dressed hair
was 'of a truly preposterous size'. 'I have gone to Ranelagh', he said, 'in a coach with a lady
who was obliged to sit upon a stool placed at the bottom of the coach, the height of her
head-dress not allowing her to occupy the regular seat.'[60] This—the lady on the floor of the
coach—is a common trope, recurring in antifashion texts, satirical prints, and the work of
some subsequent scholars (Figure 4). Mary Coke recounted it as a gossipy anecdote for her

sister, telling her that the headdresses in Paris had run to excess and '*it was said* the other day that two Ladies were obliged to kneel down in their Coach'.[61] It is just one of many recurring and recycled stories about fashionable extremity that prove so tenacious because they are bizarre, funny and memorable. Basically, people *want* to believe them. Lady Mary's choice of words, however, makes it clear that the Parisian whisperings were an anonymous rumour, and the inclusion of a similar tale in a collection of the remembered highlights of Rogers's after-dinner chat certainly needs to be treated with some caution. The context is one of amusing anecdotes, told—and recalled—for their humour and entertainment. Other of the stories within the collection are undoubtedly exaggerated. If this one is literally true, it certainly does not describe a typical and ordinary occurrence.

Comment more reliably indicative of everyday experience must be sought elsewhere. Mary Coke, for instance, when staying in Vienna, taught an English dance to the Austrian court. She explained in her journal, written daily for her sister, that one evening the Empress had ordered this to be performed, 'but desired they wou'd leave out that part of the

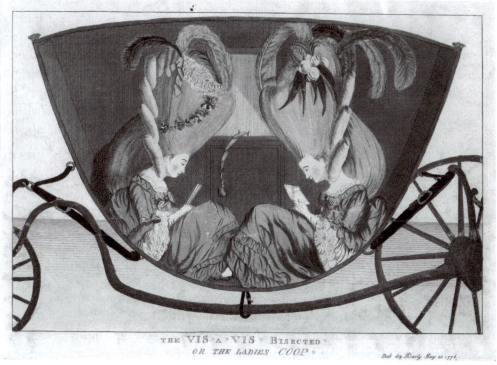

THE VIS·A·VIS· BISECTED·
OR THE LADIES COOP·

Pub by MDarly May 26, 1776.

Figure 4 'The Vis a Vis or the Ladies Coop', hand-coloured engraving published by Matthew Darly, 1776, © Trustees of the British Museum. A satire on big hair. A carriage is cut in half lengthwise to reveal the two occupants sitting on the floor to accommodate their outsized headdresses. One of them holds a fan (left), the other a 3d subscription to the Pantheon, the famous assembly rooms that housed masquerades and concerts. The hair of the lady on the left is adorned with lace, ribbon, feathers and flowers. The figure on the right carries feathers and vegetables in her hair.

Ladys passing under the arms of the Gentlemen, as it discomposed the Ladys head dress: some of them had complained the diamond pins had run into their heads'. A little over a week later the dance was performed again. This time the Empress 'approved the change I had made. It was much better She said then the ladies spoiling their headdress.'[62] Of the English court, Charlotte Papendiek remembered that the ordinary mode of dressing the hair used a 'high *toupée*, large *chignon*, and pinned curls'.[63] Looking back from a much later date, she thought it unbecoming to most people, though she may also have thought it at the time, for around 1780, finding it very inconvenient to dress her hair, she took the unusual step of cutting it off 'close to my head; but took care to have a cap most becomingly made'.[64] Mary Frampton (1773–1846), also writing her reminiscences in the Victorian age, explained that 'at that time everybody wore powder and pomatum; a large triangular thing called a cushion, to which the hair was frizzed up with three or four enormous curls on each side; the higher the pyramid of hair, gauze, feathers, and other ornaments was carried the more fashionable it was thought.'[65]

Mary Frampton's memories bring into focus the technology required by such elaborate hairdressing. The most vital part was probably the pomatum. This came in two varieties, hard and soft, and the principal ingredient was animal fat. Hairdresser James Stewart advised that great care be taken to ensure that this fat came from a young and healthy animal, and also that the pomatum be sweet—wholesome, and in this context, probably also perfumed—and of the correct consistency.[66] Sellers of pomatum claimed that different animal fats were possessed of different beneficial properties. Deer's grease was good for rheumatism, sciatica and gout; hare's grease promoted digestion; eel's fat was esteemed for reducing the pits left by smallpox, and so on; though the extent of belief in these claims is impossible to know.[67] The best pomatum fat came from bears. Author and hairdresser David Ritchie, in describing the wares he had available for sale, included:

> Also Bears fed and killed, in order that such Ladies and Gentlemen, as please to honour
> me with their commands, may be supplied with Grease of the most genuine kind; the
> great efficacy of which, for the valuable purpose of making the hair grow thick and
> strong, is so well known, from long experience, that it needs no encomium here. It is
> sold at 1s. 6d. 2s. 6d. and 5s. *per* pot; each sealed with my name, and directions how to
> use it.[68]

Pomatum stiffened the hair and held styling in place. It made combing easier. It was thought to cleanse the head, and it nourished and strengthened the hair.[69]

Pomatum was essential, and it possessed this remarkable versatility. Indeed, except for its supposed health benefits, we have continued to endorse the range of its applications, developing specialized products for each, such as hairspray, conditioner, gel, mousse, wax, regrowth formulas and leave-in sprays. The ingredients of pomatum may sound unsavoury, yet presumably differed little from the cosmetics based on animal products that until recently were the norm. Indeed, during the 1994 BSE (bovine spongiform encephalopathy) outbreak, the Health and Agriculture Councils of the European Commission discussed the safety of bovine-derived substances in beauty products. According to a statement issued by the Cosmetic Toiletry and Perfumery Association in 1999, around 80 per cent of cosmetic products contain tallow derivatives.[70] Moreover, changing the focus only slightly, there are now concerns growing over the chemical toxicity of modern cosmetics, which may yet turn out to be a much less desirable harvest than mere beef tallow or bear's grease.[71]

Inseparable from pomatum was powder, the two together being fundamental to styling and haircare. It is less easy to determine powder's ingredients though, as they varied according to the quality of the product and the means of the consumer. The best powders were made of starch, extracted from cereal crops like corn, wheat and rice, though it could also be obtained from potatoes and even horse chestnuts.[72] Cheaper, 'adulterated' powders—and there were laws against this—used flour, alabaster, plaster of Paris, whiting and lime.[73] The way to tell a good-quality powder was by its clear cream appearance and light, feathery texture, 'like snow falling'.[74] Powder was scented, and sometimes coloured, too. Although greys and browns were standard, Stewart gives directions for making yellow powder by adding ochre and essence of lemon to a plain mixture, rose powder with carmine and essence of rose, and also pink powder.[75] In 1782 Hannah More, again disparaging and witty, wrote in another letter: 'what do you think is the reigning mode as to powder—only tumerick, that coarse dye which stains yellow … It falls out of the hair and stains the skin so, that every pretty lady must look as yellow as a crocus, which I suppose will become a better compliment than as white as a lily.'[76] It seems that the chemicals used for colouring hair were harsh, and powdering was perhaps an easier, safer way to achieve a similar effect, with the added advantage of being easy to alter. David Ritchie not only held that dye was harmful to the hair, but was confident that through the pores of the head it also penetrated the brain. It is easy to mock, but Ritchie's worries are not so different from the concerns raised by recent scientific research that some chemicals in shampoo, by being absorbed by the mother, are harmful to unborn children.[77]

The quantities of powder used to dress hair were surprisingly large. Mary Frampton tells us that 'one pound, and even two pounds' of powder might be put into the hair in one dressing, though she perceptively adds 'or wasted in the room'.[78] From excise office accounts, we know that before 1795 over eight million pounds of starch was made in Britain annually, most of which went into hair powder.[79] Various devices were used to dredge this vast amount of powder onto the heads of its wearers. Blowers and different types of powder puffs were used with various techniques, according to the desired effect and the stage of dressing. The wearer, and his or her clothing, was protected from the resulting fine mist by a powdering jacket or gown, and a mask.[80] Sometimes the whole performance took place in a special room set aside for the purpose, the powdering closet. At the end, a powder-knife, six or seven inches long and carefully tempered, 'though not so sharp as to cut', was used to scrape the forehead clean of any surplus.[81]

While powder helped achieve the right thickness of texture necessary for styling and tinted the hair, it was also held to be cleansing, and thus essential for personal hygiene. This is only counter-intuitive to very modern sensibilities, for until a few decades ago it was quite common to give greasy hair a dry wash by combing it through with talcum powder. In fact, according to media coverage and sales figures, dry shampoos, in recent years probably used most by the bedridden, are currently enjoying a fashionable revival, with growing numbers finding them a more convenient alternative to a daily wash and blow-dry.[82] The well-known New York company Bumble and bumble actually manufacture a range of aerosol hair powders in five different shades. In the following extract the benefits of hair powder, if not the language in which they are described, are identical to the advantages claimed for them over 200 years ago:

> Hair Powders add sexy va-va volume, extend the life of a blow-dry by absorbing excess oil and provide a dry texture that keeps pins and clips from slipping (so styles stay put). The shades enhance or shift hair colour, these fantastic (and fun) forms of temporary colour can be used to blend away roots between colour appointments (Hallelujah!)
>
> A one-stop shop for instant fullness, blended roots, no-slip updos and dry cleansing. Ideal for oily hair, styling fine hair and root touch ups.[83]

Perhaps partly because of its identification with cleanliness and its importance in presenting the dressed, social person, powder also functioned as a sign of gentility, marking the boundaries of propriety and self-respect.[84] For Mary Frampton, it described her coming of age and entry into polite society. Although not yet out, she very clearly remembered being allowed to attend a fête given to celebrate George III's recovery from 'madness'. She was sixteen and 'was dressed as a grown-up person for the first time'. 'I ... wore powder, then the mark of distinction of womanhood.'[85] It is a small step from here to the rather sordid fetishization described by Charles Greville. He noted with contempt the 'trinkets and trash' of the late George IV's hoarded effects, including 'the prodigious quantity of hair—women's hair—of all colours and lengths, some locks with the powder and pomatum still sticking to them'.[86] Even after its fall from fashion and grace, powder continued to connote status, although only when worn on the heads of one's servants, most typically the powdered footmen of the 'upstairs downstairs' world of the nineteenth century. In 1825, Elizabeth Spencer Stanhope decided to engage redheaded John Ramsden as a footman, assuring her husband that the colour of his hair would not show through the powder. As late as the early years of the twentieth century, Osbert Sitwell (1892–1969) remembered that his family's household included 'Fat James, an enormous footman with powdered hair, who was apt to fall asleep while handing round the dishes'.[87] For employers, powdered hair continued to be a mark of gentility; for the wearers, it was a badge of their servitude.

Aside from the big two, powder and pomatum, there were also other, lesser tools required by the hairdresser. Different kinds of comb, pins, scissors, varieties of curling papers and curling irons, and the cushion, were all utilized in the performance of eighteenth-century hair.[88] The cushion, vital to the foundation of the biggest coiffures, was a small pad placed on top of the head. Hair was built over this, or false hair attached, either pinned or sewn. Today, synthetic hair padding is employed by hairdressers for the same purpose. The irons, though, were particularly difficult to use. They were heated in the fire, and the hairdresser needed to judge when they were the right temperature. Too cool, and the irons would not curl; too hot, and they singed the hair, despite its protective papers. Gossip related that actress Mrs Barry beat her hairdresser and kicked him downstairs, 'and on being asked for what reason, replied, only for catching hold of her ear, in a hurry, with the hot pinching irons, instead of her curl'. He vowed he would dress her no more.[89]

Of course, the technology and effects of eighteenth-century hair did not meet with universal commendation. Every fashion has a dissenting voice. There were plenty of texts that articulated disapproval, plenty of people for whom powder, pomatum and the prosthetic additions of cushion and false hair were immoral, irrational and unhygienic. As so often, it was the prospect of the fashion's female wearers that produced the most disgusted comment. In the middle of the decade of the largest styles, *The Lady's Magazine* ran an article, 'Thoughts on Dress', which included typical censure. 'I must not forget', the writer made certain, 'the present ridiculous mode of dress amongst our fantastical females. I mean that detestable and filthy fashion of wearing a load of false hair … which is matted together by an infinite quantity of grease and powder, which … composition of filth, cannot fail of *creating* some *lively* ideas to a squeamish stomach.'[90] The two discourses—the descant of objection and the dominant norm of accepted social custom—existed side by side. Hannah More, for example, although professedly preferring the scars of smallpox to current fashion, still wished to remain within the broad sweep of polite convention. She therefore submitted herself to a hairdresser's ministrations—'one of the most fashionable disfigurers'—in order that she 'avoid the pride of singularity'.[91]

The elaborate artifice of the hairstyles produced by this technology came at a price though, a price that the wearer paid in time. Fanny Burney says dressing took two hours, which for creating a full style from scratch was not an exaggeration.[92] Alexander Stewart talks in terms of two to three hours, understandably advising ladies against trying to do it themselves.[93] A hairdresser came to Sophia Baddeley (Figure 5) and stayed around three hours.[94] Mary Frampton explains that 'such was the labour employed to rear the fabric that night caps were made in proportion to it', covering over the hair so that it was ready for the next day.[95] In this, she was probably only partly right. Both David Ritchie and Alexander Stewart give instructions for preparing the wearer at night; preparations which, after removing ornaments and fixing the curls in rollers, comprised tying the hair with a 'very large net fillet' on a drawstring, which closed around the face and the neck.[96] However, hair did not emerge from a night's repose immediately ready for wear. The next day it was all unpinned, the loose powder removed, the hair partially repomaded, and also powdered anew. With daily attention in this manner, hairstyles could last 'for two or three months'.[97] Big hair, then, was not an impervious and permanent edifice, but a continuing style that needed regular maintenance to remain intact and healthy. Once the hair got messy, dirty and matted, 'it is absolutely necessary to comb it out'.[98] Presumably, at this point the performance began again. It is undeniable that many rich men, and particularly women, of the eighteenth century spent a lot of time sitting for their hair. To put it in perspective once again, however, we must bear in mind that a salon today will generally allow

Figure 5 'Sophia Baddeley', mezzotint by Robert Laurie after Johan Zoffany, 1772, © Trustees of the British Museum. Actress and singer Sophia Baddeley (1745?–86), one-time lover of the Lord Melbourne who sold Holland House for £16,000. Baddeley wears an elaborate coiffure decorated with ribbons and pearls. Unlike satirical representations, this print gives a more realistic sense of big hair. Feathers, a popular adornment, would give even more height. Baddeley's biography records a hairdresser taking around three hours to style her hair.

three-quarters of an hour for merely a simple wash and cut. Special occasion hair—the sort we are usually reading about in eighteenth-century sources—can take several hours. Considering this, and the specialized range of products, materials and electrical equipment we have available, helps us better appreciate both the skill of the eighteenth-century artisan and the 'reasonableness' of the undertaking.

One question remains, though: how big was big hair? Was it really so tall that mechanical contrivances were required to lower the height so that ladies could pass safely under chandeliers?[99] Was Samuel Rogers right—was London full of carriages with ladies perched on small stools or sitting on the floor? Again, the hairdressing manuals are probably our best guide, and they tell a less exaggerated tale. Stewart suggests to his readers that unless they are very tall, or the lady very low, they might have difficulty in raising the curl papers properly. When explaining the difficulties of a wearer dressing her own hair, he stresses the fatigue she would experience, it being particularly tiresome for the arms, 'as they will want to be almost a foot above her head the whole time she is dressing'.[100] On top of this twelve inches of hair—both real and false—and cushion, powder and pomatum, any ornamentation, of course, added extra height. But we are talking caps, feathers, flowers and bows here, not caged birds.[101] David Ritchie reflects on the propriety of ornaments, advising dressers consider the person of the wearer and the event for which she is dressing: for example, the styling and ornamentation suitable for a ball would be inappropriate at church. He suggests that no one be dressed in a manner too gaudy or superfluous, 'for if any person overcharges their dress and ornaments, it hath this bad effect, it gives the person a diminutive look'.[102] Wearers might wish to appear 'fanciful'—inventive and original, that is—but not ridiculous: 'no genteel lady will ever be seen with a bungling crouded head'.[103]

Learning a little about the technology behind such sculpted hair helps us appreciate the level of skill possessed by successful hairdressers. There is no difficulty in believing Stewart when he warns 'the male and female operator' that the work they are contemplating 'will require much more attention, and exertion of abilities, than they are aware of or imagine'.[104] Usually hairdressers visited their clients at home. Charlotte Papendiek frequently mentions 'Kead' coming to dress her for special occasions such as the christening of her eldest child on New Years Day 1784, or for a performance given by Haydn, when Kead charged two shillings and sixpence.[105] At the extreme end of the social and financial scale, Sonardi, Queen Charlotte's hairdresser, planned to charge £200 for attending her over the summer. The queen thought this excessive, but agreed instead to pay him at that rate for any times she might need him—pro rata, in other words.[106] Cecil Beaton's (1904–80) memories of his Edwardian childhood attest to how long such practices continued. He recalled a man coming to the house with the tools of his trade in a brown leather bag. 'He was shown to my mother's bedroom, where, armed with a spirit lamp or stove, he heated his tongs over a blue flame. I can still, in memory, conjure up the exciting scent of methylated spirit and singed hair.'[107]

Some people wished to have hairdressing services on call all the time. For this they needed a valet or maid who possessed the requisite skill—the sort of person at whom Alexander Stewart aimed his compendious 'how to' manual. When Mary Coke's maid gave notice to return to France, Lady Mary anticipated difficulty in replacing her 'as the understanding dressing of hair is a necessary qualification'.[108] The memoirs of servant John Macdonald contain very frequent references to his dressing the hair of his employees, and others. He is particularly pleased with his success in India, where, by adding candle wax to the pomatum, he could get dressed hair to stand all evening, despite the heat.[109] When Richard Cumberland and his family travelled to Portugal and Spain in 1780, Cumberland hired especially 'a London hair-dresser of the name of Legge, whom I took for the convenience of my wife and daughters'.[110]

Mrs Papendiek used the services of a particular hairdresser over a span of some years. Charlotte writes warmly of Kead's abilities, and after his attentions feels she looks becoming. The intimacy of the relationship between hairdresser and client was the butt of suggestive innuendo. John Macdonald was—innocently, he claims—on the receiving end of this when his frequent visits to Mrs Innes's room before breakfast led to accusations of sexual impropriety.[111] Baddeley's biographer, however, probably describes the more common relationship:

> The hair-dresser came, and put an end to our conversation. This kind of gentry, having access to the ladies, frequently hear things in one house, which they carry to another.

> Ladies are too apt to converse with these fellows, and ask questions; and, for every piece
> of intelligence they communicate, they are rewarded with news in return; so, that many
> women are as much diverted with their slander, as embellished by their art.[112]

Given the hours for which a lady, or gentleman, sat while being dressed, it is no wonder
that, despite Stewart's admonition to his readers to work silently,[113] both client and dresser
passed the time in conversation.

It is easy to see what the person who does the dressing brings to the 'polite' performance of eighteenth-century hair. But what of the wearer? What skills and disciplines were
needed by the person upon whose head the work was done? First, and most obviously, the
wearer had to be willing to spend up to two to three hours in what was probably quite a
chore: sitting through a dull, relatively uncomfortable period of enforced inactivity. Elaborate hair was the work of the leisured, as were so many practices of elite dress.[114] This com-
mitment of time, boredom and immobility was not one that all were able, or prepared, to
make. When Charlotte Papendiek found it 'very inconvenient' to dress her hair, one of the
reasons she gave for cutting it off was thereby escaping the accusation of 'being too long at
my toilet'.[115] Jane Austen adopted a cap for similar reasons, although at the age of twenty-
three still quite young for this symbol of mature years. However, she wrote that caps 'save
me a world of torment as to hair-dressing, which at present gives me no trouble beyond
washing and brushing, for my long hair is always plaited up out of sight, and my short hair
curls well enough to want no papering'.[116]

A second requirement concerned the need to remain inviolable. The wrong sort of movement or physical touch risked disarranging the hair and a scatter of powder. In a letter to
The Gentleman's Magazine of 1733, 'Infortunatus' recounts how the traces of his powder on
a young woman's dress betrayed his improper embrace:

> I dress fashionably, and therefore wear a great deal of Powder. Yesterday I visited a young
> Lady, whom I found without her Mother at home, you may be sure I was neither *tongue-
> ty'd* nor *motionless;* nor did she expect I shou'd; but as *Milton* says,—From my *Mouth,*
> Not *Words* alone pleased her.
>
> In comes Mama; and before she could get up Stairs, we had the whole Room be-
> tween us. After she had sat a while, looking accidentally on her Daughter, she found her
> black Silk Gown … whiter than ordinary, and guessing we had been *closer* than we then
> were, she civilly desir'd me to walk down, and told me, her Daughter was never after to
> be seen by me, but in *her Company.*[117]

While the letter itself was a spoof—a reprimand to young, overly fashionable men—the
propensity for powder to shake loose was real enough. Indeed, 'not being tidy with powder'
was a disgrace Charlotte Papendiek had often fallen into before cutting her hair short.[118]
This carelessness was conceived as being slovenly and ungenteel. Appropriate bodily decorum required neatness and containment. It also required protection from assaults by wind
and rain, either of which could ruin a dressed head and a reputation at one inclement blow.

Owing to their more domesticated lives and reduced physicality, this was less of a problem for women. For men though, lapses in the decorous presentation of the head carried the sort of shame and derision found in the unwilling removal of a wig. However, caution before the elements also laid men open to charges of effeminacy, as in the manner of this satire on languid and fashionable youth:

> Hapless that Youth, who, when the Tempest flies,
> Unarm'd each rushing Hurricane defies!
> In vain on Barbers or on Gods he calls,
> The Ringlets yield, the beauteous Structure falls.
> Nor less, when soft-descending Show'rs prevail,
> Dread the moist Influence of the Southern Gale:
> Oft will it's [*sic*] tepid Breath the Curls unbend,
> While dropping Dews from ev'ry Spire depend.
> Yours be the Care to watch, with cautious Eye,
> When threat'ning Clouds portend a Tempest nigh.[119]

Dressed hair, then, imposed on the wearer a physical restraint, which swathed in a powdering gown started with the toil of its production, and while it lasted continued to determine the limits of a wearer's exertions. Its artifice was an elegant improvement on nature, a triumph of civilization and craft; and for most in polite circles, dressing was a requirement of decorum and gentility. Mistakes and misadventures in presentation upset propriety and left that gentility in question. As with the preceding section on wigs, the last word on the subject goes to those 'disreputable' women, whose determined voices so scandalized and titillated the beau monde of their time. The anecdote concerns Margaret Leeson, who had, she writes, been insulted, assaulted and robbed by Pietro Carnivalli, a well-known musician, and two of his henchmen. In revenge she obtained warrants for their arrest and four 'ill-looking ruffians of bailiffs' to apprehend them. Having been tricked from the theatre, Carnivalli emerged into the street 'without his hat', and at Leeson's signal was set on by the bailiffs. 'I accordingly had the satisfaction of seeing them escort their prisoner *Carnivalli* without his hat, his well-powdered hair drenched in rain which providentially fell at that time.' So delighted with the manner of her revenge, Leeson ordered the bailiffs to arrest the other two. '[B]e sure', she added, to 'conduct them in the rain without their hats'. That night, Leeson wrote, she slept sweeter than she had for some time.[120]

NECKWEAR: PROUD AND HAUGHTY

At first consideration, the neck might seem a peculiar part of the body on which to concentrate. Surely, its role in the presentation of the desirable self has been negligible: an overlooked, unregarded, 'unfashioned' bit of anatomy. However, sandwiching the eighteenth-century era of wigs and hair, two very different garments for the neck achieved immense influence. Physically prominent, and with a corresponding cultural assertiveness, these two fashions have become sartorial icons. Just as they sculpted the stance of their wearers, so they continue to shape our visual imaginings of the past. Like an afterimage, the garments hang in our memories long after their wearers, and their time, have disappeared from view.

The first of these was the archetypal Elizabethan fashion, the ruff. Having its origins in a small frill adorning the neckline of shirts and smocks, by the mid sixteenth century the ruff was an independent garment, worn by both men and women. It was with the production of English starch in the 1560s, however, that the ruff really came into its own. With this stiffening agent, and the added help of a wire frame beneath called a supportasse or underpropper, by the 1580s the ruff had assumed inventive variety and an immense size. Contemporary Puritan commentator Phillip Stubbes, whose moral framework had no place for pride and vanity, attacked the wearers of these 'great and monsterous ruffes' that 'stand a full quarter of a yarde (and more) from their necks'.[121] While Stubbes frequently employed hyperbolic language, his figure here of nine inches seems a reasonable estimate for the larger styles that so anatomized their wearers and isolated head from body in such a dramatic manner (Figure 6).

The other fashion that effectively framed the face and separated the wearer's head from, in this case, *his* body, was the early-nineteenth-century neckcloth. This came in two forms: a folded cravat that passed round the neck and tied at the front in a variety of ways; or a stiffened, reinforced width of fabric called a stock, that fitted the neck snugly and was buckled or hooked behind. In combination with a very high shirt collar—the points of which, popularly called winkers for obvious reasons, might reach nearly to the eyes[122]—the neckcloth created what we, fed on a diet of costume dramas, might think of as the 'Mr Darcy look'.[123] We would be more accurate, however, if we thought of it as the 'Mr Brummell look', for it is this most famous of dandies who is credited with first starching his neckcloths—to the stiffness of 'fine writing-paper'[124]—so that the fabric held its carefully made creases. Prince Pückler, an impoverished German aristocrat visiting England a little while after Brummell's debt-laden, and it turns out syphilitic, retreat to the Continent, wrote fluently, if ironically, of Brummell's fame:

> When at last he turned his back on Great Britain, he left to his native land, as a parting gift, the imperishable secret of the starched neckband. The elegants of the capital had been so tormented by their inability to fathom it that, according to the *Literary Gazette,* one of them, a young duke, actually died miserably of a broken heart ... And as great men live on in their works when they themselves are long since dust, so Brummell's starch remains visible at the neck of every fashionable, and proclaims his lofty genius.[125]

As a ballad of around that time sniggeringly put it,

> Some gents you'll see are so starched up
> As through the streets they do sail,
> With much more linen round their neck
> Than they have in their shirt tail:
> The ladies laugh now in their sleeve,

Figure 6 'Mrs John Croker (née Frances Kingsmill)', oil painting attributed to George Gower, 1580, ©
Victoria and Albert Museum, London. Frances Croker wears blackwork trunk sleeves, a Spanish farthingale,
and a large cartwheel ruff edged with lace. Her outfit is generously ornamented with aiglets, decorative
metal tags sometimes made of gold or silver.

As after them they follow,

And say young man, you'll pardon me,

But pray who starch'd your collar?[126]

It is in memoirs of the Beau that we see something of the performance behind the wearing of the Regency neckcloth. Rather like a Renaissance monarch, Brummell's ablutions and adorning were a semi-public spectacle carried out before a court of friends and admirers. According to Captain Jesse, his first biographer, the ritual of Brummell's neckcloth began with the folding of his shirt collar—a collar so large that before this was done 'it completely hid his head and face'. The neckcloth—'at least a foot in height'—was put on and crisp folds achieved by Brummell, chin poking to the ceiling, gradually and repeatedly bringing down his lower jaw to form the creases. If unsatisfied with the result, the Beau would discard the neckcloth and start afresh with a new one (Figure 7).[127]

Whether or not Brummell was the originator of this manner of preparing and wearing neckcloths, the paradigm of erect masculinity that he embodied was hugely influential. A contemporary man about town, R. H. Gronow, recalled that 'All the world watched

Figure 7 'George Bryan Brummell', engraving by John Cook after unknown miniaturist, 1844, © National Portrait Gallery, London. Brummell (1778–1840) wears a high, lightly starched neckcloth, a fashion for which he became famed.

Brummell to imitate him.'[128] Imitators, however, achieved varying degrees of success. Gronow, himself a dandy, neutrally explained that 'it was the fashion to wear a deep, stiff white cravat, which prevented you from seeing your boots while standing', and Georgiana Sitwell recollected 'the large white neckcloths' that were de rigueur.[129] However, Sarah Spencer (later to be Lady Lyttelton), writing to her younger brother Robert, poked fun at a visiting 'county coxcomb', a 'humble imitator' of metropolitan style, who was wearing 'the highest neckcloth and lee boards I ever beheld; stiffer than a poker'. In another letter, she recalls Robert's own youthful efforts: 'I remember you there, just arrived from Cambridge, much the finest college coxcomb I ever saw, with yards of neckcloth.'[130] From such teasing private comments, it is a short step to public mockery (Figure 8):

> Quite a new sort of creatures, unknown yet to scholars,
> With heads, so immoveably stuck in shirt-collars,
> That seats like our music-stools soon must be found them,
> To twirl, when the creatures may wish to look round them![131]

The ubiquity of the fashion even spawned a series of 'how to' texts that tutored aspirants in the selection, maintenance and arrangement of their cravats.[132] The relationship of these sartorial manuals to each other, and to real practice, is complicated; in varying degrees they echo and repeat one another, entertain with parody, and instruct with practical advice. One particularly funny but, alas, presumably apocryphal story concerns a tall young man, 'at least six foot three', who paid a hapless visit to a friend's aged aunt, a small woman and something of a tartar. Wearing a high starched neckcloth, and consequently 'very much erected', he advanced to pay his respects 'to the nearest *visible* female figure; but was suddenly and, certainly, most unexpectedly stopped in his career, by stumbling against, and falling over [the] poor old aunt, whom he had hitherto not seen'. A slapstick, domino effect of disasters ensue: 'He was precipitated headlong into the lap of an old dowager' who was sitting on a low ottoman, admiring a large jar. As the man arrives in her lap, the jar, full of water from the flowers it had recently held, slips from her hands and falls over the head of 'a little foreign baron', who at that minute had been gallantly picking up the dowager's pocket handkerchief that had fallen at her feet.

The significance of the phenomenon on which these recollections, observations and parodies so variously comment is, however, unmistakable. The collar and neckcloth established the standard of upright male propriety that is still with us in the collar and tie of today. Even our favoured knot, the four-in-hand, derives from the nineteenth century, it being a method of driving a carriage with a team of four horses. The tie, whose phallic possibilities are so easily referenced, is practically redundant but symbolically alive and well as modern buttoned-up and dominant masculinity.[133]

Although separated by over 200 years and completely dissimilar in form, these two iconic fashions, the ruff and the high neckcloth, had much in common. For a start, though this is true of probably every fashion, there were the detractors. In the Renaissance,

Figure 8 'Dandies Dressing', hand-coloured etching by Isaac Cruikshank, 1818, © Trustees of the British Museum. A satirical print showing six dandies at dress. All of them wear exaggeratedly high neckcloths and collars, the seated figure on the left struggling to put on his lower garments, exclaiming, 'D—n it, I really believe I must take off my cravat or I shall never get my trowers on'. The figures on the right are tying their neckcloths in the mirror, one standing on a chair behind the other to get a better view. The higher gentleman complains, 'Dear me this is hardly stiff enough I wish I had another sheet of Fools cap', the other replying, 'You'll find some to spare in my breeches'. This alludes to the practice of reinforcing the stock (a stiffened neckband) and padding trousers. It also suggests an effeminate emasculation. The figure in the middle is being laced into stays by a dandiacally dressed servant or hairdresser, and on one leg is tied a false calf. His thighs may be similarly padded. His companion wearing gloves who appears to be taking snuff remarks, 'Pon honour, Tom you are a charming figure! You'll captivate the Girls to a nicety!!' 'Do you think so Charles?' he replies. 'I shall look more the thing when I get my other calf on.' The neglected calf lies on the carpet near his feet. Other items scattered about include boots and an umbrella. A pincushion and pot of makeup (paint) sit on the dressing table. Most of the figures are wearing very tight pantaloons. The dandy standing on the chair, and perhaps also the one sitting down, have got an alternative baggy style of trousers that was briefly fashionable, known as cossacks or Petersham trousers.

the objections of Stubbes and others like him were driven by moral imperatives. The main points of their not groundless concerns were as follows. Flamboyant garments typical of elite styles were so expensive they drove their purchasers into debt and diverted money from charitable, socially responsible uses. They misrepresented status, allowing their wearers to buck a God-given position in life, an escape that carried the seeds of dissension, unrest and societal chaos. Their external splendour sidetracked attention and effort from matters of deeper, spiritual significance. They were not necessary, they were luxurious, they were excessive. This package of anxieties lies behind Stubbes's assertions that it was the Devil, 'in the fulness of his malice, first inuented these great ruffes'. So hath the Devil, Stubbes continued,

> now found out also two great stayes to beare vp and maintaine this his kingdome of great ruffes ... the one arch or piller wherby his kingdome of great ruffes is vnder-propped is a certaine kinde of liquide matter which they call Starch, wherin the deuill hath willed them to wash and diue [dive] his ruffes wel, which when they be dry wil then stand stiffe and inflexible about their necks. The other piller is a certain deuice made of wyers ... calleth a supportasse or vnderpropper.[134]

By the dawn of the nineteenth century, moral disapproval was on the decline, or at least was being recast in a more 'rational' guise. Thus, in *An Essay Concerning Modern Clothing* of 1792, a Rochester physician warned of the grave medical risks attendant on tight collars, stocks and neckcloths. 'They render Swallowing difficult, because they compress the *Oesophagus,* and they may induce Giddiness, *Stupor,* and Apoplexy.'[135] Over a quarter of a century later, an article in *The Times* entitled 'Tendency of Cravats to Produce Apoplexy' repeated this medical advice, warning dramatically that corpulent elderly men in particular, with tight and voluminous neckcloths, are, when sitting down to their evening bottle, '*tête-à-tête* with death'.[136]

The second point of similarity, and perhaps the most significant, was that ruffs and the collar-neckcloth combination physically determined a 'proud' stance. Chin up, head held high, the wearer assumed the carriage of haughty disdain. '[W]hat an apparent superiority does not a starcher [neckcloth] give to a man? It gives him a look of *hauteur* and greatness, which can scarcely be acquired otherwise.' Warming to the theme, this writer goes on in a parodic, but illustrative, vein:

> This is produced solely by the austere rigidity of the cravat, which so far, by any means, from yielding to the natural motions of the head, forms a strong support to the cheeks. It pushes them up, and gives a rotundity of appearance to the whole *figure* [face], thereby unquestionably giving a man the air of being puffed up with pride, vanity, and conceit, (very necessary, nay, indispensable qualifications for a man of fashion) and appearing as quite towering over the rest of mankind, and holding his fellow-creatures covered with the deep disgrace of his disgust.[137]

The superiority of stance also asserted dissociation from labour: dressed in a starched neck-cloth or ruff, any manual occupation was out of the question. Those who wore these fashions of privilege did not need to spend their lives tilling the fields or relentlessly at work in a factory. Instead, they had money, time and servants in abundance, enough to satisfy the requirements of these most demanding items of dress. For demanding they were: time consuming to arrange, labour intensive to maintain, and expensive to make. A ruff, for example, had to be laundered and restarched after every wearing, and then its pleats reset into shape with heated 'poking sticks'. Jenny Tiramani, Head of Design at the Globe Theatre, reminds us that this was 'a very time-consuming business'. In the Globe's quest for authenticity they have discovered that even without the washing and starching, just to set one neck and two wrist ruffs takes over three hours.[138] The matter of laundering, starching and ironing was of a comparable importance for neckcloths. 'No perfumes', Brummell famously advised, 'but very fine linen, and plenty of country-washing'.[139] And plenty of linen was needed, too. Prince Pückler, on the authority of his washerwoman, stated the weekly requirements of a man of fashion as including twenty-four shirts and thirty neckcloths, explaining that a great quantity was needed as such a man could not get away without three or four changes of raiment a day.[140] Even larger amounts of fabric might be swallowed up by a ruff: in one extant example, an astonishing twenty yards of linen is concertined into a neckband just a single inch wide and fifteen inches long.[141] To do this, fabric must be extraordinarily fine. When first making reproduction costumes at the Globe, staff had difficulty even finding a suitable modern equivalent; although not coarse, their linen 'fell a long way short of the fifty threads to one centimetre in the warp and weft that the surviving ruffs consist of'.[142] These fabrics of cobweb delicacy—'Camericke, Holland, Lawne, and the finest cloth that maye bee got anie where for money'—were a source of anger for Stubbes. So, too, were their intricate lacework, and gold and silver embroidery 'speckled and sparkled heer & there with the sonne, the moone, the starres and many other antiquities straunge to beholde'.[143]

Tempting though it is to dismiss Stubbes and his disapproval as the product of killjoy puritanism, finding fault for the sake of it, we should be very wrong to do so. The ruff was flamboyant and beautiful. It spoke to contemporaries of privilege and wealth and social status. It spoke so confidently and loudly that it claimed not only the attention of Stubbes and his ilk, but also the juridical notice of the state. The Tudor acts and proclamations of apparel policed the consumption of clothing in an attempt to regulate appearances, in theory controlling an individual's dress according to his or her rank and income.[144] That ruffs were socially assertive is confirmed by their fast becoming a target of regulation, with only wearers of sufficient status being legally allowed access to the boldest varieties. In 1562, the wearing of 'outrageous double ruffs which now of late are crept in' was prohibited by proclamation. Single ruffs only were acceptable, and these to be of 'due and mean sort', and 'orderly and comely'. In 1580, another proclamation charged that no person was to wear 'great and excessive ruffs in or about the uppermost part of their necks'. Such styles were 'insupportable' and 'indecent', and observation of the proclamation was commanded upon pain of Elizabeth's 'high indignation'.[145] In practice, though, 'insupportability' was not so much in the eye of the beholder as on the neck of the wearer, for a ruff's acceptability was constituted by its context and owner rather than its dimensions or cost. Thus it was that Elizabeth herself, and those in her court, continued to wear them unabashed.

Ruffs and neckcloths, then, were the ultimate fashions of waste. They had no practical function, cost a great deal in time and money to make and maintain, and wearing them restricted movement. Equally, though, were they beautiful, a testament to the skill of the artisans who made them and, in the case of the latter, the wearer who arranged his own cravat. As an inescapable expression of a particular elite self-consciousness, the ruff and neckcloth were a triumph.

STARCH IS THE THING

According to Prince Pückler, when Brummell fled the country, the uncontested *arbiter elegantiarum* left on his writing desk a sealed packet. 'When they opened it, they found nothing but the following, written in large letters: "My friends, starch is the thing".'[146] And indeed, starch *is* the thing. Essential to Brummell's neckcloths, but also indispensible to the powdered wigs and hair of the long eighteenth century, and vital to the ruffs of the sixteenth, it connects these widely divergent clothing practices. It is also inseparable from the crisp shirt fronts and high collars of Victorian manhood, and is present in the production of textiles used in nineteenth-century female fashion. Even up to, say, fifty years ago, the careful housewife's stiffened shirts and household linens testified to its ubiquity. In addition to stiffening material, starch also provides a medium to which dirt adheres. As starched garments are usually white, and so often worn in contact with the skin, the grime of wear is soon noticeable. When laundered, the starch and its accompanying dirt are washed free of the fabric, dissolving together to leave the soiled garment clean. A commodity of extraordinarily long-lived utility then, starch has played a fundamental role in the presentation of well-dressed propriety, cleanliness and respectability. For 400 years, starch really mattered.

While imported from the Low Countries from the 1530s, the commercial, as opposed to the domestic, production and use of starch in England was due to the enterprise and acumen of just one woman. In 1564, Mistress Dinghen van der Plasse, a refugee from Flanders, settled in the Dutch community in London and began a starching business. She both made the starch and used it to set her clients' ruffs. The quality of her work attracted those from outside the community, and English women, too, began to bring linens to be starched. Eventually the successful Mistress Dinghen took on trainees, charging the young women 20 shillings to learn starch making, and £4 and £5 for the more skilful accomplishment of starching and setting ruffs.[147] The popularity of the product and the income generated by its sale was matched by the growth in the numbers of workers and the rapidity with which starch manufacture spread. A Jacobean proclamation stated that although it was 'a thing newly taken up', starch making had 'growen in few yeers very frequent'.[148] Although only a relatively small number of starch makers were listed in official documents, it seems these were the visible tip of a burgeoning industry in which subcontracting and outsourcing were common.[149] As far as the government was concerned, 'dayly more and more doe set up and beginne Starch-making in sundry places'.[150]

Although not difficult, starch manufacture was a time-consuming and smelly business. Robert Plot described the process as it was undertaken in Oxford in 1677, but there is no reason to suppose that this differed significantly from the methods of the preceding century or, indeed, from the century to come. First the grain was placed in large tubs and steeped in a solution of water and alum for fourteen days. Then a process of washing this mixture produced a fine flour, which in turn stood in water for about a week. At the end of this time it was strained through a fine sieve, and after settling for a day more, the remaining water was drawn off. It stood for a further two days, by which time the matter had solidified and was ready to be cut into pieces and dried, initially over cold bricks for two days, and then over a baker's oven for four to five days more. If intended for hair powder, it could be ground at this point. If intended as laundry starch, it underwent further drying with a stove. From beginning to end, the process took over a month.[151]

Although, in the urban surroundings in which its manufacture was sited, the fires used for drying starch were a potential hazard and the 'noysome stench' was considered a breeding ground for the plague, the real problem came with the grain from which starch was derived.[152] For making starch with wheat, corn or other cereal crops meant taking what would otherwise be used by ordinary people for food, and turning it into a commodity used principally for the pleasure of the rich. When harvests were good, this was less of an issue, though demand still drove up the price. When the harvest was bad, the morality of starch making, and ruff wearing, was suddenly cast in a new and very dubious light. As William Cecil (1520–98), Elizabeth's chief minister, said: 'Is it not a very lamentable thing that we should bestow that upon starch to the setting forth of vanity and pride which would staunch the hunger of many that starve in the streets for want of bread?'[153] It also helps us reassess Philip Stubbes's impassioned denunciation of starch as 'the deuils liquore', this now appearing less like a zealot's ranting and more like a reasoned cry for social justice. As his contemporary Thomas Nash put it, 'the lawne [fine linen] of licentiousnesse hath consumed all the wheat of hospitalitie'.[154]

What with one thing and another, for 200 years starch manufacture and starch use provided successive governments with quite a legislative headache. For a start, although agreeing that starch production consumed large quantities of wheat which would otherwise be available as food, governments were also uncomfortably aware that increasingly large numbers of people worked in starch-related occupations, and that prohibiting its manufacture would mean destroying their livelihoods. A 1607 proclamation put the dilemma clearly. On one hand, 'the waste of Corne spent and consumed in the making of this Stuffe … is so excessive, as it is not fit to be spared from peoples Food, to serve in so vaine and slender an use'. On the other hand, 'a great number of our loving Subjects' are economically dependent thereon, and 'utterly to take away the making of Starch … would be a great hinderance to them in their trades, and bereave many of them of the meanes of their necessary living and maintenance'.[155] Those who worked in starch manufacture were not the only ones implicated. As time went on, so the range of occupations related to this commodity increased to include, at the very least, washerwomen and starchers, grocers and other shopkeepers who retailed it, the makers of hair powder, and barbers and perruquiers. The second complication to the regulation of starch was less transparent but equally troublesome. The better sort of the sixteenth and seventeenth centuries, and the emerging middle class of the eighteenth, was the group on which legislation and its enforcement depended, and yet these represented the highest, most committed consumers of starch. The conflict of interest, although possibly never articulated or recognized, is clear on hindsight and must surely have contributed to the problems surrounding its control.

Different governments responded to the dilemma in different ways. Elizabeth and her Privy Council sought to limit the amount of starch produced and thus the quantity of grain consumed, and in 1588 granted a patent monopoly on starch making. However, this proved so unpopular among the populace—'reducing that into few mens power, which in common libertie of the Subject was free to all'—that in 1601 it was revoked, and starch manufacture and its profits were free for anyone to pursue.[156] Only six years later, however, Elizabeth's successor, James I, found that so great was 'the wasting and consuming of Corne fit for peoples food' that starch making again needed to be curbed. James and his advisers instituted a licensing system, requiring also that these certificated makers set up their trade where no one dwelling nearby would be annoyed by the stench and infectious air, and in addition, that they use only poor-quality grain, unfit for human consumption. The system was to be policed by specially appointed officers, with the cooperation of local magistrates. The extent to which these measures were 'so often iterated and renewed'[157] by subsequent legislation, however, shows how very limited was their effectiveness: unlicensed starch making proliferated, as did the use of good-quality wheat. After a scatter of proclamations, some repeating the licensing provisions and some banning starch production altogether, in 1622 James finally gave up on enforcement, and instead incorporated the starch makers into a self-governing body with responsibility for regulating its own members and ensuring their compliance with the law. In 1628 his son, Charles I, incorporated a similar body, the Society of Starch-Makers.

Although seeking to protect food supplies, the avowal of public good in these measures was neither as frank nor as uncomplicated as the rhetoric would seem to insist. Beneath concern for the welfare of the populace was further concern for the welfare of the crown coffers, for Elizabeth's patents and James's licensing and incorporation of starch makers were all sources of income, with the Exchequer getting a proportion of the revenue that the starch production generated. For example, two months before James's first proclamation on compulsory licensing, a report on the crown debt estimated that this move would bring the government £1,000 a year.[158] This aspect of fiscal self-interest is also at work in the taxes laid on starch throughout subsequent reigns, with the governments of William and Mary, Anne, and Georges I and II all carefully regulating—and receiving money from—the import, manufacture and sale of this commodity. By the latter part of George III's reign the revenue produced was around £200,000 per year.[159]

This mix of governmental altruism and self-interest crystallized in the closing years of the eighteenth century. By this time, the main use of starch was for hair powder. Contemporary estimates of the amount of wheat consumed in this way vary, but as we saw earlier, excise office accounts show that at this time over eight million pounds of starch were being made every year, and there was some agreement that it took two pounds of wheat to make a pound of starch. John Donaldson thus maintained that annually, this meant the equivalent of four million four-pound loaves were being dredged over the heads of the wealthy.[160] Reverend Septimus Hodson estimated that in prohibiting hair powder altogether, 700,000 people would be nourished once a week for a year.[161] Murmurings against the use of foodstuffs in this way were not new. In 1770, for example—when hairstyles were reaching their most extreme dimensions—Ellis Pratt's comic poem addressed such dedicated followers of fashion thus: 'For You their hoarded Grain Contractors spare, / And starve the poor to beautify your Hair.'[162] In the 1790s, however, the murmurings became harder to ignore. An extremely hot summer in 1794, followed by an equally extreme winter, meant that the harvests were meagre, and by early 1795 many were expecting famine.[163] Added to this, England was in the middle of a long and expensive war with Republican France, and the government was desperately looking for sources of revenue to pay for it. The response to both of these pressing demands was the passing, in April 1795, of 'An Act for Granting to his Majesty a duty on certificates issued for using hair powder'.[164] Briefly, this required all people wishing to powder their hair to take out a certificate annually, at the cost of one guinea (and those who did so popularly became known as 'guinea pigs'). Lists of certificate holders were to be displayed in public places such as church doors and the market cross, as a means towards policing the act through the easier identification of uncertificated wearers. The penalty for illegal powdering was £20. Thus it seems that William Pitt, the Prime Minister, hoped both to raise money through tax and husband the limited amount of wheat available. The latter was made more emphatic by a complete prohibition on the production of starch or hair powder from anything that might be used as food, in an act passed on 1 December that same year.[165]

The turmoil and debate generated by the hair powder tax was considerable.[166] The income it generated was less spectacular. Even in the early years, the total raised fell well short of Pitt's hoped-for annual amount of £210,000 (a net sum taking into consideration the costs of collection and administration), and the subsequent decline was rapid. Thus in the first six years, the tax raised an average of £158,000 per year; such money collected from the likes of the hairdresser William Dowling, who was informed on 'for wearing hairpowder without first obtaining a certificate'.[167] In 1801–2 the sum dropped to £75,000. In 1814 this plummeted to £700, and by 1820 the net annual income generated by the tax on hair powder was just £12.[168]

So, powder wearing dropped off rapidly after it was taxed. Did the tax thus cause the decline, or was the legislative measure in fact lagging behind an inevitable fashionable change? I think there is little doubt that it was the latter. Republican ideals from France, linking with emerging concepts of modernity, were already being visualized in dress forms that turned away from the heavy and ornate aristocratic styles of old, towards neoclassical lines and a new simplicity. For women this would mean the straight muslin dresses of the Regency, and for men a new ideal of manliness as embodied by, for example, Beau Brummell. Cropped, unpowdered hair was merely one part of this already evolving sartorial attitude. Looking back in his memoirs from only twenty years later, Sir William Wraxall described 'the Era of Jacobinism and Equality' and dated this very precisely to '1793, and 1794', that is, un-questionably before the powder tax. 'It was then', he wrote, 'that Pantaloons, cropped hair, and shoe-strings [shoe laces], as well as the total abolition of buckles and ruffles, together with the disuse of hair-powder, characterized the men.' The women 'cut off those Tresses' and donned drapery that, while 'classic' and 'elegant', was also 'ill-calculated to protect against the damp, cold, and fogs'.[169] In its monthly fashion column, *The Lady's Magazine* of November 1792—predating the issue of guinea certificates by nearly three years—advised its readers to follow the modish society leaders 'who have entirely abolished the large heads, and introduced the present elegant mode of dressing'.[170] Short, unpowdered hair appears as a target of lampoon in graphic satire slightly earlier again. For instance, the cartoon 'Front, Side View and Back Front of a Male and Female Crop' dates from 1791, four years before the powder act (Figure 9). William Pitt's tax may have rung the death knell for powder-ing, but its eventual demise had already been ensured by the tide of changing fashion. The guinea certificates just nailed down the coffin lid a little earlier.

While this was the end of hair powder, except on the heads of the very conservative and the very menial, this was not the end of starch, and it continued to be used in the laundry and in the production of textiles. In 1800, the rector of Preston, the heartland of England's dark satanic mills, claimed that 'More wheat is consumed in the manufacture of cotton and muslin in this country in the process from the loom to the market than is used for food for the inhabitants.'[171] This comment helps explain why the manufacture of starch using wheat was again prohibited in 1800, and then twice in 1812; and also how

Figure 9 'Front, Side View and Back Front of a Male and Female Crop', hand-coloured etching by William Dent, 1791, © Trustees of the British Museum. A satirical print featuring four fashionably dressed couples, all with short hair. The men wear high-waisted tight pantaloons tied at the ankle, coats cut away to form tails, and high hats. The caption under the couple dashing on the left reads, 'A Pair of Turf-Bred Crops Running with Fashion'. By contrast, the headwear, breeches, full coats and long waistcoats of the two men on the right are dated, more typical of the dying century than the dawning new one. The caption beneath them says, 'A Pair of High-Bred Crops Overtaken by Fashion'.

this measure came to be repealed the following year when found to be unworkable.[172] By now the commodity was too far implicated in England's newly industrialized economy for prohibition to work, even to protect the food supply. When we next come across starch, it is in the shaping of the ideal womanly waist and *poitrine*, and as a flame-retardant substance on muslin dresses. But this, as we shall see as we travel down the body, is another story.

2 BREASTS AND WAIST

MALLEABLE FLESH

Plotting the whereabouts of the waist on a map of the body is a surprisingly tricky undertaking. Like a fashion version of pin the tail on the donkey, the waist has ended up in unexpected places. Drifting up and down the torso as decade has followed decade, its location—particularly, but not exclusively, on women—has altered with a ready adaptability: as fashions change, the waist decamps and wanders off in search of a new, albeit temporary, residence. In *Anthropometamorphosis,* a seventeenth-century proto-anthropological study of body modification and cultural difference, John Bulwer comments disparagingly on this tendency with regard to the male anatomy:

> When we wore short-wasted Doublets, and but a little lower than our Breasts, we would
> maintaine by militant reasons that the waste was in its right place as Nature intended it:
> but when (as lately) we came to weare them so long wasted, yea, almost so low as our
> Privities, then began we to condemn the former fashion as fond [foolish], intollerable,
> and deformed, and to commend the later as comely, handsome, and commendable.

For Bulwer, the inconstancy of our aesthetic framework and our reinscription of what is 'natural' is a source of concern. Writing around 1650 when breeches were wide legged and increasingly decorated with dangling ribbons, he pointed out that the visual effect was to draw the waist down even lower 'to the knee', and worse, 'more lately the waste is descended down towards the Ankles'.[1] Over 350 years later, Bulwer's disgruntled description resonates remarkably with our own low-slung fashions. Of those young men whose sliding trousers rest lower than their underwear, and the crotch and seat of which flap well below the body's fork, well might John Bulwer say again that their waists were come to the knee, or very nearly to the ankle. However, this is a look with which we have become familiar, and most of us, even dressing in a more moderate and higher-waisted way, look at much of twentieth-century men's fashion, particularly its formal registers, and receive a buttoned-up impression of waist bands pulled a little too high.

The female waist has migrated even further around the anatomy's terrain. Around 1794, it rose perhaps to its highest, coming to rest just beneath the bust (Figures 10 and 39). This is the Jane Austen look, popularized over recent years through film biography and numerous adaptations: an industry devoted to the recreation of empire line dresses. Back in 1794, however, the style had not so much romantic charm as the brashness and oddity of the new. It is satirized in one print (Figure 11) that has a fashionable woman averting her gaze in the manner of a tragic heroine, refusing the refreshments offered her by a footman. Beneath the picture runs a verse:

Figure 10 'Harriet and Elizabeth Binney', watercolour by John Smart, 1806, © Victoria and Albert Museum, London. The two sitters wear high-waisted dresses of muslin or a similar lightweight fabric. The gowns are worn without a tucker or neckerchief, and the short sleeves expose their arms to well above the elbow.

Shepherds I have lost my Waist!
Have you seen my Body?
Sacrificed to modern Taste,
I'm quite a Hoddy Doddy!
For Fashion I that part forsook
Where Sages place the Belly,
Tis gone—& I have not a nook
For Cheese cake, Tart, or Jelly!![2]

The fashion endured for over twenty years—a generation, in fact, of short-waisted women whose long, columnar figures embodied the normal way of looking. By 1818, though, this

Figure 11 'The Rage or Shepherds I Have Lost My Waist', hand-coloured etching by Isaac Cruikshank, 1794, © Trustees of the British Museum. A satirical print commenting on the new high-waisted styles in women's dress, in which the short, stout figure on the right is made to look ridiculous. Her companion in the centre refuses the refreshments brought her by a footman. The verses beneath read,

Shepherds I have lost my Waist!
Have you seen my Body?
Sacrificed to modern Taste,
I'm quite a Hoddy Doddy!
For Fashion I that part forsook
Where Sages place the Belly,
Tis gone—& I have not a nook
For Cheese cake, Tart, or Jelly!!

Never shall I see it more,
Till Common Sense returning,
My Body to my Legs restore,
Then I shall cease from mourning:
Folly & Fashion do prevail
To such extremes among the Fair,
A Woman's only Top and Tail,
The Body's Banished God knows where!!!

A painting on the wall behind shows the wide side hoops of earlier in the century, fashionable in the 1740s.

particular norm was on its way out, and *The Lady's Magazine* was calling the high waist a fashionable deformity, likening its wearers to humpbacks, or 'snails carrying their houses on their backs'.[3] A hundred years later saw the opposite extreme, as in the 1920s waists dropped to lodge on the hips. *The Lady* forecast for its readers in 1919 that 'Waists are a negligible quantity; there is rarely a suggestion of one, and most new models are cut on straight lines.' Five years later *The Queen* described 'the ever-descending waist-line', saying it was the 'most significant note of fashion in 1924'. The article added that 'Venus of Milo would have held up her hands in horror, if she had any, so different is the present standards of beauty. The mere cynic with the humorous outlook has been known to exclaim at the prevailing flatness—hips that passed in the night.'[4] By the end of 1929, however, *The Times* was regaling its readers with very different news: 'Definite Return of the Waist' ran a headline in September, and a month later, 'The Restored Waist' was announced.[5]

The garment that for women controlled the waist and tracked its passage up and down the body was the corset, known earlier as stays, and earlier still as a 'pair of bodies'. Its different names and its evolving forms signal the garment's very long history. And this point is important: for most of the last 400 years, Western women have worn some type of corset to support, shape and smooth their malleable flesh. Probably we most associate corsets with the hourglass Victorian figure and rabid controversies over tight-lacing. In doing this we forget that the boned corset first appeared in the second half of the sixteenth century, and was worn continuously well into the twentieth. Even when the traditional, rigid corset gradually fell from favour in the 1920s, for decades to come many women still wore some kind of foundation garment, a way of dressing that was common through to the early 1970s.[6] Looking back with amused astonishment at a world and a self so changed, an elderly woman of my acquaintance once told me that in the air raids of the Second World War, she remembered making her father lace her stays first, before hurrying to the shelter; and as a young child in the 1960s, I can remember my own grandmother's pink corsets. Even in those periods when fashions urged a straight silhouette—such as with those high-waisted neoclassical dresses or the flapper's flatness—foundation garments were used not to enhance curves, but to reduce them. Furthermore, until the development of bust bodices and then the brassiere, corsets provided the only means of support for a woman's breasts. Historically the shape of the bust has therefore been fundamentally influenced by the shape of the waist and the rest of the torso: the upper body has been fashioned as a single anatomical chunk. Finally, and to situate the corset still further within the historical norm, from at least the eighteenth century these garments were universally worn; by women of every age and in every class, rich and poor alike. Whether labouring in the fields or factories, caring for a household or performing the social rituals of the leisured, women got up every morning and put on their stays. While the poorer amongst them may have made their own or obtained them second-hand, by the late nineteenth century shrewd manufacturers were catering specifically for the working-class market. Symington, for example, produced the Pretty Housemaid model, durable, cheaply priced, and reinforced over the abdomen to withstand the added strain of a working woman's physical exertions.[7]

In England, corsetry first appeared in the second half of the sixteenth century, initially as an elite garment. Known as a 'pair of bodies' they were usually sewn from stiff, quilted fabric, with whalebone or dried reeds known as 'bents' inserted to give the garment rigidity. In addition, a removable busk, again made of wood or bone, was slipped into a casing at centre front to provide extra stiffening. These garments get piecemeal mention in widely divergent sources. In a case of demonic possession at the turn of the century, a thirteen-year-old girl is alleged to have demanded of her demon the finest clothes, including 'a french bodie, not of Whalebone, for that is not stiffe inough, but of horne, for that will holde it out; it shall come low before, to keepe in my bellie ... My ladde, I will haue a buske of Whale-bone, it shalbe tyed with two silke pointes.'[8] In a less dramatic context, there are frequent mentions of 'bodies' in Elizabeth I's wardrobe warrants. For example, in 1597 William Jones, the queen's tailor, made for Thomasina, Elizabeth's dwarf, 'a payer of french bodies of damaske lyned with sackecloth, with whale bone to them'. Jones made bodies for Elizabeth, too, and supplied her with busks, including, in 1586, 'xij Buskes of Whalesbone and wyer coverid with sarceonet quilted'.[9] In a conversation manual written to help in the teaching of French (the English and French versions of the dialogue run parallel), the rather imperious Lady Ri-Mellaine calls to Joly, her waiting woman, 'Will you keepe me heere all the day? where be all my thinges? goe fetch my cloathes: bring my petty-coate bodys: I meane my damask quilt bodies with whale bones.'[10] Meanwhile, in real-life Norfolk, a tailor sent in his accounts to the Bacons, a local gentry family. Included in the 1591 bill are the charges for 'a paier of french bodies for m^resA. Bacon', which covered the two shilling cost of making them up, and eighteen pence for the whalebone.[11]

These early bodies were sewn without darts or gussets, and so they compressed and flat-tened a woman's waist and breasts. The effect, and the desired ideal, for a woman's fleshly reality was a long, slim and tapering torso. Rather than exaggerating curves, the body sculpted its wearer into an inverted triangle, wider at the top and narrowing to a point above the crotch (Figure 12). This effect was often emphasized still further by the stom-acher, a stiffened triangular insert worn point down and fastened to the bodice on either side. Functionally, the stomacher filled in the gap between the two front edges of a bodice; visually it made the torso appear even longer, carrying the eye down until, somewhat au-daciously, vision came to rest at the wearer's groin. Sometimes ribbons or jewels decorating the skirt further snagged the gaze, fixing it on where the fork would be, demonstrating that although revealing nothing of the body, clothing can yet be suggestive (Figure 30).[12]

The construction of stays, as bodies eventually became known, remained much the same throughout the later seventeenth and eighteenth centuries, with their complexity and bon-ing increasing but their basic shape unaltered. Under the high-waisted dresses of the early nineteenth century, however, things took a different turn.[13] No longer was the shaping of the waist an issue; instead, the corsets of the period moulded the breasts, and their shape, whereabouts and exposure became matters of criticism. For some, these 'newly-invented stays or corsets' saw the 'bosom shoved up to the chin, making a fleshly shelf, disgusting to the beholders, and certainly most incommdious to the bearer'.[14] Others held the simplicity of modern dresses tasteful and elegant, but thought that their thinness lacked decency, and that their exposure of the bosom and back was repugnant.[15] Comment on the 'too adhesive and transparent' robes also commonly pointed out how unsuited were such fashions to our climate, being 'but ill calculated to protect against damp, cold, and fogs'.[16] It must be remembered, however, that complaints about the revealing nature of women's apparel were sempiternal, and over the centuries the exposure of the breasts, in particular, was a com-mon and recurring trope in the literature of satire and complaint. First-person narrative, on

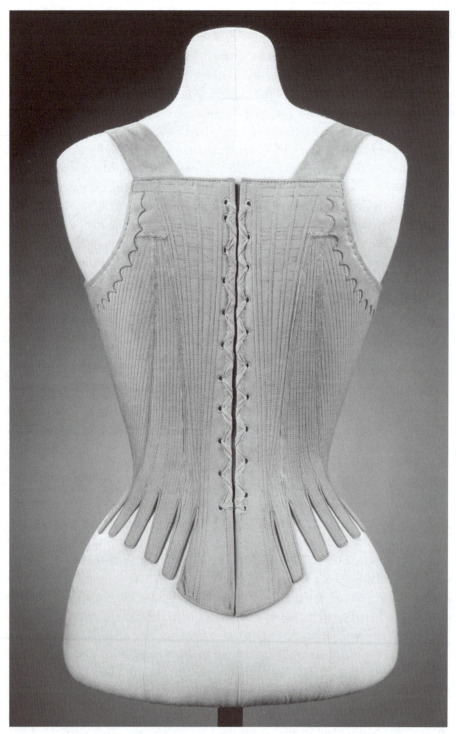

Figure 12 'Stays' (T.172-1914), 1780–9, © Victoria and Albert Museum, London. Back view of a pair of eighteenth-century linen and leather stays, reinforced with whalebone. The lacing down the centre back is clear. Like the 'bodies' of the sixteenth and seventeenth centuries, corsets at this time modelled the torso into an inverted triangle, or cone.

the other hand, usually has a less polemical take on life. Jane Austen, as one might expect from the tenor of her fiction, was cutting rather than outraged. Writing to her sister Cassandra, she witheringly dismissed a Miss Langley as being 'like any other short girl with a broad nose & wide mouth, fashionable dress, & exposed bosom'. Again to Cassandra, the confidante of so many letters, she described the melancholy part of being at a ball, seeing 'so many dozen young Women standing by without partners, & each of them with two ugly naked shoulders!' Finally, she reported with unconcealed delight on the inconstancy of fashion, pleased both at the arbitrary silliness of its adherents and the new direction the style was taking:

> I learnt from Mrs Tickars's young Lady, to my high amusement, that the stays now are not made to force the Bosom up at all;—*that* was a very unbecoming, unnatural fashion. I was really glad to hear that they are not to be so much off the shoulders as they were.[17]

The emphasis on the bust around this time also seems to have given rise to a prosthetic device, the false bosom. A writer in *The Lady's Magazine* of 1789 calls such 'fortification bosoms' unnatural and deplores their mendacity. Nine years later, the magazine adopted a gleeful tone in a punning essay on 'bosoms made of wax': ladies begin to *wax* wanton, they have *melting* moments, and one can *make an impression* on them.[18] Also about then, *The Times* combined the critique of exposure with comment on artificiality, noting, 'The fashion of false bosoms has at least this utility, that it compels our fashionable fair to wear something.'[19] Perhaps needless to say, such patronizing or derogatory comment on the widespread use of breast enhancers is not supported by evidence from the less contentious source of related personal experience. As with stories of the ubiquity of huge hair, most real life was more mundane.

It was in the Victorian period, when waists became the focus of fashion—and fetish—that the moulding of flesh became most dramatic. Industrialization and technology mass-produced shaped corsetry into which the malleable body fitted, filling out the predetermined form. The materials used were stronger and more resilient than before, more resistant to the strain of wear and less compromising to bodily demands. In the relationship between garment and wearer, it was the body that adapted most. Important steps towards the achievement of the curved, unyielding torso include the addition of gussets for the breasts and the hips, which occurred around the 1820s. Metal eyelets, also invented at this time, both made threading a corset easier and meant that it could be pulled tighter without the lace holes tearing with the strain.[20] In 1829, a French corsetier developed the first steel front-busk fastening. Although this did not come into widespread use for another twenty years, it enabled a woman to put on or off her own corset, without help.[21] The spoon busk appeared in 1873, formed, as the name suggests, into a spoon shape which curved into the waist then widened out over the lower abdomen (Figure 13). Also, steel was increasingly used to reinforce corsets, partly because whalebone—owing to demand—was becoming

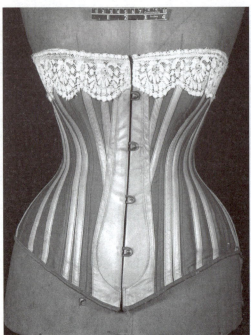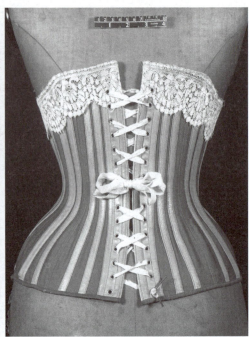

Figure 13 'Corset' (T.84&A-1980), 1883, © Victoria and Albert Museum, London. A front-fastening nineteenth-century corset made of sateen (a cotton fabric with a satin-like, glossy finish) and leather, and reinforced with whalebone. The steel spoon busk at centre front gives the corset greater rigidity and allows a more accentuated curve at the waist. The lacing at the back could be adjusted as the wearer desired.

scarce, and partly, because of the extremity of curve, it was subject to breakage at the waist.[22]

In 1868, Portsmouth corset maker Edwin Izod invented the steam moulding process in which the garment, having been wet in a solution of starch, was placed over steam-heated copper torso shapes until it dried to the correct form.[23] Not only was this a further use for that protean substance, starch, but it also represents the triumph of the standardized and ideal form over the particularities of real bodies. The mass-production of corsetry—as with all items of dress, but more dramatically—meant that a garment no longer took its dimensions from a specific wearer, but rather the reverse. Edwin Izod's career is also a study in miniature of the industrial march of the nineteenth century. In 1863 he was calling himself a stay maker; by 1867 a stay manufacturer; and by 1881 a corset manufacturer, employing 23 men and 337 women in his factory.[24] Fashion historian Valerie Steele has pointed out that some corset makers produced trade cards illustrated with industrial buildings, their chimneys smoking with the fires of manufacture, thus 'linking their products to notions of technical innovation and progress'.[25] The epitome of this—the corseted figure as modernity, the technological body—has to be the appearance of stays at the Great Exhibition of 1851. Included in the manufacturing division, within the class devoted to clothing, nineteen entrants exhibited an inventive variety of corsets. George Roberts, manufacturer of Oxford Street, showed stays made from twenty-one bias-cut pieces designed for maximum flexibility. Other of his garments had patent spring fastenings at the front or back with no lacing or unlacing required, as did examples displayed by Birmingham manufacturers Hurst and Reynolds. Charlotte Smith, 'inventress', submitted stays which she had designed to enable their wearer to regulate at will; and Emma and Elizabeth Martin of Oxford Street produced a bodice made with panels of 'vulcanized India rubber', whose superior elasticity aided easy breathing. Nicholas Geary exhibited a perforated gossamer corset for hot climates, and Mary Sykes, inventor and manufacturer of Regent Street, showed a corset weighing only five ounces, for which she was awarded a medal. The Great Exhibition, visited by one-quarter of Britain's population, was a paean to progress, innovation, industrialization and modernity. Shown in this context, the ingenious fashioning of the female anatomy was something of which the nation could be proud.[26]

The ways in which stays and their wearers have been viewed span the range of possible responses. Corsetry has been situated both within the strict boundaries of moral probity, and outside in the wastes of lascivious indulgence. It has been regarded as physically beneficial, and then again, as the cause of a huge array of illnesses. The woman in a corset improves on nature, and she is a freak of artificiality. Tight-lacing, to pick at just one of the discursive threads, has always been condemned and its dangers abhorred but, as Steele has noted, with little agreement on what it actually constitutes, it remains an amorphous—albeit potent—concept. Thus in John Bulwer's 1653 text *Anthropometamorphosis,* he censures the 'pernicious' habit of those 'who thinking a slender waste a great beauty, strive all that they possibly can by streight-lacing themselves to attaine unto a wand-like smalnesse of waste, never thinking themselves fine enough untill they can span their Waste'. He then marshals the weight of the classics to his argument, citing Terence to claim tight-lacers have 'a stinking breath'.[27] *The Gentleman's Magazine* of 1743 fills nearly four columns in detailing the seriously bad effects of straight-laced stays, including—perhaps in homage to Bulwer—the information that 'a STINKING BREATH' is always the result.[28] In her memoirs, Mary Frampton remembers that in 1780,

> the perfection of figure according to the *then* fashion was the smallness of the circumference into which your unfortunate waist could be compressed, and many a poor girl hurt her health very materially by trying to rival the reigning beauty of that day, the Duchess of Rutland, who was said to squeeze herself to the size of an orange and a half.[29]

That the Duchess, a powerful political hostess and famed for her looks, had a corseted waist as small as one and a half oranges is obviously absurd, but also illustrative of the way claims about corsetry have tended to exaggeration and prurience (Figure 14).

The ink spilt in the cause of the abolition of nineteenth-century tight-lacing would fill copious vats, and that spent in defending the practice a few more again.[30] As we have seen, in some contexts the corset wearer's curves were a technical triumph; in others, they were evidence of a dark and barbarous practice. So, how small did women actually lace themselves? There is no way of checking the veracity of contemporary claims, as advertisements and fashion illustration present a stylized ideal, and the photographic image was—then, as

Figure 14 'Tight Lacing, or Fashion Before Ease', hand-coloured mezzotint published by Bowles and Carver after John Collet, 1777, © Trustees of the British Museum. A woman's husband, maid, and page together tug at her stay laces. She has the large coiffure so fashionable in the 1770s. Tied around her waist and hanging at her side is a pocket, which would normally be hidden beneath the skirts. In the foreground a monkey—a common motif in anti-fashion satire—points to an open book on which is written, 'Fashions Victim a Satire'.

now—able to be manipulated. 'As one Victorian photographer observed, "The retoucher may slice off, or curve the lady's waist after his own idea of shape and form and size." '[31] We are left, therefore, with the evidence of extant garments. The status of material objects from the past is also uncertain, however. Do things survive because they were typical and numerous, or because, on the contrary, they were atypical and their unusual qualities prized? All we can say is that the stays that do remain from the eighteenth century suggest that the waists were not particularly small, corsets in some collections measuring from twenty-four to thirty inches, and in others, twenty-one to twenty-six inches.[32] As we have seen, the production and technology of nineteenth-century corsets meant both that they came in standard sizes, and that it was possible to lace them more tightly than their sixteenth- to eighteenth-century predecessors. Even so, manufacturers' advertisements show the usual range of corset sizes to have been from eighteen to thirty inches at the waist, although larger, and occasionally smaller, sizes were available. The Leicestershire Museums Service collection of 197 corsets, presented by the Symington foundation wear company, only has one with a waist of eighteen inches, and a further eleven that measure nineteen inches. The majority of corsets in the collection range from twenty to twenty-six inches.

When considering the 'reasonableness' of these measurements we must also remember that as a population, our bodies have changed shape, and our sense of what makes for a comfortable size has also therefore altered. We know this with some accuracy thanks to the National Sizing Survey carried out in 2001–2, a collaborative project between major retailers, University College London, London College of Fashion, and the Department for Trade and Industry. Using three-dimensional body scanning, or 'shape capture devices', SizeUK measured 11,000 subjects, taking over 150 measurements from each.[33] The results of the survey revealed that over the last fifty years, the average waist size for women has increased by an astonishing six and a half inches, from twenty-seven and a half inches in 1951 (the date of the last survey) to thirty-four inches today. While the body has enlarged all over—getting taller, wider and with bigger feet—it has not expanded in proportion with this thickening waist. Busts and hips, therefore, are now only one and a half inches larger than the 1951 measure. All this means that the shape of the modern woman is far less curvy than formerly, more straight up and down and 'masculine'. It is therefore likely that the idea of forcing our cylindrical torsos into an hourglass is much worse than the actual shaping of their curvier bodies was for our foremothers.

Also pertinent when considering the size of eighteenth- and nineteenth-century stays is that while the above are waist measurements of corsets fully closed, they were in fact variable garments that a woman could lace more or less tightly at will. A corset might be worn so the edges laced together, but equally 'it might also have been left open one, two, or more inches in the back'.[34] This more moderate picture of the modification of women's upper bodies is supported by contemporary comment that castigated tight-lacing but endorsed moderate corsetry. *The Ladies' Pocket Magazine* of 1828 denounced the 'evil' of tight stays and recommended that all women wear instead stays made of some soft and warm material 'which protect them from the cold, and afford a moderate support'. If stiffened with whalebone or steel, wearers should take care that they have freedom of movement.[35] *Woman* magazine 'consistently defended corsetry'; and although opposed to tight-lacing, Queen Victoria also believed their support most necessary, even during pregnancy.[36] Even Lydia Becker, a radical campaigner for women's suffrage and education, thought corsets indispensable. 'Stick to your stays', she urged, 'they improve the form, give warmth and assist you. Stick to your stays, ladies, and triumph over the opposite sex.'[37] Nineteenth-century advertisements for corsets were cast in terms of the garment's benefits, promising the wearer comfort, back support, flexibility, and the graceful elegance of a good figure. Steele has suggested that most women 'believed corsets served some useful function', and they certainly trimmed the waist, supported heavy breasts and flattened the larger abdomen. Instead of suppressing natural amplitude, still other corsets were padded to make up for a wearer's 'deficiencies'.[38]

The perception that a foundation garment was an indispensable part of a woman's wardrobe persisted well into the twentieth century, and it was only in the last decades that the idea of fit, strong femininity really took hold, where a woman's figure was corseted by her own taut muscles. Thus, as late as 1954, costume historian Norah Waugh was still able to write of 'the new corset phase' of nylon and lightweight elastics, speculating on 'what strange distortions of shape the artist-corsetière, inspired by his new technique, will devise for woman's malleable flesh'.[39] Furthermore, while the ideal of the 'muscular corset'[40] is perhaps more potent than ever, the number and variety of 'control' garments seem also to be increasing—from tights and underwear to support buttocks and hold in the stomach, to full-body garments to smooth and redistribute the flesh from thigh to bust. Moreover, the belief that a prosthetic device is necessary to hold and shape the breasts has never gone away. Despite being frequently informed that the majority of women are wearing an ill-fitting bra, we persist in believing them to be functional, attractive and, above all, necessary. Indeed, we could push this comparison a little further, for obviously braless women in some small way transgress the boundaries of 'polite' behaviour. Whether prompted by a politicized belief as in the 1960s, sexual assertiveness, or merely a personal choice of comfort or convenience, breasts that are overtly loose are outside the conventions of day-to-day propriety.

That this unease at the unrestrained, braless chest should persist—however slightly felt—must help us better appreciate just how and why for so many generations, loose dress was morally so very dubious. Whereas neat stays were 'a physical embodiment of solid virtue, decent self-control and respectability',[41]

> *The Negligence of loose Attire*
> *May oft' invite to loose Desire.*[42]

A woman with her upper body unconfined thus stepped beyond the whaleboned boundaries of propriety. She was open to suspicion and such various charges as immorality, slovenliness, sexual laxity and plain eccentricity. A bawdy poem of 1724, 'A Lover to His Fat Mistress with Stays', makes its argument quite clear: the uncorseted woman is both physically and morally repulsive.

> Pray charming Silvia, do not think you raise
> My modest Passion by your want of Stays;
> I do not for your dangling Breasts adore ye,
> That hang like new-milk'd Udders down before ye:
> Or do I in those flabby Sides take pride,
> That do your Aprong-strings in Wallups hide.
> You look like one from Vertues Bonds just freed,
> Whose Dress declares you little Courtship need;
> If so, at one Request, your Favours grant,
> And please your self with what you seem to want.
> But if you think my jealous Eyes to please,
> And would be gently Conquer'd by degrees,
> Raise my Esteem, and make me speak your praise,
> Pray hide the Slit, and hasten on your Stays.[43]

The sense of slovenliness lurking within this poem is also identifiable in the 'very diverting' description of Lady Rochford that the outspoken Princess Amelia recounted to Lady Mary

Coke for her amusement. '"She was dressed so loose & so naked, that I told her I cou'd see I did not know where, upon which,' said the Princess, 'She pulled up two napkins that She said She always wore upon her stomack & very dirty ones they were."'[44]

In the nineteenth century, the few women who, influenced by pre-Raphaelite ideals, wore what was known as 'artistic' or 'aesthetic' dress were a 'tiny and isolated group' from the artistic and intellectual fringes. Their uncorseted, flowing dresses made in softer, non-aniline colours were generally considered eccentric and ugly; they 'were given a critical and unsympathetic reception'.[45] For dress designer Lucy Duff Gordon (1862–1935), 'the straight-backed rigidity of the Victorian reflected those dreadful straight-backed corsets they wore'—temporarily ignoring the fact that in her memoirs she includes a photograph of her corseted younger self with, she declares, a twenty-one-inch waist.[46] Writing about the same time as Duff Gordon was being photographed, Elizabeth von Arnim, in her semi-autobiograhical novel *The Solitary Summer*, describes the death of an old woman who has saved to leave 'a very good black silk dress' and 'real whalebone corsets' in which to be buried. 'They are beautiful corsets', explains one character, adding, 'It would be a scandal not to be buried decently.'[47]

If these were the moral consequences of corset wearing, what were the physical? According to tracts opposed to tight-lacing they were many and varied, and ranged from halitosis to gastric discomfort, sluggish bowels and deformity of the spine. The medical profession, in such respected publications as *The Lancet*, also repeatedly warned of dangers, and in some cases even had no hesitation in explaining the aetiology of a woman's death as her tightly laced stays. But tight-lacing, as we have seen, was a demonized practice, probably engaged in by just a few. What of the countless women who for countless years lived ordinary corseted lives? These women stuck by their stays, altering the extremity of lacing according to occasion, time of day, stage of life, and mood. What physical effects would they have been likely to feel?[48] The first is muscular weakening. While in the short term wearing a corset would have supported the frame and even provided relief from back pain, long-term use would probably have resulted in muscular atrophy and the onset of, or increase in, back discomfort. Ironically, if this happened a corset would have been felt to be 'needed' to ameliorate what was actually a garment-induced condition, further wear in turn leading to further weakness and a worsening pain. The second effect of wearing stays is breathlessness, for the compression of the chest reduces a wearer's lung capacity. It was because of just this, music lover Mrs Papendiek discovered, that the opera singer Mara laced so loosely when about to perform. '"You look very smart in that white silk"', said Mr Papendiek to Mara, '"but how loosely it is put on!" To which she answered, "You forget what my voice must do this day—it must have room to do itself justice."'[49] Unlike muscle wastage, shortness of breath was temporary and quickly relieved by rest. However, it does mean that the hackneyed motif of corseted women fainting was probably well grounded in fact, as too the clichéd cutting of a corset's laces. Princess Lieven (1785–1857), the wife of the Russian ambassador to England, describes just such a case when Madame de Princetau 'had an attack of nerves, a fainting fit and another attack of nerves—all in public. We cut her stay-laces.'[50]

There is one further consequence of corset wearing to be noted, although not one visited upon the anatomy of the wearer. Rather, it was the whales from whom the bones were sliced who suffered most for this fashion. The 'whalebones' of a corset are actually baleen, found in the fins, but principally making the long (up to thirteen feet), teeth-like blades through which a right whale sieves the ocean for the fish and small creatures that make up its diet. Baleen is hard like horn but its fibres lie in parallel like hair, so it can be split lengthwise into very thin sections.[51] It is light, strong and pliant. If heated and cooled into shape, it will retain any new form. For everyone except the whale, baleen was the ideal substance for corsetry.

There were three main fisheries. The first was the hunting of the Atlantic right whale in the Bay of Biscay, a trade that supplied Tudor women with the whalebone for their 'bodies'. As the stock of Biscayan whales was exhausted, fishing around Spitzbergen took off, especially when the baleen was found to be of extremely good quality. The extent of the trade in the eighteenth century, the smuggling, the profits and the slaughter, can be gauged from a 1722 enquiry, which found:

> As to the Whale-Fins, it appears by the Custom-House Books, that there hath been imported in the Port of London, from the Year 1715, to 1721, one Year with another, about 150 tons yearly, even when the Price hath been very dear, viz. 400 *l.* per Ton, little more or less, which is, one Year with another, 60,000 *l.* a Year, over and above what is imported in all other Ports of Great Britain and Ireland; which may moderately be supposed to be 100 Tons more. Then the Sum paid for Whalebone amounts to 100,000 *l.* per Annum, besides what probably may be run clandestinely.[52]

By the end of the century the Greenland waters in turn became depleted, and the American Whale Fishery, which hunted bowhead whales, took its place. Even after 1859 when it was discovered that petroleum could be used instead of whale oil, the market for whalebone kept the fishery thriving. 'The output of whalebone for the whole of the nineteenth century exceeded £90,000,000 worth, about 450,000,000 American dollars.'[53] As the century progressed, the techniques for producing flexible steel improved and baleen was less in demand. Nevertheless, whalebone continued to be used in the most expensive stays, even into the twentieth century. By then, the demands of corsetry, coupled with the seriously depleted number of bowhead whales, meant that whalebone cost up to £2,800 for a single ton.[54] It was the transformation of boned corsetry into elasticized foundation garments, which finally meant that women were no longer dressed by the kill.

MASCULINITY SHEATHED AND STIFFENED

While the story of women's upper bodies has been one of containment and constriction, we should be wrong if we imagine the narrative of the male torso to have been a simple opposition. Where one was confined, the other was neither free nor unfashioned. Rather, the doublet, the basic garment that covered a man's upper body, was tight fitting and well wadded. It sheathed the body in a smooth carapace, articulating the anatomy in a sharp-edged presentation that drew its influence from contemporary plate armour.[55] In the 1570s the fashion took an unusual turn, sculpting the front of the doublet into an overhanging paunch. The peascod belly, as it was known, lasted for about thirty years and meant that the doublet was further stiffened and padded. 'For my parte, handsomnes in them, I see none', wrote Phillip Stubbes, predictably distressed at their exaggerated form. He matched it, however, with an exaggerated description, claiming that the 'monstrous' doublets 'hang downe to the middest of their theighes, or'—backtracking a little—'at least to their priuie members' (Figure 15). Indeed, some portraits of this time do show a certain symmetry between the belly above and, by this stage, the dwindling codpiece below. Stubbes claimed that such doublets were stuffed with 'foure, fiue or six pound of Bombast at the least'—surely an unlikely figure. He also made the interesting assertion that wearers are so 'stuffed, bombasted and sewed, as they can verie hardly eyther stoupe downe, or decline them selues to the grounde', so 'styffe and sturdy' do their doublets stand about them.[56]

Stubbes, of course, had his own agenda: his commentary on clothing forms part of a moral polemic, and he writes to expose fashion to derision. However for all that, there is some truth in what he said. Doublets were stiff, heavy garments, sometimes reinforced with boning, in which the wearer would have found it hard to slouch, or perhaps bend over easily. While the doublet style that succeeded after 1600 looked more relaxed and loose, the internal construction remained similar. Indeed, in place of the stuffed peascod belly, such doublets now had

Figure 15 'Sir Francis Drake', engraving attributed to Jodocus Hondius, c. 1580, © Trustees of the British Museum. Drake wears a doublet with a large peascod belly.

'belly pieces'—stiffened triangular inserts—to maintain rigidity. Furthermore, at this time doublet sleeves were not cut and sewn straight, but with a pre-shaped bend at the elbow. This accommodated the inward movement of the arm without straining the seams. It also lured the wearer towards the arms akimbo stance, so prevalent in Tudor and Stuart portraits as to be known to us as the Renaissance elbow. Arm jutting out and resting nonchalantly on the hip, we see this image of assertive masculinity rendered in paint and canvas (Figures 23, 34 and 35); it was also rendered in flesh with the help of the doublet's structure.[57]

The second half of the seventeenth century saw the doublet in transition as men's dress evolved its way towards the coat and waistcoat, garments that would be as universal and long-lived as had been the doublet and jerkin that preceded them. The demise of the doublet did not mean the disappearance of upright masculinity though; it just meant that stiffening might be worn as an inner layer, for late-eighteenth- and nineteenth-century mentions of men wearing stays are not unusual (Figure 16). For example, in one of the many amusing and slightly scurrilous stories from Sophia Baddeley's biography, the actress (Figure 5) receives a visit from Count Haslang, an unpopular and elderly Bavarian minister, always 'full of his compliments'. She turns to remove her cat from the sofa so the Count can sit down, but he takes the opportunity to grasp her hand and desire a kiss. Angrily she refuses

Figure 16 'The Protecting Macaroni', etching published by Matthew Darly, 1772, © Trustees of the British Museum. A caricatured man of fashion is laced into stays by a servant or stay maker. The wig or hair of the latter is dressed in a club typical of the macaroni style. The man on the right wears a bag wig with the ribbon brought to the front to be tied in a solitaire style. The falls at the front of his breeches can be clearly seen.

and pulls her hand away suddenly, which, as the Count's foot is entangled in her long gown, causes him to lose his balance and fall on the floor. Overcome with laughter and not having sufficient strength to help him to rise, Sophia goes for the maids, who eventually get him into a chair. The Count, more wounded in pride than body, hobbles to his carriage, whereupon the maids 'laughed as heartily as we did' and 'declared the Count had stays on'.[58]

In the closing years of the eighteenth century, Walter Vaughan's medical treatise on clothing included a section on the compression caused by stays. 'It has been reported', he wrote, 'that a certain Class of finical Gentlemen have begun to wear them: but, for the Sake of the Age, I hope this Report is groundless.'[59] Alas for Vaughan, it was not, for with the rise of dandiacal masculinity at this time, stays or corsets were worn by 'at least a conspicuous minority of fashionable men'.[60] Among their numbers was the portly Prince Regent, future George IV. It was common knowledge that as he got older and fatter, the Prince restrained his increasing corpulence with the help of corsets (Figure 17). As Lord Holland snidely commented to politician Thomas Creevey, 'They say the Prince has left off his stays, and that Royalty, divested of its usual supports, makes a bad figure.'[61] Whether pictured graphically or in text, a cinched middle and an enormous neckcloth soon became the shorthand for a dandy (Figure 8). Again and again in description and satire, he is found laced into stays:

Figure 17 '1812, or Regency a la Mode', hand-coloured etching by William Heath, 1810–15, © Trustees of the British Museum. The Prince Regent (the future George IV; 1762–1830) stands at a mirror and, with a brush, applies what appears to be rouge. Meanwhile, a servant pulls hard to lace him into his corset. As well as the pot of rouge, the dressing table contains tooth powder, a skin wash, and perfume. A monkey—so often used in representations of the foolish who 'ape' the fashions—perches on top of the mirror and tries on a wig identical to the Regent's own hairstyle. The Prince's coat is ready on a stand, and on the shelf above there is space for bills (on the left) and receipts (on the right). There are, however, no receipts. The unpaid bills include demands from the hairdresser, tailor, silversmith, hatter, butcher and fishmonger.

A skeleton's the taste, scarce five inches round the waist,

My body belt, tight buckel'd in so handy O ...

My stays are lac'd so tight, that I'm forc'd to walk upright

My chin pok'd out, my neckcloth stiff, so handy, O ...

Some stare, but all declare, that I'm a Dandy, O.[62]

In *The Fudge Family*, a series of comic letters describing fashionable types (Figure 18)—and all in a metre reminiscent of a Dr Seuss book—the vicissitudes of the corset-wearing beau are vividly described, as the pressure of a heavy meal causes him to burst his laces. 'Dear DICK,' writes Dandy Bob to his friend, 'old DONALDSON's mending my stays':

Which I *knew* would go smash with me one of these days,

And, at yesterday's dinner, when, full to the throttle,

We lads had begun our desert [*sic*] with a bottle

Of neat old Constantia, on *my* leaning back

Just to order another, by Jove I went crack!—

Figure 18 'A Dandy', hand-coloured etching by Charles Williams, 1818, © Trustees of the British Museum. A print illustrating *The Fudge Family in Paris* shows Bob (misnamed as Phil by the artist) arrayed for the evening in familiar dandy style—an excessively high neckcloth and collar, a cinched middle and skintight pantaloons. He stands before the mirror trying on rings, and on the washstand is a collection of cosmetics, perfumes and a patch box; a scarf, hat and boot on a boot-stretcher hang at its side. Littered on the ground lie bills from the makers of stays and pumps (such as he is wearing), as well as a packet of chicken skin gloves and a discarded pair of stays. The open wardrobe with a bust of Adonis on the top has a pair of trousers spilling out of the drawer that clearly show the new vogue of stirrup-like straps worn to achieve a tighter, smoother fit. On the back wall a gun hangs limply from a nail, with a sign saying, 'not loaded'. The inference is abundantly clear. The verse beneath, part of a letter from dandy Bob to his friend Dick, is copied from *The Fudge Family*. It plays on typical dandy motifs—the high gloss of the boots, the corset, the tailor's skill—and also draws a parallel between tight neckcloths, a horse's harness and the hangman's noose:

A lad who goes into the world dick like me,
Should have his neck tied up, you know, there's no doubt of it;
Almost as tight as some lads who go out of it.
Whith [*sic*] whiskers well oil'd, and boots that hold up
The mirror to nature;—so bright you could sup

Off the leather like china; with coat too that draws
On the tailor who suffers a martyrs applause,
With head bridle'd up like a four in hand leader
And stays—devils in them—too tight for a feeder,
I strut to the Old caff [café] Hardy.

Or, as honest Tom said, in his nautical phrase,
'D—n my eyes, Boв, in *doubling* the *Cape* you've *miss'd stays*.'
So, of course, as no gentleman's seen out without them,
They're now at the Schneider's—and, while he's about them,
Here goes a letter …[63]

So pervasive was the cultural type of a corseted dandy, it turns outs that one petty thief used it as the basis for his pickpocketing scam. Dressed 'in very tight stays, and decorated with all the other insignia of a dandy', W. Clarke was, as *The Times* reported, 'brought up on the vulgar charge of picking a brazier's pocket'. Although the theft was witnessed, at first there was no suspicion attaching to Clarke and his companion, for sauntering along unconcernedly they 'appeared to be men of fashion'. When the witness, a Mr Bushell, called out, 'stop thief', though, Clarke's companion lost his nerve and bolted. Bushell was easily able to detain Clarke; indeed, he was so feeble in his struggles that a child could have stopped him. The reason for such physical impotence soon became clear as Bushell over-heard Clarke mutter, 'Curse the stays'.[64]

While much of the comment surrounding men in corsets took place in a context of disparagement and satire, Jonathan Gray's speculation about England's foremost military hero, Wellington, is cast a little differently. 'The Duke', wrote Gray to his family, 'appeared stiff, as if he wore stays.'[65] Here Gray, with perfect accuracy, is linking the upright military carriage and pouter-pigeon chest with the use of corsets. While the 'girding of fighting men's loins' has a long history, in the nineteenth century 'military dress uniform reached extremes of rigidity and display' and corseting was 'frequently undertaken to preserve' its 'stiff perfection'.[66] In a dress manual of 1830, the anonymous 'Cavalry Officer' author pointed out the advantages that uniform gave to a bad figure, including the way stays made the wearer's waist small.[67] This was not just a stylistic choice, however. Certainly stays gave the military wearer—especially the cavalry officers who most favoured them[68]—a panache and élan. But they also provided support, particularly while riding, and some civilian wear-ers adopted them for the same benefits. A modern parallel are today's weightlifters who wear wide, tightened belts to help their most strenuous exertions.[69]

Advertisements for men's corsetry usually emphasized postural and strengthening ben-efits. Some also made these military and sporting associations overt. Hunting belts sold by the India Rubber Web Depot in Regent Street were said to support the figure and repress corpulency.[70] The Melton Riding and Cricketing Belt promised abdominal sup-port, improvement of the physique and, for the more mature wearer, 'the lightness and elasticity of youth'. This model came with a testimonial from J. Hare Esq., who recom-mended it in preference to all others.[71] Amidst advertisements for riding boots, saddles and other equestrian equipment, the pages of *The County Gentleman: Sporting Gazette, Agricultural Journal, and 'The Man about Town'* also featured 'belt band drawers'—a garment endorsed by 'army surgeons' and advertised with frequency in a variety of publications—and abdominal belts for ladies and gents.[72] Then there were electric stays: belts that combined the traditional benefits of corsetry with the modern wonders of medical science, a blessing to men with a nervous or weakened constitution. The maker of Harness' Electropathic Belts urged that they 'should be worn by all in search of Health, Strength, and Energy'.[73] It is also noteworthy that amongst the corsets entered in the 1851 Great Exhibition were a small number for men, including the 'anti-rheumatic belt and drawers' patented by G. Bradshaw.[74] In the opinion of one corset maker, all men would benefit from wearing stays. In youth, a properly constructed belt prevents rupture, making the wearer stronger and exertion safer. In a man's middle and later years, they guard against obesity and contribute to well-being. Indeed, according to her, 'almost every gentleman who has arrived at a "certain age" wears a belt or stays for comfort and for health's sake.' Although it has to be said that the status of the correspondence in which this view is aired is suspect—both contemporaries and modern historians are uncertain whether these communications were genuine or fictional—either way, the sentiments in this letter were at the least consistent with its audience's frame of reference.[75]

The similarities between the trim-waisted dandy and the clipped and upright military figure are probably not coincidental, for not a few society dandies had in fact been officers.[76] On one hand, then, corset wearing was associated with the effete man of fashion whose manliness had attenuated to the point of effeminacy, and whose mincing steps proclaimed his physical timidity. In his inability to struggle or run away, W. Clark, hailed before the courts in his stays and dandy's dress, had, readers would have inferred, reaped the just rewards of his disguise. On the other hand, corsets were also imaged as garments of potency and self-discipline, whose wearers' hard bodies glittered with strength and prowess. These two very different views existed side by side, but in some contexts, and some men, merged—almost as if you go far enough in one discursive direction, you come back around in another. It was perhaps in the person of the Regent that such divergent readings most clearly coalesce. In the abstract, George represented royal authority. In the particular, he was a corpulent and unpopular man, yet still possessed of an enduring personal charm and the ghost of his dashing and handsome youth. With a passion for flamboyant clothes and militaria,[77] under Brummell's influence the Prince espoused the severe restraint of dandy cut and colour. Constraining his body, the corset was at once powerful, fashionable and ludicrous.

Most men, however, did not have to contend with obesity; neither did they strut on the parade ground, nor spend disciplined hours in the grooming required by serious dandyism. Most men existed somewhere in the middle ground and, most emphatically, they did not wear stays. Nevertheless, military and dandy chic—with their shared aesthetic of tightly fitting garments revealing a broad chest and narrow waist—were extremely significant, and found their way into the average male wardrobe and onto the average male body. The influence of the military look was a pan-European phenomenon. The Napoleonic Wars, fought in every corner of the Continent, 'disseminated a new social respect for the soldier'. Many citizens enlisted in national armies where, for the first time, success brought the possibility of social advancement.[78] The career of Napoleon himself, rising through the ranks to become ruler of the biggest empire since the Roman, was just the most notable. In this period, the uniform came into its own: in the military's showy formal dress, in the clothing adopted by early civil services, as a badge of membership to the growing number of sporting clubs, and adapted in decorative detail on women's fashion.[79] Jane Austen, for one, observed society's dalliance with military chic. In *Pride and Prejudice*, Lydia Bennet's determined pursuit of the militia quartered at Meryton owed more than a little to the handsome appearance of the officers. As her silly mother, Mrs Bennet, fondly remarked, 'I remember the time when I liked a red coat myself very well—and indeed so I do still at my heart ... and I thought Colonel Forster looked very becoming the other night ... in his regimentals.'[80]

The echoes of military uniform are found in many aspects of early-nineteenth-century attire: in garments such as pantaloons, which we will return to later; in the cut of coats; and in detailing like epaulettes, braiding and buttons. Underlying the bravado of dress uniform and its translation into civilian style, however, was the interest in classical art and architecture that had gathered momentum over the second half of the eighteenth century. For it was in the heroic male nude of classical sculpture that the nineteenth century found a pattern for modern masculinity.[81] Unlike the full-bellied manliness of previous centuries—typified by the peascod doublet—which swaggered big hipped and large thighed with an out-thrust cocky elbow, modern man was lean and hard. He was statuary made flesh, with defined musculature, a large chest, a flat stomach and long legs; and he continues to be recognizable in our ideal of today.

How was this Pygmalion myth to be realized? How was the perfection of cold marble to be brought to life? The answer was through the skill and creativity of the tailor. Subsequent commentators are emphatic about this. Bespoke tailoring 'formed the male body during the nineteenth century', redefining ordinary flesh according to the heroic ideal.[82] Such transformation through dress was made possible by a number of advances and innovations in tailoring at this time. The one that perhaps underpins the rest was the invention of the measuring tape. In widespread use by 1818, this simple device 'revolutionized tailoring', allowing customers' measurements to be taken with both greater speed and accuracy.[83] Up until this point, tailors had used strips of parchment, one per client, with notches cut to indicate various measures, a relatively clumsy way of recording the anatomy. With the standardized tape, English tailors 'could cut cloth and mould it to the body so that it fitted like a second skin'.[84] Along with the tape measure came a particular etiquette attaching to its use, enabling the tailor and customer to negotiate 'an intimate social terrain in which the potential breaching of corporeal, sexual and class taboos was dangerously real'.[85] Tailors' guides advised those in the trade on how to maintain a discreet social distance, even while physically intruding on the most private areas of the body. Standing to one side rather than in front 'of your man', being deft and swift in all movements, and being deferential, were all important.[86] For the complexity of a bespoke garment the measurements taken were comprehensive and ranged over the entire body, for in the pursuit of classical proportions the length of a coat, for example, was decided by the length of the wearer's legs as much as by his upper body. Altering the garment's cut—where, for example, the waist was placed—could make a client's anatomy appear to more closely resemble the antique ideal.[87] Accompanying the measuring, the tailor was also adept at 'discreet note-taking':

> Did the gentleman stoop or hold his chest too far forward? Was the waistline a reality still, or a fictive projection of the tailor? How rounded was the seat? To all these questions, small enciphered marks could be make against a sketched 'tailor's doll' to re-order the man according to the new ideals of masculine perfection.[88]

Once the measures were taken and the cloth was cut, a further raft of techniques came into play. These included the addition of painstakingly stitched padding, set between the lining and the outer fabric, and placed so as to make the most of what nature had supplied and disguise what she had seen fit to withhold. Typically, this might mean ameliorating a set of rounded shoulders, or enlarging a chest not sufficiently defined. Darts and seams that curved into the body, particularly at the back, ensured a tight fit and an upright posture. Combining with small armholes set relatively far back, the wearer was forced by his garment to draw back his shoulders and throw out his chest. By comparison, the suits of today are cut large and loose, with the back seam encompassing a slight curve out rather than inwards, and the roomy armholes set forward. A contemporary jacket thus allows for ease and stooping and slouch; its nineteenth-century equivalent was far more rigorous, and insisted its wearer remain erect.[89] During the construction, careful steam pressing, stretching and working of the cloth also helped mould the garment to the desired form. Finally, the complex collar was perfected, tailored so as to stand around the neck and then flatten into the lapel. 'There is as much art in cutting a collar as in cutting a coat', instructed one tailor's manual, 'for if the collar is not properly cut to fit the neck, it easily spoils the fit of the coat over the shoulders, which runs in creases and may roll the lapel and breast from top to bottom.'[90] By contrast, skilful tailoring of this feature would flatter the wearer's neck, shoulders and chest.

The tailor's creation of the idealized figure features in Edward Bulwer Lytton's immensely popular novel of 1828, *Pelham*. The eponymous, first-person hero is the ultimate dandy, and in the following, he is being measured for a coat:

> 'We are a very good figure, sir, very good figure,' replied Mr Schneider surveying me from head to foot, while he was preparing his measure. 'We want a little assistance though; we must be padded well here, we must have our chest thrown out, and have an additional inch across the shoulder … all the Gentlemen in the Life Guards are padded there sir, we must live for effect in this world, sir. A *leetle* tighter round the waist eh?'[91]

In real life, Brummell's biographer Ian Kelly suggests vignettes like this would have been the 'prologue to the series of scenes that would mark the creation of a particular garment'. Up to six fittings in this—quite literally—costume drama were not uncommon, the Prince of Wales once taking seventeen before he was happy with the appearance of his coat.[92]

Other garments also had their roles to play on the fashionable stage. Like the coat, carefully shaped seams fitted the waistcoat to the body snugly, and at the back, straps and buckles, or lacing—reminiscent of corsets—could be tightened to further suggest a flat stomach and small waist.[93] Restraint for the waist might also be built into the fastenings of breeches and trousers. Some extant examples have boned panels sewn into them, and the standard design incorporated a vent at the back, which was fastened with corset lacing to achieve a tight fit.[94]

So, garments in the nineteenth century actively fashioned the male torso. While some men, for reasons connected with their body shape, their sense of aesthetics or their pleasure, took this to the level of corset wearing, for most it was achieved through the cut and construction of the coat, waistcoat, drawers and trousers. Tailors who successfully fashioned their clients in this way might also succeed in fashioning themselves considerable wealth. Despite the long credit they offered—usually around six months, but sometimes only sending their customers an annual bill[95]—some London tailors achieved greater fame and fortune than those they dressed. A significant number of these were foreign refugees who, having developed their skills meeting the demand for military uniforms, then fled the turmoil of war-torn Europe.[96] Although a bootmaker rather than a tailor, Hoby's career is illustrative. He catered to George III and his brothers the royal dukes, the Prince of Wales, and many naval and military officers including the Duke of Wellington. According to Captain Gronow, a dandy of the day, Hoby was said to employ 300 workers and a great deal of insolent conceit. 'If Lord Wellington had had any other bootmaker than myself', he is meant to have said, 'he would never have had his great and constant successes; for my boots and prayers bring his lordship out of all difficulties.'[97]

THE PLEASURES OF CONTAINMENT

Any garment that lasts for over 300 years has to have something going for it. There are probably few who would wholeheartedly condemn the corset, so well has revisionist history done its job of rehabilitating this most demonized of garments.[98] But equally, there are probably few who would immediately leap to its defence, appreciating that it offered its own advantages and specific pleasures. Most certainly, not everyone subject to whalebone and lacing found it a conducive regime. Some wearers experienced corsetry as a confinement that had to be silently endured, like so many of life's discomforts. Artist Gwen Raverat (1885–1957) remembered her rebellion against stays when first made to wear them: 'to me they were real instruments of torture; they prevented me from breathing, and dug deep holes into my softer parts on every side, I am sure no hair-shirt could have been worse to me'.[99] For most though, corsetry was a normal part of getting dressed which may, like most garments, have had its drawbacks, but which, again like most garments, had also its satisfactions and advantages.

So what might have been the advantages of a corset? What is there about the fashioning of the midriff that could be experienced positively? Gwen Raverat described her uncorseted state as 'soft shelled', a condition that she obviously preferred. But there is also in this image a sense of something vulnerable, of something pinkly exposed, its protective carapace peeled away. For the corset and other reinforced garments like the doublet, gave the wearer containment. They sheathed the soft and visceral bits; they protected a person's core.

One consequence of this containment was support. As noted earlier, before the development of the separate brassiere the breasts were held and shaped by the stays. This garment also supported the belly and back, obliging the wearer at the same time to adopt an upright posture. As dance re-enactor Jackie Marshall-Ward describes it, this was not a hindrance, but a help: a well-fitting corset gives comfortable support and can be worn for most of the day.[100] This may not have been an unalloyed benefit. Steele suggests that prolonged corset use weakened the wearer's own musculature, thus inducing back pain and perpetuating reliance on the corset's support. However, it is debatable whether the generations of women post-1950s who adjure corsetry's embrace in favour of a 'soft-shelled' condition have fewer back problems as a result. And it is certain that our general stance—men and women alike—is more stooped, slouched and round shouldered than that of our forebears who were laced and tailored into a reinforced erectness. This upright posture and carriage of theirs was built not only into clothing, but into theories of health, courtesy, and the figuring of moral rectitude.[101] A slumping body was neither attractive nor healthy, and suggested a corresponding moral sluggishness; a straight body was essential for strength and beauty of both the physical and spiritual varieties alike. *A letter of genteel and moral advice to a young lady*, an improving work published in the mid eighteenth century, is perfectly explicit. 'Stooping in a young Person', it states, 'bespeaks a Meanness of Spirit; therefore endeavour after a strait Carriage, and an erect Countenance.' Similarly, 'Leaning and lolling are often interpreted to various Disadvantages.'[102] According to *The young ladies conduct*, a slightly earlier text, the positioning of the feet, the head and 'the Uprightness of the Body' together immediately show one's sense and education.[103] We all make moral judgements like this on the basis of physical information; it is just that in the past they were more explicit about it. As late as the Jazz Age what shocked society about the flapper figure was not only what she wore, but also how she wore it. It was because of her slouching and angular deportment as much as her clothing, that she was considered to be a new, and not necessarily nice, manifestation of femininity: 'No nice girl in pre-war days crossed her legs in public. No nice girl lifted her hands to rearrange her hair in public … So the little girl pal slouched in her chair, went in for the cult of the leg, and lifted her arms frequently.'[104]

There is also, in the containment offered by corsetry, the possibility of a certain empowerment. Like the girding of loins, the binding of the midriff signals a gathering of energies and an arming for battle, if only that of social engagement. Anne Hollander talks about the 'serious inner and outer power' conferred by stays on both their male and female wearers. She considers this partly sexual, but also describes the presence that corsetry conferred, and that sense of readiness and completeness that a wearer experienced. The undergarment's firm grip was 'more reassuring than troublesome' and gave the wearer 'countenance'.[105]

This understanding of corsetry's benefits is echoed in the writings of Anne Fogarty, a dress designer working in the 1950s through to her death in 1980. 'When feeling drab or upset', she maintained, 'a tight or firm foundation will make you feel alert.'[106] Weightlifters pulling in their belts in preparation for a lift and athletes who favour the sheathing of Lycra demonstrate the continuing understanding of how containment can enhance the performance of the mind and body. And on the subject of the enhanced body, there is no doubt that foundation garments smoothed and redistributed the flesh to produce a sleeker and less lumpy form. Being able to use dress to temporarily enhance flawed reality—to have the wherewithal to mould actual substance towards ideal appearance—might be a kinder, and more creative, regime than contemporary modernity that insists that poor flesh struggle to perfection unaided; unaided, that is, except by corporeal interventions such as dieting, exercise, drugs and surgery. As far as emancipated attitudes to the body go, it is unclear whether our society's obsessive mix of glorification and self-loathing is superior to our foremothers' corseted experience.

In presenting the person for social engagement and view, the corset clearly marked out the territories of public and private. Stays kept 'secrets intact'[107] and clearly demarcated the boundaries of privacy. The body above the layer of corsetry was for public view; what lay beneath was for intimate revelation only. Similarly, dressed in stays a wearer took up a public persona, one ready for social, and perhaps physical, demands. In the domestic setting, however, she might loosen or dispense with this undergarment, a circumstance that from the 1870s contributed to the popularity of the tea gown, an unboned loosely fitting garment worn in the late afternoon, a social and sartorial relaxation sandwiched between the day's activities and evening's more formal demands. This adoption of 'undress' when 'off duty' continues today, as anyone of us who has returned home and cast off the restraint of work clothes in favour of looser informality, surely knows. The importance of maintaining the distinction between the private and public self was emphasized by advice literature. 'Never appear to Company without your Stays.' Indeed, 'Make it your general Rule to lace in the Morning before you leave your Chamber.' Failure to do this, failure to observe an appropriate formality of presentation in company, opened an individual to censure. She might be thought indolent, a creature of supine thought, sluttish and—as *A letter of genteel and moral advice* ominously, albeit intriguingly, warns—'very often worse'.[108]

Much has been said of the eroticism of corsetry, though chiefly only of the scopophilic satisfactions. It seems hardly necessary to mention the pleasure of viewing the corseted body, or the importance of the garment as an erotic motif or fetishized object. Steele discusses this at length, finding that the excitement generated by the sight of corseted women, in particular, was a pleasure shared by both men and women, and experienced in observing others or the self. She concludes, at least of the nineteenth century, that 'the idea of looking at a woman in her corset was regarded as erotic, whether the gaze was male or female, autoerotic, or voyeuristic'.[109] Outside the consideration of fetishized practice and extreme tight-lacing, however, less has been written on the somatic pleasure of stays—the sensations felt by the wearer in her state of corporeal containment. To cite Anne Fogarty again, this might be described as an 'awareness': a feeling of constraint that is not so pronounced as to cause discomfort, but is firm enough to stimulate a heightened sense of the body.[110] Feminist activist and writer Beatrice Faust considers the enduring popularity of the corset in just these terms, especially in conjunction with high heels. Together, these 'provide intense kinaesthetic stimulation for women', remembering herself the 'modest but sustained arrousal from comfortably tight girdles and well-fitted high heels' that she, like Anne Fogarty, wore in the 1950s and 1960s. For another wearer, the sensation of her basque was like an embrace:

> A cool, sophisticated constriction, smooth on the skin and then warming to a firm, sleek secret under other, more ordinary cloth. Pleasantly sly when out of sight, it made posture and movements more formal and reserved while unbuttoning the mind and will entirely . . . Its sensuality appealed to me, its lessons of repression and release. Here it controlled flesh, kept it pleasantly confined: elsewhere it left me tangibly exposed, complicity free.[111]

Faust further explains that 'Girdles can encourage pelvic tumescence and, if they are long enough, cause labial friction during movement.'[112] Before the adoption of drawers in the early years of the nineteenth century, it may be that this pleasure was further emphasized by the contrast between the wearer's constrained midriff and her near naked buttocks and vulva, covered only with a shift. It has also been noted that by reducing the expansion of the rib cage, a corset forces the wearer to breathe from the upper diaphragm, taking more shallow, higher, lighter breaths that are more akin to the panting of sexual arousal.

Of course, the various pleasures of containment—ranging from mental alertness to sensual enjoyment—should not be overstated. There were many who experienced corsetry as an enforced confinement—a garment that blunted, rather than heightened, an appreciation of their bodies in action. And, presumably, any one individual might have felt both pleasure and penance, depending on time, context and age. However, for all that, it would be equally misleading to disregard or overlook what were perceived by the majority as the benefits of fashioning the waist and breasts. Above all, what must be kept in mind was the overwhelming normality of the practice; a normality within which a stiffened and contained midriff was a mark of civilized dress.

3   HIPS AND BOTTOM

DOES MY BUM LOOK BIG IN THIS?

'Does my bum look big in this?' For most of the time from the start of the sixteenth century to the opening years of the twentieth, the answer would have been a glorious, resounding and opulent yes.

The key fashions for women that draw forth this emphatic affirmative are probably familiar. They linger in the mind's eye—surprising, theatrical and surely emblematic of all that is irretrievable in the past. The first of these, the farthingale, appeared in England around the middle years of the sixteenth century. It had two basic styles of which the earlier, known as the Spanish farthingale, was conical in shape, narrow at the waist but flaring out as it descended. It is familiar from countless Tudor portraits, where the predominantly flat treatment by the sixteenth-century artists tends to gives its wearers the look of having been assembled in triangular sections. A sitter's torso in her 'pair of bodies', or corset, forms a small inverted triangle on the top; the farthingale is the large base triangle, within which is the triangular repetition of the overskirt and contrasting forepart beneath (Figure 19). Frequently, large hanging sleeves add further lateral triangles to this neat stack of shapes. By contrast, the French or wheel farthingale—the later style, which lasted until about 1620—was cylindrical in form. As its name suggests, it resembled a wheel or hoop suspended around the wearer's hips, from which the skirt then fell all but horizontally to the ground (Figure 20). Typically the wheel farthingale was worn at a tilt, higher behind than at the front: 'I will haue a French fardingale, it shalbe finer then thine; I will haue it low before and high behinde, and broad on either side, that I may lay my armes vpon it.'[1] If the Spanish form made its wearer into a cone, however, the French variety formed her into a barrel. As one contemporary wrote, 'Fardingales aboue the Loynes to waire, / That be she near so bombe-thin, yet she cross-like seem's foure-squaire'—or to paraphrase, no matter how 'bum thin' a woman might be, see her side on in one of these, and she appears square and squat.[2]

The second of the fashions to dramatically extend the hips and bottom, known to its contemporaries as the hoop petticoat, appeared in the first decade of the eighteenth century and was not to disappear until around sixty years later. Generations of women were born, lived and died, but the hooped skirts went on. It does much to establish their normality to consider that by the time they were left off for all but ceremonial wear at court, barely a single person could have remembered a time when hoops were not worn. Their common currency in the eighteenth-century imagination is apparent in the naming of a spring bulb that flowered in borders about the middle of May, the hoop-petticoat narcissus: the botanist responsible had observed that the nectary was 'formed like the ladies hoop petticoats'.[3]

Figure 19　'Catherine Parr', oil painting attributed to Master John, c. 1545, © National Portrait Gallery, London. Catherine Parr (1512–48) wears a Spanish farthingale. Its distinctive cone shape—rendered as a flat triangle in the painting—is echoed by the skirt's contrasting forepart and the hanging sleeves of her gown. Her torso, shaped by her 'pair of bodies', forms another triangle at the top.

Figure 20 Untitled, pen and ink drawing by Nicholas Hilliard, 1547–1619, © Trustees of the British Museum. It is suggested that the sitters are Elizabeth of Bohemia (1596–1662) and her son Frederick Henry (1614–29), and that the drawing dates to around 1610–15. The woman wears a large flounced French farthingale tilted up behind, a standing band (collar), and carries a pair of gloves. Her son wears an infant's long skirts and a ruff.

Eighteenth-century hooped skirts started out as dome shaped, but after a time they flattened at the front and back, forming more of a fan silhouette. By the 1740s this had further flattened and extended into a kind of lateral oblong. Side hoops held the wearer's skirts out horizontally at her hips, from where they fell straight to the ground, while the front and back were flat. In effect the wearer's lower half was transformed into a vast, but skinny, rectangle. Seen front on, she was huge; viewed from the side and she narrowed into a comparative nothing. The last and most recent of these fashions was the Victorian crinoline (Figure 21). Like the early-eighteenth-century hoop, initially this was dome shaped. Later it, too, flattened at the front, and also at the sides, leaving a skirt whose bulk flowed out at the rear.

These, the farthingale, hooped petticoat and crinoline, were, quite literally, the big three. However, there was a range of lesser styles that, while perhaps not as dramatic as these, also fashioned their wearer by enlarging her hips and behind. In the sixteenth and seventeenth centuries, for example, bum rolls—long, sausage-like bolsters—were tied about the hips to bear out the skirt. Towards the end of the seventeenth century bustles presaged the arrival of hoop petticoats, and in the nineteenth century the crinoline not so much declined as metamorphosed into the tournure, the enormous bustle structure at a woman's rear that might extend sixty centimetres, or two feet, behind her.[4]

Even the apparently 'simple', neoclassically inspired fashions of the late eighteenth and early nineteenth centuries were not innocent of additions beneath. From the 1770s a

Figure 21 Fashion plate, hand-coloured lithograph, 1864, © Victoria and Albert Museum, London. Appearing in the women's periodical *Englishwoman's Domestic Magazine*, this print shows fashionably large crinolines as day dresses. The girl's costume follows the same line. As well as fashion plates, the magazine published paper patterns for home sewing and, more controversially, the infamous tight-lacing correspondence.

padded cushion that was often bolstered with lightweight cork, was worn to give fullness to dresses increasingly made from softer cotton fabrics. Commentary became delighted with the possibilities offered by the cork rump, as it soon became known (Figure 22). 'There is something, it is alledged by connoisseurs in female proportion, in the hindmost movements of a fine woman, peculiarly elegant and beautiful. The Cork Rump originated in this lascivious idea; and it gave apparent elasticity to those parts, about which the imagination of most men are often busily employed.'[5] Notwithstanding any erotic appeal that the rump may or may not have held, in the pages of the press at least, the male imagination was almost exclusively exercised around the propensity of cork to float. In a recurrent topos that was tossed from paper to paper, and text to cartoon, a damsel suffers an accident and falls into the water, only to be saved from drowning by her buoyantly bolstered bottom. In some cases the incident is clearly a humorous spoof; in others—such as the following—it is presented as news:

> On Sunday evening a very ludicrous accident happened at Henley upon Thames. A large party from town went after tea to enjoy the coolness of the evening on the banks of the river. Youth and spirits hurried them into such follies of vivacity, that in running with too much precipitation, a lady's foot tripped, and she fell into the Thames. The consternation was general; but how much was every body surprized, to see her swim like

Figure 22 'Chloe's Cushion or the Cork Rump', etching published by Matthew Darly, 1777, © Trustees of the British Museum. A satire on fashions of the 1770s. The lady's enormous, mountainous hair is decorated with yards of ribbon and streaming lace. Her dress is so excessively bolstered with a cork rump that a small spaniel sits on it behind her. The presence of a lake or river in the background may allude to the floating cork rump motif common at this time.

a fishing-float, half immersed, and half above water! It seems, this unfortunate lady had been furnished with an immoderate sized cork rump, which buoyed her up … She was towed to shore by a gentleman's cane, without the least injury but wet petticoats.[6]

As the waistline migrated upwards, so, too, did the rump, until it came to lodge as a pad that prevented the soft muslins of the new long-bodied styles from curving into the small of the wearer's back. Knowing this helps contextualize certain criticisms of the fashion: complaints that women were deformed, rendered ill made and humpbacked, like a snail carrying its shell.[7]

If it wasn't pads, hoops, bustles, rolls or rumps, a fashionable woman's wardrobe furnished her with layers of petticoats beneath, or an overskirt pinned up or gathered at the back. Not as sculptural or pronounced, these nevertheless added bulk. Taken all in all then, from 1500 to 1900 or so, there were very few times in which a woman's rear and hips were not extended by her garments. Enlargement was not the sartorial exception, it was the anatomical rule. But while the fashioning of this part of the body is primarily a story about women, there is also a quieter narrative here concerning masculinity. In the previous chapter we saw that the early nineteenth century envisaged a particular style of manliness, a type that they have bequeathed to us and which we continue to 'see' to the exclusion of all others. Through tailoring and dress they constructed the form of modern masculinity. He is lean and muscled. Wide shoulders, slim hips and a flat stomach make him an inverted triangle. He is classical statuary made flesh, or rather, fabric. Before this, the embodiment of manhood was very different. In swelling doublets, he was bulkier and big bellied. Below the doublets, too, padded hose and full breeches increased the girth of his hips and buttocks and thighs, until he strode into the idealized performance of gender with a rolling and swaggering gait.

Superb demonstrations of this are the trunk hose that became popular around 1550. These were the short, full breeches that thrust out from the waist but extended, at most, only to the mid thigh, with a girth achieved with wadding and linings (Figures 23, 33 and 34). John Bulwer, looking back from nearly a century later, illustrated what he considered to be the folly of these hose with the story of a conceited gentleman who stuffed his pair with bran. In chatting up some ladies—or, as Bulwer put it in the seventeenth century, showing off his 'bravery and neatnesse [fine apparel and handsomeness, elegance]', 'talking merrily' and being 'taken with delight'—he did not notice that a nail protruding from his chair had made a small tear in the fabric, out of which the bran had begun to fall. The ladies, however, did notice, and exchanging glances with one another they began to laugh. Thinking them impressed, the gallant redoubled his efforts to entertain, which of course only made the bran fall the faster. Eventually, however, he 'espied the heape ... which came out of his hose', and hiding his shame and embarrassment as best he could took a chastened farewell, leaving the ladies to their mirth.[8]

This sounds apocryphal, but who knows? More unlikely to us, but certainly true, is that these breeches were the object of legal control. In 1562, Elizabeth and her Privy Council issued a proclamation enforcing the statues of apparel—laws that, in theory at least, regulated what might be worn according to status and income. Generally, these sumptuary laws were concerned with controlling access to different textiles, the most expensive and beautiful being prohibited to all but the most wealthy. This proclamation, however, included a new provision, aimed at 'the reformation of the use of the monstrous and outrageous greatness of hose, crept alate into the realm'. It made it illegal for tailors, or anyone else, to put too much material into trunk hose, or too much or too large a lining. The proclamation specified the maximum amount of fabric allowed and stipulated that the linings were to be neither loose nor bolstered, but were to fit neatly to the leg. To enforce this, hosiers were required to pay a £40 bond, and every eight days their premises were to be searched. Moreover, any man found unlawfully wearing hose exceeding the allowable size risked forfeiture of the garment, imprisonment and a fine.[9]

At the next parliamentary session, which occurred the following year, there was an attempt to strengthen the proclamation with statute law. A bill for the punishment of such as shall make or wear great hosen was introduced to the House of Commons on 9 March 1563. It proved contentious and failed after its second reading but was reintroduced eight years later, in 1571. This time the bill passed its three readings, though the last of them only by a majority of one. Although at this point it should have gone to the House of Lords, for some reason it neither reached the upper chamber nor was reintroduced in the

Figure 23 'Robert Dudley, Earl of Leicester', oil painting by unknown artist, c. 1575, © National Portrait Gallery, London. Dudley (1532/3–88) adopts the classic manly pose of the time, with one arm nonchalantly jutting from his hip. He wears large paned trunk hose with gold linings, and a modest-sized codpiece. There are matching neck and wrist ruffs, and a short black coat, open over his doublet, matches his hat. Around his neck Dudley carries the Collar hung with the Great George, part of the insignia of the Order of the Garter.

Commons.[10] While no further efforts were therefore made to pursue the prohibition of large breeches through parliamentary channels, some enforcement of the earlier procla- mation did occur. Leant on by the queen and the secretary of state, William Cecil, the corporation in London appointed watchers to see that the provisions were obeyed in their wards, took bonds from tailors and hosiers, and hauled some offenders before the court of aldermen.[11] For example, servant Richard Walweyn was arrested on 24 January 1565 'in a very monsterous and outraygous great payre of hose'. On 23 November 1570, Thomas Bradshaw came before the court. It ordered that the stuffing and lining of his hose be im- mediately cut and pulled out and that, wearing the garment thus, he be led home through the streets.[12] In Essex in 1565 a tailor was fined for the size of his hose 'contrary to the proclamation', and three years later a further three tailors were charged with the same offence.[13]

As with other instances of enforcement of apparel orders—and these are not common— those who bore the brunt were of a relatively low estate. Men with money, status and power wore their big hose with impunity. Furthermore, as we saw in the attempted regulation of the size of ruffs, the impetus for the clothing laws came from the court, but so, too, did the impetus for fashionable display and the drive for novelty. With such a conflict of interests, the privileged would always be able to swagger it out in the bulkiest of breeches.

Although John Bulwer was ready to ridicule trunk hose, the bottom-heavy male figure was no less a part of his sartorial landscape. The styles of breeches that succeeded trunk hose, while never as truncated, were nearly all generously full; some were positively baggy and voluminous. Even the more restrained and coordinated wardrobe typical of Charles I's reign and the Commonwealth period that followed, conforms to the same pattern. While the political landscape of the seventeenth century changed dramatically, the silhouette of its political actors remained very similar. The typical Cavalier was distinctly pear shaped, but so, too, were those of a more godly persuasion.

The 1660s saw the restoration of the monarchy, and also the emergence of the breeches, coat and waistcoat (then called a vest) ensemble, an arrangement of garments that turned out to be the prototype of the three-piece suit. Once established, the style changed little over the eighteenth century and is ubiquitous until the closing years. Its composition is fa- miliar from, and identical in, untold numbers of portraits: a man in a wig—another fashion development from the Restoration court—and a long waistcoat that buttons down the length of his torso and over a rounded belly. Frequently we are carefully shown the puckers in the fabric where it fastens across his middle. On top of this the coat is fuller towards the bottom, and until mid century had stiffened skirts that flared out over his hips and rear. Being generally collarless and without lapels, it made the wearer's shoulders seem small, and the very large cuffs pulled the proportions even further downwards. So while the breeches were fitted, rather than full as in the preceding century or so, the ideal male figure until the 1780s was pear shaped, bottom heavy and with a kind of roundedness (Figure 24). Art historian Anne Hollander describes him thus:

Figure 24 'Thomas Nickleson', oil painting by unknown artist, c. 1755, © Victoria and Albert Museum, London. Nickleson (1717–88) is painted here in the pear shape so typical of eighteenth-century masculinity. The collarless coat narrows his shoulders, while its deep cuffs and full skirts give his figure a bottom-heavy look. The waist is below his rounded belly, over which the long waistcoat is seen to pucker.

Art of all kinds shows that throughout the period from 1650 to 1780 men's shoulders ideally looked very narrow and sloping and their chests somewhat shrunken, and that even on slim figures the stomach swelled out prominently between the open coat-fronts and above the low waist of the breeches … The entire effect [of his garments] tended to emphasize a man's hips, belly, and thighs, shrink his chest and shoulders, lengthen his torso and shorten his legs.[14]

It is hard not to see this figure as effeminate. In shape and proportions he is the inverse of the modern masculine ideal, and it takes an imaginative leap to reinvest him with a per-suasive physicality. Yet there is nothing less essentially manly in the pre-1780s aesthetic than in the construction that followed, and that we happen to endorse. One takes its inspiration from a younger, athletic physique, perhaps; the other reflects a more mature, heavier frame. Making an imaginative effort allows us to appreciate something of the swaggering brag-gadocio in the dressed male figure of the sixteenth and seventeenth centuries, the courtly bravura and élan he embodies and, as his codpiece testifies, the cocky bravado (Figure 23).[15] Likewise, in changing our viewpoint we can see a cooler, more restrained masculinity in the pear-shaped figure in a wig and eighteenth-century clothes. He is, in the Earl of Chester-field's (1694–1773) words, 'unruffled'. He is dressed for a world of civic virtues, ready to cultivate the performance of politeness and espouse the causes of reason and rational thought (Figure 25).[16] In this polite new world, influence in society is grounded in bodily control, and discipline exercised over others reflects discipline over self. Lord Chesterfield the quintessential eighteenth-century man, wrote hundreds of letters of advice, threat, ex-hortation and admonishment to the various young men in whose futures he was concerned, though principally to his son, trying to prepare them for success in just this milieu. It was a milieu into which he himself—aristocrat, politician, diplomat, acknowledged wit, patron of the arts—appeared to fit perfectly. Essential to the accomplished gentleman, he said, were dignity of manners, elegance of deportment, quiet but faultless clothes, a graceful bearing and carriage, and ready address. These were 'the qualifications necessary to make him well received in the world'. Without them a man could neither fulfil his own ambi-tions, nor perform the duty he owed to society. They were the requisite accomplishments for every gentleman.[17]

I want, however, to leave this story of the changing performance of masculinity in the background for now, and return to women and their truly outsized hips and haunches. For they were, at their biggest, seriously huge. Of course, each of these styles was not uniform in amplitude. Differently sized skirts were worn depending on the time of day, the prefer-ences of the wearer, the wearer's place in the social scheme, and the context in which she was to appear. But when we talk of their variation in dimensions, what sort of sizes do we mean? Just how big were big skirts? It seems fairly certain that no sixteenth-century far-thingales have survived from which to take measure, but the instructions for making the Spanish variety can be found in a tailoring manual dating from 1580. The writer of this text says that 'the width round the hem [is] slightly more than thirteen handspans'. This,

Figure 25 'Sir George Lucy', Pompeo Batoni (1708–87), Charlecote Park, The Fairfax-Lucy Collection (The National Trust), 1758, © NTPL/Derrick E Witty. Although his garments are more ornate and expensive, Lucy is cast in the same mould as Thomas Nickleson (Figure 24). The coat is collarless, its skirts and cuffs are full, and it has pockets—the flap of one of which is visible on the right—set low down. Although apparently a slim man, his waistcoat puckers and curves over his full belly. The ribbon on his wig, possibly part of a bag, is just visible at the back of Lucy's neck.

in his opinion, is large enough, but he says that if required, more fullness can be added. Costume historian Janet Arnold estimates a handspan at about 22.8 centimetres, which would give a circumference at the bottom of the skirt of nearly three metres. For the French farthingale there seem to be neither any garments nor tailor's patterns.[18] One estimation of their size, however, suggests they extended anywhere from eight to forty-eight inches.[19] This would mean that dressed in a wheel farthingale of the maximum size, the diameter of a woman's skirt across the hips would be getting on for one and a quarter metres. This accords with a description given by the Venetian ambassador in 1617, who was astounded by the size of the skirt worn by Anne of Denmark: 'Her Majesty's costume was pink and gold with so expansive a farthingale that I do not exaggerate when I say it was four feet wide in the hips.'[20]

Figure 26   Gown and petticoat (T.120 to B-1961), c. 1760, © Victoria and Albert Museum, London. The side hoops that hold out this Spitalfields silk dress are fan shaped and at their widest measure sixty-four inches, that is, a little over five feet. This is not the largest petticoat in the Victoria and Albert Museum's collection. A court dress of the 1740s (T.227&A-1970) fits over narrow oblong hoops that are six feet across at their widest point.

It is much easier to accurately gauge the size of eighteenth-century hoops and nineteenth-century crinolines, for there are many more written sources available and some extant garments. In 1739 one woman wrote that hoops, flattened out into a sideways shape by then, were 'two and three-quarter yards wide'—that is, a fairly massive two and a half metres, though it is hard not to believe this to be an exaggeration.[21] Less extreme was the hoop petticoat ordered by Elizabeth Purefoy on 11 June 1741. Although then aged sixty-eight, she wanted it 'of the newest fashion', specifying a circumference of '3 yards & a quarter round ye bottom', or nearly three metres, remembering that this was distributed in an oblong, rather than circular, shape.[22] One dress in the Victoria and Albert Museum collection dated around 1760 measures over five feet at its widest point; another court dress from the 1740s stretches six feet from side to side (Figure 26).

The evidence for nineteenth-century crinolines is relatively abundant, whether for smaller daytime dresses or the larger formal gowns (Figure 27). The collection of the Kyoto Costume Institute includes examples of both. One small crinoline cage from *c.* 1875, for example, has diameter measurements of fifty-eight centimetres from left to right and fifty-nine centimetres from front to back, and has a circumference at the hem of 1.89 metres. The diameter of a much larger specimen from around 1865 is around 1 metre, and its circumference measures 3.18 metres. It is important to bear in mind that these are the dimensions of the actual supporting structure worn beneath. The dress itself billowed over the top, frothing to the ground at the front and very often forming a train behind. One pink silk taffeta evening dress from the 1860s, again from the Kyoto Collection, measures 1.5 metres from front to back at the hem, and has an astonishingly impressive circumference of about 4.7 metres.[23]

OH, WHAT A RIDICULOUS FASHION!

The drama of garments of this size—their massive alteration of the wearer's body, their unignorable claims on public space, their materiality and dominance—could hardly be missed by contemporaries. Satire, unsurprisingly, had a field day. With relish, the voices of disapproval levelled humour against a target so big that even the wildest gibe could hardly fail to find its mark. It was indeed 'a theme, whose diameter and circumference afford so large a scope to eloquence'.[24] In an issue of *The Spectator* devoted solely to hoop petticoats, Joseph Addison (Figure 2) had plenty of text with which to playfully deride what he saw as their folly. Although in actual fact still relatively small, Addison complained that if the fashion proved popular—which of course it did—'our publick Ways would be so crouded that we should want Street-room'. Church going, he said, was already problematic in fashionable parts of town. 'Should our Sex at the same time take it into their Heads to wear Trunk Breeches (as who knows what their Indignation at this Female Treatment may drive them to) a Man and his Wife would fill a whole Pew.'[25] *The Female Tatler*, a more or less contemporaneous periodical, ran a spoof advertisement that simultaneously greatly exaggerated the size of the skirts and identified them with sexual immorality—the conflation of fashion and lewdness is, incidentally, a discursive ploy probably as old as clothing itself.

Figure 27   Day dress (T.2-1984), c. 1862, © Victoria and Albert Museum, London. This vivid blue silk dress was probably coloured with the new synthetic dyes. It fits over a crinoline cage beneath, and although it is very large it was nevertheless designed for day wear.

Lost: The second instant, from under one of the modish petticoats of twelve yard circumference, in a new-fashioned hackney coach, a gem called Honour, supposed to be taken by some of Higgins Scholars, who, whilst the lady was descending from the balcony of her coach, very dexterously cast himself into one of the folds of her coat, and lay concealed.[26]

The most well known and subsequently influential of these early attacks on the hoop petticoat were found in the pages of *The Tatler*. Particularly memorable, and a favourite with cartoonists, is the winch that lowered women into their open-topped coaches—'tried by a Lady's Woman in one of these full Petticoats, who was let down from a Balcony, and drawn up again by Pullies'.[27] Addison's intended last word, though, is the trial in which Isaac Bickerstaff, *The Tatler*'s censor, subjected the petticoat to judgement. At first, the woman wearing it is unable to come in 'by reason of her Petticoat, which was too large for the Entrance of my House, tho' I ordered both the Folding-Doors to be thrown open for its Reception'. She is therefore 'stripped of her Incumbrances' until 'little enough to enter'. The petticoat itself, arranged on an umbrella-like contraption, is furled to bring it indoors. When Bickerstaff orders it to be raised on a pulley and opened to its greatest extent, it forms a splendid and ample canopy above them, covering the court like a silken dome. It is, in point of fact, 'in its Form not unlike the Cupolo of St. *Paul*'s'. At the end of the hearing Bickerstaff orders the canopy ballooning overhead to be made into ordinary petticoats for five indigent young gentlewomen, with the remainder of the silk to be turned into accessories for himself. Bickerstaff's—and Addison's—judgement on the hoop is uncompromising: 'I neither can, nor will allow it' (Figure 28).[28]

As fashion is impervious to rational or moral strictures of any sort, *The Tatler*'s attempts at reformation through parody and discursive disapproval failed. The popularity, and circumference, of hooped skirts continued to grow, and satire kept pace. An issue of *The Female Spectator*, a periodical written by Eliza Haywood that appeared more or less monthly between April 1744 and May 1746, dwelt on the hazards faced by wearers in simply walking through the streets. Warning that many very ugly accidents had lately occurred, Haywood's narrator described one that she claimed herself to have witnessed. A young woman had the misfortune to choose the wrong time to come

> tripping by with one of those Mischief-making Hoops, which spread itself from the Steps of my Door quite to the Posts placed to keep off the Coaches and Carts; a large Flock of Sheep were that Instant driving to the Slaughter-House, and an old Ram ... ran full-butt into the Foot-way, where his Horns were immediately entangled in the Hoop of this fine Lady, as she was holding it up on one side, as the genteel Fashion is, and indeed as the Make of it requires.—In her Fright she let it fall down, which still more encumbered him, as it fix'd upon his Neck;—she attempted to run, he to disengage himself,—which neither being able to do, she shriek'd, he baa'd, the rest of the Sheep echo'd the Cry, and the dog who follow'd the Flock, bark'd, so that altogether made a most hideous Sound.

The ram plunges wildly, the lady falls, and the mob is hugely entertained. With a filthied gown and her false hair slipping from her headdress down her shoulder, she is eventually disentangled from the frantic animal, only to be jeered at by the crowd. Such, Haywood concludes, are the potential embarrassments of enormous hoops.[29]

Figure 28 'The Review', etching and engraving, *c.* 1733, © Trustees of the British Museum. A satire on big skirts that draws its inspiration from the attacks on hoop petticoats in *The Tatler*. The woman in the foreground—who incidentally has three patches placed fashionably on her face—is causing an obstruction with her skirts. The lady facing her gestures towards the figure at the far left, who is pulling her hooped skirt up with a contrivance of drawstrings or cords. The black servant who stands at the centre seems to be doing the same with his mistress's skirt. To the right, a hooped petticoat is raised over Bickerstaff's court scene in the manner of an architectural dome. A system of pullies and ropes in the background lowers a lady from a balcony into the opened roof of a waiting carriage. The verse at the bottom explains,

Ladies for you this ample Scene I vend,
A new Invention by your Sex'es Friend,
With which you may securely trip along
Each narrow Lane, or shun the rustic Throng.
Had our fair Dames, when gay Sʳ Isaac liv'd
Such a convenient Scheme as this contrived,
With silken Cords to guide yᵉ huge Machine,

On such Occasions as above is seen.
Of coach and pullies he had never thought,
Nor the pois'd Nymph to such Disgrace been brought
The wide Machine, aloft in Nikey's Court
Displays its Orb, to public jeer and Sport;
The weeping Maid, while she her Sentence hears,
Wails her lost Hoop, and melts in pearly Tears.

About this same time two related publications appeared; one an attack on, the other an apology for, the huge skirts. *The Enormous Abomination of the Hoop-Petticoat* elaborated on what the author saw as the inconveniences and absurdities of the fashion: sitting down a woman occupies an entire couch; two or more women can only travel together in a coach in the greatest discomfort—'cramp'd, squeez'd, bruis'd, and crush'd'—and the silken skirts, with nowhere else to go, billow out the windows; public assemblies are intolerably crowded, with each woman taking up as much room as two or three men; and Sunday worship has become positively violent—'We can neither kneel, sit, nor stand … One with the stiff Ribs of her Petticoat *dashes* against me, and almost breaks my *Shins*: Two, or Three more *attack* me in the *Rear*, banging my *Hams*, and the *Calves* of my Legs.'[30] As the widest hoops of the time necessitated that the wearer either make a sideways movement through a door or squash her petticoat upwards, even entering a room provided grist for the humorists' mill:

> First *enters* wriggling, and sideling, and edging in by degrees, Two Yards and a half of *Hoop,* for as yet you see nothing else. Some time after appears the *Inhabitant* of the Garment herself; not with a full Face, but in Profile; the Face being turn'd to, or from the Company, according as they happen to be situated. Next, in due time again, follows Two Yards and half of *Hoop* more. And now her whole Person, with all its Appurtenances, is *actually* arriv'd, fully and completely in the Room.[31]

Interestingly, hoops proved too tempting a target for the small matter of their fashionable decline to altogether halt the tide of complaint. In 1782, after their use had ceased for all but ceremonial occasions at court, *The Lady's Magazine* ran an essay misleadingly titled 'On the Universal Fashion of Wearing Hoop-Petticoats'. In it, the author, 'A Foe to Hoops', describes his domestic situation. Although a man of tolerable fortune, with four hooped daughters his rooms are too small, the staircase is dangerously narrow and his post-chaise diminutive. In short, solely on account of the enormous size of the female part of his family, he must be obliged to obtain new furniture, a new coach and a new house.[32]

So much for the eighteenth century. The burgeoning crinolines of the middle years of Victoria's reign received similar, and at times all but identical, treatment. *The Ladies' Cabinet*, in its fashion pages for August 1853, reported that skirts were becoming wider and wider. If this continues, the paper said, there were but two options: reception rooms must either increase their dimensions, or hostesses limit their invitations.[33] Two years later it printed a letter, promoted by the 'excessive use (or abuse?) of crinoline', which purported to be from the proprietor of a Parisian omnibus. In it he explained first, that no vehicle had an entrance large enough for the passage of the most fashionable crinolines; second, that if by luck a lady squeezed herself in, no one could sit beside her; and third, that the fashion was ruinous to his profession 'from the fact that his omnibus containing twenty places can only hold four persons'. The omnibus owner urged that ladies wearing crinolines should therefore pay a higher fare. The columnist concurred, and unknowingly echoing the correspondent from *The Lady's Magazine* of seventy-three years earlier, went on to describe the difficulties of a mother with a bevy of crinoline-flounced daughters in packing her progeny into carriages. Even should she hire an omnibus, 'six really fashionable crinolines could not place themselves therein', and heaven forbid that a well-brought-up young lady should mount to the roof. To conclude, 'let us hope that serious measures will soon be adopted for moderating the extent of crinoline, or the consequences may be very serious.'[34]

While the ladies were reading such humorous disparagement in women's magazines, the man in the street was humming ballads. 'Crinoline: or What a Ridiculous Fashion' was typical of these musical lampoons. Printed as a single sheet costing a penny or less, people could sing along to a chorus that ran: 'Balking, walking all the day, / Always getting in the way, / All, except the ladies say, / Oh, what a ridiculous fashion!'[35] Perhaps of all contemporary publications, however, *Punch* made the most copy with anti-crinoline humour. The periodical was, according to some, 'the perfect mirror of Victorian bourgeois mores',[36] and if this was the case, it reflects a society profoundly affected by the fashion of its women. There are, quite literally, hundreds of scathing references to crinolines in its pages, and during the 1850s and 1860s, when crinolines were at their biggest, their size was a staple for cartoonists and copywriters alike (Figure 29). As a source, it is rather like an immense lucky dip: plunging in you are guaranteed a prize, but which of the tantalizing offerings, all of them intriguing and entertaining, to choose? One letter from a 'female' correspondent blamed men for selfishly taking up too much space so that the crinoline swept into them, for being so absent-minded as to stand on the skirts, for carrying their umbrellas and walking sticks so as they snagged and caught in its folds. There again, servants were also at fault for inconsiderately leaving objects where they might be upset and overturned, and railway companies and theatre managers had most thoughtlessly made their seats too narrow. Another piece, addressing 'Crinolinomaniacs'—and what a wonderful neologism— asked 'To what lengths (and widths) do you intend indulging in your fashionable frenzy?' The article advocated that railways charge extra for taking crinolines, both those carried in trunks and those carried on the person, for the purposes of which each lady should be measured when she takes her ticket. If this echoed the omnibus owner's letter printed in *The Ladies' Cabinet* of three years earlier, a letter of complaint from 'John Stout' picked up on the grumbles voiced by opponents of the hoop petticoat over 100 years before. Mr Stout explained that although he paid two guineas for his pew, he could no longer occupy it on account of the crinolines. Standing up he was crammed between them, and in sitting he had to perch on the extreme edge of the hard seat. 'Kneeling is altogether out of the question.' The discommoded gentleman called on the vicar to either refund him his two guineas or stick a notice on the church door: 'No hoops admitted, unless an extra-sitting is paid for, for their accommodation.' Once again, as in the previous century Victorian disapproval also showed itself unwilling to stop flogging what, with the passage of time and changing fashions, had long since proved to be a dead horse. In 1893, for example, a good twenty years after the crinoline's heyday, *Punch* ran with an illustrated poem warning against the fashion's return:

> Rumour whispers, so we glean
> From the papers, there have been
> Thoughts of bringing on the scene
> This mad, monstrous, metal screen,
> Hiding woman's graceful mien ...
> Vilest garment ever seen!
> Form unknown in things terrene;
> Even monsters pliocene

A WHOLESOME CONCLUSION.

Lady Crinoline. "Yes, Love—a very Pretty Church, but the Door is certainly very Narrow!"

Figure 29 'A Wholesome Conclusion', *Punch*, 1858, with thanks to the Library and Archives, University of York. A tongue-in-cheek comment on the size of crinolines (Saturday 6 February 1858, p. 54). Two women in enormous dresses stand in a churchyard and look doubtfully at the doorway ahead of them. The caption reads, *Lady Crinoline.* "Yes, Love—a very Pretty Church, but the Door is certainly very Narrow!"

Were not so ill-shaped, I ween.
Women wearing this machine,
Were they fat or were they lean—
Small as Wordsworth's celandine,
Large as sail that's called lateen—
Simply swept the pavement clean:
Hapless man was crushed between
Flat as any tinned sardine.
Thing to rouse a Bishop's spleen,
Make a Canon or a Dean
Speak in language not serene.
We must all be very green,
And our senses not too keen,
If we can't say what we mean,
Write in paper, magazine,

Send petitions to the QUEEN,
Get the House to intervene.
Paris fashion's transmarine—
Let us stop by quarantine
Catastrophic crinoline.[37]

Although much of the preceding is clearly exaggerated for comic effect, other sources
do confirm that the size of the really big garments did indeed impose themselves on both
their wearers and those in the vicinity. John Chamberlain, in a letter of 1613 detailing the
entertainments at the wedding of Princess Elizabeth, daughter of James I, said that it had
been decided no woman with a farthingale should be admitted. This policy 'was to gaine
the more roome'.[38] Some hosting dances in the following century followed the same course
with respect to hoops. Lady Mary Coke was scolded for attending a ball in a hoop petticoat, 'but as I don't dance, nor ever stay Supper at those places, I cou'd not see why I was
to be without': showing by her answer the contexts in which hoops were troublesome, and
also that, for some occasions at least, she nevertheless liked to wear them. Very shortly afterwards the Duchess of Queensbury invited Lady Mary to another ball, warning however
that 'She wd not have a bone [whalebone] (meaning She admitted no hoops)'.[39] We will
come back to Lady Mary later, but for the time being move on yet another century to the
reign of the crinoline. In old age, Lady Dorothy Nevill remembered it as 'an odious, hideous, and dangerous fashion', explaining that because of 'the amplitude of women's skirts,
great inconvenience was caused in churches, theatres, and public places generally'.[40] Many
observers at the time agreed. According to one, the four o'clock afternoon promenade in
Hyde Park featured ladies 'in an amplitude of crinoline difficult to imagine and impossible
to describe'.[41] As another saw it, the evening hours from five until seven constituted a dress
parade of crinolines 'monstrously overfull', 'badly draped' and 'like geometrical cones'.[42]
Letters to the editor printed in *The Times* from this period bear an uncanny resemblance to
those entirely spurious examples invented for the delectation of *Punch* readers. John Stout
was fictionalized, but we can assume that the R. N. who wrote to the editor on 11 June
1860 was real enough, and that his tongue-in-cheek tone gave voice to a genuine griev-
ance. 'Ladies will persist in attending Divine worship in crinoline', he wrote. 'Pews hired
out to accommodate four persons will, therefore, now barely contain two.' R. N. explains
that he rents two seats at his parish church but that his neighbours, attired 'from the waist
downwards in a sort of steel-ribbed apparatus, like a carriage umbrella inverted, over which
acres of silks and muslins and ribands are festooned', make occupying the pew well-nigh
impossible. Like John Stout before him, R. N. calls on crinoline to be banned from Sunday
service, or alternatively suggests that the ladies wearing them be charged not for their pew
place, but by the cubic foot. The following year another correspondent, signing himself
'Musicus', complained that he had been unable to obtain tickets for a fund-raising concert,
for the equivalent of nearly 400 seats had been set aside to allow for the expansiveness of
the crinolines. The year after, a letter appeared from a gentleman who reported that he

was made to miss his station, for by the time he could get past some ladies' crinolines, the train was in motion and he was being carried away. He changed trains at the next stop but was late and, owing to having to pay an extra fare, also out of pocket.[43] Interestingly, his complaint is actually against the railways; being inconvenienced by crinolines he seems to have taken, rather literally, in his stride.

KEEPING MEN AT A DISTANCE

Such dramatic extension of a wearer's personal space could not help but affect a woman's interaction with her environment and with people. From the vantage point of free-moving modernity, we might assume that far from enlarging her dominance, these skirts actually reduced a woman's sphere of influence, confining her within a walking prison of whale-bone, silk and gauze. On hindsight, we might picture the garments as a particularly subtle materialization of the 'angel in the house' topos, that did not so much trap the wearer within the domestic realm, as gave the domestic realm sartorial form and then draped it about her person. Even in leaving the house, there was no escape. Contemporary reality, however, suggests otherwise. By and large, big skirts were experienced as assertive by both their wearers and the men around them.[44] Their claims on space were not to be denied—as the many complaints from the eighteenth and nineteenth centuries testify—and perhaps this very assertiveness helps explain the reluctance of satire to leave them alone, even after they had vanished from actual view. Although gone from real bodies, satire gave hoops and crinolines a discursive afterlife, a lingering presence that outlasted their fashionable death. Furthermore, wearing huge dresses did not prevent women from appearing and acting in the public realm. Hundreds, thousands, of now anonymous Victorian women travelled on trains, rode omnibuses, and went to work in factories, dressed in crinoline. Perhaps the supreme example of a woman working in her clothes, and making her clothes work for her, is Elizabeth I. In the portraits from the closing years of her reign, her encircling farthin-gales, massive and assertive, are essential to the iconography of her representation. In the Ditchley Portrait, for example, she literally stands over England, her farthingale sweeping from one coast to the other, her realm covered by the mantle of her authority (Figure 30). In this case, a smaller dress just wouldn't have done as well.[45]

One interesting comment made repeatedly through the eighteenth and nineteenth centuries is that big skirts kept men at a distance. This phrase became a sartorial truism and was either handed down the generations, or was discovered—or invented—anew by each hoop-wearing era. Addison, in 1711, reported that 'I find several Speculative Persons are of Opinion that our Sex has of late Years been very Saucy, and that the Hoop-Petticoat is made use of to keep us at a distance.' In 1741 a correspondent to the *Universal Spectator and Weekly Journal* wrote that although some said hoops 'serv'd to keep Men at a proper distance' and the wearer within 'a spacious verge sacred to herself', this was in fact falla-cious. Five years later, the *True Patriot* chimed in, agreeing that although women generally believed the hoop petticoat served 'as a Sort of Fortification', with 'the Assailer kept at a Distance', a fortification such as this was bound to fail. The year before this, however, *The*

Figure 30 'Elizabeth I (the Ditchley Portrait)', oil painting by Marcus Gheeraerts the Younger, c. 1592, © National Portrait Gallery, London. Elizabeth stands over her realm in a dress of extraordinary size and magnificence. Most obvious is the large French farthingale sewn over with pearls and jewels. Behind her, hanging sleeves fall from her shoulders to the ground. She wears a laced open ruff and her head is framed by a wired head rail, a kind of huge gauze collar. The long stomacher narrows to a sharp point, and ropes of pearls hang down to her crotch. She carries a folded fan in one hand and a pair of gloves in the other.

Hoop-Petticoat Vindicated had asked its readers to consider the modesty of dress 'which keeps Men at a distance'. Then, in 1747, an article in *The Gentleman's Magazine* humorously arguing the merits and demerits of hoops, repeated nearly verbatim that 'the compass of the coat serves to keep the men at a decent distance, and appropriates to every lady a spacious verge, sacred to herself'. Swapping centuries and fashions, *The Ladies' Monthly Magazine* of 1859 described the witticism with which a woman had depressed the pretensions of a conceited youth decrying crinoline: 'You are not aware, sir, of its use: it keeps foolish people at a distance.'[46] This was finally repeated by Dorothy Nevill just before the First World War. In looking back on the crinolines of her younger days she, being no advocate of the fashion, said that the sort of silly women who defended them gave out that 'they at least kept men at a distance'.[47]

At first sight all this seems quite true. Big skirts created an enlarged personal territory, the dimensions of which precluded physical contact. Lady Nevill illustrates this with another of her anecdotes, this time about a doctor summoned to remove a fish bone stuck in the throat of the imperious Lady Londonderry. When adjured testily to begin, Dr Fuller explained he was 'quite unable to get within many yards of her ladyship's throat in consequence of her crinoline'.[48] Reflection, however, suggests things may not have been so straightforward and that the chaste encounters the garments dictated were by no means without their own frisson, nor necessarily innocent of lurking sexual promise. Putting aside our own contemporary fixation on the exposed body for a moment, we might see that being amply clothed is not a sartorial shorthand for asexuality, and that garments that cover do not automatically banish desire. In terms of big skirts, extending the self might actually extend the territory of potentially sexualized contact. Garments are identified with the wearer anyway. They become imbued with his or her being—or they are treated as such, which comes to the same thing. As any medieval collector of saints' relics or modern pilgrim at the shrine of celebrity memorabilia could tell you, dress holds a special place in that jumble of material things that help build and shore up individual identity. Walking about with your hips and bum—sartorially speaking—swaying and swishing in all directions could not, therefore, be further from a diminution of self. Instead, it extends the wearer's body in a fashion that borders on the unseemly. Add to this the somatic pleasures of such garments: the sheen, the silken rustle—Samuel Rogers talked about 'the *whishing* sound' of ladies' trains[49]—the folds of fabric, the sway and tilt. Then further add the frequency with which, as we know, hoops and crinolines pressed into others, obtruded themselves onto another's person, and we get a situation where garments do not so much barricade bodies as bridge between them. Consider sitting in church or the proximity of a railway carriage, a crinoline billowing over a man's knees, drawing him into its folds (Figure 31); or the lingering glide of a woman's skirts as they wrap about his legs and ankles as she passes. Here these big garments do not set the wearer in the midst of an inviolable space, but instead conjoin the two in a shared geography, enforcing a temporary—and on either part, not necessarily willing—intimacy. The ladies in my pew, wrote one man in mock complaint, 'exercise the right of rustling their dresses and swinging their crinolines against my legs, and entangling

Figure 31 'The Travelling Companions', oil painting by Augustus Egg, 1862, © Birmingham Museums and Art Gallery. Two identically dressed women sit opposite one another on a train. Their crinolines billow in a silky mass, expanding to dominate the carriage.

me in a mass of skirts'. Describing the effect with the breathlessness of sexual suspense, he finds he is afraid to move and unable to speak; while the 'sinuous folds of the train sweeping rhythmically after the wearer' exercises a 'fascination' and invites him to 'come along'.[50]

In 1859, as crinolines were reaching to their most protuberant, *Punch* ran a verse that capitalized on this propensity of the large skirts to intrude, making what had been public space into an extension of a very private terrain. In 'The Dangers of a Vis-à-Vis', addressed to the single gent who commutes daily to town, a Rev. Maguire shares a railway carriage with Miss Louisa Lettington: 'Three feet of breadth between the seats— / And in that narrow space, / A Crinoline to stow away, / And a pair of legs find place!' Despite being 'all innocent of evil thoughts', after various squeezings and encroachments, Maguire ends up being equally entrapped by the skirts and their wearer:

> But if this sort of peril
> Is to haunt each railway line,
> We dwellers in the Suburbs
> Must in self-defence combine:

By an Anti-Crinoline Bill
To put down these steel and netting tuns [large casks],
And save possible MAGUIRES
From probably MISS LETTINGTONS.[51]

This was not mere mischievous whimsy on the part of the editors of *Punch*. Eight years later in April 1867, in a curious instance of life imitating art, a case came before the Southwark magistrates court. The charge was made against Rev. George Keppel, who was accused of indecently assaulting a young woman called Mary Ann Fraser while she was alighting from a railway carriage at the London Bridge terminus. Miss Fraser stated that he had 'put his hand on her clothes roughly and in an indecent manner', at which she turned round and called him 'a nasty beast'. At this point a railway inspector had come up, and upon having her story corroborated, took Rev. Keppel into custody. Keppel's defence lawyer, Mr Mackenzie, claimed that his kind and benevolent client had merely been trying to assist the young woman, but in his zeal Keppel's hand had become 'somewhat entangled in her crinoline'. Mackenzie produced plans of the carriage showing the compartment to be five feet wide, and stated that the complainant could not have passed Keppel 'without his being compelled to put his hand out to avoid her crinoline'. He added that it was not feasible a clergyman 'should in broad daylight wilfully commit such an act' as Miss Fraser alledged (a linguistic construction unfortunate for his defence, implying, surely, that clerics inevitably wait until the hours of darkness to do that sort of thing?). Miss Fraser, however, asserted that her crinoline was very small—the same that she was wearing in court—and was adamant it was not large enough to incommode Keppel. Her story was supported by two witnesses: Miss Fraser's mother and Charles Martin, a railway porter, both of whom were also travelling in the carriage. Mr Martin agreed that ladies got in and out of carriages 'with such large crinolines that gentlemen have been compelled to put their hands out to keep them off'; however, he was certain that this had not been the case here. 'No, Sir, he deliberately committed the act complained of.' With two corroborating witnesses, the magistrate saw 'nothing to throw the slightest doubt' on Miss Fraser's testimony and accordingly ordered that the case go to jury trial. The Rev. Keppel, in the company of two friends, left the court on bail. Of course, in this context the actual guilt or innocence of George Keppel is not important. What is at issue is that women's garments could be so big that they forced a familiarity, that men were compelled to 'put their hands out to keep them away'. Whether this intrusion was welcomed or not, and it is easy to imagine scenarios for either, there is no doubting that the biggest dresses managed both to carve out a space for their wearer and to engage her and others in moments of sudden intimacy.

PERFORMANCES

Big garments had big possibilities. For sure, any item of dress holds certain performative potential, but equally certain, little else in the wardrobe quite matches up to the drama of bustle, hoops and a train. Although the garments and their owners have long since crumbled to dust, we can recapture some sense of how wearers undertook the performance of their skirts—how the garments were managed, the idealized schema that formed the pattern for real life, and the varying degrees of skill and success that different individuals displayed. While there are few contemporary references to sixteenth- and seventeenth-century dress in motion, the experiences of costume recreation suggest that to manage a wheel farthingale successfully a woman needed to take small steps, as the larger paces that a modern woman is accustomed to cause the skirt 'to sway out of control'. The ideal motion was gently undulating, likened to 'a gondala rising and falling on a lagoon'.[52] Also, portraits often depict a wearer with her arms resting lightly on the farthingale—'I will haue a French fardingale, it shalbe ... broad on either side, that I may lay my armes vpon it'—a stance that helped her keep the garment under control.[53]

By the eighteenth century, however, sources were positively voluble on the subject of 'the strutting Petticoat'.[54] It was recognized that managing hoops could be done with grace, with coquetry, with impudence perhaps, and with relish. In short, manipulating a big skirt entered the realm, discursively at least, of feminine arts and wiles. By pushing with her hands, perhaps swaying or leading with her hips and varying her speed, the wearer could exploit its dynamic possibilities: 'swinging her Hoop with a grave or frisky Air, just as she happens to be in a Temper, either gay or melancholly'.[55] *The Female Spectator* found some too hoydenish, complaining that ladies did not so much walk as 'straddle; and sometimes run with a Kind of Frisk and Jump', which would 'throw their enormous Hoops almost in the Faces of those who pass them'.[56] More modestly, merely negotiating doorways, furniture and people required pulling and pushing at the hoops to compress them or guide them past obstructions. Virtue out of necessity, according to Eliza Haywood in *The Female Spectator*, holding it up on one side was both 'the genteel Fashion' and a requisite of the design.[57]

In this action, another of the hoop's characteristics was revealed. Despite being so huge and covering so much, in movement the eighteenth-century hoop petticoat was liable to disclose the wearer's feet and legs in a way impossible in dresses composed of unsupported drapery. The 'Visible Play of the Foot' peeping in and out of the petticoat was frequently, and repetitiously, remarked.[58] Artfully lifted up, a hoop 'gives a Woman an Opportunity of shewing a Pair of handsome Legs'; it reveals 'the Beauty of the Leg and Foot which play beneath it'; it is 'that fashionable Way of shewing their Legs' (Figure 32).[59] Unsurprisingly, some felt this display to be immodest. One contributor to *The Gentleman's Magazine* suggested that hoops had been designed not to conceal pregnancy—a perpetual and, given their shape, quite impossible origin myth for big skirts of all periods—but were the creation of an inventive lady of pleasure seeking to show more widely the beauty of her limbs.[60] Certainly hoops did have a propensity, if mishandled, to reveal more than the wearer may have bargained for, becoming, indeed, 'a treacherous Covering to the Unwary'.[61] Such accidents, or clumsy performances, were the delight of the satirical press. Anecdotal stories and verses abounded, delightfully dwelling on the plight of women embarrassed by their hoops:

The *Petticoat*'s of modest Use;
But should a Lady chance to fall,
The *Hoop* forbidden Secrets shews,
And lo! Our Eyes discover all.[62]

Bearing in mind that at this time women did not wear underpants of any sort, accidental revelation certainly had plenty of scope for public mortification. It also more accurately informs our understanding of the fascination that the sight of a foot or ankle was said to exercise: all

Figure 32 'Taste a-la-Mode 1745', etching and engraving by Francis Patton after Louis Philippe Boitard, 1745, © Trustees of the British Museum. A print caricaturing hoop petticoats. The short, squat woman in the centre overwhelmed by her hoops recalls Lady Delacour's later description of her ungainly acquaintance 'as much a prisoner—and as little able to walk as a child in a go-cart' (Maria Edgeworth, *Belinda*). The tall figures on either side look much more elegant. The woman on the left, eyed by a nearby gentleman, coquettishly lifts her skirts to show her ankles and her shift. Eliza Haywood, writing at just this time, described the way ladies would 'throw their enormous Hoops almost in the Faces of those who pass them' (Eliza Haywood, The Female Spectator). The drawing also illuminates the incident in which Lady Mary Coke described how Miss Montgomery accidentally 'threw her hoop over the Queen' (Letters and Journals of Mary Coke). Beside these expansive women, the men appear slender and a little insignificant. Anne Hollander says they might be seen as a child beside an adult, or else the keeper of 'a large decorated beast on a leash or a full-rigged ship in tow' (Sex and Suits, p. 73). In the midst of such extravagance of fabric, the men's stockinged legs have an unadorned anatomical quality. Close examination shows their variety of wigs: the indistinct figure at the far left has a tye wig, the queue held with a bow at the nape of his neck; moving a little to the right, the man in the background has a pigtail wig, its tail visible hanging down his back; of the two men embracing centre back, the one on the left has a different variation of the tye. At the far right, two gentlemen stand with their backs to the viewer. The wig of one has a ribbon bow just a little lower than his hat; his companion has a large bag wig.

knew that above a woman's knee-length stocking, the garments ended and flesh began. While actual vision might not travel all the way, to the imagination it was but a short journey.[63]

Sharing the same dynamic qualities and responsiveness to movement, Victorian crinolines swayed, swung and rustled their way across the middle decades of the nineteenth century in the way hoops had queened it through the Georgian world before them. Like their eighteenth-century predecessors, they were also renowned for showing their wearer's legs, whether by accident or design. R. N., who wrote to *The Times* about being so incommoded at church, had it that crinoline wearers simply swaggered and hoisted their skirts in a manner 'alarmingly disclosive of their legs'. He could not help but notice their very decorative stockings, adding in a wryly convoluted double negative that he presumed they were not put on 'in order that they should not be looked at'.[64] Not so, one imagines, the Duchess of Newcastle's scarlet tartan knickerbockers, which she presumably put on for warmth or wore as drawers, that garment having come into use in the early years of the century. According to Lady Eleanor Stanley's diary for 1859, the duchess,

> in getting too hastily over a stile, caught a hoop of her cage in it and went regularly head over heels lighting on her feet with her cage and whole petticoats remaining above her head. They say there was never such a thing seen—and the other ladies hardly know whether to be thankful or not that a part of her underclothing consisted in a pair of scarlet tartan knickerbockers (the things Charlie shoots in)—which were revealed to the view of all the world in general and the Duc de Malakoff in particular.[65]

The ability to manage big skirts did not necessarily come naturally. Then, as now, some wearers were more graceful than others, seeming more at home in their garments and probably garnering considerable enjoyment from the performance. By the time Maria Edgeworth's novel *Belinda* was published in 1801, hoops had long since ceased to be fashionable. At Queen Charlotte's insistence, however, they remained de rigueur at court. There is a scene about this in the novel, and it makes clear both that a clumsy performance lowered a woman's social credit and that a graceful bearing was a test of true gentility. The witty and elegant Lady Delacour begins:

> Every body wears hoops, but how few—'tis a melancholy consideration!—how very few can manage them. There's my friend lady C—in an elegant undress; she passes for very genteel, but put her into a hoop and she looks as pitiable a figure—as much a prisoner— and as little able to walk as a child in a go-cart.—She gets on, I grant you, and so does the poor child, but getting on you know is not walking.[66]

Lady Delacour illustrates her comments by proceeding to mimic 'the hoop awkwardnesses of all her acquaintance', earning much laughter from her entertained audience as she does so.

As Lady Delacour suggests, hoops were the props in a performance of cultivated, elite sensibility. They offered women the opportunity to demonstrate a particular physical skill, but they were equally effective in exposing awkwardness.[67] This was not just the stuff of novels. In her journals, Lady Mary Coke observed that the Princess Dowager of Prussia had the ungainly habit of kicking out her leg, as though annoyed by the train of her gown. She described other people who were clumsy of carriage—such as the Comtesse de Provence, who had 'the most ungraceful manner of walking I ever saw'—or situations that went sadly awry, including moments of her own embarrassment. On one occasion she had been offered a lady's hand, only to be outfaced by the lady's garments: 'her fan hoop was so in the way, and her Gown hung so ill, that I trod upon it the first step I took, and we stumbled together out of the room'. Another time, Lady Coke's hoop petticoat got entangled with the queen's. She had no compunction about tearing her own to release them, but still 'it was some little time' before the two hoops were separated. In a masterful demonstration of *noblesse oblige*, the queen said with a smile, 'Lady Mary seems to have no mind to part with me.' Even over 200 years later, it's hard to resist a sympathetic wince on Lady Mary's behalf. At least on the following occasion she was the retailer, and not the subject, of amusing gossip. In mishandling her skirts, a Miss Montgomery 'threw her hoop over the Queen'—evidence that supports the more partisan assertions that hoops were liable to be lifted or squashed up unbecomingly high. This does not mean, of course, that poor Queen Charlotte actually disappeared beneath her hapless subject's draperies. Rather, the edge of Miss Montgomery's hoop swung up against her. Unfortunately it caught on the queen's jewelled stomacher—that triangular decorative section at the front of a woman's bodice— and tore off a diamond, which then fell upon the ground. Lady Mary assured her sister that this piece of news came from Lady Holderness, and therefore 'this you may depend upon for truth'.[68] It was presumably to guard against such unrefined ill grace that before her presentation in a court hoop and train, Queen Charlotte's fourth daughter, Princess Mary, undertook lessons in their management.[69]

The sociologist Erving Goffman has talked about every performance in which a social persona is presented to others as having a front and a back region. The front is where the public face is seen, where the polished act that conveys a particular impression or identity is played out before an audience. Where this public face is prepared, where the fostered identity is knowingly put aside, where the hidden effort behind the act becomes apparent, Goffman terms the backstage.[70] This construct works remarkably well when considering a woman from the eighteenth or nineteenth century who has dressed in her huge, hooped skirts. As we have seen, the ideal performance was graceful. The woman manipulated her gown dextrously, and without apparent effort. It could be worn modestly, provocatively or with gravitas, depending on her movements, bearing and age. Yards and yards of fabric were carefully arranged to achieve a 'natural' elegance, a becoming vision: 'dress assumes those deep and rich folds in which artists so much delight'.[71] In the ideal performance, life did not imitate art; life *was* an art. However, beneath these rich folds, beneath the flounces and brocades and lace so captivating to the eye and the ear and the touch, was the unsightly structure upon which the whole endeavour rested.

Hooped petticoats and the cage crinoline were skeletal contraptions that buoyed up the whole big-skirt project. Ugly pieces of technology as far removed from the outward performance as is imaginable, they are the quintessence of a Goffmanesque backstage prop. In his terms, they are 'the vital secrets of a show', the 'suppressed facts'.[72] In the sixteenth century, the secrets of the Spanish farthingale were the canes or whalebone sewn into casings in a series of graduated circles, which formed the skirt's conical shape. The late-sixteenth- and early-seventeenth-century French variety was created either with a bum roll —the sausage-shaped bolster tied below the waist—or, more dramatically, the wheel-like frame worn out from the hips, formed again with canes or whalebone.[73] The skirts of the eighteenth century started out very like the Spanish farthingale, with the petticoat rein-forced with graduated whalebone hoops. As time went on and the silhouette flattened and broadened, so too did the framework beneath. Eventually the petticoat was separated into two *D*-shaped panniers, which were worn slung outwards, one on each hip. Still greater sideways extension was obtained by using a device that looked positively orthopaedic: a system of three metal or wood hoops held together by strips of fabric, again worn over each hip. The hoops were hinged and therefore allowed the very large skirt to be pulled upwards, helping the wearer negotiate the necessary impedimenta of doorways, furniture and carriages.[74]

As befitted Victorian technological verve, in the nineteenth century skirt supports reached new levels of industrial creativity. Crinolines started out, as their name reflects, as petticoats stiffened with horsehair (Fr. *crin*). By the late 1840s the many layers of these re-quired for a fashionable outline made the gown heavy, cumbersome and uncomfortable. In 1856 the first cage crinoline appeared, which immediately dispensed with the need for the underlayers, enabled the skirt to extend its dimensions, and within the circumference of the cage allowed the wearer's legs free and unfettered movement. A triumph indeed, though perhaps not so very different to the farthingales of three centuries before. The following year though, the whalebone hoops were replaced by flexible steel rings, and from here, this sartorial technology never looked back. Many different varieties were made. In some, the steel was threaded through casings in the fabric of the petticoat. In other skeletal structures, the metal hoops were strung together with tapes—like the bare bones of a garment—which, suspended from the wearer's waist, swayed with her every movement. Some combined the technology of both. There were even inflatable alternatives invented, and those in which the steels were covered in gutta-percha, a kind of india rubber substance. One variety was hinged at the bottom so that, with the help of a hidden string passing up the inside of the skirt to the waist, the wearer could draw it up to make climbing stairs more decorous.[75]

A broadside ballad mocking the crinoline asked,

> How long will English ladies troop,
> About encircled by a coop,
> Composed of air tube, bar and hoop?
> Oh, what a ridiculous fashion![76]

As the rest of the ballad makes clear, partly the ridicule came from its sheer size and out-ward appearance. However, it also arose from the audience's knowledge of the hidden mechanism that kept the whole thing afloat (Figure 33). In Goffman's terms, people's perception of the backstage paraphernalia leached through their appreciation of the front-stage performance. In clumsy and mismanaged presentations, such as the Duchess of Newcastle's tumble over the stile, the backstage contrivances eclipsed the front-stage view, and the illusory performance was shattered. Jean-Paul Gaultier may have made fortune and fame by dressing Madonna in underwear as outerwear, but for most of us getting our skirts tucked into our knickers does not make for a winning look.

However, as they say, no one ever actually died of embarrassment. But perhaps all that shows is that we do not live in the nineteenth century, for in a crinoline a clumsy perfor-

Figure 33 'The Bum Shop', hand-coloured etching published by S.W. Fores, 1785, © Trustees of the British Museum. This satirical print plays with difference between the dressed figure and the anatomical reality that lies beneath, acknowledging openly the 'props' of the fashionable performance. On the back wall are displayed various types of supports used to bolster out skirts—side hoops are tied at the top of the display, a bum roll is mounted lower left—ready for the insufficiently endowed women to select and try on. The lady about to leave has been fitted with a cork rump. The dog, whose back quarters have been shaved, stands on his hind legs. According to the caption,

> DERRIERE begs leave to submit to the attention of that most indulgent part of the Public the Ladies in general, and more especially those to whom Nature in a slovenly moment has been niggardly in her distribution of certain lovely Endowments, his much improved (aridæ nates) or DRIED BUMS so justly admired for their happy resemblance to nature. DERRIERE flatters himself that he stands unrivalled in this fashionable article of female Invention, he having spared neither pains nor expence in procuring every possible information on the subject, to render himself competent to the artfully supplying this necessary appendage of female excellence.

mance could lead swiftly, tragically, to death. As is abundantly clear from eighteenth-century comment, hoop petticoats from that era from time to time involved their wearers in accidents, usually of a minor nature. By the time the cage crinoline dominated the drawing rooms of the following century, the world was a very different place. Urban growth, rapid industrialization, mass production and the democratization of fashion had all transformed how and what was worn. In short, more people were wearing bigger skirts in more crowded spaces. The result was that serious injury or death became a kind of occupational hazard for crinoline wearers. The most common danger came from fire. The large, mobile skirts easily swept against a grate or caught sparks, often without the wearer noticing. Once alight, the cage's airy structure was rapidly engulfed in flames, and it made smothering the fire, or even getting close to the victim, extremely difficult. Helplessly watching as someone burned to death was not an uncommon outcome. Many newspaper reports and proceedings from coroner's inquests tell us these forgotten stories. We will be coming back to fire hazards in a later chapter, and so for now will leave it with the words of Lady Dorothy Nevill, for whom the crinoline 'once came near costing me my life'. She and a party of ladies were in the drawing room after dinner, waiting for the gentlemen to join them. 'Somehow or other my voluminous skirt caught fire, and in an instant I was in a blaze.' Lady Nevill kept her presence of mind, and rolling herself in the hearthrug eventually beat out the flames. Just as well she was able to help herself, for 'None of the other ladies present could of course do much to assist me, for their enormous crinolines rendered them almost completely impotent to deal with fire, and had they come very close to me, all of them would have been in a blaze too.' The scarring on her arms remained with Lady Dorothy for the rest of her long life, and although she survived the experience, one assumes it did much to establish her detestation of 'that monstrosity, the crinoline'.[77]

The other accidents resulted simply as a consequence of the crinoline's size. They got entangled round people's feet, caught in machinery, dragged into the wheels of passing carriages or even blown against hazards. In January 1860, for example, Ann Watts suffered the most appalling injuries when her dress was snagged in the machinery that ran under a workbench at a Sheffield button factory, where she had gone to visit her sister. Miss Watts was drawn down and whirled about the shaft before the machine could be stopped. She sustained terrible injuries to her head, shoulders and spine, and died a few days later.[78] Just a few months afterwards, seventeen-year-old Caroline Marshall died at a paper mill. She was leaning over to oil the shaft that ran the glazing rollers when her 'extensive crinoline' got entangled in the machinery. By the time they could extract her she was dead, the back of her head beaten to a pulp. The coroner and jury 'expressed a strong opinion as to the extreme impropriety of girls wearing crinoline in mills'.[79] Harriet Moody was twenty-two, and she worked in a Leeds cloth mill. On the afternoon of Wednesday, 29 July 1863, she was on the fourth floor apparently waiting for a friend to join her. Mrs Cudworth, an eyewitness and fellow employee, saw her turn around as though to make way for someone, and then immediately heard her scream. Mrs Cudworth ran to find Miss Moody's crinoline entangled in shafting, which had continued to revolve. It took nearly fifteen minutes for the foreman to succeed in having the machinery turned off, by which time Harriet Moody was hideously damaged and her crinoline steel wrapped repeatedly round her. She died a few minutes later. Mrs Cudworth said she had never considered the shafting to be dangerous, but added that she never wore a crinoline and 'would not allow a person who wore one to work in a mill'.[80] However, even such a prohibition could not necessarily prevent this sort of industrial accident. In 1864, a young woman who worked at a hosiery factory near Nottingham was dragged into the machinery by her 'expansive crinoline'. Her screams were 'heartrending'. According to the report in *The Times*, the company's employees were not allowed to wear crinolines at work, and the manager had provided a room where women were expected to change before beginning their shift. Unfortunately, the victim had not done so.[81]

Not surprisingly, in the pages of the press these and many, many other women were seen to be victims of fashion and folly. *Punch*, emphasizing the self-inflicted nature of the accidents, began calling them 'suicide by crinoline'.[82] However, the ill consequences were not necessarily limited to the wearers. The circumference and design of some skirts were such that family, friends or merely strangers passing by, might be swept, or wrong-footed, into danger. In April 1858 a chairman—that is, in this case, one who made his living wheeling invalids in a bath chair—caught his foot in a woman's crinoline while taking a client around the park. His injuries meant he was unable to work at his usual job, and in the hope of receiving aid was forced to apply for charitable assistance through the papers.[83] An unnamed chocolate manufacturer from London was more fortunate. Being better off, he had been able to afford insurance. Injured when his foot caught in a crinoline while alighting from a railway carriage, he received a compensation payout of £15.[84] Much more seriously, James Welsh, a sixty-year-old porter, met his death when his feet became entangled in a woman's skirts. He was flung from the pavement and under the wheels of a passing van. His thighs were broken and he sustained injuries to his head and chest. The woman whose skirts had tripped him immediately went on her way and was lost in the crowd. The coroner stated 'that it was simply useless to continue to adduce arguments against crinoline. It was quite evident that ladies would wear it, without the slightest regard to the danger either to their own lives or those of other people, so long as the fashion pleased them.'[85]

Although crinolines were so greedy of space, a commodity increasingly at a premium in bustling, industrialized modernity, the consequences of their intrusions were not wholly bad. Sources from the eighteenth century present cases in which hoop petticoats allegedly save their wearers from drowning. Such was reported of a young maidservant in Norwich in December 1735. Not being able to see her way in the winter dark, she accidentally walked straight into the river. Although the current carried her along, her hoop petticoat buoyed her up until rescue arrived.[86] Perhaps knowing of this propensity, with tragic foresight a young woman who drowned herself in London in 1721 most carefully removed her hoop petticoat first. It was found hanging near the spot where she threw herself in.[87] Crinolines apparently acted in a similar way. Martha Sheppard tried to commit suicide in the Serpentine. Pacing the area for some time, she finally walked to the centre of the bridge and climbed onto the parapet. A constable on duty in the park, guessing her intentions, ran to stop Miss Sheppard just as she leapt. 'When falling, her dress, which had a large hooped crinoline skirt underneath, expanded to its full dimensions, and she came upon the water like a balloon, floating there for several minutes.' Although she then began to sink, it was long enough for the police officer to find and throw her a buoy.[88] Other lives were preserved in other, and unlikely, ways. Mrs Williamson, for example, was saved when she fell from the top of the ruins of Kenilworth Castle and her crinoline snagged on the ivy-covered walls. Although a fifty-foot drop, her fall was broken to such an extent that all she suffered was external bruising and shock.[89]

Further stories are less easy to believe. A nursemaid is said to have fallen 102 feet off the cliffs at Newquay, only to have her crinoline expand with the air, helping her rather to float than fall, so that she landed 'without a scratch or bruise'.[90] The idea of a Mary Poppins figure drifting downwards and alighting unscathed, with or without a carpet bag surely strains the limits of credibility. It seems to me that the history of big skirts is interesting enough without the dubious addition of parachuting nursery maids. The varying relationship of real women to these garments and the different performative possibilities they experienced in the ordinary round of their daily lives, give us a far richer sense of the past. Lady Nevill, narrowly escaping burning to death, loathed crinolines, whereas Lady Charlotte Lyster and her friend Lady Forester obstinately clung to them decades after their disappearance from fashion.[91] Mary Coke appreciated the aesthetics and the formality of hoop petticoats. She thought them becoming and always observed the necessary etiquette of formal occasions. As she wrote once when she dined with the royal children, 'I had put on a hoop to be respectfull.'[92] However, she was also alive to their disadvantages, explaining often that they were uncomfortable, inconvenient for walking, and troublesome at dinner.[93] Lady Leconfield, who wore crinolines throughout their period of fashionability, found their awkwardness objectionable, especially when trying to sit in a hurry or enter a crowded carriage. On the other hand, she also enjoyed the 'unfettered liberty to one's legs', and remembered that as a little girl she had thought them 'very comfortable for running in'.[94] And artist Gwen Raverat (1885–1957) once asked her Aunt Etty what it had been like to wear a crinoline. 'Oh it was delightful!' Aunt Etty replied. 'I've never been so comfortable since they went out. It kept your petticoats away from your legs and make walking so light and easy.'[95] For a correspondent to *The Times* writing to defend her right to wear what she chose, the crinoline was 'that graceful and much maligned necessity'.[96]

Whatever meanings big skirts held for these women of privilege, for Ann Allington their significance was entirely different. Perhaps it was the price of a meal, a source of ready cash, or the aspirational lure of fashionable appearances. Whichever of these, in 1724 Ann was tried at the Old Bailey for the theft of a hoop petticoat, found guilty and, for her sins, sentenced to transportation.[97] The connection between garments and crime is no haphazard or fleeting one. Representing considerable financial value, portable, and easy to sell on or, alternatively, enjoy oneself, in the past clothing was one of the most frequently stolen of commodities. Until the second-hand market dwindled, the importance of the pawnshop as a source of credit declined, and garments became more cheaply available to a large sector of the population, clothing and theft went, if not hand in hand, then hand in glove.[98] It is therefore no surprise to see such advertisements as the one that appeared on 18 January 1783, listing the many items, mostly apparel and dress accessories, stolen from a gentleman's house. Gowns, shoes, stockings, jewellery and 'one Hoop Petticoat': if any of the items were offered for sale or pawn, then the person apprehending both the culprit and the goods would, upon a successful conviction, receive a five guinea reward.[99]

Interestingly, the added dimensions of hoops and crinolines gave an added dimension to their involvement with crime. The capacious and private space they formed about the person of the wearer was a gift for smugglers and those drawn by the temptations of shoplifting. For example, customs searches undertaken by Mr Foster revealed a considerable quantity of tea hidden under women's petticoats, while another revenue officer, named Mr Draper, was reported to have apprehended twenty-three articles illegally secreted under another set of hoops.[100] Likewise, shoplifter Christiana Lougham was detected in trying to steal a short cloak. Upon being searched she was found to have muslin, ribbons and pieces of fabric hidden about her person.[101] It was instances of this sort that led to the assertion that the hoop 'was the invention of some *shoplifter* for facilitating the conveyance of stolen goods', a sentiment that *Punch* echoed the following century with regard to crinolines.[102] 'Crinoline for Criminals' announced a *Punch* headline of 1860, and although the article then takes flight to the realms of exaggeration, the phenomenon of goods being stashed beneath the big skirts was real enough. That same year Mrs Louisa Toula, aged thirty-eight, was charged with smuggling foreign tobacco. The suspicions of the customs officer were aroused because 'she looked very bulky'. The officer, Mr Grey, asked Mrs Toula if she had anything about her that was liable to duty. 'She said that her crinoline spread out her dress, and made some remarks about the absurdity of the fashion.' Mr Grey, sensing dissimulation, insisted she be searched. Mrs Toula relinquished four pounds of tobacco of her own accord, and a further five pounds, also hidden in her dress, came to light in a police station search.[103] Isabella Freeman appeared before the magistrate Mr Cooke, charged with shoplifting—a crime for which she had already served the 'lenient' term of one year's imprisonment. A sales assistant, catching her with various pieces of material fallen from the counter and her crinoline and dress 'drawn up as high as her knees', decided to follow her from the shop. He 'intentionally pressed against her dress, which confirmed his suspicions', and then 'shook her skirt'. Fifteen yards of silk rolled out onto the pavement.[104] The following year Mr Cooke had to deal with a duo of crinolined shoplifters. Elizabeth Hart and Ellen Sweeney were given into custody for stealing thirteen pairs of 'leno window curtains' wrapped up in two packages and hidden one each beneath their crinolines. The packages 'were more than two feet long and five inches thick'. Although once discovered Miss Sweeney offered to pay for them, the draper whose goods they had stolen was adamant that they be brought to court, for, he said, he had already lost £20 worth of goods in a similar way just that one week. Ellen Sweeney had been convicted of stealing some silk four years earlier, for which she was sentenced to 'three years penal servitude'. Six years before that, in 1856, she had served six months' hard labour for the theft of thirty-three yards of dress fabric. She was, at that time, eighteen years old.[105]

These small and very human stories of theft and punishment serve as a final reminder of the polysemous nature of big skirts. Their outsized dimensions have made them capable of sustaining multiple overlapping and conflicting meanings: assertive, alluring, absurd; concealing and revelatory; ugly and graceful; wilfully dangerous. These are all qualities that hoop petticoats and crinolines, in particular, have been thought to embody—or have been thought to be embodied by their wearers. And now Ann Allington, transported for stealing a hoop petticoat, and Ellen Sweeney, serving three years in a Victorian prison for shoplifting, add yet another cluster of meanings to these garments, reminding us that behind the performance and artistry of fashion, there is almost always a harsher story.

4   GENITALS AND LEGS

THE BREECHES PART

What is the one thing that frogs and properly built men alone have in common? The answer, according to John Doran's nineteenth-century study of costume history, is calves.[1] For until modernity reinscribed their attractions as female, the desirability of good calves, thighs and legs has been positioned securely within the realm of the masculine. Hidden beneath their enveloping dresses, until the twentieth century women's legs were all but invisible. At most revealed to the ankles, or peeping forth from hooped skirts, the lower part of a woman's anatomy was shrouded from view, its form disguised by the mass of her skirts. Ideal deportment and the need to manage these skirts made her movements smooth and graceful. The workings of her legs mysteriously hidden, the desirable motion was a kind of glide. Pacing and striding, and the varieties of biped action, were reserved for men with their visible and virile lower halves. So if, since the medieval period, the story of the fashioning of hips and buttocks has primarily been about women, the dressing and display of legs is a history of men.

As, sartorially speaking, only men had legs, the bifurcated clothing that covered them were *the* defining garments of gender. Breeches were only ever worn by the male part of the population. Every other item from their wardrobe was at some point appropriated by women's fashion: doublets, hats, jackets, ties, and military cut and decoration were all translated into female garments, and riding dress in particular consistently echoed the motifs of menswear.[2] A long and peevish history of complaint about manly women, amazons and immodesty attests to this propensity of women's fashion to plunder more masculine styles. But, and this is significant, these styles never included bifurcated garments worn over the crotch and legs. Hose, breeches and trousers were so overwhelmingly 'not female' that they were beyond the imaginative reach of even fashion's invention. Of course, there were individuals who cross-dressed, some of them famous, some forgotten: Mary Frith, born in the sixteenth century, whose activities became legendary; a handful of women from the lower orders whose existence we know of from court records; pirates Anne Bonny and Mary Read; writers George Sand and Radclyffe Hall; the nineteenth-century 'pit brow women' working on the coal fields of northern England. The deeper one delves, the larger the number of transgressive, determined and perhaps desperate women who appear, about each one of whom a fascinating history could be written.[3] However, these are individuals in some way on the margins, who were generally cross-dressing for purposes of practicality, preference or disguise. They were not dressing as women in women's trousers; they were dressing as men. Female fashion, and the accepted construction of female gender, left breeches well alone. Indeed, so thoroughly are trousers imbued with notions of masculinity that even now—when women wear them more commonly than dresses and most opprobrium or uncertainty about this vanished decades ago—we all understand that the phrase 'she wears the trousers' describes a domineering, 'unfeminine' woman and a man who has relinquished his potency.

I want to look at three periods in which the legs of men were particularly in evidence, when their importance to notions of elite manhood can be seen in clothing and its painted representation, in the discursive realm of texts and embodied in cultural practices. The first of these straddles the sixteenth and seventeenth centuries: an age of monarchs and courts, and an age of courtiers. Theirs was a small and intense world of clients and patrons, gift and obligation, favourites and favouritism, in which appearance, presentation and self-fashioning were essential to success. In the deadly serious game of court politics, how you looked was a vital stake to play. Robert Carey (1560–1639), who eventually became the Earl of Monmouth, believed he partly owed his preferment to his good taste in dress—not just his actual garments, which were 'as good clothes as any', but the way he selected and wore them, in which 'he exceeded in making choice of what he wore to be handsome and comely'.[4] Similarly, in 1611 Thomas Howard told Sir John Harington that he must be well turned out if he wished to succeed at James I's court. He advised getting a new jerkin, not too short and with plenty of colour, and to make sure his ruff was well stiffened. 'We have lately had many gallants', he warned, 'who failed in their suits, for want of due observance of these matters.'[5]

Fundamental to this matter of appearance were legs. In the portraits of the period it is easy to mark the ubiquity of the Renaissance elbow, the stance in which ease, elegance, assertion and privilege are all rolled up together in one gesture. Within the frame at least, it is the corporeal shorthand for elite manliness. Because so few of these extant portraits are full length, however, it is also easy to miss what is going on below. The placing and appearance of the subject's legs are as significant as the negligent thrust of his elbow. One is planted slightly forward of the other, the toes of both turned somewhat outwards. Legs are never shown in parallel; they are always angled to show the definition of muscle, the swell of the calf, and the shape of the ankle. It is a pose repeated again and again. Clad in silk stockings that are rendered on the painted canvas without even a hint of wrinkle or sagging, these idealized legs of the time were long, slim and well defined. Often they appear, improbably smooth and unrealistically elongated, from beneath those large, full, hip-enhancing breeches and trunk hose. There is, particularly in the contrast between the two, a daintiness about these limbs, a neatness: the sort of legs on which the phrase *well-turned* would sit nicely.[6] In the early years of the seventeenth century, they were further embellished with outsized garters and elaborate shoe roses—decorative rosettes, often laced and spangled, that adorned footwear. These were courtier's legs, made for elegance, for those courtly arts of salutation and bowing, of dancing, of riding and martial display (Figure 34).[7]

Unlike the modern bow in which the body is inclined, in the sixteenth and early seventeenth centuries it was the legs that did the work of deference. Developed from the simple kneeling homage of the medieval period, early modern conduct books taught their readers

Figure 34 'George Villiers, Duke of Buckingham', oil painting attributed to William Larkin, c. 1616, ©
National Portrait Gallery, London. This picture exaggerates the length of Villiers's legs, making them the
arresting focus of the painting. Placed in a rather balletic posture, the swell and shape of his ankle, calf and
knee are rendered clearly, and from mid thigh his trunk hose swell to a high waist. One arm rests on his
hip, making a classic Renaissance elbow. His head is isolated from his body by a standing band, and at his
feet large, spangled shoe roses adorn his high-heeled shoes. Villiers is dressed in ceremonial robes and
wears the Garter collar, with the Garter itself tied just below his shapely left knee.

to draw one foot back and then bend the knees. The depth of the reverence was indicated by the depth of the knee bend. A bow in passing was slight; in the deepest bow the back knee might touch the ground, for 'the bowing of the knee declareth that we submit our selues vnto him, & that we wil not remaine equal, but wil humble'.[8] To perform these finely studied acknowledgements of relative status with grace was a requisite achievement of genteel civility: 'O, fine courtier! How comely he bowes him in his court'sie!'[9]

Conduct books advised that the way to learn this grace and comeliness was through the study and practise of dance. 'I thinke it', wrote James Cleland in his book devoted to the correct upbringing of youth, 'one of the best exercises that a Noble man can learne in his young yeares'.[10] Edward Herbert, Lord Cherbury (1582–1648), recommended to posterity the three exercises of fencing, riding and dancing. He advised, however, that dancing be learnt first, 'as that which doth Fashion the Body giues one a good presence in and addresse to all Companyes'. Herbert describes the suppleness and agility of limbs that an early start in dancing gives a man, and informs his readers that good dancing masters will teach the skills of courtesy such as how to enter and leave a room gracefully, how to bow handsomely and 'according to the seuerall degrees of persons he shall encounter', and how to doff and hold his hat.[11] Dancing as a fundamental part of the curriculum is perhaps surprising to us, but contemporaries indicate that this was so. Educated with a tutor at home until he was nearly fifteen, Sir John Reresby (1634–89) related that when he then attended school, he and his brother 'were instructed in Latin, French, writing, and danceing'. He also says that aged two, he fell from an open window and dislocated his knee. Fortunately it eventually mended so that it was nearly as strong and nimble as the other for dancing and fencing.[12] Scottish courtier Sir James Melville (1535–1617) recounts being sent to France at the age of fourteen. While in Paris he had masters to teach him French, fencing, playing the lute and dance.[13] Similarly, when John Reresby travelled on the Continent as a young man, he learnt French, the guitar and dancing in Blois, and when later in Italy and Paris, studied mathematics, music, fencing and dance.[14]

Perhaps not surprisingly with all this practice, in 1598 Paul Hentzner, a German visitor, described the English as a people who 'excel in dancing and music'.[15] Elizabeth I famously loved it: delighting in the exercise herself when she was younger and its spectacle as her years advanced.[16] The court masque, that genre of entertainment that combined music, acting and dance in theatrical and politicized display, gave courtiers a highly visible arena of performance. John Chamberlain described three masques staged to celebrate the 1613 marriage of Elizabeth, daughter of James I, to Frederick, the Elector Palatine. The one performed by the men from the Middle Temple and Lincoln's Inn on the evening after the wedding was particularly successful, with 'theyre apt invention, apparell, fashion, and specially theyre excellent dauncing'. The king 'was so much delighted that he gave them many thancks, and much commendation'.[17] One can see how chances of preferment at court might be much improved by notable prowess on the dance floor.[18]

The movements themselves challenged the virtuosity of male dancers. The sartorial focus on legs—so visible in tight stockings and short breeches—encouraged choreographers to

Figure 35 'Henry, Prince of Wales', oil painting by Robert Peake the Elder, c. 1610, ©
National Portrait Gallery, London. Another classic representation of early modern
manhood. Henry (1594–1612) stands with bent elbow, hand on hip. In the other
hand he holds a single glove. Like the portrait of George Villiers (Figure 34), his
legs are rendered as long, slim and shapely, the silk stockings achieving an idealized
clinging smoothness. He wears shoe roses and the Garter. Above his waist, Henry's
doublet forms the same stiffened triangular shape as women's bodices of the time.
A delicate standing band and matching cuffs frame his face and hands, and from the
blue ribbon around his neck hangs what appears to be the Lesser George, a further
part of the Garter insignia.

create steps and movements to test their control, strength and stamina.[19] This provided some with an opportunity to shine and made public and humiliating the shortcomings of others. Prince Henry (1594–1612; Figure 35), as befitted the king's promising eldest son, at ten years old danced 'very gracefully'. He performed the galliard at a court banquet and ball of 1604 'with much sprightliness', 'cutting several capers in the course of the dance'.[20] In a masque of 1606, 'he danced brilliantly'.[21] Sir Henry Bowier was also 'a fine dauncer'. Unfortunately, in the course of strenuous practice for a masque he overheated, and this, it was believed, brought on smallpox, of which he quickly died.[22] By contrast, while he lived to dance another day, Sir Thomas Germain's performance in a masque of 1605 was lacklustre indeed. The dancing of the other eight gentlemen was 'full of life and variety'. Only Germain sometimes forgot his steps and had—a witness complained—'lead in his heels'.[23]

Duelling, and display fighting in the tilts and tourneys that were played out before the Tudor courts, were further tests for strong and skilful legs.[24] With graphics and text, illustrated fencing manuals, for example, showed how these legs should look and the ways they should move. In the basic posture for defence and attack, the duelling novice was taught to stand with his right foot forward and knee bent—or 'somewhat bowing'—and his weight on the left leg. The stance must not be 'stedfast and firme' as one who seems 'to be nayled to the place', but rather ready and nimble, as though about 'to perform some feate of activitie'.[25] Whether thus able in fencing or fighting, in dancing or even simply leaping, in this society these were personal achievements of which one could boast. In the memoirs of her husband, Lucy Hutchinson (1620–81) described his qualities and aptitudes in glowing terms. These included a gentlemanly skill in fencing, and 'he could dance admirably well'.[26] According to John Reresby, his father (also Sir John) was an extremely active man who 'danced in perfection' and 'leaped further then most men'. We might not think the ability to jump high much of a recommendation in a genteel parent, but it certainly cut the mustard with Reresby *fils* and, if he is to be trusted, with Charles I too, who himself leaping with Reresby senior, did acknowledge his virtuosity. Apparently the elder Sir John seldom used a stirrup, and instead usually vaulted onto his horse.[27] Lord Cherbury also writes about leaping and vaulting onto horseback as being valuable skills, recommending them as achievements of great use.[28]

This cluster of elite manly performances—bowing, martial combat, riding, dancing, leaping—foregrounded the looks and skill of the legs. A little like a top footballer today whose nimbleness and strength of limb on the pitch make him famed and wealthy, in the work of social advancement 400 years ago, a pair of elegant and agile legs were a distinct advantage. Romeo's face was good, indeed 'better than any man's', yet his leg was still better—'his leg exels'.[29] Such considerations contextualize a passage from *Every Man in His Humour*, a comedy by Ben Jonson first performed in 1598. In it, the country dupe Master Stephen fancies himself as a Renaissance man about town. 'How dost thou like my leg', he asks the cunning servant, Brainworm.

Brainworm: A very good leg, Master Stephen! But the woollen stocking does not com-
mend it so well.

Stephen: Foh, the stockings be good enough, now summer is coming on, for the
dust. I'll have a pair of silk again' winter, that I go to dwell i' the town.
I think my leg would show in a silk-hose.

Brainworm: Believe me, Master Stephen, rarely well.

Stephen: In sadness, I think it would: I have a reasonable good leg.

Brainworm: You have an excellent leg, Master Stephen, but I cannot stay to praise it
longer now, and I am very sorry for it.[30]

Like Brainworm, we cannot stay any longer to praise the early modern leg, but casting
our eyes upwards must inevitably come to the fork and that most unforgettable of sartorial assertions, the codpiece. The name makes its purpose and location explicit, *cod* being a
contemporary term for testicles. It originated in the triangular flap at the front of the hose,
which being laced up functioned as a modern fly. Staking a sartorial claim, gradually this
section was stuffed and decorated, reaching its most protuberant in the middle years of
the sixteenth century (Figure 36). It diminished in size from about 1570 (Figure 23), and
by 1600 its wear had ceased altogether. Surprisingly little has been written about the codpiece, either at the time or subsequently. Dress historians agree it is a symbol of virility, but
beyond that can find nothing to say.[31] Contemporaries were similarly reticent. You would
think that men walking about with artificial erections would occasion some comment—
some sniggering, outrage, or admiration. Extreme codpieces are to us like priapic jokes:
surely the sixteenth century must have thought them significant? In 1654, around 100
years after their heyday, Edmund Gayton described the codpiece as '*Umbonically* prominent', adding that if one should appear now, 'what twittering and peeping through the
Fingers we should have'—an observation as true of the early twenty-first century as the
mid seventeenth.[32] But in the sixteenth century there seems to have been little twittering,
peeping or—more to the point—satire or disapproval. Even Puritan writer Philip Stubbes,
who found so many clothing forms disturbing and immoral, did not expend any ink on
the codpiece. Partly, this may have been because the codpiece no more exaggerated its bit
of anatomy than other parts of contemporary dress did theirs. Doublets swelled the belly,
trunk hose inflated the hips and bottom and thighs, ruffs isolated the head, and the puff-
sleeved and padded gowns made Henrician shoulders simply enormous. This was the era of
the anatomized body and of extreme embellishment, where every part had separate visual
significance and its own claim to decorative fame. Almost anything that could be embroidered, jewelled, slashed or padded, was. It was an aesthetic of parts, not a blended whole.
The codpiece was just another part.[33]

This is not to say that comment, including reference to its sexual significance, was entirely absent. Prefiguring Gayton, Michel de Montaigne (1533–92) called the codpiece a
'laughter-moving, and maids looke-drawing peece'—though his essays were not translated

Figure 36 'Henry VIII', ink and watercolour by Hans Holbein the Younger, c. 1536–7, © National Portrait Gallery, London. Striking in this portrait of Henry VIII (1491–1547; his father Henry VII stands in the background) is the prominent codpiece pushing though the skirts of his jerkin. The shoulders are made more massive by the short gown with puffed short sleeves. Henry wears the Garter below his left knee.

into English until 1603, that is, after the codpiece had actually ceased to be worn.[34] As to be expected from Rabelaisian humour, enormous and exuberant codpieces make regular appearances in François Rabelais' (d. 1553) satire. However, this also did not appear in English until Sir Thomas Urquhart's translation of the first two books in 1653, a good half-century after the codpiece's demise.[35] In fact, the most interesting thing about what was said of the codpiece seems to be *when* it was said. In English, its appearance in text overwhelmingly postdates its life as a material object.[36] After the decline and disappearance of the fashion, the codpiece was born again in a textual incarnation. Why this should be so is a moot point. Perhaps earlier references have not survived, or perhaps the kind of texts in which later mention is made, such as stage plays, were not yet being written. However, surely in part the continuing awareness and literary life of the codpiece must have something to do with the fashion being so very memorable. Once it was no longer worn and people no longer expected to see it, *then* the idea of a padded penis decoration became, well, noticeable. Even today, over 400 years later, when most would be hard-pressed to name many items of Tudor dress, everyone can identify—and speculate on—the codpiece. I also suspect that linguistically the term was useful. Writers were able to make good conceptual mileage out of it—it was both rich in connotation and innuendo—and in more neutral usage, it was descriptively accurate. Thus sometimes codpiece was used merely to denote an area on the dressed body, as we might do with the term crotch or fly. Even as late as 1737, in describing the sort of opening he wanted in his breeches, Henry Purefoy stipulated that they 'must not have a flap at y[e] cod peice but only buttons & buttonholes'—that is, a fly fastening rather than a fall closure.[37] At other times the word was brandished for its explicitly sexual meanings, as in the French monsieur who came to London and was 'hot in the Codpiece', for the remedy of which he 'desired a Cooler'.[38] Or the man aroused, whose pulse beat so he thought his codpiece point—the lace that tied the codpiece to the hose—would fall asunder.[39] Another had a codpiece 'as big as a *Bolognian* sawcedge'.[40] In 1674, a six-page satire attacking the masculine sociability of the coffee house played extensively with the idea that coffee caused impotence. The 'continual sipping of this pittiful drink' was enough to 'tie up the *Codpice-point*'. 'It renders them that use it as *Lean* as Famine … they come from it with nothing *moist* but their snotty Noses, nothing *stiffe* but their Joints, nor *standing* but their Ears'.[41]

At the same time as talking of codpieces, this linguistically robust age gave a certain discursive life to female genitals through playing with the allusive nature of busks. As we saw in Chapter 2, the busk was a wooden, horn or whalebone strip that was inserted into a casing in the front of a corset. Running vertically down the corset's centre, the top of the busk lodged between a woman's breasts, while the bottom lay at her pelvis, or as Randle Home put it in the seventeenth century, 'it reacheth to the Honor'.[42] The erotic potential is obvious. Sometimes busks were decorated, carved with 'amorous images or phrases', and sometimes they were given to the wearer as suggestive, intimate gifts.[43] A seventeenth-century example worn by the Duchesse de Montpensier combines gift and text, carrying the words as from a lover: 'How I envy you the happiness that is yours, resting softly on her ivory white breast. Let us divide between us, if you please, this glory. You will be here the day and I shall be there the night.'[44] Like codpieces (and many other garments), busks were tied into place with ribbon-like lengths of silk. Just as a woman might be given a busk, so she in turn might give a busk point as a gift, or favour: 'he forsooth / Is in such longing heate, / My busk-poynt euen on his knees, / With teares he doth intreat'[45]; or, 'Loue is a childe contended with a toy, / A Busk-point, or some fauour stils the boy'.[46] When busks and their fastenings were combined in text with codpieces, the talk could become dirty indeed. A text of 1685 has a group of fictional ladies and gentlemen playing a risqué game of questions and commands:

> A Lady was commanded to put her busk in a Gentlemans codpiss.
> Another Lady was commanded to pull it out, which occasioned some sport, for she laying hold upon somthing else, after two or three pulls gave over, excusing her disobedience, by pretending that the busk was tackt to the Gentlemans belly.[47]

Although when this was written, the actual garment had not been worn for nearly 100 years, no one could possibly misunderstand the reference of 'codpiece' to both the breeches opening and the genitals beneath.

The next image I want to evoke is that of elite masculinity from the eighteenth century, particularly as it is represented within the heavy gilt frames of portraiture. This incarnation of physical manhood cuts a very different figure from his sixteenth- and early-seventeenth-century predecessor. His wig or powdered hair crowns a pear-shaped body. A long waistcoat forms a rounded belly, the collarless coat narrows the shoulders and its flaring, stiffened skirts obscure his hips and thighs. He is not at all leggy: on the contrary, he is distinctly long-bodied. Nevertheless, from the knee down his stockinged legs were disposed with careful elegance, their appearance of discreet, but considerable, significance (Figures 32 and 37).

The ideal eighteenth-century limb was trim and neat, neither long nor too muscled. In this regard, women were held to be unfortunately chunky. A mid-century work of medical science described the body's proportion thus: 'The Legs, as well in Men as in Women, ought to be of moderate length, and the Calf should not swell too much. Although the Legs of Women are commonly thicker than those of Men, yet this is by no means a Perfection.'[48] In keeping with the emphasis on bodily control and decorum, the disposition of all the limbs was of overt importance to polite demeanour. The aim was 'Standing, Walking, Dancing, or performing any genteel Exercise in a graceful, easy and becoming Manner'.[49] As with the dressing of hair, however, culture was better than nature. When it came to deportment, the rules of elegance needed to be learnt: left to its own devices, the untutored body would betray itself in coarse and common awkwardness. To attain 'Decency and genteel Behaviour', it is 'absolutely necessary *to assist the Body and Limbs* with Attitudes and Motions easy, free and graceful, and thereby *distinguish the polite Gentleman from the rude Rustick*'.[50]

First must be taught the art of standing, 'the Foundation of all Exercise'.[51] Deportment guides typically devoted their opening sections to getting this right, delineating the body's demeanour from the correct positioning of the head down to the approved placement of

Figure 37 'The Duet', oil painting by Arthur Davis, 1749, © Victoria and Albert Museum, London. The woman sits at a harpsichord, while her companion hands her a page of music. She wears a hooped petticoat, and her skirts spill in silken folds around her. Her gracefully posed forearms are bare. The gentleman wears the bottom-heavy eighteenth-century ensemble of long coat, waistcoat and breeches. His white stockinged legs catch the eye and are elegantly disposed. His powdered wig probably has a bag and bow behind.

the toes. Ideally the head was erect—the face expressing 'manly Boldness' tempered with 'becoming Modesty'—shoulders relaxed, arms neither stiff nor angular but disposed easily, with perhaps a hand in the waistcoat or at the sword hilt. The legs were positioned one ahead of the other, 'and both Feet must be turn'd outwards'.[52] 'Always turn out your Feet', explained another text, 'because that makes you stand firm, easy, and graceful.'[53] Subjects shown standing in eighteenth-century paintings are usually depicted so, and if their composition has a balletic cast to it, it is because the five classical positions were taught as the foundations for deportment both on and off the dance floor.[54]

From this easy stance at rest, the body 'is ready to do what you would have it, either to Walk, make a Bow, or Dance'.[55] In all three, the open-toed and balletic posture was important. As Pierre Rameau directed in his dancing manual, in 'walking well' the hips must be turned outwards 'because the lower Parts are governed by this commanding Joint, which gives a Disposition to the Knees and the Feet'. While women were also taught to move in this way, long dresses made into a hidden ideal what was constantly conspicuous on men. To walk with one's feet and legs too straight was ungainly, was unrefined: 'the *Toes* turn'd in, or placed in a strait Line with the Bone of the Leg; will lessen all the Dignity and Gracefulness of the other Parts of Attitude'.[56] Thus the desirable motion of the eighteenth century turns out to be very different from our ideal carriage, which designates walking in parallel as most attractive. To turn the toes outward seems lumpish and clumsy. Modern locomotion, incidentally, finds its extreme expression on the runway, in the walk taught to female models. Here the feet are placed one directly in front of the other in a single straight line, or even with the front foot crossing over—a fault, according to Peirre Rameau in 1731, to be carefully avoided.[57] This gait helps the hips sway and gives the model that look of, as we interpret it, strutting insouciance. According to one source in the fashion industry, the 'little body-jiggling stamp' that is now a fairly common characteristic of this walk is designed to bounce breast implants in a way that mimics the movements of real flesh.[58]

As one might expect from an age that was energetically exploring notions of civility and in which bodily discipline was enjoined to a hitherto unprecedented degree, the ceremony of the bow, which marked the boundaries of personal interactions, was formalized and elaborate. These movements of the body that acknowledged arrival, acquaintance, departure, offering and receipt, were all codified, and the aim was to perform them with fluent ease, respecting both the context of the interactions and the relative status of the parties involved. Rameau divides bows into those 'made forwards', those made in passing, and those 'made backwards', the latter of which did not actually involve any backwards movement of the feet and were the most respectful. He distinguishes 'the Quality of the Person' saluted and also the places. A passing bow made in the streets, for example, may be made with less exactitude; 'but those in publick Walks, where Persons of the best Fashion resort, they must be made with more Care and Regard'.[59] François Nivelon instructs his readers on the passing bow, the bow forwards, on the 'agreeable Disposition of Body and Limbs' when offering and receiving, and how to make a compliment upon retiring from a room. In the last, which seems to be a variation of the bow backwards, it is important 'to shew the Shape of the Leg in the best Manner'.[60] Apart from the increased complexity and variations of type, the eighteenth-century bow differed in one fundamental way from its sixteenth-century precursor, and was worlds away from the kneeling medieval obeisance. To simplify what took pages for conduct manuals to describe, now a gentleman did not step back in a kneel; rather, he took a pace forward, then, keeping the front leg straight and his weight on the back, he sank down, thus bending the back knee and bowing from the body. This was more assertive, more theatrical and, quite literally, foregrounded a man's lower limbs, bringing them to immediate notice. This was 'making a leg'.[61]

Obviously, the version of life that we get from the pages of dance manuals and conduct books is a theoretical and idealized one: civility and performance as some thought it should be embodied, rather than as it necessarily was. In addition, the dancing master was a stock figure of satire, the butt of derisory humour levelled at effeminacy, lewdness, pernickety fussiness and, very often, the crime of being foreign.[62] For all that, however, first-person observations tell a not dissimilar story, suggesting that self-presentation was important and that if good, a man's legs were an asset. For example, on the day preceding the coronation of George III, writer Richard Cumberland (1732–1811) found newly ennobled Lord Melcombe 'before a looking-glass in his new robes practising attitudes and debating within himself upon the most graceful mode of carrying his coronet in the procession'.[63] Society courtesan Margaret Leeson, whose memoirs punctured the *amour propre* of quite a few, described the vain self-satisfaction of a young man of her acquaintance whose habit it was also to preen in the mirror. Visiting this demi-monde more to enjoy his own physicality than hers, according to Leeson:

> Young *David* indeed used generally to employ the time he was at my house, in admiring himself in my large looking-glass; he would contemplate his person with a great degree of complacency and self-approbation, then would turn round to me cut three or four capers and cry out 'well *Leeson!* ar'nt I damned handsome fine fellow? pray do admire my legs, shape and divine figure'.

In the interests of personal gain, Leeson reports herself as more than happy to play pander to his self-love:

> whatever I thought, it was my business to praise him in order to coax him out of something genteel, and therefore my constant reply was, 'that there was not a handsomer man in town, nor in my opinion a finer dancer or more elegant figure'.[64]

Ann Sheldon, another courtesan turned memoirist, found herself, however, unable to sacrifice real opinion to financial prudence. Being presented to a wealthy merchant, she bore with his tedious supper-table conversation, which turned upon no other subject than 'the elegance of his dancing'. After some while, however, he got up to demonstrate 'his grace and agility'. The table no longer hiding his lower half, he revealed 'such a pair of bandy legs' as to determine Sheldon on an immediate departure. While the merchant concentrated on performing a dance step, Sheldon performed her exit. Her pander Mr Pratt remonstrated

with her for whistling such wealth to the wind, but 'he was not a sufficient master of ora-
tory to talk the Merchant's legs into a decent shape'.[65]

All in all, gents to whom nature had not been kind had a bit of a problem on their
hands, for in a society that admired a good limb, the flip side meant that insufficiently attractive legs were the subject of jokes. Amputations and wooden legs, for instance, figured
in jest books.[66] Margaret Leeson recounts a story in which, during a gathering at her place,
the company fell to ridiculing one of the gentlemen, whose misfortune it was to have
crooked legs. Rising to the challenge, he held out his right leg, saying pleasantly that they
might make what fun they pleased of him, but he wagered that 'there is a worse leg than
that in the company'. Thinking this impossible, the bet was promptly accepted, on which
the gentleman 'produced his left leg, which was much more deformed than the right) [sic]
and won the wager'.[67] A satirical publication, *The Midwife*, impugned the masculinity and
morals of men with feeble legs: 'What wondrous little Legs the Men have here, I can't see
'em even with my Lanthorn, and my Spectacles.' These small-membered men—and the
inference is clear—are unable to impregnate their wives; instead 'they carry their Calves to
Covent Garden', an area notorious for prostitution, where the only sex they get they must
pay for.[68]

In stockings there was no hiding a disappointing limb: it was therefore fortunate for
those let down by nature that there was always padding. Placed in the stockings this could
supply a deficiency, and swell the muscle to a more elegant dimension. John Vanbrugh's
1696 play *The Relapse* was reworked around the middle years of the following century to
include a hosier by the name of Mendlegs. Another character, Lord Foppington, complains
that Mendlegs has thickened the calves of the stockings a little too much: 'They make my
Legs look like a Chairman's [i.e. a man who carried a sedan chair].' Foppington orders that
the next pair be 'the thickness of a Crown-piece less'.[69] The play appeared on the stage at
various London theatres throughout the eighteenth century, its list of characters published
in the newspapers along with the notice of its forthcoming performance.[70] It is unlikely,
of course, that many wore calf pads. What their presence in satire really articulates is not
that individuals might have used artificial means to attain an ideal appearance, but of what
that ideal appearance consisted.

Surprisingly, false calves, or talk of them, persisted even after the breeches and stockings combination gave over to the new fashion of trousers (Figure 8). While, as we shall
find, around the turn of the century these and pantaloons were worn very tight, this does
make sense. Thus Mr Eddy of 43 Dean Street, Soho, advertised in various newspapers
over the period from 1798 to 1800, offering a range of prosthetic devices from trusses to
leg irons, and also 'False Calves to shape the Legs'.[71] And as late as 1830, a gentleman's
dress manual regarded tight pantaloons as 'the most proper and becoming' garment for
evening dress, yet also advised that either these be avoided by men without at least toler-
ably good legs, or else the defects of their person be remedied with the judicious use of
'a slight degree of stuffing'.[72] Meanwhile, in some conservatively minded venues such as
Almack's Assembly Rooms, knee breeches and stockings—'the terror of the bow-legged

and thin-shanked'[73]—had remained de rigueur. Thus, in 1828 a society column printed a verse about the Almack's patronesses refusing entry to gentlemen 'who, not complying with the rules laid down respecting tights, / Present themselves in shapeless trowsers, vulgarly call'd whites'. This was quite true: the Duke of Wellington was once famously turned away for wearing trousers. The paper added, ''Tis rumour'd, that in consequence large orders for false calves' were made 'to grace the spindle shanks of those whom Nature made by halves'.[74]

But even when stockings had become a thing of the distant past and the fashionable cut of trousers had become looser, talk of artificial calves remained current. Very interestingly, most of it appeared in one specific context: lampoons of aging, sexually active, senior politicians.[75] For satirists, false calves connoted the elderly dandy grotesquely attempting to retain youth who pursued sexual exploits inappropriate to his years, and whose anatomical deceptions reflected his untrustworthiness in political life. As if this weren't rich enough, an added bonus for the press was the variant meaning of calf as a 'dolt' or 'stupid fellow'—a usage that gives the point to the observation, 'If men wear false calves, it may at least be said in their behalf that they themselves are real ones.'[76] So we find that in the pages of the fairly scurrilous *Satirist*, the Duke of Wellington was scorned for painting, patching and padding, and Lord Palmerston was found obnoxious for his 'coxcombry'. In 1834 when this was published, Wellington was sixty-five, had been known as a womanizer and was continuing to show interest in very much younger women. Palmerston was nearly fifty. In his youth as a good-looking man about town, his nickname 'Cupid' was earned by his habit of frequent liaisons, a habit that he was to keep up most of his life. His affair with Lady Emily Cowper was the most notorious: Palmerston acknowledged as his, three of the five children she bore while married to her first husband. Although on opposite sides of the benches, Wellington and Palmerston have this in common: both men, said the paper, 'wear false calves, which, in honest truth, become them amazingly. Legs, they state are nothing unless sustained by *calves*'.[77] In May 1838 the same column played on Palmerston's affair with Lady Emily and their illegitimate children, one of which is alluded to here by the gratifyingly polysemous term, calf:

> It is untrue that Palmerston wears false calves—it is a malicious and unfounded report of the enemy. His Lordship, it is well known, has no necessity for anything 'false' in that particular—he has, as all the world must be aware, and old Lady Cowper can avouch, a most excellent *calf*—one quite natural to him, in good keeping and just proportion with his other qualities of person and figure![78]

The next month, the paper followed up with the observation:

> Some of Palmerston's political acquaintances declare that he has a false tongue. We know that he carries about him false hair, false calves, false teeth, false eye-brows, and other false articles, but a false tongue is rather too great a stretch of the power of art over nature.[79]

In November *The Age*, a periodical also given to libellous attacks, drew a picture of Palmerston as dying his whiskers, speculating on a special pomatum to fill up crow's feet, and with 'false calves, false hips, false shoulders, and everything false'.[80]

Two months previously *The Age* had published a ditty about the Lord Chancellor, Henry Brougham: 'One fears, now so often the first Whig is able / To tuck his false calves under Royalty's table'.[81] Baron Brougham and Vaux, then just turned sixty, had had more occasional affairs, but they included one with the well-known courtesan Harriette Wilson. Wilson, whose memoirs had made scandalous and entertaining reading for the higher echelons in society—the four-volume work had run to thirty editions in the first year alone[82]—had also had a relationship with Wellington, whom she had unsuccessfully tried to blackmail. Wilson offered to remove from the memoir the names of individuals who immediately paid her £200, an extortionary 'offer' she was to repeat as the book went into further editions. Wellington is meant to have responded with the famous 'publish and be damned'. Where she had failed with Wellington, however, Wilson succeeded with Brougham, and for several years he paid her to keep their relationship quiet.

In 1840 *The Satirist* again attacked Palmerston, asserting that thieves had visited his home and from his dressing room stolen materials for 'making up'. These included wigs, padding to swell out the chest and shoulders, rouge, and 'two pair of false calves'. The next year *Punch*, then in only its second month of publication, got into the act. This time the target was Lord John Russell, at that point the outgoing Home Secretary. In July, Russell had married for the third time. He was just turning forty-nine; his new wife, Lady Fanny Elliot, was more than twenty years younger. In August, *Punch* advertised that Lord Russell was shortly to start a matrimonial agency. There followed a barbed list of the agency's requirements of prospective clients, including that 'Gentlemen who wear wigs, false calves, or artificial teeth, or use hair-dye &c., will be required to state the same, as no deception can be countenanced by Lord J.R.'[83]

In 1853 Palmerston was again the subject, this time of a vitriolic, vituperative letter to *Reynold's Newspaper*. Palmerston, by now sixty-eight, was flayed for being 'still ambitious of the form of an Adonis' and attempting to conceal the 'ravages of age' with cosmetic paints and padding. '[Y]ou have even condescended to take a lesson on symmetrical proportion from your own footman; in fact, that your lordship's calves are cork.' Thus prinked out, this 'Cupid of the Cabinet'—utilizing Palmerston's early nickname—lays siege to elderly female hearts and fancies. 'If this be not true', said the author, 'it ought to be, for in that case the falseness of your lordship's calves'—and here he reaches the heart of the metaphor—'might typify the hollowness of your heart.' He closes with the accusation that Palmerston is 'a man of false pretences—false calves, false heart, false teeth, false faith, false all over'.[84]

This last example is interesting, for in it two contexts of the 'false calves' conceit overlap. From about this point, the trope lost its satirical potency, perhaps as the memory of eighteenth-century elegance faded and dimmed, or perhaps as it came only to signify the livery of the typical Victorian footman. For as with hair powder, breeches and stockings had slid from elegance, to conservative unfashionability, and then to a final incarnation as servants' uniform. In this last descent they were apparently accompanied by the stocking's accessory, the padded calf. False calves thus became, as in this letter, equated with footmen—a species of servant, being typically tall and well built, whose appeal to their employers was at least partly visual. *Punch* therefore observed that the skill of a first-class footman might be satisfactorily shown in a mould of his false calves; and it became a jest that pins might be stuck into a footman's leg without him feeling a thing.[85] And thus it was that old Lady B— was said to have turned off her footman, James, for obtaining employment under false pretences. His character was blameless; his height, at six foot two, was beyond reproach; but about the 'manly proportions' of his legs there was doubt. In the end, by virtue of some maliciously wielded scarf pins, the secret of his 'falsely fatted calves' was revealed.[86]

For the third look at the fashioning of the male leg, we have to go back to the closing years of the eighteenth century, to the point when breeches began to be replaced by trousers, that type of bifurcated garment familiar to us today. When we looked at the dressing of the upper body, it became apparent that around this time a new vision of masculinity began to emerge. The older, bottom-heavy aesthetic that favoured bellies and hips gave way to an ideal that 200 years later is still going strong, and is thus very easy for us to approach sympathetically. Taking its inspiration from antique statuary—the chiselled perfection of marble gods, warriors and heroes—this look prizes broad shoulders, a lean torso and slim hips. Below the waist, as we shall now find, the emphasis was on long, strong legs—the sort of legs, to go back to the classical statues, that might carry a latter-day Achilles to victory in the drawing rooms, even if not on the battlefields. And just as the 'natural' anatomy of the upper body was given a helping hand by its garments, so, too, legs were dressed so as to embody the new desirability.

Most notably, this was achieved by pantaloons, a garment halfway between breeches and trousers which, like the coats they were worn with, were influenced by contemporary military dress. Chiefly, pantaloons were characterized by a smooth, body-hugging fit achieved through skilled tailoring and the use of semi-elastic materials such as cloth cut on the bias, knitted fabrics and supple leathers (Figure 38). They were kept from riding up by being tightly fastened at the bottom of each leg, either at the calf or the ankle, depending on the style. At the centre back, a vent, closed with corset-style lacing, enabled the garment to be pulled higher and tighter still. The favoured colours were pale: their cream and buff hues spoke tantalizingly of naked flesh, and whereas dark colours smooth a form, the light tones revealed the swell and shape of the body beneath.[87] For this sort of fashion 'thin thighs' are 'intolerable', complained *The Taylor's Complete Guide* of c. 1796. Conversely, as a newspaper of 1800 observed, pantaloons were an ornament to a thigh well formed.[88] During the day, pantaloons were most usually worn with Hessians—tasselled boots ending at a rounded point just below the knee but lower behind, again modelled on a military chic. The emphasis on the upper leg—and also on the crotch—was even further underscored by the short-waisted, cut-away style of the coat above; aesthetically a world away from the flaring garments of just a few years previously, whose long bodies and full skirts effectively hid this part of the anatomy from view. According to one commentator, it was 'to please the Ladies' that gentlemen wore such high waists, 'this causing their legs to appear the longer'.[89]

As the new century dawned, men's clothes were therefore designed to reproduce a fashion in bodies as much as a fashion in dress, a fashion perfectly encapsulated by the wording of this advertisement: 'shoulders down; arms back; chest open; Body gracefully erect; and waistband properly HIGH up'.[90] In painting, the effect of the ensemble, though discreet, is visually arresting: the pale-clad thighs and crotch luminous, swimming into focus against the dark surrounds of coat and boots (Figure 39). If, on the canvas, this part of the body leaps out, it is a pretty fair guess that in real life the effect was similar. This is a style that rivets the viewer's gaze on the upper legs and the fork.[91] It is no wonder that pantaloons were sometimes called 'inexpressibles'. An additional eroticism came from their fall-down, the flap around five to nine inches wide that, buttoning near the waistband on either side, functioned as a fly opening does today. For obvious reasons a loose fall-down was deemed

Figure 38 'Le Bon Genre, No. 68. Costumes Anglais', hand-coloured etching published by Pierre Lamésangère, 1814, © Trustees of the British Museum. The three men on the left are dressed alike in tall hats, neckcloths, fitting cut-away coats and very tight trousers. The one on the left wears pantaloons at calf length with top boots; the man in the centre has full-length pantaloons tied at the ankle; the man on the right of the group wears breeches and gaiters. The military officer in the centre of the print also sports tight pantaloons and tailored coat, the short tails of which are fastened back.

'indelicate' and 'indecent' by *The Taylor's Guide*.[92] However, even the most fitting of closures made a feature of this section of the body in a way that, except for the codpiece, has been seen neither before nor since in mainstream fashion.

As far as bifurcated garments go, however, the period was transitional, breeches, pantaloons and trousers all having their place in the wardrobe.[93] Indeed, in paintings it is not always possible to tell which of them a subject is wearing. And although a fashion column of 1798 advised that breeches, being less tight than pantaloons, 'are more decent', they drew on the same aesthetic and their looks were very similar.[94] They were all constructed with a laced back vent and a frontal fall opening. Light colours were favoured for daytime wear, and a smooth, close fit was essential. To guard against 'disagreeable wrinkles',[95] braces—a new invention—were worn to pull them taut from the high waist. In addition, many trousers and longer varieties of pantaloons were made with another innovation, 'trouser straps', a kind of stirrup worn under the instep to anchor the garment at the bottom.[96] Pulled from above, stretched from below, and moulded around the wearer's body, the garments covering the lower half of the early-nineteenth-century gent fitted his contours closely. It was in this context that a tract on the relationship of contemporary clothing with the health of its wearers spent some time considering the injurious effects of tight leather breeches. 'They are certainly handsome', the author allows, 'and very fit to expose a muscular Thigh.' However, the physical discomforts should dissuade men from wearing them: they are inconvenient for walking, liable to cause numbness and coldness on the outer part of the

Figure 39 'Sir Mark Sykes, Henrietta Masterman Sykes and Tatton Sykes', oil painting by Thomas Lawrence (1769–1830), accepted by HM Government in lieu of tax and allocated to York Museums Trust (York Art Gallery). In the centre of the picture, Henrietta wears the high-waisted muslin fashion that some considered both immodest and unsuitable for the climate. To the right, Tatton Sykes's coat is also cut on high-waisted lines that elongate the lower half of his body. The tails of the coat fall away to the back, revealing his crotch and thighs clad in pale pantaloons. A modestly sized neckcloth, a dark overcoat and top boots complete the ensemble. Sir Mark (seated) is dressed in the older style of breeches and stockings.

thigh and, some report, pain in the testes. The author also disparaged the sort of man who would wear boots made too small 'for the silly Purpose of showing the exact Shape of his Legs'.[97] Looking back at her younger days it was the trousers, though, that Lady Dorothy Nevill remembered, bringing to mind 'the extreme tightness which fashion ... prescribed'. They were so tight, she said, that, much to the merriment of onlookers, a furious gallop in Hyde Park caused one gentleman's 'tight white trousers' to 'burst right up the side'.[98]

The tightness of breeches, trousers and pantaloons, and their high-placed seam at the fork, compelled wearer and tailor to negotiate a matter of delicate intimacy. The high crotch, taken from cavalry garments and thus adapted for riding, 'obliged the wearer to dress to one side'; that is, with no room above the crotch seam, the wearer's genitals had to be positioned down either one trouser leg or the other, with extra material allowed accordingly on that side.[99] Taking the measurements for this required discretion and circumspection, and a willingness by both parties, as it were, to mentally avert the gaze. Thus the matter could be glossed over; while the eye was elsewhere, the hand was deft and to the point. As a tailor's guide advised:

> Remember always that your hands are going about a sensitive, intelligent, animate man, and not a horseblock. First rule—Never stand while taking any measures in front of your man, but on his right side. To do so is to commit a gross piece of familiarity, rather offensive in all cases ... [T]he leg measure is one of the chief, if not the very chief measure in a pair of trousers, and is often taken very faultily. With great quickness place end of your measure close up into the crotch, then pass down your left behind his thigh to knee joint ... If a man's dress is right, well two measures thus 24, 22, will at once indicate on which side that has to be cut out.[100]

The most complete embodiment of the fashionable impulses of the early years of the nineteenth century crystallizes in the figure of the dandy (Figures 8 and 18). Just as he was portrayed in the highest of collars and neckcloths, and the most fitting of coats with the smallest of waists, so too, in the cultural imagination, was he clad in the tightest of trousers:

> A collar to his eyes, which contains an ounce of gum, Sir,
> So close his mouth surrounds, its [sic] a wonder he's not dumb, Sir;
> A neckcloth, three or four yards square, his baby chin protects, Sir,
> And keeps his head from falling off his long and scraggy neck, Sir.
> His corsets of whalebone, three inches in diameter,
> Produce his wasp-waist, and show, of fashion he's an *amateur*, ...
> Sometimes his inexpressibles are wider than they're long, Sir,
> At others, he can scarcely move, so tight they're pasted on, Sir.[101]

Of a less satirical and more domestic nature are the letters between Elizabeth Coke and John Spencer Stanhope. In 1822 the preparations for their marriage were well under way, including the planning for what the couple should wear. Miss Coke approved of her fiancé's choice of a blue coat, but was uncertain as to whether trousers or the more dashing pantaloons would be better: 'you look so well in trousers that I am rather puzzled; perhaps pantaloons are the most correct'. Spencer Stanhope eventually decided on the latter, and Elizabeth wrote that she thought 'light coloured pantaloons—to tie at the ancles—of any light color would look very well'. However, she warned the bridegroom playfully, 'You must not make yourself too much of a dandy, or my father would take fright.'[102]

The last view of the dandy illustrates the self-absorbed coldness at the heart of his pursuit of perfection. It was perfection of restraint, performed physically through the restricted colours and tailored precision of his garments, and emotionally through the adoption of an ironic stance that refused affective engagement. The true dandy wielded social power because he never allowed himself the common vulnerability of feelings.[103] The story in question is told by Captain Gronow, himself a minor dandy figure of the Regency world, of Lieutenant-Colonel Kelly of the First Foot Guards. Dandiacal Colonel Kelly was, according to Gronow, thin, haughty and 'the vainest man I ever encountered'. 'Very fond of dress', he was particularly proud—as others were envious—of the high gloss on his boots, which were polished to an unsurpassed brilliancy. Kelly was killed in a house fire, says Gronow, 'endeavouring to save his favourite boots'. As the news of his horrible end became known, men of fashion vied to profit from his death, outbidding one another to secure the services of Kelly's valet, who now alone possessed the secret of the 'inimitable blacking'.[104]

DRESSING FOOLISHLY

So far we have looked at how men's legs were variously clad in stockings, hose, breeches and pantaloons, garments that gave their legs a visual prominence. Dressed in this way, the bits of the anatomy below the waist were essential to the proper performance of elite manliness. Legs and what they could do—dance, bow, ride, fight and even just stand elegantly— were on show, and the bifurcated garments in which they were revealed were the sole and utter prerogative of male wearers. In short, breeches categorized gender. I want to look now at those excluded from trouser wearing, to see if the customs and assumptions surrounding this exclusion can tell us anything further. Obviously the largest group among them is women. Before exploring their halting progress towards trousers and the tide of resistance against which they battled, I want first to consider the case of young boys.

It is common knowledge that in infancy boys and girls were dressed alike in long gowns (Figure 20), but it is perhaps less well appreciated how significant a milestone it was when boys finally graduated to breeches. It marked the transition from the female-dominated world of the nursery, to being more in men's company and tutelage. In other words, once in a birfucated garment, a child's social context and behaviour were meant to change. Although the age at which this happened varied over time and with social class, the attainment of that first pair of hose, breeches or knickerbockers was quietly, but nonetheless immensely, significant. In the small domestic worlds where it occurred, the event was worth recording, and usually with considerable affection and pride. Like first steps and first words, first breeches were a real achievement in the process of growing up. Donning them, the young wearer crossed a divide, leaving the neuter stage of infancy for the gendered life of manhood.

It was for this reason that in 1679 Lady Anne North (d. 1684) wrote in such fond detail about the occasion that her grandson was dressed in his first suit of adult clothes. 'You cannot beleeve the great concerne that was in the whole family here', she said, as the tailor came to fit little Frank. What with the buttons, the breeches, the sword and every-one pressing round to help and to watch, Lady Anne said he was barely to be seen for the hands about him. When finally buttoned and buckled to everyone's satisfaction—including Frank's own—Lady Anne thought him 'taler and prettyer' than before. 'This day', she wrote, Frank was 'wholly to throw off the coats [petticoats] and write man.'[105] A clearer statement of the assumption of gendered maturity it would be hard to find. The tenor of Lady Anne's letters is remarkably similar to that of the diary entry in which, thirty years earlier, Sir Henry Slingsby had recorded sending a suit of clothes from London for his son Thomas, 'being ye the first breeches and doublet yt he ever had'. Although the actual vestimentary rite of passage was not to happen until Easter, to assuage Lady Slingsby's impatience Sir Henry dispatched the breeches and doublet in good time: 'his mother had a desire to see him in ym how proper a man he would be'.[106]

In Lady North's family the day set aside for Frank's breeching was accounted a special event—she esteemed it 'great good fortune' that the weather was fine, as we all do for cel-ebratory occasions. Similarly, the breeching of Thomas Slingsby was a planned event, not just something that would happen whenever the suit of clothes was ready. Both boys got to try on their new garments before the actual transition was to take place in a more formal-ized context. Nearly 100 years after Thomas received his first 'man's' garment, the breeching of Charlotte Papendiek's brother was timed to coincide with the queen's birthday, a formal court celebration that, for a family in royal service in the queen's household—Charlotte's father had come to England in the queen's entourage and remained with her ever since—was a very important day. It is also significant that Charlotte, writing her memoirs many years later, thought the occasion noteworthy enough to describe:

> On the Queen's birthday, January 18, 1777, my brother was to appear in a new dress. He was to be 'breeched,' the term used in those days, and literally so it was. A pair of breeches with a buckle at the knee; a coat with a falling shirt collar hanging over; a waistcoat with pockets long over the thigh; and a cocked hat, round ones not being known; was the costume.

Further on in her memoirs she described the breeching of her own son, 'dear Frederick'. It was, she said, a total change of dress for a boy: a shirt like a man's, jacket, trousers and gaiters, strong shoes, coat, hat and cane—'and the sweet dear child looked, as he was, beautiful'.[107]

It is easy to see how sentiments such as these might become construed as sentimentality. 'Tom's First Knickerbockers', a story in the Victorian periodical *Good Words for the Young*, is a prime candidate. In it a young boy is delighted both with his 'real rifle-green cloth knickerbockers', and the opportunity they give him to crow over his big cousin Tom, who, despite being taller and older, is still kept by his mama in 'short socks and frilled drawers'. Triumph turns to chagrin, however, when Tom appears in a far more adult-looking pair of his own with 'smart stripes down the seams', in which he looks 'like a gentleman growed', a regular 'six-foot hossifer'.[108] Adding to the sentimentality of this improving tale so typical of its period, there is also a death, a motherless child and a moral; though all three fortunately of no concern here. Of more relevance is another story that pictures a fond and doting spinster fingering the 'little relics' of her adoration of her one-time nurseling: 'a soft downy curl', 'a faded photograph of a very fat little boy in petticoats', and 'a tiny scrap of cloth, the pattern of his first knickerbockers'.[109] Dress historians Jo Paoletti and Carol Kregloh have found that in America at this time, popular literature often described first breeches, and the haircuts that might accompany them, as 'traumatic for a mother, first steps toward the inevitable day when she would lose her son forever to the world outside the home'. They also suggest that breeching was a moveable feast, so to speak, depending not only on a boy's age, but also on his physique and behaviour. Thus 'acquiring masculine clothing was not merely a matter of being old enough, but also of looking and behaving in a masculine manner'.[110] Mothers anxious about this transition, or having trouble knowing when it was appropriate, could always turn to the pages of the burgeoning periodicals market for advice. The correspondence section of the November 1876 issue of *Myra's Journal of Dress and Fashion* replied to 'Violet', reassuring her that the 'prettiest style for little boys' dresses, under five years old', had box pleats front and back and a wide sash tied behind. But boys of seven, the journal advised, should be in a knickerbocker suit or equivalent.[111] Similarly, fashion reportage tended to make it explicit at what age certain ensembles were deemed appropriate. Thus, a velvet frock with lace at the wrists worn over what we would call drawers, also edged with scalloped needlework, was a costume suitable for a 'Little Boy from three to five years'. His older companion of seven to nine should be dressed in a long blouse belted over long trousers.[112]

The Taylor's Complete Guide in the late eighteenth century was less prescriptive and more practical. In the section on making a jacket and trousers for a boy—'the first change the parents give their children, when they are tired of seeing them in frocks'—the author gives suggestions on how to measure these infants, for, as he points out, there is no previous set of clothes from which to take guidance nor, for obvious reasons, can their dresses provide the tailor with any clue.[113] At almost the exact same time, the Austen extended family was dealing with the exact same problem. Passing on a message from her sister-in-law Mary, for Cassandra to then pass on to another sister-in-law Elizabeth, Jane wrote: 'Mary has likewise a message—. She will be much obliged to you if you can bring her the pattern of the Jacket & Trowsers, or whatever it is, that Eliz[th]:'s boys wear when they are first put into breeches.' Mary had only one son, at this point nearing three, whereas the more experienced Elizabeth already had four sons and was to give birth to two more. Even better than a pattern, though, would be 'an old suit itself', of which Mary 'would be very glad'. However, perhaps because such suits were so much in demand in Elizabeth's household, Jane concluded practically, 'but that I suppose is hardly do-able'.[114]

Austen, writing before nineteenth-century perceptions of childhood expanded the wardrobe and apparently complicated the breeching transition, had similarly no sentiment to spare when she had written to Cassandra to tell her that 'Little Edward'—their nephew, Elizabeth's eldest boy—'was breeched yesterday for good & all, and was whipped, into the Bargain.'[115] Her comment does, however, illustrate the expectation that masculine raiment brought masculine behaviour in its wake, in this case the corporal punishment suitable for a youth but not an infant. This is echoed mid century in one of those throwaway lines whose significance lies in what it reveals of the normative understandings of its time. A newspaper columnist reassures his readers that his spoof autobiography will not commence in the usual way 'at first breeches and birch'.[116] This then—trousers and a beating —is the conventional way of dating the start of a man's life, his beginning moment, the point at which his identity hardens into its thereafter recognizable form.

Another of the traits a child was expected to put on with his masculine habit was rationality. Along with physical robustness, he was meant to assume its intellectual equivalent: the sort of mental capacity that marked him off from infants and females, and gave him access to rights and responsibilities that under law were denied to them.[117] The development of this specifically masculine intellect began when he put on his specifically masculine garments. It was something like this that Bulstrode Whitelocke (1605–75) had in mind when, in his memoirs, he wrote of his seven-year-old self 'having changed his habit'—that is, been breeched—his father delighted 'to see him more & more inclinable to his book'. Bulstrode was 'taught musicke, dauncing, fencing, & writing & was no unapt schollar in them'.[118]

Breeches, as well as signifying masculinity then, were markers of the particular gendered qualities of self-determination and rationality. For the boy child, the ceremony of breeching opened up the conjoining promise of adult status, manliness and mental acuity. But what of that other sector of the population barred from the wearing of breeches? What of women, whose wit 'is but weak and crazy'?[119] What of their relationship with that garment that promised the wearer so much? 'If the wife go in breeches, the man must wear long coats like a fool'[120]: between this articulation of 1611 and the practice of fashion today, there lies a yawning gulf of cultural change. On one side of it, a breeched woman was symptomatic of a world upside down—a subversion of authority and a perversion of the natural order. Nowadays, on the other side of that gulf, the wearing of trousers by women has become the norm; most women wear trousers most of the time. How, then, did we get from there to here? We will now spend a little time peering into this chasm of historical difference, tracing the key moments in the process of this particular fashionable change. It was an inching advance that took over a century, was firmly resisted at every step, and depended not on consistent progress but on the gradual establishment of contexts of acceptability. At the end of it, after hundreds years of skirts, fashion finally came to dress women's legs separately, each limb in its own tubular envelope of cloth.

Considering the many hundreds of years in which bifurcated garments were associated with that bundle of attributes so long held to be essentially masculine, it is perhaps not so surprising that women's fashion took such a long time to successfully lay claim to their form. Their first participation in mainstream fashion dates to the closing years of the eighteenth century, when pantaloons appeared as garments worn under the high-waisted muslin gowns of the period, though, it seems, designed to be glimpsed below the hem.[121] 'Our *modern Eves,* instead of the *fig leaf* decoration against intrusive eyes, have assumed the Gentleman-like inexpressibles against *bold* and *piercing winds.*'[122] French women in particular were held to favour flesh-coloured varieties.[123] While by modern standards such undergarments, long to the ankle, could rarely be thought anything but dauntingly modest, at the time their adoption was generally felt to lie somewhere on the scale of dashingly risqué to disgustingly shameless. According, for example, to the *London Packet* of June 1798, the 'rage of the French Ladies for fantastic and indecent novelties in dress' led three of them to deserved discomfiture. Appearing in public 'in the most voluptuous and shameless dress, *without shifts*, with flesh-coloured pantaloons', they were hissed and pelted by the crowd until a police commissary intervened. The writer of the article undermined the morality of the fashion and its wearers still further by slyly suggesting that the commissary was neither disinterested, nor that his services went unrewarded by the ladies.[124] Similarly, the wearing of pantaloons coupled with a revealing dress was held by some in the French republic to be sufficient grounds for divorce. In an illustration of the benefits of 'Incompatibility of Disposition' as the basis for marital separation, a young man is described as coming home one night to find his naked wife surrounded by four women 'who were fitting her with a pair of *flesh-coloured* pantaloons'. He remonstrated with her, but in vain: 'a robe of transparent lawn was all the dress this Lady chose to wear over her pantaloons'. Indeed, in this state she insisted on attending a ball, where—owing to her immodest dress—she was surrounded, caressed and insulted by gallants and coxcombs. The following day, her husband sued for divorce.[125]

By 1806 however, pantaloons, also known as pantalettes, were being introduced into the fashion pages of English periodicals. In the general observations on fashion for its June issue, *La Belle Assemblée* described 'walking dress pantaloons' made of cambric and trimmed around the bottom with lace. That they were still daring, though, is obvious, for the journal took care to reassure readers that 'the novelty of this dress' was rendered less 'conspicuous' by the thin muslin overdresses which, in some measure, disguised 'the singularity of its effect'.[126] From about this point, pantaloons, though still worn by a few, in general seem to have shrunk to just below the knee, transforming themselves into the undergarments that became known as drawers. Slowly, these became acceptable wear. By 1811 for instance, fifteen-year-old Princess Charlotte, the rather racy daughter of George IV and Queen Caroline, had adopted them. Lord Glenbervie, who had it from his wife who was present at the time, wrote that on one occasion in company with her mother, the princess was sitting with her legs stretched out, thus showing her drawers 'which, it seems, she and most young women now wear'. Her governess, Lady de Clifford, felt it necessary to give Charlotte a hint:

'My dear Princess Charlotte', she said, 'you shew your drawers.'

'I never do, but where I can put myself at ease', replied the princess.

Lady de Clifford persevered: 'Yes, my dear, when you get in or out of a carriage.'

'I don't care if I do', came the insouciant reply.

'Your drawers are too long.'

'I do not think so—the Duchess of Bedford's are much longer, and they are bordered with Brussels lace.'

This was apparently a clincher. ' "O," said Lady de Clifford in conclusion, "if she is to wear them, she does right to make them handsome." '[127]

Drawers thus began as indecent, were then dashing, and eventually even nice girls were found to be wearing knickers. By the end of the 1830s they were generally accepted throughout society's wealthier and more fashionable ranks, though even in the 1850s there were those who refused to wear them on the grounds of modesty.[128] Similarly, although drawers had been advertised since the early years of the century, it was not until the 1880s that illustrations in fashion magazines began picturing the garment unfolded, clearly demonstrating its true, bifurcated nature.[129]

As the increasing acceptance of drawers so ably demonstrates, decency was a culturally constructed category and therefore subject to change. This argument was often utilized by campaigns for women's dress reform that began to appear from mid century onwards. The first of these came to be called Bloomerism, after the costume that it championed. Originating in America and worn most famously by Mrs Amelia Bloomer, after whom the design took its name, the costume consisted of baggy, Turkish-style trousers gathered at the ankle, with a loose over-tunic reaching to around the knee. Although clearly influenced by the full silhouette of the period, the ensemble had the distinct advantage of dispensing with the many layers of heavy petticoats that, before the development of the under cage, supported the voluminous crinoline dresses. However capacious though, the bloomer costume was distinctly bifurcated. Whereas pantaloons and drawers had initially been seen as too sexually emphatic, trousers as outer garments were perceived as desexualizing their wearers and raised the spectre of the manly woman (Figure 40). As *Punch*'s characteristically patriarchal mockery put it:

Wearing what-d'ye-call-'ems—Gracious! brass itself ain't so brazen.

Why, they must look more audacious than that what's-i-name—Amàzon!

Ha! they'll smoke tobacco next, and take their thimblefuls of brandy,

Bringing shame upon their sex, by aping of the jack-a-dandy.

Yes; and then you'll have them shortly showing off their bold bare faces,

Prancing all so pert and portly at their Derbys and their races.

Oh! when once they have begun, there's none can say where they'll be stopping,—

Out they'll go with dog and gun, perhaps a-shooting and a-popping ...

Sitting in a pottus tap, a-talking politics, and jawing;

Or else a-reading *Punch*, mayhap, and hee-hee-heeing and haw-hawing.[130]

BLOOMERISM!

Strong-Minded Female. "Now, do, pray, Alfred, put down that Foolish Novel, and do Something Rational. Go and play Something on the Piano; you never Practise, now you're Married."

Figure 40 'Bloomerism!', *Punch*, 1851, with thanks to the Library and Archives, University of York. One of *Punch*'s many cartoons and articles to capitalize on the brief bloomer phenomenon. Most of them ridiculed the bloomer figure and showed her adopting an unbecomingly masculinized role. In this drawing ([October] 1851, p. 189), the woman stands before the fire in a manly attitude. Above the waist, she is dressed like a man; below the waist, her bloomer costume is much shorter than its real-life equivalent. Along with her male garb, she has put on a manly and rational cast of mind. In a change of roles, her husband droops on a sofa, wasting his time reading fiction. The text beneath says,

> *Strong-Minded Female.* "Now, do, pray, Alfred, put down that Foolish Novel, and do Something Rational. Go and Play Something on the Piano; you never Practise, now you're Married."

Starting around September 1851, the pages of the British press began to flutter as the costume and its advocates made their way from the New World to the shores of the Old. Over the months that followed, bloomer devotees proselytized through a series of aware-ness-raising lectures and appearances, and even a bloomer ball. So frequent did bloomer appearances apparently become that *The Times* described the professors as having 'sprung up as thick as blackberries'.[131] Three ladies attired in bloomer fashions, for example, took advantage of the thousands attending the Great Exhibition to walk around Crystal Palace distributing leaflets advertising a forthcoming talk to be given on the subject.[132] These frequent lectures were well attended and reported in metropolitan and provincial papers: Bloomerism was news, and most editors wanted a part of it. Even such far-flung organs as *The Aberdeen Journal* ran several articles commenting on the phenomenon.[133] As one contributor to *The Lady's Newspaper* declared, 'One can hardly take up a newspaper with-out reading of a Bloomer mobbed, or addressing an audience on the advantages of this new mode, or distributing handbills in which it is advocated.'[134]

However, the impact of Bloomerism had more to do with entertainment value than any serious consideration of its message. While bloomer devotees argued that the trousered costume was more practical, decent and healthy than the fashionable dress of the time, the majority of their mostly male audiences listened with only eager amusement. Rather like Dr Johnson's walking dog, the wonder of it was that it should be done at all. Speakers were subject to raillery and laughter, written comment tended to the benignly condescending, and the crowds heckled and jibed bloomer wearers. Bloomerism was also as short-lived as it was entertaining, flaring into sudden prominence in the closing months of 1851 and then all but disappearing. Even the founding figure Amelia Bloomer herself, gave up the costume later in the decade when the crinoline cage dispensed with the layers of petticoats that had so encumbered women's dress in the years beforehand.[135]

The movement's lasting legacy, however, was twofold. First, the term 'bloomer' and the concept of women in trousers bubbled along over the ensuing decades, occasionally rising to the surface of public notice, until reappearing with renewed energy in the debates over dress reform that took place in the 1880s and 1890s. Although not strictly accurate, in this later context 'bloomers' was sometimes used to denote the divided skirt being promoted by this second generation of activists. Second, from the very outset, the bifurcated garments advocated by Bloomerism were, and continued to be, associated with the question of wom-en's rights. Wearing trousers was a politicized action. Mrs Bloomer, although later denying importance to the costume, was a lifelong campaigner for women's emancipation,[136] and the Bloomerism lectures almost invariably included discussion of the position given to women in society and their rights under law. But it was in the public's mind, perhaps even more than in the beliefs or activities of its partisans, that bloomers really came to stand for demands for suffrage, education and political reform.

As early as October 1851, only a few weeks after the bloomer costume first appeared in the capital, and in the context of revolution in Europe and the struggle for political reform at home, *The Times* ran with a leader that made overt connection between the two. Both movements, the editor warned, sought to implement too violent and radical a change for British society, and performing a rather spectacular elision of identity declared: 'The Chartist, the Socialist, and the extreme Radical are your true political BLOOMERS.' The article then spent several column inches on the absurdity of the beliefs and appearance of those advocating dress reform, before striking out at the 'cognate efforts of the political Bloomers', which were equally 'ridiculous'.[137] The following year, at a meeting of the Marylebone constituency, Lord Stuart began his address to the electors by noting the number of women who were there. It was a pleasure, he said, 'to see so many of the fair sex present'; at which a voice interjected, 'They're Bloomers', and 'loud laughter' was heard.[138] A few months later, reporting on the Women's Rights Convention being held at Syracuse, another editorial described for its English readers the kind of women who attended, of which a 'large proportion of them were Bloomers'.[139] Back in England, in 1855—several years after its brief incandescence—the bloomers' after-image was still imprinted on the public consciousness as the garment of female stridency. 'Miss Nightingale', wrote the *Bristol Mirror*, 'has done more towards proving that women are capable of acting a great part in the world, than the harangues of all the Mrs. Bloomers who ever talked philosophically, and rejoiced in trousers.'[140] The following year, in discussing the Divorce Bill then before Parliament, yet another *Times* leader denounced those who proposed such amendments to the law as should make wives into ' "Bloomers," or Amazons, or anything else more masculine'.[141] By 1868 the arguments about female education were in full swing, with the University of Cambridge notoriously instituting examinations and, two years later, in 1870, lectures for women—though it must be pointed out that the University did not actually grant them degrees until 1921. These sorts of developments at least one writer thought a 'serious mistake', asserting that it was possible to want better education for women 'without desiring to make them Amazons or Bloomers'.[142] In an 1875 parliamentary session debating an attempt to introduce the franchise to unmarried women of sufficient property, one Member of Parliament, who opposed the bill, said that this sort of political agitation had been brought from America by women who 'usurped male attire' and 'clad themselves in breeches'. At this the House laughed. 'They were called "Bloomers"', the MP added.[143] These are just a few examples of the sorts of connections that were being made between women in bifurcated garments on one hand, and agitation for equal rights under law and access to education and employment, on the other. This is not to say that all women who supported emancipation also favoured trousers—quite the opposite was almost certainly the case—but that the two were conventionally linked, and that the term 'bloomers' was a handy and modern label for strong-minded, 'unwomanly' females. By the time Mr Smollett, the speaker in the 1875 parliamentary debate over suffrage, had been calling on this metaphor however, the next programme of dress reform was on the horizon.

The Rational Dress Society was established in 1881. Its mission was 'to promote the adoption, according to individual taste and convenience, of a style of dress based upon considerations of health, comfort, and beauty, and to deprecate constant changes of fashion, which cannot be recommended on any of these grounds.'[144] An annual subscription cost half a crown, and the society aimed to advertise their doctrine through drawing-room meetings, the circulation of pamphlets and leaflets, and by issuing patterns of approved dress designs. Although people continued to bracket the movement with Bloomerism, it had just as much to do with the many other groups working for social, health and aesthetic reform at the time. Thus, a very measured assessment of the Society in *The Liverpool Mercury* applauded its aims and, while shrewdly cautious about the likely practicability of enforcing reforms on fashion, stated that if it could succeed in ameliorating those aspects of contemporary dress that were 'notoriously hurtful' as well as 'unlovely and unbecoming', 'it will deserve to be ranked as a useful factor among the many societies of the present day'.[145]

While the Rational Dress Society opposed tight-lacing, high heels, and the draperies of long skirts that unhygienically swept through the dust and dirt—and in terms of this latter concern it is important to remember the context of cholera, typhoid and tuberculosis that ravaged Victorian Britain—it quickly became almost exclusively identified with the promotion of the 'divided skirt'. Despite its euphemistic name, this was rather like the bloomer costume in style: full Turkish trousers reaching to the ankle, surmounted by an overskirt of varying lengths. It did not take long for *Punch* to make its comment:

> Nothing succeeds like a little variety,
> Novelty still is the craze of the day;
> Here is the latest, the newest Society,
> Bidding folks dress in a sensible way.
> Formed upon principles quite international, ...
> Dress, it declares, must henceforward be rational,
> What then are Ladies in future to wear?
> Surely reform comes with too much velocity,
> Bloomers, it seems, are to startle again;
> Skirts be divided, Oh, what an atrocity!
> To 'dual garmenture' folks must attain.
> True that another skirt hides this insanity ...
> Yet it should flatter our masculine vanity,
> For this means simply the trowsers of Man![146]

In 1883 the Rational Dress Society staged an exhibition at which various garments and patterns were shown, and the following year occupied a section of the immensely popular International Health Exhibition, held at Kensington. There was much interest in both these events, and the issue of divided skirts and trousers was hotly debated: as dress historian Stella Mary Newton puts it, 'the bifurcated garment, whether worn outside or beneath, was to be a controversial issue during the rest of the 'eighties'.[147] In actual fact, this controversy spilled not only into the following decade, but also into the century beyond.

Objections to women dressing in trouser-like garments were made for moral, medical and aesthetic reasons, and their wear was justified on exactly the same grounds. What really made the difference to this debate, turning the argument from a fringe concern to one of wider-reaching significance, was the growing importance of sport, and in particular, of cycling. By the late 1880s the safety bicycle, essentially the same as a modern machine, was being produced commercially. This simple vehicle transformed society, in one inexpensive stroke providing transportation to millions who had previously been unable to afford the commodity of mobility. As well as profoundly impacting on social class, cycling offered an unprecedented freedom to women that was yet deemed acceptable even by the very conservative. Huge numbers embraced that freedom and—supported by clubs and associations, and the establishment of specialist magazines—took to the roads.

A renowned early rider was Tessie Reynolds, who in September 1893 aged sixteen, made the journey from Brighton to London and back in eight hours and thirty-eight minutes. This feat was widely reported, partly because she chose to wear a knickerbocker-like cycling garment, known most commonly as 'rationals'.[148] The link with the Rational Dress Society is of course plain, but how interesting that in this case trousers, for so long the defining garment of masculinity and its attributes, were christened with this name. Arguments ranged back and forth, with both sides marshalling the ammunition of safety, suitability, modesty and looks. *Hearth and Home* magazine, for example, held a Rationals vs. Skirts essay competition, offering prizes to the best entries of either persuasion. The first prize of a guinea went to Miss E. Prettyman of Edinburgh, who opposed rational dress for cycling, as did the three runners-up who each won two pairs of gloves. Indeed, the competition's organizers remarked that its chief feature was the 'enormous preponderance' of entries that were against the new costume.[149] By contrast, readers of less conservative periodicals might be expected to be more sympathetic. In September 1894—just days before Miss E. White was to break Tessie Reynolds's record, achieving the same London–Brighton–London journey in seven hours, fifty-six minutes—the progressive *Woman's Signal* ran an interview with committed cyclist Miss N. G. Bacon. The article, 'Through the Air on Wheels', discussed with Miss Bacon her recent cycling tour, the demands of the sport—'Oh dear no, an ordinary girl like myself can do sixty or seventy miles per day quite easily'—and her crusade for rational dress.[150] Some advocated a middle road, such as the editor of *Cycling: An Illustrated Weekly*, who advised that knickerbockers be worn while actually riding but that women have with them a skirt to put on over the top when they dismount.[151]

Although the rationals controversy was widely discussed (Figure 41), only a minority of women actually wore the knickerbocker garments, and many of these were socially privileged and thus more able to flout convention. The most famous of these was Viscountess Harberton, not only the founding president of the Rational Dress Society, but also a member of the Cyclists' Touring Club. On 27 October 1898, Lady Harberton cycled to Ockham in Surrey, where she was refused lunch at the Hautboy Hotel because of her bifurcated garments. This was not an isolated incident—a high-profile case of a similar nature had been reported in Dorking earlier that year, with the *Daily Mail* receiving letters to the editor both supporting and condemning the proprietor's actions in refusing admittance to the lady cyclist in question.[152] Therefore Lady Harberton and the Cylists' Touring Club decided to test the principle and take the Hautboy's landlady, Martha Sprague, to court.

Martha Sprague won the case, the jury finding that she had not actually refused to supply a paying customer with food and drink—which was against the law—but only that,
because of Lady Harberton's dress, the landlady had insisted the Viscountess be served in
the bar parlour and not the coffee room. Mrs Sprague made no secret of the fact that 'She
had never admitted ladies in rational costume into the coffee-room unless they put on a
skirt first.'[153]

What this case so ably demonstrates is the importance of context to acceptability. Knickerbockers were more or less suitable as sportswear, but not in day-to-day life; similarly, the
bar parlour was an appropriate venue but the coffee room was not. The resistance of more
formal activities and interactions to the claims of equality of dress was only gradually
eroded and still, over 100 years later, occasionally makes itself felt. Even the redoubtable
Florence Harberton admitted that she would never wear rational dress to the theatre or
to church.[154] However, what had been established by the end of the nineteenth century

RATIONAL COSTUME.

The Vicar of St. Winifred-in-the-Wold (to fair Bicyclists). IT IS CUSTOMARY FOR MEN, I WILL NOT SAY GENTLEMEN, TO REMOVE
THEIR HATS ON ENTERING A CHURCH!"
Confusion of the Ladies Rota and Ixiona Bykewell.

Figure 41 'Rational Costume', *Punch*, 1896, with thanks to the Library and Archives, University of York. This
cartoon (Saturday 13 June 1896, p. 282) plays with the idea that in trousers women lose their femininity;
that breeched females blur the gender distinction and are made unwomanly. The scene is set in a church,
where the two androgynous-looking ladies dressed in cycling costume are mistaken by the cleric for young
men. The caption runs:

> *The Vicar of St. Winifred-in-the-Wold (to fair Bicyclists).* "IT IS CUSTOMARY FOR MEN, I WILL NOT SAY GENTLEMEN, TO
> REMOVE THEIR HATS ON ENTERING A CHURCH!" *Confusion of the Ladies Rota and Ixiona Bykewell.*

was that sometimes it was all right for women to dress their legs in separate envelopes of cloth. Gymnastics, cycling and climbing, among other sporting pursuits, were the accepted exceptions that proved the rule of skirted femininity. This, it turned out though, was the thin end of the wedge, and as the new century advanced and particular concepts of fitness and health became increasingly influential, the situations where one might legitimately see trousered women increased in number and variety. By the 1930s women might wear shorts for hiking, and wide, loose trousers—'beach pyjamas'—not only on the beach, but for a variety of holiday and leisure pursuits. And although strictly limited to the exigencies of war work, the 1914–18 conflict had seen the establishment of yet another context of acceptability.

However, it is important not to overstate the extent of trouser wearing at this time, or to misrepresent what continued to be a contested, piecemeal and hesitant practice. Notwithstanding the iconic images of glamorous 1930s movie stars and the rich at play in their Mediterranean resorts, in day-to-day life, outside a few accepted contexts there was 'widespread and very strong condemnation of trousers by much of the general public'.[155] Even in the early years of the Second World War relatively few ordinary women wore trousers, and never in their daily routines of work or shopping, or to go out. This widespread conservatism, though inflected by class and age, is borne out by the findings of the Mass Observation investigations. For instance, in 1941 short 'trouser counts' were undertaken in Bolton, Worcester and London. An investigator observed passers-by for three fifteen-minute periods, noting their age (under or over thirty), their social status (A = 'rich people', B = 'the middle classes', C = 'artisans and skilled workers', D = 'unskilled workers'), and dress. Collating the information revealed that in Bolton, of a total of 264 women, not one was wearing trousers. In Worcester 300 women were counted, of whom just 2—that's less than 1 per cent—were wearing trousers. These two women were both under thirty and both of a higher social status (AB). In London, out of 364 women, 15, or 6 per cent, were in trousers. Fourteen of these were under thirty, and eight were in the upper social bracket. The one wearer over thirty was also in the AB group.[156]

A questionnaire added flesh to this rough statistical outline. In the provinces women reported wearing trousers owing to the nature of their work and respondents in London were more likely to consider how the garment looked, but overall the importance of context remained paramount. The recorded comments of these anonymous women give us a fragmentary yet intensely vivid glimpse of a period of history that, while being so close in time, is yet so distant in mores and attitude.

'At the seaside I don't abhor them, but I do in a place like Worcester', said a wealthy provincial housewife, aged thirty-five.

'I rule them out. They're too masculine looking. Let men be men and women stay women', was the opinion of a fifty-five-year-old middle-class housewife from Bolton.

A London housewife, aged thirty-five, whom the interviewer put in the skilled worker category, had decided: 'I wear them if there's a raid. I think they're more decent than a skirt, really, for the bombs, you know. But not at ordinary times, I wouldn't like them.'

'When I'm on my holidays—not otherwise', responded a thirty-year-old Bolton bus conductress; and a London typist, aged twenty, said, 'I wear them at home, to save my other clothes.'

Finally, there is the uncompromising judgement of a sixty-year-old housewife from Bolton, categorized as an unskilled worker with little money or education, for whom trousers were utterly unacceptable: 'No, I never wear them. Good gracious, woman, who do you think I am?'

Inevitably, by the end of the war, there were fewer women or men who felt as she did. As a *Times* editorial amusedly noted, 'Trousers for women all round the clock did well out of the war, and it is hard to recall that, not so long ago, the now common sight of shopping queues of matrons in slacks would have caused policemen to stop short, aghast on their beats.'[157] But although the war can be considered to be the watershed—the beginning of the beginning, as it were, of trousers as garments for everyday wear by everyday women[158]—again, the capitulation of the more conservatively minded in the more formal of contexts has been, by our way of thinking, astonishingly slow. Wearing trousers to work, for example, was unacceptable for many years. As Monica Cartright complained in a letter to *The Times* in 1962, women were not 'allowed' to dress in trousers to keep out the winter cold.[159] Seven years later, in 1969, Gillian Thomas, a twenty-one-year-old maths teacher, was sent home from the comprehensive school where she worked because she had arrived wearing brown flared trousers. She returned in a miniskirt.[160] The year before, Jayne Harris, debutante daughter of property-owning millionaire William Harris, had also run into the paradox of decency, finding that in some situations it was more acceptable for a woman to reveal her body than to cover it in too challenging a fashion. At the 1968 Ascot, Harris was refused admittance to the Royal Enclosure because she was wearing a trouser suit. She returned dressed in a baby doll minidress that skimmed to barely beneath her crotch (Figure 42). Wearing this, she was admitted.[161]

In 1970 Judge Anthony Bulger made the news by rebuking Edith Merchant for wearing a lemon-coloured trouser suit when appearing before him in a divorce case filed against her husband on the grounds of cruelty. Judge Bulger said, 'I don't like women wearing trousers in court … It is not like coming to a fun fair.' Understandably piqued, Mrs Merchant, who had made the suit herself, offered to take the offending garments off.[162] The National Union of Students (NUS) conference in 1974 was held in Margate amidst fears of police infiltration and terrorist reprisals. As well as discussing Irish Republican Army bombing, the NUS adopted a campaign opposing discrimination against women in higher education, which included the banning of women wearing trousers by some colleges of education.[163] The conservatism of these training colleges probably reflected the tenor of some workplaces. In 1978 one Reading head teacher banned nine women from the classroom for breaking his rule against trouser wearing. The dispute escalated to involve the board of governors and the National Union of Teachers.[164]

These cases that made it to the news are, of course, atypical in their high-profile nature. The fact that they were reported at all, it might be argued, demonstrates their unrepresentative character. However, anecdotal evidence from many women of middle age and over

Figure 42   Jayne Harris in minidress, 1968, © TopFoto. Jayne Harris (hand on hip) in the Royal Enclosure, Ascot, 1968. Wearing a trouser suit, she had been earlier refused admission.

suggests that there have been not infrequent situations in which wearing trousers, although not openly prohibited, was certainly frowned upon. In 1983, for most of us a time not from history but of lived experience, forty-year-old Mrs Jeanne Turnock was fired from a north London crematorium after wearing a trouser suit. Mrs Turnock brought a case of unfair dismissal against her employers, telling an industrial tribunal that she had begun wearing a navy blue business trouser suit because of the cold, particularly as her job included showing people about the crematorium grounds in all weathers. The crematorium's managing director, although he had 'no personal objection to women in trousers', said the garment was inappropriate in the context. 'We are dealing with elderly people recently bereaved and a large number may find some offence in a lady in trousers coming to deal with them.' Despite there being no contractual obligation to dress in a particular way, the tribunal upheld the crematorium, unanimously deciding that 'the dismissal was fair'.[165]

So although the twentieth century brought two world wars, universal suffrage, contraception and the Equal Pay Act, it did not give women equal access to trousers. In a few areas even in the new millennium, the convention still persists that dresses and skirts are

more appropriate. At weddings and balls, for instance, few women will be wearing trousers; and while the haute couture collections by no means exclusively feature dresses and
skirts, the theatre of the catwalk showcases them to a much greater extent than does more
ordinary life on the sidewalk. In 2000, the Equal Opportunities Commission (EOC) took
up the challenge of school uniform, forcing at least one secondary school to change its
skirts-only policy under threat of legal action. Two years later, in 2002, the EOC began
preparations to sue another school that had refused to alter its uniform code to allow girls
the option of trousers.[166] Also that year, Helen Clark, then New Zealand Prime Minister,
wore a designer trouser suit at a state dinner given for the Queen. According to Television
New Zealand, the Prime Minister's choice of outfit 'earned barely-veiled derision from the
BBC'. Unphased, Helen Clark replied that 'the BBC should realise this is 2002 and not
1642'.[167] And of course, we do realise this; since the seventeenth century, we have changed
immeasurably in our manners, customs and practices of dress. But it is ironic that more
than 350 years after the time when the real scandal was Parliament's war with, and eventual beheading of, the monarch, that a woman Prime Minister in trousers dining with the
Queen could still cause even a minor flutter.

5   SKIN

HIDDEN BODIES

Wrapping us into flexible parcels of flesh, skin holds the inside and outside apart. It is our boundary with the rest of the world, keeping us contained and discrete: skin defines where we stop and everything else starts. Histories of its fashioning usually view it as a kind of blank canvas on which decoration is inscribed, as in the case of tattooing, scarification, piercings, and cosmetic adornment. In this chapter, however, I want to look not at how our cutaneous envelope has been decorated, but at its changing relationship with the garments in which it has been clothed. For instance, what has been skin's contribution to the concept of beauty; what might its concealment and disclosure signify; what conditions of materiality and belief make the revelation of the body unthinkable in one period, and the norm in another?

The most fundamental point about skin is that until the twentieth century, it was hardly ever seen. For hundreds of years, most of the body, for most of everyday life, was covered by garments. Encasing the feet, legs, torso and arms, a textile membrane secured the skin from visual or physical contact with the surrounding world. Clothes were, to use Erasmus's (c. 1466–1536) phrase, 'the body's body'.[1] Even hands were subject to the regime of cloth. Pulling on gloves on a chilly morning, we can of course appreciate this. But with abundant heating that we take for granted, we are less likely to imagine biting cold indoors. 'The weather continues still so violent', remarked John Chamberlain shortly before the Christmas of 1621, 'that I am forced to write in my gloves.'[2] Gloves also protected against the roughening effects of exposure. In 1599 Antwerp merchant Emanuel van Meteren recorded that English women knew well how to protect the complexion of their hands with gloves.[3] More or less 200 years later, in making her infant daughter long cotton mitts without fingers that tied round the arm 'high above the elbow', Charlotte Papendiek was doing the same thing. As her girls grew older Charlotte continued the practice, dressing them in leather gloves always tied high 'to preserve the arm in beauty for womanhood', and always with the fingers cut off 'so that they [the gloves] were always on'.[4] The length of the gloves worn by Mrs Papendiek and her daughters relates to the shortness of their sleeves. From around the mid seventeenth century, for the first time a woman's dress could be cut to reveal her forearms, and gloves correspondingly increased their length to cover what was newly exposed. Thereafter, they tracked the passage of sleeve length, for reasons of practicality and looks becoming shorter as the sleeve grew longer, and vice versa.

The importance of gloves to our forebears was not confined to the merely useful. It is in less practical contexts that gloves most often appear in our sources. Far from languishing as the wardrobe's optional extra, in the sixteenth and seventeenth centuries gloves fig-ured highly in expressions of status, obligation and love, holding a small but persistently recurrent part in the affective worlds of their wearers. It is presumably their association with the hand that gave gloves this symbolic value. Clenched in anger, pledged in loyalty, extended in friendship, plighted in love and even tied when powerless to act, the hand is busy in the most public, and private, of moments. Through our hands we are able to reach out and touch the world. From acknowledging the hand's myriad guises, it is but a short metonymic step to the glove as a textile proxy. On a less abstract note, adding this symbolic potential to their one-size-fits-all and conveniently portable nature, made gloves the ideal gift in a wide range of situations. Tokens of affection, remembrance, loyalty and esteem, gloves were given in the humblest and the grandest of contexts. Lady Brilliana Harley (1598–1643) writes to her son, a student at Oxford. She encloses a little purse of small change to help him in the necessaries of life (including charitable giving) and also 'a pare of gloufs'. Touchingly, she explains that she is sure he could get better in Oxford, but that wearing these Edward might sometimes remember her 'that seldome [h]as you out of my thoughts: the Lord blles [bless] you'.[5] In a more obligatory act of gift giving, in 1666 the widow of diplomat Sir Richard Fanshawe (1608–66), in paying her respects at the palace and petitioning for monies owed her husband, presented the king and his family with '6 dozens of gloves'.[6] Bulstrode Whitelocke (1605–75), Interregnum ambas-sador to the Swedish court in 1653–4, describes something similar. When introduced by Queen Christina to the Countess de la Garde—'a beautifull & gallant Lady', the queen's favourite and quite possibly lover—the countess 'pluct off one of her gloves, & gave it to Wh[itelocke] for a favour'. The next day, Bulstrode reciprocated the gesture, sending 'a dozen payr of English gloves to the Lady for a present'.[7] There are several interesting things about this incident. The first, of course, is the giving of a glove as a mark of favour, a token of partiality; in this case still warm from the wearer's hand. The second is that the countess—attending court in the evening 'to discourse' and hear 'Musicke'—was wearing gloves in the first place. Of relevance here are the observations of another ambassador, this time to the English court. In 1597 Monsieur de Maisse's description of Elizabeth granting audiences and listening to music on the spinet also shows her to have been wearing gloves. It has been suggested that this may have been a matter of etiquette, but also a way of stav-ing off the December cold in the chilly palace rooms.[8] It is likely that either, or both, of these reasons—etiquette and warmth—held true nearly fifty years later, in the February temperatures of the Swedish court. The third thing to note is that Whitelocke had a dozen pairs of gloves at hand ready for him to send the following day, perhaps part of a store of diplomatic gifts and sweeteners.

The gift of gloves could also be made to reflect distinctions of status, nuanced to acknowl-edge differences in relationships. At Martin Fotherby's consecration as bishop of Salisbury in 1618, he gave 'rich gloves to his frends that were present'. The archbishop, the earls and the bishops received gloves with five laces, or bands of decorative work; the barons' gloves had four laces; and the knights' had three.[9] When Colonel Edward Phelips was buried in

1680, the executors gave gloves to the mourners in three grades: 8 shammy pairs went to close kin; 96 of cordovan leather and kid were given to friends and other relatives; 118 of the coarsest grade, a sheep's leather, were distributed to servants, tradesmen and others.[10]

As is suggested by the number and variety of gloves given at Colonel Phelips's funeral, their distribution to mourners was customary; it continued, in fact, into the late nineteenth century. So important was this observance to a well-conducted burial that following Lady Honywood's death, Rev. Ralph Josselin (1617–83) complained in his diary that 'not a glove, ribband, scutcheon, wine, beare, bisquett given'.[11] Custom also decreed that gloves were distributed to guests on the occasion of a marriage, an observance that also only disappeared in the nineteenth century. Henry Machyn (1496/1498–1563), chronicler of early-sixteenth-century London life, records the 100 pairs of gloves given at a wedding in 1559. More modestly, after performing a private ceremony, Ralph Josselin wrote in his diary that the groom's father 'gave mee gloves and my wife'. Remarking on his friend Dudley Carleton's absence from nuptial celebrations, John Chamberlain wrote, 'You have lost your wedding gloves by being away at the marriage of the younge couple.'[12] In the words of a poem of the time: 'Come to our wedding, to requite your loves, / Shew us your hands we'l fit you all with Gloves'.[13]

Gloves were in evidence in other exchanges that celebrated friendship and affection. For instance, Samuel Pepys and his wife Elizabeth received and sent gloves to friends as Valentine's gifts; and around this time, a slim volume, sold from a shop on London Bridge, supplied the would-be lover with little verses suitable for sending with rings, handkerchiefs and gloves.[14] As a simple couplet quipped, 'If that from glove you take the letter g, / Then glove is love, and that I send to thee'.[15] As well as gloves for every relationship, there were gloves for every budget. Elizabeth Masham sent her mother, Lady Barrington, 'a small remembranc of my duty, sum plaine gloves', whereas Bulstrode Whitelocke gave a pair to the Swedish Master of Ceremonies with gold coins stuffed in the fingers, to the then very handsome tune of £40.[16] Queen Elizabeth received a pair as a New Year's gift, perfumed and the cuffs embroidered with gold thread and pearls.[17]

In looking at these records of gift exchange, there is a danger that all there is conveyed is a slice of 'ye olde England'. It seems to me that the distancing effect of time and the difference between text and lived experience, sharp with sensation, threatens to leave us with altogether too anodyne and too bland a picture of the past. Lest this be the case, in the account of the late George IV's effects, we can glimpse something more sharp edged and visceral. 'He had never given away or parted with anything.' Amongst 'the quantity of trinkets and trash that they found' were 'heaps of women's gloves, *gages d'amour* which he had got at balls, and with the perspiration still marked on the fingers'.[18] These garments, peeled from the skin and stained with sweat, hint at the glove's private erotic potential. In their smell, their feel and their look, they whisper of the body; and hoarded in the absence of their wearers, they become something like objects of fetish.

In the sixteenth and seventeenth centuries, then, gloves were used to cover—and also to disclose—the hands for a variety of purposes, ranging from the practical through to the affective and sexual. As the eighteenth century dawned and progressed, gloves continued to be used in similar ways and certainly remained a fundamental part of daily costume. Around 1788 Mrs Papendiek even records the interest taken by George III and Queen Charlotte in a Worcester glove factory.[19] A year or two before this, the ever-resourceful William Pitt, with a desperate need for revenue and a mounting public debt, sought to capitalize on the ubiquity of gloves by raising a tax on their sale and purchase. In the budget presented to Parliament on 9 May 1785, Pitt calculated that there were three million people—that is, over a third of the population—who wore gloves. These three million, he reckoned, would purchase at least one pair annually, and many of them, 'indeed twenty, thirty, or forty pair in that time'. Taking, he said, a conservative average of three pairs a year, the Chancellor of the Exchequer thus estimated a consumption of nine million pairs annually. Assigning a stamp duty of one to three pence per pair, depending on the value of the gloves, and adding the revenue to be obtained from obliging sellers to purchase licences, Pitt expected the tax to raise £50,000 every year. In the debate that followed, Pitt's opponent, Charles Fox, gave the opinion that not taking sufficient account of children and labourers who never consume this article, the Chancellor had overestimated the number of glove wearers and therefore the tax's revenue-collecting potential. This caveat aside, Fox and his colleagues were satisfied enough with the bill, and it duly passed into law with little discussion.[20] In the event, Fox's reservations about the tax as a source of revenue were proved correct, though not necessarily for the reason he stated. A report the following year from the select committee on public income and expenditure, on the basis of the takings of the first seven months added to outstanding sums from outside London, put the stamp duty's annual produce at £10,000—just a fifth of the sum Pitt had hoped for.[21] It was not that the commodity being taxed was any less popular; gloves continued to be purchased and worn in the same numbers as before. It was rather a problem of enforcing payment. In the end, the government had little choice but to accept that 'in its present form it [the tax] is unproductive, and very much evaded'.[22]

Although Pitt had been unable to utilize gloves as a financial commodity, subsequent governments also turned their attention in that direction. In 1826, as part of a new policy of free trade, the prohibition on the import of foreign gloves hitherto in place, was lifted. Opinion was divided about the effects of the new policy. Some—including those in the trade who petitioned Parliament—blamed the abundance of imported gloves for distress within the domestic manufactories. Others asserted the contrary, saying that levels of production and employment had increased. Still others decided that the distress was real but only local and temporary, and would soon pass. A further camp felt that far from bringing an end to clandestine trade, opening the borders to foreign gloves had actually increased smuggling in the commodity—presumably owing to the 30 per cent duty now payable. Some championed the rights of the manufacturers, others the interests of the consumer, who ought to be able 'to procure every species of article as cheaply as possible'. Another view saw the policy as divisive, advantaging the rich who were getting wealthier and impoverishing still further those who were already poor.[23] Within the small matter of gloves, there clearly lurked much larger issues of political economy, state responsibility and individual rights. So what kind of numbers were involved here? In the parliamentary debate that witnessed these arguments, it was stated that in the five-year period from 1827 to 1831 inclusive, 792,000 dozen kid gloves were manufactured in Britain; that is, nine and a half million in total, or just under two million annually. Added to these were the foreign-made gloves from Germany, Italy, Austria and, in particular, France, which flooded the market. For example, in 1832, imports into Britain of French gloves alone exceeded one and a half million pairs.[24] Added to this huge number were home-manufactured gloves made from materials other than leather, like cotton, worsted and silk. The honourable member Mr Morrison, for example, showed the house that he was wearing the 'white cotton gloves' that had lately come into fashion.[25]

It is clear that the problems of the glove trade, touching as they did upon irreconcilable differences in political and moral thought, could never be settled to the satisfaction of all. However, usage of the commodity itself continued oblivious to the wider issues at stake. In the words of one advice book of the time, 'Nothing can give a more perfect finish to a handsome dress than the covering for the hands.'[26] Indeed, in the nineteenth century the importance of gloves to the dress regime of the wealthier classes grew into a social necessity: custom 'required gloves to be worn in almost every possible circumstance'.[27] Thus every hand with pretensions to gentility was covered by a glove. Perhaps because of this, the nineteenth century saw a complex etiquette established around their wear.[28] For example, ladies and gentleman ought to wear gloves in the street, at public assemblies, and at church and the theatre, keeping them on even when shaking hands. In warmer weather particularly, 'it is more agreeable to both parties that the glove should be on'. However, if wearing a dark-coloured pair, a gentleman should 'never offer to shake hands with a lady' for fear he soil her white ones. When at the altar, a sister or favourite friend will be on hand to hold the bride's gloves, 'when she ungloves for the wedding-ring'. 'Gloves are indispensably necessary in a ball-room'—indeed, 'nothing is so revolting as to see one person in an assembly ungloved', especially when the exercise and heat have made their hands 'redder than usual'—but they must always be removed when eating: 'It is as vulgar to eat in gloves as it is to dance without them.'[29] It was this sort of etiquette as gave rise to the Language of Gloves, surely a tongue-in-cheek creation?

> For 'Yes,' drop one glove from the right into the left hand. 'No' is said by rolling both gloves in the right hand. If you want to express that you are indifferent to a partner take the right hand glove partly off. If you wish a male friend to follow you into the next room, strike your left arm with both gloves. 'I love you still,' is expressed by slowly and carefully smoothing both gloves. If the fair one desires to know whether her affection is reciprocated she is to put on half the left-hand glove, one finger at a time. As certain unpleasant old fogies go to balls and social gatherings merely to observe the conduct of the young people an elaborate code has been drawn up having them in view. 'Be on your guard against the governor,' or 'my mother-in-law,' as the case may be, is a message often

sent, and is given by delicately twisting the glove fingers round the thumb. If the damsel is in a quarrelsome mood she simply makes a cross with both her gloves and proceeds to lay them on her lap in this position.[30]

The era of gloves continued well into the twentieth century, during the first three decades of which they 'remained an essential item of both male and female dress'.[31] In his autobiography, Osbert Sitwell vividly evokes the Edwardian ladies of his youth, with their very low cut dresses and correspondingly very long 'white kid gloves without which at dinner the women would have deemed themselves naked, and which could only be worn once'.[32] As they 'were one of the most expensive items of a woman's wardrobe, for they could only be worn once or twice, and after a visit to the cleaners they invariably split somewhere, generally at a critical moment—and had to be discarded', a newspaper correspondent reporting on Paris fashion trends in 1928 was confident that women would meet 'with relief' the news that such long gloves were no longer in demand.[33] In these early years of the century styles proliferated, and there were gloves for every occasion and activity: for travel, motoring, riding, evening wear, daywear and visits to the country. Their popularity as gifts also remained undimmed. An entry in Lady Cynthia Asquith's diary for 1917 reads, 'I opened the boxes he had brought, to find one dozen white washing gloves, one dozen beautiful suede ones, and a handsome fur-lined pair thrown in, too!'[34] A pre-Christmas shopping column in *The Times* in 1928 assured readers that 'Gloves are always a good and acceptable present for men and women and also for children'—although, parenthetically, one might wonder just how acceptable their more youthful recipients actually found them.[35]

As late as the 1930s, the Mass Observation data continue to show gloves as significant and frequent gifts, with most of the female respondents reporting that they 'wore gloves year round for going out of the house'.[36] The opinions of a selection of women interviewed in 1939 are probably fairly typical. A forty-eight-year-old Bolton housewife said she wore gloves 'when going out or shopping in town'. Interviewed together at Bible class, eleven young women aged between eighteen and twenty-five said that they all wore gloves for going out, regardless of the season. Many of them also wore gloves for work, even in summer. They preferred it if their clothes, shoes and gloves made a matching outfit. A rather well-off housewife of thirty-one explained that unfortunately gloves were a social necessity, the requirement of a polite demeanour: 'I don't like gloves, but you have to wear them, they don't think you are dressed without gloves.' Like the young women from the Bible class, she liked matching outfits. 'I buy my gloves so that they go with anything', she said. 'I have plenty of gloves, let us say 6 pair.' She reported that she gave a good price for the best gloves, probably kid, but explained that cotton and artificial silk varieties were cheaper.[37] It was the material want and social upheaval of the Second World War that really did for gloves, and finally, after hundreds of years, began their inexorable metamorphosis from an essential requirement of polite dress to an occasional and practical afterthought.

So feet, legs, body, arms and now hands: the sum of coverage seems to be mounting. This catalogue of body parts neatly wrapped up in cloth leaves only the face exposed, and at times even that bit, of a woman's anatomy at least, was subject to concealment. Around the mid sixteenth century, the fashion for masks arrived in England. Except for holes cut for the eyes, these silk or velvet ovals covered the entire face (Figure 43). Sometimes the mask was held in place by a bead or button on the inner side that the wearer gripped between her teeth. The effect of these blank, staring faces, in contemporary drawings at least, is rather frightening. One has to sympathize with Phillip Stubbes, who described the wearers with their faces hidden but their eyes glittering forth, 'So that if a man knew not their guise before, should chaunce to meet one of them hee would think hee met a monster or a deuil.'[38] At this stage they seem to have been worn principally to protect the complexion, and perhaps also as a shield to dust, when outdoors or travelling. Stubbes says these 'inuisories or visors' were worn 'to ride abroad', and the testimony of Emanuel van Meteren broadly agrees. The visiting Antwerp merchant had already observed that English women preserved the appearance of their hands with gloves. They also, he wrote, wore hats and veils to protect the complexion of their faces. He added further that 'ladies of distinction have lately learnt to cover their faces with silken masks or vizards, and feathers'.[39] The ladies of distinction of whom van Meteren spoke included the queen herself: astrologer John Dee recorded in his diary the graciousness shown by her majesty in 'putting down her mask' to speak to him 'with mery chere'.[40] Another account describes her walking in the palace gardens, taking off her mask to bow to a visiting dignitary.[41] While observers often comment on how good was Elizabeth's complexion, it seems the same could not be said for her successor, James I's wife, Anne of Denmark. Dudley Carleton, gossiping about the new queen's arrival in 1603, allowed that she was 'of herself a comely personage'. Unfortunately though, 'for her favor she hath done it some wrong, for in all this journey she hath worn no mask'.[42]

The extent to which masks were worn by women of the better sort can perhaps be inferred from Peter Erondell's dialogues.[43] Written to help in the teaching of French to English speakers, each dialogue is structured around a typical scene as, for instance, 'In the Nursery', 'Table Talke' or 'Going to Bed'. In the dialogue entitled 'The Rising in the Morning', the lady, assisted by her maid and waiting woman, attires herself in the full intricacies of elite dress. The list of garments Lady Ri-Mellaine calls for is long indeed, presumably as a method of introducing language learners to as large as possible a vocabulary. Once she is finally dressed, she orders her fan, her gloves and her mask. Lady Ri-Mellaine's real-life counterpart we might find in someone like Lady Margaret Cecil, descendant of William, Elizabeth's chief minister. Included in the list of apparel and necessaries for Margaret for 1633 is a taffeta hood and a mask (Figure 44). As a poem from later in the century put it, 'Loo [half] masks, and whole, as wind do blow, / And miss abroad's dispos'd to go.'[44]

On several occasions in his diary Pepys mentions masks—not because they were especially noteworthy, but as contextual information. One morning, in his coach, he takes up Mr Hater and his wife. Tom Hater is his clerk at the Navy Office and obviously well known to Pepys. Mrs Hater he has not met before. He writes that through her mask she at first seemed to be an old woman; it was only afterwards he found her to be very pretty. Another

Figure 43 'Here Be Your New Fashions Mistris.' This illustration from the antiquarian Frederick Fairholt's *Costume in England* (Vol. 2, p. 310, author's copy) is based on a woodcut from the Roxburghe Ballads, a collection of seventeenth-century broadside ballads. It shows a mercer (a seller of textiles and haberdashery) displaying fashionable wares to his female customers, including a feather fan, which he holds in one hand, and a black mask, which hangs from the other. On his face he wears shaped patches, also for sale.

time he records going with his wife to buy her a mask, and on a visit to Bartholomew Fair, mentions that she was wearing her 'vizard'. In 1663 he recorded that it had become the fashion for ladies to wear masks at the theatre, 'which hides their whole face'.[45] Along with this fairly neutral reportage, in parts of Pepys's narrative there is discernable a particular assumption about women in masks, for it was becoming a cultural commonplace that

Figure 44 'Full-Length Seasons, Winter', etching by Wenceslaus Hollar, 1643, © Trustees of the British Museum. A woman fashionably dressed against the winter cold. Her muff, furs, hood and half mask (loo mask) keep her warm and also protect her skin. Her overskirt is gathered up out of the dirt as she walks abroad. According to the verse beneath,

> The cold, not cruelty makes her weare
> In Winter, furrs and wilde beasts haire
> For a smoother skinn at night
> Embraceth her with more delight.

wearers were up to no good. The mask could as equally hide ugliness as preserve beauty, and its anonymity was a licence for depravity. In short, a woman in a mask was immoral and dishonest. Mask wearing probably always had a somewhat ambivalent status. Back in the 1570s, William Harrison had stated that masks had come via France from Italy, where they 'were first devised and used … by Curtezans'.[46] This set of connotations of course existed side by side with the knowledge that masks were worn by women of impeccable lineage and character—Queen Elizabeth, for example, or Lady Mary Cecil, or even Elizabeth Pepys herself. In his diary Pepys holds both 'truths' simultaneously in the text. As just one example, in February 1667 he wrote about his visit to the theatre and annoyance at not being able to concentrate on the play for the talking going on around him. Yet not all the evening's pleasure was lost, for the conversation that he was inadvertently overhearing was very witty and entertaining. One of the talkers 'would, and did, sit with her mask on all the play', yet, noted Pepys, she 'was, I believe, a virtuous woman and of quality'.[47]

Part of the problem came from the context of wear; playhouses, in particular, having always been considered places of dubious morality. There is a rather satisfying irony in Lady Mary Cromwell—daughter of Oliver, under whose Puritan rule the theatres were closed during the Commonwealth period—attending a play at all, let alone, as Pepys tells us, in her vizard mask, which she kept on the entire time.[48] The threat the woman with her face hidden in public seemed potentially to pose to good and decent order persisted, whether she wore a full cover or the half (loo) mask that had also come to be popular. A royal command issued by Queen Anne in 1704 for the regulation of the Drury Lane and Lincoln Inn Fields theatres, included the order that 'no Woman be Allow'd or Presume to wear a Vizard-Mask'. The decree gave rise to a song, 'The Misses' Lamentation, for Want of Their Vizard Masques at the Theatre', but probably little else, at least in the long term.[49] In a letter dated 1733, a German visitor to London described the appearance of women who 'turn out in a Morning with a black velvet Mask on their Faces, a Coif on in Form of a Hat, with the Brims down, a round Gown, and a white Apron, and in this Trim they go to the Park, or where else they please'.[50] While the excruciatingly mediocre verse 'On Seeing the Duchess of Devonshire in an Half-Mask at the Opera House Gala in 1787' tells us little, it does at least confirm that masks remained fashionable: 'O quite reveal that heav'nly face, / Where LOVE and all his CHERUBS play! / So Morn's first blush in shades we trace, / And anxious wait the brilliant day.'[51]

Indeed, it was the eighteenth century that played most freely with the fashion for concealment, using the masked ball, or masquerade, as a specialized venue in which to experience the frisson and intrigue of fluid identity: *Do you know me? Who are you? and I know you*; with the sly pointing of the finger, the arch nod of the head, and the pert squeak of the voice.'[52] Such a context, however, could only underscore the ambivalence attending the masked figure: hidden faces allowed a freedom and familiarity of behaviour, and at a masquerade, the beau monde, the *demi-monde*, and everyone in between mingled without restraint. 'Shun Masquerades', warned one conduct manual:

> there you will see, and hear,
> What will offend your Eye, and hurt your Ear;
> There Wit licentious reigns, there Jest obscene
> Your Fancy, with Impurity, will stain;
> There conscious Shame, fair Virtue's best Defence,
> Lost in a Mask, will yield to Impudence;
> Mask'd Virgins, when their Blushes are conceal'd,
> Grant Freedoms, which they would deny unvail'd;
> But Pow'r of blushing, Nature's inborn Grace,
> Will soon forsake a masquerading Face.[53]

Such affairs quickly gained a reputation for immorality and licence, a reputation that no doubt helped secured their long-lasting popularity. To be fair, this was not the only eighteenth-century context where masks were viewed with distrust. According to wider cultural preoccupations, the figure described in a 'vizard mask' was more likely to be a highwayman or footpad, disguising his identity in the same way as modern criminals caught in security footage or played for fictional entertainment, with their faces, grotesque and threatening, behind stocking masks.

Public masquerade balls came to a fairly sudden stop towards the close of the century, and this seems also to have been the end of masks, whether worn for protecting the complexion or for more playful reasons. In the last decade of the eighteenth and throughout the following century, however, the wearing of veils by women became common (Figure 45), taking over from masks and fulfilling much the same purposes.[54] 'The Veil', a popular song of 1793 complaining at the concealment of the wearers' 'glowing charms', is witness to the emergence of this fashion; so too is a single-page notice printed around 1800: 'lost since Sunday evening 7 o'clock, from Curzon street, May Fair, a Brussels lace veil'. An expensive accessory, whoever could give information leading to its recovery was assured of 'a handsome reward'.[55]

But why should hiding the face, as a predominantly female fashion, have been so popular as to endure, in one form or context or another, for over 300 years? I think the answer partly lies in the empowerment felt by the figure behind the mask or veil. To withhold expression, to stand aloof, to receive but not return impressions, is enormously potent. Rather like the disadvantage felt in a conversation with someone in dark sunglasses, the impassivity of a mask potentially gave the wearer the upper hand. Observing, but herself giving nothing away, the masked face was difficult to judge, difficult to place, difficult to gauge. It is an appreciation of this, which presumably lies behind the nineteenth-century advice on manners that 'It is ill-bred to wear your veil over your face while paying a visit.'[56]

Figure 45 'Full-Length Seasons, Summer', etching by Wenceslaus Hollar, 1644, © Trustees of the British Museum. A woman stands before a garden scene (the Banqueting House in Whitehall), dressed for warm weather. She wears a low collar, and her shoulders and chest are uncovered; however, she also wears gloves and a veil. In one hand she holds a fan. The other hand seems to be holding up her overskirt—a practical response to the environment, but also an engagement with the performative possibilities of her garments. The verse reads,

Now Phoebus, crowns our Sumer dayes
With stronger heate and brighter rayes
Her louely neck, and brest are bare,
Whilst her fann doth coole the Ayre.

Now Phœbus, crowns our Symer dayes Summer Her louely neck, and brest are bare, With stronger heate and brightermus Whilst her fann doth coole the Ayre.

Figure 46 'Half-Length Seasons, Winter', etching by Wenceslaus Hollar, 1644, © Trustees of the British Museum. As with Figure 44, a woman in a muff, stole, hood and half mask.

It also explains the discomfort so evident in the seminal sixteenth-century conduct book *Instruction of a Christen Woman*. Written early in the century in Latin, and then translated and reprinted through multiple editions over the next seventy or so years, the text urges that women not 'wrappe their head' as is the custom, for 'that is to go vnknowen, and vnsene of other folkes, but theym selfe bothe to see and knowe other': that is, women with their faces covered go unknown and unrecognized, but can themselves both watch and comprehend the people they meet. This, the text goes on, is 'an occasion of viciousnes'—or, as we might put it, an opportunity for immorality—and opens for women 'a wyndowe of libertee', a peephole on the world for roving eyes and a roving imagination (Figure 46). 'Therefore', the author Juan Luis Vives concludes, 'let the womens faces be bare of clothes.'[57] Rather than working as a garment of exclusion then, the mask, and to an extent the veil, freed the wearer from the obligations of reciprocity. She could take without giving; a position that women, historically categorized as soft, generous and emotional, could otherwise rarely occupy.

DISCLOSURE

One effect of such an enveloping vestimentary regime was that more attention was paid to those areas that were revealed. This was where all cutaneous adornment was concentrated, and all the desire and disgust that uncovered flesh could provoke. It is under this scrutiny that hands became significant parts of the anatomy in a way now lost to us. In early modern portraiture this is very noticeable: hands—so often framed against a backdrop of dark cloth—have an insistent presence, long, slim fingered and white skinned. Very often the sitter's pose and props further direct the viewer's attention: holding a pair of gloves (or wearing one and holding the other) was a common motif, as was lightly grasping an object, or fingering material, displaying jewellery or pointing. Queen Elizabeth was notably proud of the shape and appearance of her hands, and employed some of these painterly techniques in life off the canvas. '[S]he drew off her glove and showed me her hand', wrote de Maisse, 'which is very long and more than mine by more than three broad fingers.'[58] Paul Hentzner described Elizabeth conferring a particular favour by pulling off her glove to give her hand to be kissed. Her 'hands were slender, her fingers rather long' and they were 'sparkling with rings and jewels'.[59] In later years, another foreign visitor at court used to say that at each of his audiences with her, Elizabeth would draw her gloves on and off her hands at least a hundred times, to show how very beautiful and very white they were.[60] The gloves of this time reflected the aesthetic of tapering, slim hands in their form and decoration. All the extant examples 'seem to have excessively long fingers', far longer than the wearers' real hands; lines of wear actually show that their finger tips usually stopped one and a half to two centimetres short of the glove's end, leaving just space beyond. A pair of gloves Elizabeth presented to Oxford University has a middle-finger measurement of twelve centimetres. This 'elongated effect' might be emphasized by decorative stitching that further tricked the eye.[61]

While perhaps most clearly articulated in the sixteenth and seventeenth centuries, the appreciation of hands as potentially beautiful only receded gradually. In the mid nineteenth century, a manual of politeness could still advise that even in the house ladies should always wear gloves, it being both 'a very elegant fashion' and a preserver of 'the delicacy of the hands'. Another advice book suggested that the only circumstances in which it was permissible for a lady or gentleman *not* to remove their gloves at the dinner table was if 'their hands, for some cause, are not fit to be seen': a sentiment that these days is just not thinkable.[62] I suggest that it was only really in the twentieth century that the concept of beauty in hands lost potency. With more skin on show, attention was distracted or dispersed; the importance of hands in the visual scheme of the body dwindled and drained away.

Although, gloves and masks allowing, the space above the neck and below the wrists composed the usual extent of public disclosure, there were exceptions to the rule of concealment. Practised more often in the realm of female dress—for then, as now, showing the body was a gendered matter, with a greater amount of a woman's skin being seen than a man's—these exceptions can be envisaged as peepholes through to the body, or better, as places on the corporeal landscape where the tide of cloth receded to leave new areas uncovered. The terrain of exposure was, by our standards, very modest indeed: forearms; a lowered neckline at the front, sides or back; décolletage. Such limited disclosure was also only a feature of formal wear and not a part of more ordinary, daytime interactions.

As readers of *The Lady's Magazine* were reminded in 1811, custom regulated decency according to the time of day. 'In the morning, the arms and bosom must be completely covered to the throat and wrists.' In the evening, 'as far as delicacy will allow', the arms may be bare to above the elbow and the neck and shoulders unveiled.[63]

Although restricted in scope and social context, the revelation of anatomy lying either above the wrists or below the neck was accompanied by comment, and very often also by the disapproval of the conservatively minded. When so little was on show, each new ebb of the vestimentary tide was noticed. Joseph Hall (1574–1656), first bishop of Exeter and then Norwich, warned in a sermon that revealing, fashionable dress tempted and ensnared beholders. '[W]anton dames', he said, even come to church 'with their breast bare almost to the navel, their arms to the elbow, their necks to the shoulder points'—his comments picking up on contemporary wide, low necklines and, new in the seventeenth century, shorter sleeves.[64] Earlier in the century, in 1605, Dudley Carleton had found the masque costumes worn by the queen and her ladies to be 'too light and courtesanlike'. Partly this was because they showed their arms, 'bare up the elbows'.[65] In 1653 one anonymous author, in a chapter charmingly entitled 'An Invective against Bad Women', complained of those whose 'neck and brests are left bare unto the open view of the world'; and in 1678 a treatise called *A just and seasonable reprehension of naked breasts and shoulders* really went to town, listing the many reasons why such disclosure was unacceptable. In the words of Robert Codrington, 'Fashions are every day invented to Sell naked Bodys, than to cover them.'[66]

Moving into the new century, *The Guardian*, published in 1713, made quite a thing of the declining use of the tucker. Also known to us as a fichu or handkerchief, this triangle of fine fabric was worn by women around the neck and shoulders and fastened to the front of the bodice. Over a number of issues Joseph Addison (Figure 2), author of these particular essays, complained that dress has sunk 'so that when we now say a Woman has a handsom Neck, we reckon into it many of the adjacent Parts'. 'The disuse of the Tucker', he went on, 'has still enlarged it, insomuch that the Neck of a fine Woman at present takes in almost half the Body.'[67] Roughly twenty years later, in its very first volume, *The Gentleman's Magazine* took occasion to 'animadvert on the present Mode among the Ladies, of exposing their naked *Breasts* and *Shoulders*'. At intervals, the periodical continued to advise ladies against '*unmasking their beauties*'. However, it was the high-waisted, low-necked evening gowns at the turn and first quarter of the nineteenth century (Figure 10) that provoked its concerted comment. According to one correspondent of 1804, this 'nakedness of appearance' threatened to 'overthrow the whole moral constitution of our country'. In an argument with strangely incestuous undertones, the writer maintained that men, inflamed by the sights of their fashionably dressed—or underdressed—sisters and mothers, would rush out to indulge in 'revels of debauchery'. Other correspondents around that time said baldly that otherwise polite, genteel women looked like common prostitutes and women of the town. Bond Street, wrote one, was 'the London Market-place for the *exhibition* and *sale* of fashionable women'.[68]

As we see, this kind of complaint was generally made from a position of indignation, was often exaggerated and usually revealed a paternalism bordering on misogyny: indeed, the arguments voiced by some of these writers come chillingly close to the 'she asked for it' school of justification. However—and this needs to be borne in mind before dismissing even this exaggerated complaint—from our experience of constant visual access to the anatomy it is easy to become blasé, to forget the impact that partial disclosure must have held when the body was otherwise cocooned in cloth. Even without straying into the world of pornography, the bodies of strangers are today so often revealed to our eyes. Calves, thighs, bellies and bum cleavage are commonplace on the streets; the world of entertainment and advertising routinely discloses more; and by changing the context slightly, we can view the anatomical reality of countless strangers by merely going to the local swimming pool. For a culture in which nakedness presupposed intimacy, however, seeing a woman's arms or breasts in public, or even the top of her back, to some degree must have been shocking. At the very least, such revelation was noticeable and worthy of comment.

Looking through the words of personal experience gives us some sense of the impact of this very partial disclosure. There is less exaggerated outrage, but the interest in revelation, and its strangeness and discomfort, remains. By way of example, in 1597 Henri IV's ambassador described Queen Elizabeth's appearance in a spectacular sounding dress made of white and crimson cloth of silver, its sleeves slashed to show a red taffeta lining. The collar of this robe stood very high, and the inner part was lined with pendants of rubies and pearls. According to de Maisse, Elizabeth 'kept the front of her dress open, and one could see the whole of her bosom, and passing low'. As Elizabeth was then sixty-four, it is hardly surprising that de Maisse also noted that her 'bosom is somewhat wrinkled'.[69] Prefiguring Addison's complaints in *The Guardian* by nearly forty years, Samuel Pepys fell out with his wife on coming home to dinner at noon to find she had cut away 'a lace hankercher so wide about the neck, down to her breasts almost, out of a belief, but without reason, that it is the fashion'.[70] Given his extramarital activities, subsequent readers of his diary find that Pepys's concern for his wife's modesty is not without an uncomfortable edge. Unsurprisingly, Jane Austen has a much lighter touch, sketching a young woman she had met in the assembly rooms as 'like any other short girl with a broad nose & wide mouth, fashionable dress, & exposed bosom'. At another ball she described the melancholy view of 'so many dozen young Women standing by without partners, & each of them with two ugly naked shoulders!' Further setting her remarks apart, even from Addison's equally sharp wit and ready pen, is Austen's acknowledgement of her own participation in that very human occupation of self-presentation. Thus, preferring to cover her own arms—in defiance, she fears, of customary evening dress—Austen tells Cassandra that she plans to wear her gauze gown, 'long sleeves & all'. She has, however, 'lowered the bosom especially at the corners'. Interestingly, at the end of the evening she is home early enough to finish her letter. Jane is able to tell Cassandra that in covering her arms she was not, after all, so singular. 'Mrs Tilson had long sleeves too, & she assured me that they are worn in the evening

by many.' Jane, like most of us when fashion happens to march in step with our prefer-
ences, 'was glad to hear this'.[71]

Lady Dorothy Nevill recounts a story, which may well be apocryphal, concerning Bishop
Bromfield, a clerical gentleman remembered for his ready wit. The bishop was 'at a party
where a lady in an extremely *decolleté* [*sic*] gown excited a good deal of attention'. Someone
remarked to him, ' "Her appearance is really quite scandalous. Did you ever see anything
like it?" "Never," replied the Bishop; "at least," '—and here Lady Dorothy pauses for the
punchline—' "not since I was weaned." '[72]

ALL THINGS WHITE AND BEAUTIFUL

'How ill Eliza Bennet looks', remarks Miss Bingley spitefully in *Pride and Prejudice*. 'She
is grown so brown and coarse.'[73] It's only a little thorn of a comment, yet it reaches deep
into a visual economy in which the only colour of desirability was white. This was not a
racial claim—or perhaps, not only a racial claim. It was primarily an aesthetic judgement
that only recognized these qualities in untanned skin, which preferably was also smooth
and unblemished. As a way of looking at beauty, it lasted for hundreds of years. Eyewitness
accounts of Elizabeth I often note the quality of her skin. Even in old age, de Maisse found
her flesh 'exceeding white and delicate, so far as one could see', and on her hands 'the skin
is still most fair'. Frederic Gerschow, seeing Elizabeth at around the same time, wrote that
'the Queen uncovered herself down to her breasts'—that is, revealed her neck and chest—
'showing her snow white skin'.[74] Much earlier in her reign, Sir James Melville, envoy from
Elizabeth's Scottish cousin and political rival, Mary, found himself between a diplomatic
rock and a hard place in being forced to declare which of the queens was the more beautiful. According to Melville, Elizabeth desired to know whether she or Mary was the fairer,
probably here using both meanings of attractive and fair complexioned. Suavely, Melville
replied that 'The fairness of them both was not their worst faults.' Whether for reasons of
personal vanity or political strategy, Elizabeth was renowned for her ego in such matters,
and perhaps predictably was not so easily satisfied. She 'was earnest with me to declare
which of them I judged fairest'. Again, Melville found a diplomatic reply, saying that she
was the fairest queen in England, and Mary the fairest queen in Scotland. Elizabeth, however, insisted. Perhaps backed into a corner, Melville answered that Mary 'was very lovely'
but 'that her Majesty was whiter'.[75] Hippolyte Taine, a French visitor to mid-nineteenth-
century London, admired the city's most beautiful women. Their 'perfect' faces were 'reminiscent of those astonishing flowers one sees in exhibitions of choice blooms, a whiteness of
the lily or the orchis'. By contrast, *The Lady's Magazine* described less well-favoured damsels
of 'a brown, dingy, or speckled complexion', the 'muddy-skinned and ill-formed'.[76]

Whiteness, an index of attraction in a woman, was equally a mark of manly beauty,
particularly when combined with a 'glowing' masculine vigour. The Venetian ambassador
thought it a pretty sight watching Elizabeth's father, the young Henry VIII, play at tennis,
'his fair skin glowing through a shirt of the finest texture'. In her memoirs of her husband,
a parliamentarian officer in the civil war, Lucy Hutchinson (1620–81) detailed his many

physical excellences. These included a fair complexion, lips 'very ruddy and graceful', and skin that was 'smooth and white'. Captain Gronow recollected that Count D'Orsay, the famed mid-nineteenth-century dandy, had a complexion that 'glowed with a radiant health'; and an etiquette manual of the same era promised to show readers how to obtain 'a soft white skin' and 'good nails': the 'two chief attributes of a lady-like or gentlemanly hand'.[77]

It is clear from these somewhat flattering descriptions that whiteness encompassed more than just beauty, whether found in either gender. Along with praise of the subjects' looks, creeping into these assessments are judgements both about their state of health and their social estate. Glowing, white skin was desirable and healthy, but it was also only within reach of those whose privilege brought them leisure and freedom from the coarsening effects of physical labour. Soft, white skin separated the genteel from their coarse and brown inferiors. It is easy to see how, as far as women were concerned, connotations of virtue and purity also came to be shackled to this concept of whiteness. A fair, unblemished visage went hand in hand with a fair and unspotted soul. Beauty, it was argued, was more than skin deep. A writer in *The Lady's Magazine* made this explicit when claiming that a man of delicacy and worth would turn in disgust from the lures of a woman in a revealing dress, and clasp instead to his warm and noble heart 'the unsunned bosom of the chaste and vestal-enwrapped fair'.[78] The reasoning half articulated here runs something like this: only licentious women expose their skin, exposing the skin makes it tan, therefore all tanned women are licentious. Of course, in real life skin tones ranged, freckles prolifer-ated, immodest hearts might beat beneath the most modest of garments or vice versa, and the sun shone without prejudice on the virtuous and depraved alike. Back in 1619, poet Michael Drayton had idealized perfect skin as being whiter than the finest and most costly of textiles. 'If thou but please to walke into the Pawne'—that area in London in which hab-erdashers, milliners, seamstresses and starchers had stalls catering to the fashion market—

> To buy thee Cambricke, Callico, or Lawne,
> If thou the whitenesse of the same wouldst prove,
> From thy more whiter Hand plucke off thy glove;
> And those which buy, as the Beholders stand,
> Will take thy Hand for Lawne, Lawne for thy Hand.[79]

While the finest, whitest fabric merging with the finest, whitest skin is a pretty conceit, Lady Spencer Stanhope reminds us of the more prosaic reality in a letter to her son of 1807. She tells him about a winter ball; how beautiful the ballroom looked hung with swathes of material and wreaths of evergreens. The only fault, she said, 'was *the pure white of the Calico made all the ladies look dirty*'.[80] The emphasis and amusement are Lady Elizabeth's own.

For these real-life women over the centuries, there have been a number of ways of obtaining a pale complexion. It is common knowledge that there were cosmetic preparations that whitened the skin, and also that very often their ingredients made them harmful. How-ever, the position of 'painting'—that is, the use of makeup—was always morally dubious, and it was not until the 1920s that cosmetics became socially acceptable and their use widespread. As we have seen, one of the functions of gloves, masks and veils was to protect the skin from sun, wind and cold. Other accessories like parasols, mufflers and hats were also important in a lady's skincare regimen. Judging from the different texture and appearance of my own skin on those anatomical areas that have not had years of exposure and engagement with the world, this cloth barrier must have been extremely effective. The skin of a woman of privilege, regardless of her colouring, must have been considerably softer, finer, and of course, whiter, than one would commonly see today. At least, unless she had caught smallpox; or suffered, say, from eczema; or had contracted an illness or sustained an accident which resulted in scarring or burns. In a world before antibiotics, steroids and reconstructive surgery, the story of an individual's health might be written far more plainly on the body. Indeed, in a morally impassioned harangue against the less concealing styles of the early nineteenth century, a correspondent to *The Gentleman's Magazine* included a vivid complaint against women whose dress shows 'the blister-marks on their backs, and inoculation scars on their arms'.[81]

One fashion that seems to have made a virtue out of this blemished necessity is the mode for patches. In evidence, though not necessarily common, for the 200 years from the end of the sixteenth to the end of the eighteenth century, patches were small shapes cut from black silk or velvet which were gummed to the face (Figures 43 and 47). Although round beauty spots were most usual, more inventive examples like suns, stars and crescents were also worn. Sometimes they were kept in special decorative boxes, similar to those used for snuff (Figure 18). These boxes might feature verses or be given as gifts. In an interesting overlap between the history of fashion and that of travel and tourism, some patch boxes were manufactured and sold as souvenirs.[82]

In some cases, certainly, spots were used to cover blemishes like scars or pimples. Pepys mentions seeing the Duchess of Newcastle with 'many black patches because of pimples about her mouth'. Although this hardly sounds attractive, she seemed to him 'a very comely woman'.[83] More often, these scraps of silk were simply worn as decoration: placed on a dimple, or used as a foil to white skin to give interest and vitality to a face, rather like model Cindy Crawford's trademark mole. Detractors, of course, found them ugly. They thought the custom of patching vain and proud, and typical of those who preferred the sins of the flesh to the purer beauties of the soul—weighty charges in the moral world of the seventeenth and eighteenth centuries. 'It is a Riddle', wrote Robert Codrington in his conduct manual, 'that a Blemish should appear a Grace, and that a Deformity should adde unto Beauty.' Hannah Woolley, another writer of conduct texts, echoed him almost verbatim, adding that wearers' inventive fashions showed them to be 'defective in nothing but a vertuous mind'.[84] *A brief anatomie of women*, a short conduct treatise of 1653, rather dramatically called patches 'pieces of darkness, which are as so many seals of *Sathan* to bind them to his pleasure and will'.[85] Only extreme opinion ventured so far, though. *The British Apollo*, an early newspaper, judged them 'Ornamental' in much the same way as jewellery, and not 'Sinful' like the 'flagrant Cheat' of painting (i.e. makeup).[86] Pepys comments on patches several times, noting their fashionable use. Although fairly conservative in his

Figure 47 'A Rake's Progress', plate 3 (detail), etching and engraving by William Hogarth, 1735, © Trustees of the British Museum. In this detail of Hogarth's well-known print, a prostitute undresses; her stays already lie with a heap of clothes on the floor. The woman's face is patched on the forehead and chin.

attitude to his wife's appearance, he nevertheless thought her 'very pretty' on the first day he had 'given her leave to weare a black patch'. His spousal sanction followed two months after he had first seen her wear them. Presumably in this time he had become accustomed to the idea, and was perhaps swayed by the Earl of Sandwich's courtly example, whose 'lady and child to wear black paches'. Pepys was quickly able to feel gratified at the sight of his wife 'with two or three black paches on and well dressed', seeming to him much more handsome than those about her.[87]

The most curious record of patching is perhaps the issue of *The Spectator* that Joseph Addison entirely devotes to the practice.[88] In it Mr Spectator recounts his visit to the theatre, where the women in the audience have arrayed themselves in boxes on opposite sides and have also patched accordingly, some on the right side of the face, others on the left. 'I quickly perceived', he says, 'that their Patches were placed in those different Situations, as Party-Signals.' Those 'on my right Hand, were Whigs; and those on my Left, Tories'. Seated in the middle were a neutral party of ladies who patched indifferently on both sides, 'whose Faces had not yet declared themselves'. On the basis of this evidence—abstracted from a satirical periodical devoted entirely to moral reformation and the promotion of a particular middle-class and masculine discourse—patching for political allegiance has become one of those urban myths of dress history. If it happened at all, it was certainly not in the systematic manner described in this parodic essay. As Mr Spectator himself wrote, 'this Account of Party-Patches will, I am afraid, appear improbable to those who live at a distance from the fashionable World'—improbable, indeed. Reading the rest of the essay, however, one arrives at Addison's real message: a fixed opposition to any interest and involvement of women within the broader political sphere. They should, he writes, pursue 'accomplishments proper to the Sex, and to distinguish themselves as tender Mothers and faithful Wives, rather than as furious Partizans. Female Virtues are of a Domestick turn. The Family is the proper Province for Private Women to Shine in.'

HEALTH

Although the partial relationship between patching and disfigurement is interesting, it is really only an aside in the much larger issue of the role of garments with respect to the skin and the body beneath. The way in previous centuries that people covered so much of their anatomy, clearly argues a different morality from ours. It points also to different material conditions: for most of the last 500 years open fires were the only heating, and for some of this time, winter weather was considerably colder.[89] It is obvious that our forebears did not have well-heated means of travel to transport them from well-heated homes to well-heated places of work, education and leisure. It is indeed obvious, but perhaps the material reality needs restating to help us imagine what the physical experience would really have been like: an enveloping cold that could only be temporarily assuaged by moments of warmth. Pepys complained after one bitter night in March that having left his stockings lying near the window, they had been covered with a rime of ice.[90] Charlotte Papendiek explained to readers of her reminiscences that the winter of 1788 was so cold her children could only rarely go out. One of her daughters suffered terribly from chilblains 'just at the top of the shoes, where the petticoats do not shelter the legs from the cold air'.[91] The harsh cold of December 1808 saw heavy frost and deep snow. Sarah Spencer, after complaining to her brother that the road was 'one sheet of ice', told him that 'poor everybody is creeping about from fire to fire, wrapped up in shawls, and shivering and chattering away deplorably'.[92]

Under these conditions, it makes sense that people used clothes much more as a way of keeping warm. There is, however, a much more profound difference to be appreciated here. In its maximal coverage of skin, the past reveals a very different understanding of physiology and how to keep healthy. By and large, contemporary western society has a sense of the body as being robust, durable and solid. Our bodies have a self-sufficiency that needs little protection from the environment, leaving good and bad health as a consequence of our internal state. Cold or excessive heat is unpleasant, but in our day-to-day lives rarely dangerous. Ordinary experience recounted from the past, however, tells a very different tale. Bodies are more porous somehow, more vulnerable to threat from without. Being inadequately covered one might catch cold, or being too well covered one might overheat; and having been taken by cold or heat, one might in turn be taken by illness, or even death. For example, in 1649 Ralph Josselin felt cautious about dispensing with too many garments, despite it being midsummer. 'This day I left off my head cap', he wrote, 'and wore a thinner stomacher, I foremerly left of my night wascoate, and found no damage thereby, and I hope I shall not now.'[93] Alice Thornton's (1627–1707) baby was not so lucky. In making the tragedy of this child's death understandable for herself, the gentry housewife explained, 'When he was about fourteen daies old, my pretty babe broake into red spots, like the smale pox, and through cold, gotten by thinner clothing.'[94] Over the years Pepys mentions these kinds of worries with regard to his own health. He catches cold by flinging off his hat at dinner and sitting in a draft, or by pulling off his wig too often.[95] Brilliana Harley's middle son, Robert, 'left of some of his cloths' and took a bad cold that left him ill and feverish.[96] Sir Henry Bowier suffered through getting too hot. A fine dancer, he overheated with practising, 'fell into the small pocks and died'.[97] Something similar was thought to have happened to Lady Worcester, over two centuries later. Having overheated herself with dancing at a ball, she was 'fool enough to take a shower bath before she went to bed'. Lady Worcester was immediately taken with an inflammation in her bowels and died soon after.[98]

If the effects of getting too hot, too wet, too cold were potentially serious—bringing on fevers or even a disease like smallpox—it is easy to see the importance of clothing as the first line of defence. A letter of 1563 from the bishop of London to William Cecil takes us further towards appreciating the role of dress in maintaining good health:

> I am gladde to heare that your disease diminsheth, so I am sorie it hangeth on you so longe. Yt is sayd your payne is in your backe: I wille be bolde to communicate unto you my coniecture off the cawse theroff & off the meanses to avoyde the lyke heraffter; nott by anie acte of physick butt upon some experience off myne owne bodye in ye lyke case. When I came firste from beyonde seas I felt greate heate in my backe & feared the stone [gallstones]. I cutte my dublettes, my peticotes in the back, I went ungyrte, I coulde nott abyde to sytte by a quission [cushion] … In continuance I strived so to coole my backe, that I felle into the contrarie; so that a smalle colde taken by that parte, under the poynte off one sholder or bothe, & sodeynly claspeth by the smalle off my backe, & ther remayneth xv or xx dayes. I doo remember one morninge a yeare and more agone, yo shewed me yor dublettes cutte, & voydett in the backe & that you feared the stoone. I am perswadett yt by resystinge heate … yo have cooled yor backe to moche, rydding and goone syngle, & so have browght those parts to greate imbecillitie. surely I thinke yor onely waye to avoyde it heraffter is to goo warme … & namely on yor backe; but specially when you ryde, thowghe it be in the myddes off sommer.[99]

Here we have clothing specially cut away to cool the back, and the unfortunate results of too much cold in turn being remedied by warm dress at the affected part, despite the midsummer heat. Clothing, therefore, represents the means through which people could intervene to better their own health. The strategic use of dress was an active way to self-medicate: it was not dependent on specialist knowledge or access; it was available to all. Such medical/sartorial prescription was offered to Samuel Pepys as a remedy for his failure to conceive any children. He listed the ten points of advice given him, including '5. Wear cool Holland-drawers. 6. Keep stomach warm and back cool. 7. Upon my query whether it was best to do at night or morn, they answered me neither one nor other, but when we have most mind to it. 8. Wife not to go too straight-laced.'[100]

This belief in a vulnerable body that can be protected by garments was long-lived. *The Polite Lady*, an epistolary conduct manual first published in 1760, warns of the dangers of exposing the neck and breast, the most delicate parts of the body, to the inclement and severe weather. 'This custom must certainly be very pernicious to the health. I verily believe that nineteen in twenty of the diseases, incident to our sex, are owing to this foolish manner of dressing.' 'It is generally allowed', the author continues, 'that most of our distempers are occasioned by colds; and what way so likely to catch cold as to leave the the [*sic*] most sensible parts of the body almost, if not entirely naked.' The wages of vanity and fashion, therefore, was to lie 'pining and languishing' in a sick room, or worse, on a deathbed.[101] *The Ladies' Pocket Magazine* reminded its readers in 1829 that the most important function of clothing 'ought to be protection from the cold'. The consequences of ignoring this are serious, for cold 'lays the foundation of the whole host of chronic diseases', including scrofula and consumption.[102] *The Gentleman's Magazine* of 1788 reported on experiments undertaken by Sir Benjamin Thompson, a Fellow of the Royal Society, to determine the absorption and evaporation of moisture by various substances. Sir Benjamin's scientific knowledge and personal experience led him to recommend warmly 'the wearing of flannel next to the skin, as contributing greatly to health', for it both kept the body warm and enabled chilling perspiration to evaporate.[103] Mlle. Clémence D'Albenas, with the stubbornness of youth, failed to heed this advice. A French noble émigrée, at the age of nineteen she was governess to Adeline De Horsey. Years later in her memoirs, Adeline, now Countess of Cardigan and Lancastre, remembered that Clémence was a little *difficile*, among other things refusing to wear any flannel garments. 'The result of this was that poor Mlle. Clémence went into a decline which caused her death, at least we were always told so, perhaps with the idea of pointing a moral to young people who hated flannel.'[104]

However, the effects of clothing were not always beneficent. Garments could, on occasion, be damaging to their wearers' health. A notable example is apparel at times of plague. The Plague Orders issued by the Privy Council in 1578, and which for nearly 100 years determined the administrative response to the illness, listed seventeen directives.[105] One of them commanded that the apparel and bedding belonging to plague victims be burnt. There are two reasons why clothing was thought especially susceptible to receiving and transmitting infection. The first was owing to its intimate, nearly organic relationship with the wearer. Remembering Erasmus, as 'the body's body' clothing was perhaps prone to the body's illnesses. A verse account describing the plague outbreak of 1603 reported sufferers maliciously seeking to infect others by casting about personal items of dress: 'Here do they Gloues, and there they Garters fall / Ruffs, Cuffs, & handkerchers, and such like things / They strow about, so to endanger all'.[106] The second reason apparel was so dangerous concerns the texture of cloth and its openness—like the pores in skin—to contamination. Softer fabrics with a looser weave, like wool, or feathers and fur, were held to be particularly treacherous. Conversely, smooth shiny textures, like that of satins, were more repellent to contagion and safer to wear.[107] While the burning of infected apparel might not seem unreasonable to us, in a society in which everyone—the richest and poorest alike—reused, recycled and remade clothing, and garments had a relatively high monetary value, such destruction represented a serious loss of resources and wealth. When outbreaks of plague were at their height in London and thousands were being entered on the bills of mortality, it is hard to imagine the vast material loss that silently accompanied the horrendous loss of life. Put like this, it more readily explains the risks that might be taken to break the law and retrieve some of this wearable wealth. The Council minute books in York record that four women and a man 'degged and raved upp Clothes and other things that were buryed in the grounde for danger of infection'. As punishment they were set in the stocks and whipped.[108]

Another problem with garments, particularly long, trailing ones, was fire hazard. With open grates providing the only means of heating and candles being used for domestic lighting, burns were always a risk. With the advent of lightweight muslin dresses at the turn of the nineteenth century, however, the danger became very much worse. Issue after issue of *The Gentleman's Magazine*, for example, report on excruciating accidents and deaths. Mrs Rachel Broxham's muslin neckerchief was set alight by a candle. In being torn off, the fire spread to the rest of her dress, 'unfortunately also of muslin' the report stated, 'and she became immediately enveloped in flames'. A small draft also blew Miss S. Smith's muslin gown against a candle, whereupon it immediately caught fire 'and burnt with great rapidity'. She lived fourteen hours in agony. An unnamed Birmingham girl, just six years old, was standing near the fire to dry her frock. It caught alight and burnt her so badly that she died three days later. Lady Warren died at Brighton, 'in consequence of her muslin-dress catching fire, in her bed-chamber'. The butler, who tried to rescue her, was also much burnt.[109] Hannah More, whose disapproval of big hair we have already seen, in 1814 was the victim of one of these household accidents. In her case it did not prove fatal, and she probably owed her life to her choice of rather unfashionable clothing for that day. It seems she was reaching across the fireplace for a book, when the end of her shawl caught the fire. As she described it, before any help could arrive, 'I was one sheet of flame'. Because she had a bad cold, however, she had chosen a thick woollen gown and three shawls to protect her from the December weather. They also protected her from the fire. The previous day she had worn a muslin dress, and she was thankful to providence for preservation.[110]

The surge in fire-related injuries prompted a corresponding surge of preventative advice. *The Gentleman's Magazine* printed a page-long article, 'Hints Respecting Women's and Children's Cloaths Catching Fire', which included the suggestion that wire fenders should be fitted before fireplaces to prevent coals and sparks flying into the room. Second, the writer suggested that the most evident means of checking the progress of flames would be to wear dresses of materials that would not readily burn, but in the same breath admitted that the use of muslins and linens was not actually going to stop. Given this, he urged that research be undertaken into making these fabrics fire resistant in a way that was practical for widespread use and would not discolour or damage the materials' appearance. Finally, while acknowledging the efficacy of rolling up in the carpet someone whose clothes have caught fire, he also pointed out that most often carpets are either tacked down or are laid under tables and heavy furniture. He therefore advised that a thick woollen cloth or blanket be kept—rather in the manner of a modern throw—in rooms where there was especial risk, such as nurseries and sitting rooms. This 'stifling cloth' would then be always on hand to smother any flames should an accident occur.[111]

The Lady's Magazine also ran with advice, this time principally concerned with what a woman should do if her clothes caught alight. This included extinguishing the flames with a water decanter (to be always kept full for the purpose) and sitting down to wrap herself in the hearth rug (which, for this reason, should form part of the furniture in every room). The article closes by recognizing that women are 'most commonly the subjects of this terrible accident, owing to their clothing being of a more combustible kind than those of men'. Not only do the woollens that comprise the male wardrobe smoulder rather than flame, but the smell of their burning raises the alarm more quickly. Therefore, the writer concludes, women who are particularly at risk—the old or infirm who spend much time by the fireside—should be persuaded into silk or woollen textiles. A few years later the periodical printed a letter that repeated many of the same ideas, and for their own sakes urged those involved in such accidents to exercise 'presence of mind'. It was placed immediately preceding the fashion pages. A third article also appeared, suggesting that every lady should provide herself with a strong woollen cloak 'for the express and sole purpose of extinguishing fire in her clothes'. In this the author echoed the writer of The Gentleman's Magazine who had advised that 'stifling cloths' be kept, and like him also looked forward to the time when 'a *fire-cloak* will be seen in every parlour and 'drawing room in the kingdom'.[112]

In the event, it was neither fire cloaks nor stifling cloths that won the day, but the development—as the far-sighted contributor to The Gentleman's Magazine had urged—of a process that made highly flammable textiles fire resistant. In December 1844 a nasty and particularly well-publicized incident occurred at Drury Lane Theatre, when the clothing of the young actress Miss Clara Webster caught the oil lamp footlights and ignited. In her terror she ran about the stage and, the coroner's inquest was told, the 'whole of her dress blazed up about her'. Witnessed by the horrified audience, Miss Webster's accident and subsequent death 'very naturally awakened the attention of the public to the possibility of the prevention of similar catastrophies in future'. Just days later, a short piece appeared in The Times reporting on trials of an anti-inflammable starch.[113] It was not until nearly thirty years and presumably many deaths later, that starch—that most useful and adaptable of substances—really asserted itself in this new guise. In the Scientific Invention Department of the International Exhibition of 1872, D. Nicolls exhibited materials prepared with his Patent Fire-Proof Starch. Upon the request of the visitors, the attendant 'daily and publicly tested' these materials by passing them through a flame. On contact with the fire the fabric was found only to char. The medical establishment evidently gave this the thumbs up.

In June of that year *The Lancet* reported on Nicolls's contribution to the International Exhibition, and praised his achievement in producing a starch that 'renders the finest cambrics and muslins … not only inflammable, but well-nigh incombustible'. *The Lancet* hailed this as an addition to the armoury of preventative medicine. 'Henceforth we are entitled to expect that the verdict, hitherto so frequent at Coroners' inquests, "Burnt to death by her clothes accidentally taking fire," will reach its minimum.'[114] The Patent Fire-Proof Starch Company was floated on the stock exchange in November, its directors including the owner of a drug company and the manager of an accident insurance firm. The company's prospectus estimated that 27,000 tons of starch were manufactured in Britain every year, and that cornering even a fairly modest slice of this market would ensure a handsome profit.[115]

With this new role for starch, we reach the end of a story that stretches from the elaborate complexity of elite Elizabethan dress to the mass production and consumption that heralded the twentieth century. Throughout this time clothing was used to shape and adorn the body, and to keep it warm, healthy and decent—although this latter concept in particular was a contested category, and subject to widely different interpretations. After hundreds of years, however, of more or less covering the skin, the decades following the First World War witnessed the beginnings of a revolution. It was a revolution in social relationships, the material conditions that surrounded them, and understandings of decorum, taste and the functions of dress. Furthermore, while begun in those years, it is a revolution that is still being played out today. We will finish, therefore, by taking a look at the fashioning of the anatomy in our own historical moment.

EPILOGUE: FASHIONING THE BODY TODAY

In the preceding chapters we have looked at the body in bits, considering some of the ways that various fashions from the past have worked on the anatomy to create a range of forms, and with those forms a corresponding set of behaviours and assumptions. The fashioned body has encompassed a remarkable diversity of shape: an opulent hourglass, the cylindrical regularity of a classical column, the distension of a big belly, a big bottom or, by dressing the hair, a big head. Notwithstanding this diversity, while current each new gestalt has become the norm, and individual subjects, while clothed fashionably, have embodied the 'natural' aesthetic of the moment. Through the course of these pages, I hope that some of this normality has become apparent. I hope that the pleasures and difficulties experienced by those who peopled the past have become more understandable according to their own frames of reference. But I also want to hold on to some of the strangeness, not only to appreciate the wild inventiveness and beautiful oddity of fashion's response to the human subject, but also to help us remember that, in countless different ways, each fashion is implicated in the larger picture of its chronological moment. Whether in the mechanisms of production, the politics of consumption, the construction of sexuality or gender, or the formation and reformation of manners and morals, fashion is there. By keeping a perspective on its image we can better appreciate the connections between, say, starched garments and poverty, or massively feathered Edwardian hats—'plumed as though they were bright fowls about to take wing'[1]—and a nascent environmental movement committed to the protection of exploited and endangered species.

I want to finish, however, by reassembling the anatomical parts to think about the fashioning of the body today. I want to consider our own place in the sweep of history as witnessed through dress, to try to appreciate whether what we do is a variation on an endlessly repeated theme or whether it is something altogether more novel, more particular. Are the impulses that drive our fashioning the same as in the past, or does something distinguish our practices from those that went before? At this point it is customary to issue a caveat, a kind of academic disclaimer concerning the difficulties of getting any kind of historical purchase on the notoriously slippery present.[2] As photographer and fashion observer Cecil Beaton put it, 'as regards contemporary events, the eye is depressingly short-sighted'.[3] Be that as it may, we can still, albeit myopically, make some sense of the image we see reflected back at us when we ourselves stand before the looking glass.

My first contention—and it is a big one—is that dress no longer really matters to us. Collectively, we are no longer upset, challenged, angered, inspired or captivated by clothes and their appearance on the body. When compared to any other time over the past 500 years, our emotional engagement with the matter of dress is slight, and our attention is found to be elsewhere. As with a dull conversation, we are only going through the motions, for our real interest has been caught by something different. This is not to say that clothes are of negligible importance to the individual—far from it. On a personal level, dress has as great a power as ever: impacting on how we feel about ourselves and how others judge us. As writer Kate Cann describes it, 'wearing the right stuff can make you feel great about yourself'.[4] And we all know the profound emotional discomfort caused by wearing the 'wrong stuff'—the clothes that do not match our sense of self at the time—and the attendant sensation of temporarily being an unwilling inhabitant of this particular physical envelope. But on a societal level, judgements about what might constitute the right stuff and the wrong stuff, and why, are manifested only very rarely.

An exception might be found in the workplace, where usually there are rules—written or unwritten—about acceptability of appearance. In this case an employee is obliged to reflect his or her employer's values and culture, and most usually conform to expectations.[5] This can work both ways on the formality continuum, however, as attested by one Cambridge graduate who, while working for Greenpeace, wore her hair in dreadlocks 'to match her boss'.[6] And some companies like Sky, are now stepping back from enforcing a dress code: 'We want people to enjoy working here, and the freedom to choose how you look at work is part of that';[7] although it is fair to say that few employers are as permissive. Another aspect of dress practice that has definitely engendered debate is the wearing of religiously charged clothing. For example, Nadia Eweida recently sued her employer, British Airways, for banning her from wearing a necklace bearing a Christian cross. Disciplined by British Airways in the latter part of 2006 for refusing to comply with uniform regulations, Eweida responded by accusing the company of discrimination. In January 2008 she eventually lost the case. In a related vein, in 2006 the BBC discussed the implications of newsreader Fiona Bruce's decision to wear a cross, though it took no action. Again in 2006, Aishah Azmi, a Muslim teaching assistant, was suspended, and later dismissed, for refusing to remove her veil in the classroom. Like Eweida, Azmi took her case to an employment tribunal, and also lost. At the same time, Jack Straw, a former foreign secretary and Member of Parliament for Blackburn (a constituency with a high Muslim population) suggested that the wearing of full veils was detrimental to positive relations between Muslims and non-Muslims.

Outside these contexts there is little evidence that clothing systems any longer get under the cultural skin, irritating, niggling, demanding notice. Our attitude to fashionable dress worn in day-to-day situations is blasé; concerns about who wears it when have all but evaporated in the powerful light of modernity. Of course there is interest in celebrity individuals and their celebrated individual outfits—Liz Hurley in *that* safety pin dress by Versace for example, or the awarding of the worst-dressed status that allows us lesser mortals the delightful but fleeting pleasures of *schadenfreude*. However, none of this really matters: it is a ripple on the surface of public attention rather than being a manifestation of fundamental interest, and it has, moreover, much more to do with the cult of fame than any kind of sartorial value system.

That our society no longer responds to the power of fashion to shock and challenge is clear in the virtual disappearance of sartorially motivated satire. What was once an energetic, vitriolic, impassioned and entertaining genre has withered away. Usually targeting the appearance of the Other—women, youth, aspirational classes, 'sexual deviants'—satire showed how much the establishment had invested in how particular people looked, and in what behaviour and beliefs their garments suggested. Macaronis, flappers, dandies, the Victorian New Woman, ruffling gallants: a list of the subjects of satire would be as long as a description of fashion itself. But nowadays, fashionable clothing is apparently no longer perceived as a threat to morality, gender identity or class systems. Its importance is a private, individual matter, and as a category of cultural anxiety it has ceased to exist.

Along with this collective relaxation of sartorial vigilance has come a massive democratization of context, a kind of levelling of the venues of display, so that almost anything can be worn almost anywhere. The demarcation of different social occasions through dress was perhaps at its most marked during the Edwardian period. If a woman was leisured and wealthy enough, she might expect to change her outfit up to seven or eight times a day, tailoring her appearance to fit her activities. Morning gowns, tea gowns, evening dress, clothes for driving, walking and visiting: a proliferation of styles nuanced for their respective social purposes. Osbert Sitwell remembered 'the continual changing of clothes' in his childhood, and fashion designer Lucy Duff Gordon (1862–1935) remarked that after World War I very few women would bother to change five or six times a day, 'yet every Edwardian, with any claims to being well-dressed, did so as a matter of course'.[8] While at its most articulated at this point, every period has seen a clear sartorial distinction between formal and informal, and domestic and public registers. Writing in the 1760s and 1770s, for instance, Mary Coke's journals are liberally peppered with her references to 'dressing'—that is, putting on formal dress—and when this was required. On one occasion she dined with some of the royal children, writing that 'I had put on a hoop to be respectfull.'[9] Always one for observing etiquette—some thought her attitude to royalty positively sycophantic—she was therefore scandalized by the behaviour of Lady Susan Stewart, who appeared at the Chapel Royal one Sunday 'without a hoop'. Notwithstanding her 'undress', Lady Susan 'sat down in the bench which is in sight of the Royal Family, & used to be alotted for those Ladys that were dressed for Court'. Then Lady Hyde came in, 'still more undressed'. Lady Effingham remonstrated with her: 'Lady Hyde, give me leave to tell you, as a friend, that you are doing a very irregular thing; those Places are only for the Ladys who are dressed for the Drawing room, & 'tis very disrespectful to appear before their Majesties in an Undress.'[10] Although a stickler, Lady Coke was pleased to escape the trouble of formal dress when she could, and in the November of 1771, for example, she several times recorded that she preferred to be comfy in her home clothes. 'I was invited to dinner to day', she wrote on the 18th, 'but excused myself; if I go out it will be only where I can go quite undressed.'[11]

By comparison with this, today informality has proliferated. The same garments can be, and are, worn in a wide range of contexts, and individual items can be dressed 'up' or 'down', acquiring a polyvalent utility. Naturally the concept of formality still exists, but it is one that is much more personally defined than before. Individuals dress to their own standards, making their own judgements of what is acceptable for them, rather than observing widely understood social norms. It is still possible to give, or take, offence in matters of dress, but again this tends to be a personal matter, to do with the lacerating of individual, rather than collective, sensibilities. By and large we adopt a much more ironic stance now, with an extreme or unusual appearance more often raising an eyebrow than the blood pressure. Some have found this modern characteristic makes it harder to dress appropriately: when nothing is wrong, what then is right? But it explains why—at the theatre, at a restaurant, at church, at the cinema—there is such a variety in registers of dress, ranging from the mindfully elaborate to the simple, shabby or skimpy. In recent years many of us have felt this shift towards the casual operate in our own clothing choices, and it is certainly evident in comparison with the generation that came before. In the 1960s, hats were worn to church; in the 1970s, television gardener Percy Thrower mulched his herbaceous borders in a collar and tie; and it was only in the 1980s that elderly women in trousers became a common sight. Today there are still events, certainly, that call most to a showier sartorial display—weddings are an example. However, in a world where there are few such elaborated contexts, increasingly the fancy dresses of participants have an aura of just that, of 'fancy dress'.

If we are no longer concerned with clothing, where then is our attention fixed? Simply put, culturally we have shed our garments, or at the least we look through them unseeingly. For now the locus of awareness, and the site of intervention and activity, is to be found in the body itself. The aesthetics, health, rights and ontological status of the body are the subject of vigorous scientific, legal and moral debate; a debate that pervades our lives daily, if not through personal experience, then through the ubiquity of media text and images. Whether the issue is stem cell research, fertility treatments, cloning, disability, obesity, pornography or eating disorders, the conversation is vocal and often impassioned. Even in certain sectors of the academic world, 'embodiment' is—to borrow a fashion metaphor—the new black.

If clothing has shrunk in a discursive sense, then it has certainly thinned and reduced its physical form (Figure 48). We cover ourselves only minimally, leaving large areas of the skin exposed to the elements and to the gaze. Some do this with a near disregard for climatic conditions, not protecting themselves very much against the sun, the rain or the cold. As will be apparent from the last chapter, compared to any other time in our past, we simply cover much less of our skin with cloth. Furthermore, when we do envelop the flesh, our garments are generally close fitting and sewn from fine, lightweight fabrics that reveal, rather than hide, the body's contours. Little is suggested; much is declared. Indeed, there has been a collapse, or blurring, of the distinction between the public and private realms. The boundary between what is on show for all and what is private and intimate has been radically redrawn. This applies not just to the parts and amount of anatomy disclosed, but also to the revelation of undergarments, which layered with other items have a stylistic outer life of their own. This is democratization of dress indeed, where we all get a visual share of the body's secrets.

The foregrounding of the corporeal, the placing of the body in the starring role centre stage, argues, I think, that we have the sense of our physicality as something dependable. Our bodies have a robust durability upon which the environment has relatively little effect. We no longer recognize a potential risk in every burning hearth, in candles used for lighting, or in the seasons and the weather, for the dangers we fear come in a microscopic form. Against the invisible legion that corrupts a healthy organism from the inside and hijacks the body's functioning for its own purposes, clothing is no protection at all. Except for the surgical mask—which in our society is confined to medicalized contexts when the body's integrity is at its most precariously uncertain—we fight our fears with antibacterial soaps, vitamin supplements, medicines and disinfectants. The relationship that we picture for ourselves in the wider world is altogether more benign. We therefore pursue an immediacy of physical contact with our environment, and the mediating properties of dress are only dimly remembered as we pull on our gloves on a frosty morning.

There are exceptions to this sense of inviolability, however, through which we can glimpse the normality of dress practices of an earlier age. One of them is the way we clothe babies and infants. Vests, socks, booties, mittens, newborn hats, sun hats, woolly hats, mitts to prevent scratching, parasols for pushchairs, and blankets and shawls for swaddling are practical responses to a physiology that we perceive as different to an adult's. We are told that babies' skin is delicate, that young children cannot regulate their own internal temperature, and that summer and winter, night and day, we need to do this for them by removing or adding covering layers. Another very different exception to the physiologically self-contained adult body of everyday life is found within the realm of outdoor activity clothing. Here, images and a discourse of fitness and strength are combined with a sense of the body's interactions with the environment, and that health and performance can be protected and enhanced by wearing the right garments. The following is taken from the catalogue of an outdoors clothing company:

> You'll enjoy the outdoors more if you select your clothing to ensure that you stay dry and are not too cold or too hot. Water conducts heat better than air does; so wet clothing transfers your body warmth away more quickly than dry clothes ... If the wind can penetrate your clothing it will carry your body heat away with it ... Layers effectively create a microclimate that surrounds your body; you can adapt this to deal with temperature, wind, moisture and exertion levels.[12]

Garments designed for outdoor activities draw out body moisture, or wick; they breathe through a hydrophilic construction that lets sweat out but does not allow rain in; they have windproof membranes; and they offer ultraviolet protection from the sun. In short, they care for the body in ways that our forbears, even of hundreds of years ago, would probably

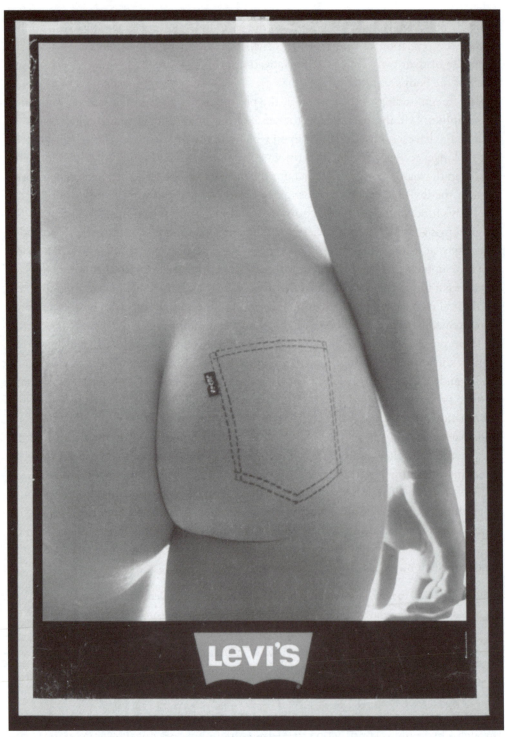

Figure 48 Levi's poster, by Ida van Bladel, 1973, © Victoria and Albert Museum, London. The Levi's advertising poster promises the viewer jeans with a skintight, figure-hugging fit. The only thing better than wearing garments like this is to wear nothing at all.

recognize. Despite the modern technology and the modernity of leisure pursuits, through 'extreme' clothing we are in direct connection with our sartorial past.

Many of our contemporary attitudes to the body have their origin in the 1920s and 1930s. In this period between the wars a whole cluster of interconnected social changes set the foundations for our own particular looks and practices. For a start, modernity cut a swathe through the yards of cloth that previously formed the dressed figure. Hem lines went up, foundation garments became lighter, and sporting and leisure activities—increasingly popular from the latter part of Victoria's reign—encouraged the development of more informal styles. Women's clothes came to be typified by Chanel's simple, reduced designs and easy-to-wear, pliant fabrics. On holiday or at the beach, swimsuits, beach pyjamas, vests and shorts publicly revealed the physique of both sexes for the first time ever. Naturally, the fashionable sloughing off of clothes was a gradual affair, with the rich stripping faster and further and the middle and lower classes setting a more modest pace and morality. However, within a relatively short time, even the most conservative in the community became accustomed to the new norms of disclosure.

Accompanying the new revelation of the body was its radical new look: 'tan was the skin colour of modernism'.[13] A number of developments conspired to overturn the centuries-old aesthetic of whiteness. Medical opinion had begun to champion the benefits of the sun, its therapeutic qualities being recognized as efficacious against certain skin conditions and diseases such as tuberculosis and rickets. Sunshine, it was argued, was 'the highest expression of preventive medicine'. According to this new conception of health, 'the wearing of unhygienic clothes' atrophied the skin, preventing 'the direct action of the air and sun' upon it.[14] A revolution of medical thought, indeed. In 1924 Dr Saleeby established the influential Sunlight League, which aimed to spread the good news of heliotherapy, particularly when combined with the benefits of sea bathing. Local and national governments were soon persuaded that intervention along these lines could substantially improve the health of the urban poor, especially the young. Mr Lansbury, the First Commissioner of Works, was particularly keen on the provision of sunbathing sites in London parks;[15] and in 1934 Tower Beach—created with the blessing of George V and over 1,500 barge loads of sand—was opened for the enjoyment of the capital's children.

This medical endorsement of judicious tanning only provided extra impetus to what was already a growing fashion for sunbathing. Following the example of the rich at play in the Riviera, millions of ordinary English began to take to the beach in sundresses, ever-diminishing swimsuits and the new invention of sunglasses.[16] Also during this same period, cosmetics swept into widespread use. It was a contested progress, with the rich, the young and the daring leading the way, but nevertheless the triumph of makeup was swift and absolute. In 1931, for instance, the *Sunday Express* reported that for every 1 lipstick sold ten years previously, 1,500 were being sold today.[17] Shadowing, or perhaps driving, demand, cosmetic advertising burgeoned. Starting in the early 1930s, the amount spent on face powder ads began to escalate in leaps and bounds, in one year rising by nearly 40 per cent. The number of advertisements for lipstick carried by women's magazines showed a similar expansion. For example, in 1936 there were 60 per cent more than in a corresponding period just one year before.[18] As Robert Graves and Alan Hodge remembered it, looking back from less than a decade later: 'All hairdressers, beauty parlours, large stores, chemists and branches of Woolworth's now sold cosmetics and nail-enamel.'[19]

If the decades following the First World War established the tanned, outdoors body as the physical ideal, they dictated that it must also be slim and young. In dramatic contrast to the full, mature contours of the Edwardian era—'magnificent, handsome, statuesquely beautiful'[20]—modernity declared itself thin and youthful. 'Slimming was now a cult', wrote Graves and Hodges of the 1920s, with a panoply of pills, diets, machines and exercises to help the willing lose weight. Lucy Duff Gordon also wrote of the 'slimming craze', contrasting the models she used to show her designs with the post-war ideal of womanhood. Her 'goddesses' were tall and heavy—several weighing considerably more than eleven stone—with 'generous curves' and 'a full bust'.[21] Maturity was the keynote of their attractions.[22] The new fashion, however, completely reversed this. Clothes were now designed for the young or were designed to make older women look young.[23]

For those who lived through these changes, the comparison between the old order and the new was often poignant, sometimes bewildering. Whether welcomed or not, a paradigm shift had occurred in the role and rights of the body. Sex began to be talked of openly; incessantly, some would say. Marie Stopes opened her first clinic in 1921; Freud entered the popular consciousness; Havelock Ellis's work began to be more widely known; and reformed laws saw a significant rise in the number of divorces.[24] Furthermore, in 1928 universal suffrage meant that, in theory at least, all adults had a say about this. While hindsight artificially smoothes the course of these developments, generalizing what was fragmented and initially a minority experience only, nonetheless, much of what we consider as ordinary had its origins in these extraordinary times.

The rise of the body as a focus of society's interest and energies has resulted in a corresponding diminution of the role of clothing in the staging of appearance. How people look remains as much a cultural preoccupation as ever, but garments now have less significance in the creation of that look, and the size, shape and characteristics of the body wearing them have more. Again, this is a trend whose origins can be discerned in the interwar years. In 1932 Lucy Duff Gordon speculated that dressing would never figure in social life as it had done at the turn of the century. 'It is regarded as of infinitely less importance nowadays.' The cult of beauty, she maintained, had actually increased—girls were 'far better groomed' and 'far more *soignée*' than their mothers—'but they think less of clothes'.[25] These were sentiments echoed, or perhaps inspired, by Chanel. 'As a dress designer, she was virtually nihilistic, for behind her clothes was an implied but unexpressed philosophy: the clothes do not really matter at all, it is the way you look that counts.'[26] The shift of focus onto the body's appearance—as opposed to the appearance of the body when dressed— helps explain the astounding rise of cosmetic surgery and techniques of body modification. Modern garments, form fitting and adaptive to the wearer's contours, have a reduced capacity to fashion our shape, and we ourselves have a reduced interest in their fashioning possibilities. Because of this, an increasing amount of the work of appearance has been displaced onto skin and flesh and bone.

Devoting time and energy to dressing, adapting to discomforts of constriction and bulk, learning to move gracefully in complicated garments, manipulating them for visual and aural effect: these disciplines and skills have given way to effort expended on diet, exercise, washing and the maintenance of health. We used to live through our clothes; now we just live. An increasingly large number eschew the decorative properties of fabric altogether, choosing instead the adornment of incisions made directly into their person (Figure 49). Tattoos and piercings have expanded their traditionally reduced range in our society, and are now found on more bodies and more body parts than a short time ago would have been imaginable. The skin of men and women is patterned with colour and shape; brows, nose, lips, tongue, bellies and genitals flash with the metallic glint of studs and rings.[27] Then there is the explosion in the popularity of surgical interventions. Again, this can be traced to the 1920s, when a few people on the quest for aesthetic enhancement began to choose from plastic surgery techniques developed to patch and repair the maimed and wounded of the battlefields.[28] Very recently, however, the small market for this elective surgery has burgeoned, as indeed has the range of interventions now possible. Working from the top down, a surgical menu of what's on offer gives us hair transplants for male-pattern baldness; eyelid surgery for a wider, more youthful gaze; nose, ear and chin reshapings; implants to fill out hollow cheeks; face and neck lifts; breast enlargements, reductions (both female and male) and uplifts; nipple correction for a perkier appearance; arm lifts to tighten sagging skin; tummy tucks, with liposuction for recalcitrant fat; buttock lifts to pull in drooping flesh and buttock implants to push it out; vaginal tightening, labial reduction and inserts for a shapelier calf. Cosmetic dental surgery, a specialism all its own, offers dental implants to fill the gaps; straightening and whitening procedures to correct the imperfections; and porcelain tooth veneers to just cover up. This list of interventions is by no means exhaustive, and new procedures are arriving on the market all the time.

Meanwhile, there are throngs of people, list metaphorically in hand, crowding to this particular marketplace to shop. For example, according to the British Association of Aesthetic Plastic Surgeons (BAAPS), in 2007 a total of 32,453 surgical procedures were performed by its members. When compared with the total UK population, this figure is not large, but it is nevertheless 12.2 per cent larger than the figure the year before. Breaking down this statistic, also between 2006 and 2007 the number of face lifts rose by 36 per cent; eyelid operations by 13 per cent; and nose reshapings by 13 per cent.[29] These are examples of a pattern of consistent increase seen over the early years of our new millennium. Overall, from 2002 to 2007, there was a rise of 300 per cent in the number of people electing cosmetic surgery.[30] In those same five years, breast augmentation—the most popular cosmetic surgery procedure in the UK—increased by 275 per cent.[31] Although the huge majority of those presenting for surgery are female, the numbers of operations on men are showing a steady rise too, with some specific procedures greatly increasing in popularity. In 2007 rhinoplasty on men, or nose reshaping, increased by 36 per cent from the year

Figure 49   Tattoos and piercings, © Shredboy Studios / Shutterstock. Adornment
cut directly onto the skin: labial, naval and ear piercings, and tattoos.

before; liposuction increased by 18 per cent; and tummy tucks by 61 per cent.[32] None of
these statistics, furthermore, include either operations undertaken by surgeons who are not
members of BAAPS or those performed on Britons abroad, who sign up for medical tourism to take advantage of cheaper rates overseas. Adding these would significantly increase
the percentages. Furthermore, it is not just the number of operations that is rising; multiple

procedures are becoming more common. One of these is the 'mummy tuck', a post-partum tummy tuck, breast lift and liposuction combined. According to one source, BAAPS identifies new mothers as the fastest growing group wanting surgery.[33] To help with the all-over transformation that patients are beginning to request, 'Some surgeons have even taken to working in pairs, one taking on the face while the other handles the body.' Says a former BAAPS president, people have started to see cosmetic surgery as being little different from a trip to the salon.[34] Certainly, in a poll commissioned by *The Observer* in September 2003, 46 per cent of women aged twenty-five to thirty have had, or would consider having, cosmetic surgery.[35] Given the rise in the number of procedures undertaken since then, this figure can now only be higher.

Then there are the non-surgical cosmetic procedures, the injections of fillers and Botox that are designed to plump or smooth away the signs of aging, and microdermabrasion, which scours it away. The effects of these interventions last from a few months to a couple years, and then need to be performed again. Injected into the face to hide lines, furrows and thinness, dermal fillers do just what it says on the tin—or rather, on the syringe. Botox, a dilute solution of the botulinum toxin, works by paralysis, freezing the muscles so that wrinkles are flattened away. Injections to the face deaden the lines of age and expression; injections to the hands smooth away the batterings of life; application to the armpits and feet stop the body sweating.[36] As Botox and fillers can be administered by beauticians, who are not obliged to keep records in the way hospitals are, it is impossible to know with any accuracy just how many people use these products, just how often. However, it is certain that they greatly exceed the numbers who opt for the more invasive surgical interventions. For Hadley Freeman, deputy fashion editor of *The Guardian*, Botox is 'the encroaching tide' that 'has tsunamied the country'.[37]

Whatever the statistics that lie behind the industry's practice, in a very short time the idea of surgical and clinical aesthetic interventions has become a normalized one. Through media coverage, advertising, and the images of the famous for whom the results have been either successful or disastrous, the possibility of body modification is ever present. And this is without our own personal experiences, or the stories reported through our networks of acquaintances and friends of friends. The ubiquity of at least the concept of physical alteration hides from us a rather large historical irony. One common response to clothes worn by previous generations is a kind of bewildered amazement at their 'unnaturalness'. As we have seen, garments sometimes worked without particular reference to the body's shape beneath; they perhaps constricted or exaggerated a portion of the anatomy; and very often the properties of the cloth from which they were constructed intruded into the performance of wearing. Today clothing is made very differently. Our garments are put on and off easily, and form a flexible adaptive envelope that demands far less of its wearer. Nowadays dress does not markedly disguise, constrain or alter the body's contours; nowadays these contours are defined by the scalpel. The aesthetic work, the 'unnaturalness', has become embodied: eyes widened, fat removed, sagging tightened and wrinkles smoothed, we take our selves and we improve on nature (Figure 50). We may find the idea of false calves pushed down a pair of stockings amusing, but who laughs at calf implants inserted in the operating theatre?

It is probably pretty clear, however, that we need to scrutinize the idea of 'naturalness' more closely. It would be easy to set the purity of the body draped with cloth against the artificiality of a body altered by surgery, but it would be wrong. All adornment is a work of culture: tying a hair ribbon or wearing a pair of shoes is as much a cultural intervention as sucking out fat deposits under anaesthetic. Washed, fed and dressed, by the time the body reports ready for duty it is hopelessly compromised by 'unnaturalness'.[38] For all that, however, a corset and a mummy tuck are not the same kind of thing. They may both be cultural interventions that affect the body, but to deny the palpable differences would be as misleading as to falsely range them on opposing sides of the nature–culture divide. How, then, does concentrating on the body as the site of fashioning differ from taking garments as the focus of the fashion project?

Most immediately noticeable is the degree to which the rise of the surgical industry has led to the body becoming commodified. It is marketed, sold and sliced up, just like any other object. Advertising techniques heavily reinforce the message. Images of ideal bodies with a price tag attached to every perfected part clearly spell out the message that you, too, can buy yourself a physique like the one pictured.[39] Prospective shoppers are encouraged with 'buy now, pay later' deals, a range of finance options, and discount offers on featured

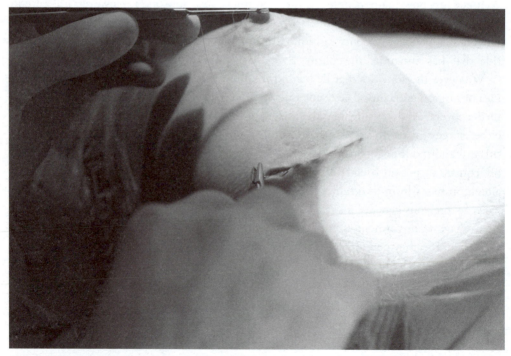

Figure 50   Cosmetic surgery, © Tomas Hlavacek / Shutterstock. Surgeon sewing the wound in a breast augmentation operation.

procedures. Some providers hold out cash incentives if customers refer friends and family; and forget the book token—vouchers that can be redeemed against surgery are 'the perfect gift'.[40] The words used by purchasers of cosmetic surgery suggest that they have internalized this objectification of their body bits. As excited by the pleasures of ownership as young children impatiently tearing the paper from presents, those newly emerged from under the knife are eager to draw attention to their new anatomy. 'I want to show the world my new body', boasted celebrity Kerry Katona in an interview given after her extensive surgery. Of her breasts, which had previously fitted implants removed, and then an uplift, she explained, 'I can't stop feeling them and showing them off! ... I love showing my body off now and I'm whipping them out at every opportunity!' Highlighting the commercialized nature of her transformation, she answers possible critics bluntly: 'Sod them! Who wouldn't do it for free?'[41] The sentiments of high-profile Katona are echoed by other, more ordinary people. After travelling abroad for surgery costing £7,500—a breast uplift, implants, tummy tuck and vaginal tightening—Linda was thrilled with 'the new-improved me', and reported wanting 'to flaunt my new body'. Surgery, she said, 'made me a whole new woman'.[42] The words that Linda and Kerry chose to describe their experiences perfectly demonstrate what Alex Kuczynski, a journalist who has recently investigated the US cosmetic surgery industry, has found. In recent years, Kuczynski writes, 'women have begun to flaunt their surgery and revel in the artficiality'.[43]

As this last quote suggests, drawn along in the wake of commodification comes a curious paradox of authenticity. Concerns about the propensity of fashion to dissimulate are very old indeed. Articulated throughout the centuries is the awareness that clothing can be utilized to alter the body and that these alterations are—that word again—unnatural. Sometimes there is complaint about the particular contours of these changes. Some held that the shaping effected by corsets, for example, was a 'monstrous distortion', a 'hideous metamorphose' by which the garment is made to 'force the figure of the wearer into whatever form the artist'—or stay maker—'pleases'.[44] Others judged that high waists 'rendered the women ill-made' and made them all '*hump-backed*'.[45] At other times anxieties hover around the misleading nature of the sartorial work itself. For garments that constrict or exaggerate can hide a multitude of imperfections, padding creates a shape not otherwise given to the wearer, and prosthetic additions to the body simulate a reality that, when they are removed, proves to be false. What does the hoop petticoat hide, speculates one comic poem:

> Within the Shelter of thy useful Shade
> The pregnant *Flora* passes for a Maid;
> Thin *Galatea*'s shrivel'd Limbs appear
> As plump and juicy as they did last year;
> Whilst tall *Miranda* her lank Shape improves,
> And, grac'd by thee, in some proportion moves.[46]

More viciously, a treatise of 1600 makes the same point, condemning whorish women for their 'periwigs, vardingals [farthingales], false bodies, trunk sleeues [sleeves], spanish white, pomatoes, oyles, powders [all cosmetics], and other glozing fooleries too long to bee recounted'. These

> doe disguise their first naturall shape, onely sophistically to seeme fayre vnto the out-
> warde views of tame and vundiscreete woodcocks [the gullible]. Yet notwithstanding,
> lette a man beholde them at night or in the morning, and hee shall finde them more
> vgly and lothsome then before.[47]

Articulated here, and in many other similar sources, is a perception of fashion as a lie that deceives the viewer. The wearer is inauthentic and a cheat.

By contrast, the position we have reached with regard to cosmetic surgery visualizes the altered body as *more* authentic. Intervention gives us not our ideal body, but the one we should have had all along if only nature had had the nouse to organize things differently. Surgery makes us real and complete. Thus, after her operation, Linda said it was the first time in many years that she had felt like 'a proper woman'—this despite the fact that it was the physical results of bearing four children that she wanted to eradicate.[48] Katona's surgery was filmed for her MTV show called, with no apparent irony, *Whole Again*.[49] And Emma Haws, who had a breast enlargement in 2002, was delighted with the results: 'For years I've been unhappy with what nature has given me ... Now I'm so happy. My boobs look natural and clothes fit me so much better.' She admitted that she had 'blank spots' on her breasts where she had no sensation, but that this was a small price to pay 'for feeling normal'. As she summed up the whole experience: 'I've finally got the body I should have had—and it feels great.'[50] Artificiality as a means of self-actualization may be paradoxical, but it is a powerful driver in decisions to buy a new appearance. Perhaps, because these alterations occur subcutaneously and cannot be taken off, they achieve the status of reality denied the deceptions practised by mere garments. A penile enlargement incorporates what the codpiece could only suggest. And while a padded bra gets dropped on the bedroom floor, a silicone insert is for life—or at least until the next operation is required, something that will be necessary in anything from 'a few years to a few decades'.[51]

One result of identifying the authentic self with the post-operative one is that it binds an individual's identity closer to his or her physical looks. Whereas those who fashion them-selves without clinical or surgical interventions in some degree assert the independence of character from body, believing the reshaped anatomy to be the real 'me' reduces the scope of that 'me' and ties it more firmly to appearance.[52] Ironically, doing so leaves the subject of surgery more vulnerable to the insecurities or dissatisfactions that prompted the surgery in the first place. Given this, the growing number signing up for multiple procedures or ongoing treatments is unsurprising. According to one plastic surgery professional, 'There's an increasing realization that it's not just one aspect of your appearance that is inadequate. Unattractive teeth will still ruin your face even if you have a nose job.'[53] Like sawing a wobbly table leg, an intervention here often shows up the 'need' for an intervention there. Added to this, the industry has now 'found more and more procedures a person can have, giving them complexes about parts of the body heretofore rarely considered'.[54] It is commonly accepted that body dysmorphia—acute dissatisfaction with one's body image that has no basis in observable reality—is on the rise. It is perfectly conceivable that this rise is linked to our emphasis on the body in general, and the influence of cosmetic surgery in particular.

The tendency of such body work to bind the subject more closely still to its enterprise, leads to recurrent and repeated interventions. Like the persistent touching of a sore spot, it proves very difficult to leave well alone. Little wonder then, the degree to which the language of addiction is used in connection with the quest for the authentic and deserved body. Scholarly critiques talk in terms of 'cosmetic surgery junkies' and the 'surgical fix',[55] and Alex Kuczynski's whole investigative appraisal of the industry—*Beauty Junkies*—is structured about this paradigm. When asked in an interview whether she was tempted by more surgery 'despite knowing you could die on the operating table', Kerry Katona replied unequivocally: 'Absolutely, I'd love liposuction on my legs—I'm addicted now!'[56]

Although there is nothing intrinsic to the enterprise that dictates that this should be so, the appearance that aesthetic surgery and its related non-surgical procedures is currently committed to reproducing is a very particular one. Anything wrinkled, lumpy, too small or too big, is out. Only the 'right' breasts, noses, eyelids, vaginas—one can substitute virtually any body part here—are acceptable. More and more it is an aesthetic that reduces the variety of nature and herds us towards a loss of individual difference. This is 'eugenics-lite',[57] where not conforming to the ideal has become something that has to be fixed. Whether it's the wrong sort of nipples, an insufficiently pert bottom, or—with a whole extra tangle of complex but unexamined moral issues—eyes that look too Asian or the distinctive features of Down's syndrome sufferers, the drive is to 'correct' the faulty.[58] Moreover, not only is the norm being defined against increasingly narrow parameters, it is being defined in spite of what is naturally possible. Thus the ideal of large bouncing breasts attached to a slender torso and slim hips is, by natural standards, a bit of a freak. A woman without fat deposits on her belly and thighs is unlikely to have the subcutaneous wherewithal to manage a large bust, and it will certainly not remain pointing cheerily skywards when she lies down.[59] Similarly impossible is a face that shows no lines or wrinkles, and has trouble registering the finer nuances of emotion. This is an insistent redefinition of the norm as something that in reality is only attainable by surgical or clinical intervention, and it results in such featureless uniformity that attempts to perceive distinguishing differences simply slide off its Teflon-coated surface.

In this respect it is not the invasiveness of surgery that marks its difference from dress, but its drive to homogeneity and, allied to that, its secretive nature. In fashion, clothes—and piercings and tattoos, incidentally—usually work to express individuality, albeit within conformity to a general look. No one wants to be dressed identically, and indeed, uniform is a sartorial shorthand for an individual's fascistic loss of autonomy. Moreover, the point of clothes is that they advertise themselves; they draw attention to what they are and how they interact with the body they adorn. As interventions, they clearly privilege the cultural over the relatively dull state of the natural, unadorned canvas. 'Clothing', to use art historian

Anne Hollander's words, 'hides the commonness of nakedness; and so, by all its variable creative means, it produces the quality of individuality—all the mysteries of uncommon-ness, all the distinctions of quality and mode.'[60] Cosmetic surgery, as we understand it, does nothing like this. It is the champion of naked uniformity. It works to reduce individu-ality and it aims as much as possible to hide the evidence of its own involvement. No mat-ter how unlikely the anatomical end product, it must seem as though nature, unassisted, doled it out. Thus, while our desire to shape our appearance according to the dominant aesthetic is the same as it has ever been, our means of achieving this, and the ramifications of our interventions, have become very different. Thanks to cosmetic surgery that peels, pins, lifts and tucks, our skin, like cloth, is cut, sewn and tailored to perfection. But, as currently constituted, it is a dead-end aesthetic without the creativity, variety or outward-looking energy that characterizes the previous centuries of fashionable dress.

Standing in the early years of the twenty-first century and looking in the mirror, one is left with a sense of the anatomy as being strangely malleable. Individuals certainly feel the intransigence of their corporeal form but, as revealed in cultural practice, there is a fluidity to our bodies. Bone, sinew and fat have become like modelling clay that can be compressed here, extended there, to make a new and 'better' self. Ironically, however, while our ability to transform our bodies is greater than ever, aesthetically we are becoming stuck in a nor-mative straitjacket which is reducing our imagination and our range of looks. Our focus on the body as the site of our endeavours has led to a fashioning of the physical; however, dress can do more. Dress can transform the mind.

NOTES

PROLOGUE

1. This anecdote comes from one of her three books of reminiscences: Dorothy Nevill, *Under Five Reigns*, 2nd edn (Methuen, 1910), pp. 337–8.

2. *Taine's Notes on England,* trans. Edward Hyams (Thames and Hudson, 1957), pp. 19, 20.

3. Lucy Johnston with Marion Kite and Helen Persson, *Nineteenth-Century Fashion in Detail* (V&A, 2005), p. 126.

4. See Johnston, *Nineteenth-Century Fashion,* p. 122; *Fashion: A History from the 18th to the 20th Century,* i: *18th and 19th Century* (Taschen, 2006), p. 238.

5. See Johnston, *Nineteenth-Century Fashion,* p. 128.

6. On the exploitation of workers in the clothing trade in the nineteenth and early twentieth centuries, see Elizabeth Wilson and Lou Taylor, *Through the Looking Glass: A History of Dress from 1860 to the Present Day* (BBC Books, 1989), pp. 33–4, 68–71. For more recent exploitative practices in Britain, see Barbro Hoel, 'Contemporary Clothing "Sweatshops", Asian Female Labour and Collective Organisation', in Jackie West, ed., *Work, Women and the Labour Market* (Routledge and Kegan Paul, 1982), pp. 80–98, and Annie Phizacklea, *Unpacking the Fashion Industry: Gender, Racism, and Class in Production* (Routledge, 1990). In addition, there is a growing literature addressing the conditions of workers in the globalized market of today, including Andrew Ross, ed., *No Sweat: Fashion, Free Trade, and the Rights of Garment Workers* (Verso, 1997), and Jane Lou Collins, *Threads: Gender, Labor, and Power in the Global Apparel Industry* (University of Chicago Press, 2003).

7. By way of a few examples: Robin Bryer, *The History of Hair: Fashion and Fantasy Down the Ages* (London: Philip Wilson Publishers, 2000), contrasts the 'elegance' of the close of the eighteenth century with the 'excess' and 'ridiculous extremes' of earlier styles (pp. 63–4, 67, 71). Also on big hair, Angela Rosenthal, the guest editor of *Eighteenth-Century Studies* 38/1 (Fall 2004), draws uncritically on earlier scholarship, perpetuating the image of rather disgusting extremity. In 'Raising Hair', she writes that powdered styles were 'plastered', 'greased' and 'often inhabited by lice, caged birds, or other creatures, all bedecked with (bottled) flowers, and toys of all imaginable kind' (pp. 9–10). Elizabeth Wilson describes fashionable dress from the fifteenth century as 'fantastical and absurd' in *Adorned in Dreams: Fashion and Modernity* (London: Virago, 1985), p. 118; and G.R. Elton, *England Under the Tudors*, 3rd edn (London, 1991), calls breeches 'enormous (and very unsightly)', says bodices were so tightly laced they squeezed the vital organs, and described dandies in 'idiotically tall hats and high heels' as

infesting the court (p. 435). A National Portrait Gallery exhibition catalogue states that 'Really tight lacing damaged internal organs' in the Victorian period. It also describes 'the most extreme excesses of eighteenth-century artificiality', including false eyebrows of mouse fur (a thing I have only ever seen referenced in satirical contexts, and then very rarely), and hair styles 'greased with lard' that 'attracted mice and insects' and caused a few wearers 'to be burnt to death when their hair was set alight by candelabras': *The Pursuit of Beauty: Five Centuries of Body Adornment in Britain*, text by Clare Gittings (London: NPG, 1997), [n.p.]. In *Dress in the Age of Elizabeth I* (London: Batsford, 1988), Jane Ashelford talks of the 'bizarre silhouette' of the dress at the end of the period (p. 11).

8. The art historian Anne Hollander has written very cogently on these issues. See, in particular, *Sex and Suits* (New York: Alfred A. Knopf, 1994 / New York, Tokyo, and London: Kodansha International, 1995), pp. 24–9, and *Feeding the Eye: Essays* (University of California Press, 1999), pp. 105–14. Also on the lack of inherent meaning in dress, see Valerie Steele, 'Appearance and Identity', in Claudia Brush Kidwell and Valerie Steele, eds, *Men and Women: Dressing the Part* (Washington, DC: Smithsonian Institute Press, 1989), p. 6.

9. Joanne Entwhistle, *The Fashioned Body: Fashion, Dress and Modern Social Theory* (Cambridge: Polity, 2000), p. 65. For Entwhistle's account of the shortcomings of explanatory theories of fashion, see pp. 57–71.

CHAPTER I

1. It seems that James and Charles II also took their time about it: Pepys does not record seeing them dressed in a wig until 15 February and 18 April 1664, respectively. *The Diary of Samuel Pepys,* ed. Robert Latham and William Matthews (London: G. Bell, 1970–83), V, pp. 49, 126 (hereinafter *Diary*).

2. The entries that chart Pepys's gradual progress towards wig wearing are *Diary,* II, p. 97, 11 May 1661; IV, p. 130, 9 May 1663; IV, p. 290, 29 August 1663; IV, p. 343, 21 October 1663; IV, p. 350, 26 October 1663; IV, p. 357, 30 October 1663; IV, pp. 357–8, 31 October 1663; IV, p. 360, 2 November 1663; IV, p. 362, 3 November 1663; IV, p. 363, 4 November 1663; IV, p. 369, 8 November 1663; IV, p. 378, 11 November 1663.

3. Elizabeth Wilson, *Adorned in Dreams: Fashion and Modernity* (London: Virago, 1985), pp. 5–6. Wilson goes on, 'To dress fashionably is both to stand out and to merge with the crowd, to lay claim to the exclusive and to follow the herd'. Joanne Entwhistle, *The Fashioned Body: Fashion, Dress and Modern Social Theory* (Cambridge: Polity, 2000), p. 139, similarly remarks, 'The individual may want to "stand out" but she or he also wants to "fit in" with a group'.

4. *Diary*, VI, p. 97, 5 May 1665.

5. Ibid.,VI, p. 74, 6 April 1665, Pepys takes a wig to the barber to be mended.

6. Ibid., IV, p. 363, 4 November 1663.

7. Ibid., V, p. 212, 18 July 1664; also VIII, p. 133, 27 March 1667, and VIII, p. 146, 4 April 1667.

8. Ibid., IX, p. 217, 30 May 1668.

9. *Diary*, VI, p. 210, 3 September 1665.

10. Lynn Festa, 'Personal Effects: Wigs and Possessive Individualism in the Long Eighteenth Century', *Eighteenth-Century Life*, 29/2 (2005), p. 47. Scholars who have considered the wig's ambivalence as a commodity and its complexity as a cultural signifier include Festa, ibid., and Marcia Pointon, 'The Case of the Dirty Beau: Symmetry, Disorder and the Politics of Masculinity', in Kathleen Adler and Marcia Pointon, eds, *The Body Imaged: The Human Form and Visual Culture since the Renaissance* (Cambridge: Cambridge University Press, 1993), pp. 175–89. Pointon repeats and expands her argument in Marcia Pointon, *Hanging the Head: Portraiture and Social Formation in Eighteenth-Century England* (New Haven and London: Yale University Press, 1993), pp. 107–39. Whether or not contemporary individuals actually experienced, or were troubled by, the polyvalent complexities described in such works is a moot point.

11. We do know that Samuel's wife, Elizabeth, had hairpieces made of her own hair. *Diary*, III, p. 51, 24 March 1662.

12. R. Campbell, *The London tradesman. Being a compendious view of all the trades, professions, arts, both liberal and mechanic, now practised in the cities of London and Westminster* (London, 1747), p. 205.

13. James Stewart, *Plocacosmos: or the whole art of hair dressing* (London, 1782), pp. 184, 302.

14. Georgiana Sitwell, *The Dew, It Lyes on the Wood, Reminiscences of Georgiana Caroline Sitwell*, in *Two Generations*, ed. Osbert Sitwell (London: Macmillan, 1940), p. 3.

15. 'A-List Beauty Treatments—Are They Really Worth It?', *Reveal*, Issue 43 (25–31 October 2008), p. 61.

16. For example, Monsieur de Maisse, Henri IV's ambassador to England, described Elizabeth wearing 'a great reddish-coloured wig'. André Hurault, Sieur de Maisse, *A Journal of All That Was Accomplished by Monsieur de Maisse Ambassador in England,* trans. and ed. G. B. Harrison (London: Nonesuch Press, 1931), p. 25. Paul Hentzner, travelling in England in 1598, also visited the English court. He wrote that Elizabeth, in her sixty-fifth year, had hair 'of an auburn colour, but false'. William Brenchley Rye, ed., *England as Seen by Foreigners in the Days of Elizabeth and James the First* (London: John Russell Smith, 1865), p. 104.

17. *The annual register or a view of the history, politics, and literature, for the year 1765,* 4th edn (London, 1784), p. 64. On the extent to which wigs were also common for more plebeian wearers, see John Styles, *The Dress of the People: Everyday Fashion in Eighteenth-Century England* (New Haven and London: Yale University Press, 2007), pp. 58, 65, 86.

18. Dorothy Nevill, *Leaves from the Notebooks of Lady Dorothy Nevill*, ed. Ralph Nevill (London: Macmillan, 1907), p. 268.

19. *Correspondence of Sarah Spencer, Lady Lyttelton 1787–1870*, ed. Hon. Mrs Hugh Wyndham (London, John Murray, 1912), pp. 348–9, letter written in September 1844.

20. *The Times* (Wednesday 18 March 1925), p. 10, col. E; (Friday 20 March 1925), p. 10, col. E; Saturday 21 March 1925), p. 10, col. C; (Monday 23 March 1925), p. 10, cols. F–G; (Thursday 26 March 1925), p. 12, col. E; (Saturday 28 March 1925), p. 8, col. D.

21. Nevill, *Leaves from the Notebooks,* p. 269.

22. *The Letters and Journals of Lady Mary Coke,* ed. J. A. Home, 4 vols (1889–96; facsimile repr. Bath: Kingsmead Reprints, 1970), II, pp. 112–13, Friday 14 July 1769. John Beresford, ed., *Memoirs of an Eighteenth-Century Footman: John Macdonald Travels (1745–1779)* (London: George Routledge and Sons, 1927; facsimile repr. Routledge Curzon, 2005; orig pub, 1790), p. 91.

23. Stewart, *Plocacosmos,* p. 204.

24. Ibid., p. 204. For descriptions of many eighteenth-century wigs, see C. Willett Cunnington and Phillis Cunnington, *Handbook of English Costume in the Eighteenth Century,* rev. edn (London: Faber, 1972), pp. 89–96.

25. J. T. Smith, *Nollekens and his Times* (London: Turnstile Press, 1949), pp. 163–4, first published in 2 vols in 1828. Whitefoord (1734–1810) was also a wine merchant and diplomat.

26. *The Memoirs of Richard Cumberland,* ed. Richard Dircks, 2 vols in 1 (New York: AMS Press, 2002; first published 1806, 2nd edn 1807), I, p. 109.

27. David Ritchie, *A treatise on the hair: … also a description of the most fashionable methods of dressing ladies and gentlemens hair* (London: printed for the author and sold by him at this shop, 1770), p. 47.

28. *Diary,* VIII, p. 136, 29 March 1667.

29. *The wig. A burlesque-satirical poem* (London, 1765).

30. William Roberts, *Memoirs of the Life and Correspondence of Mrs. Hannah More,* 4 vols (London, 1834), II, p. 112.

31. Ritchie, *A treatise,* p. 46.

32. *The Spectator,* ed., Donald F. Bond, 5 vols (Oxford: Clarendon Press, 1965), II, pp. 91–2, No. 150, Wednesday 22 August 1711. On *The Spectator* and *The Tatler* and the relationship of these periodicals to the emerging bourgeois ethic, see Erin Mackie, *Market à la Mode: Fashion, Commodity, and Gender in the Tatler and the Spectator* (Baltimore and London: Johns Hopkins University Press, 1997).

33. *Letters and Journals of Lady Mary Coke,* II, p. 203, Monday 29 February 1768; III, p. 136, Thursday 17 August 1769; p. III, 282, Friday 7 September 1770; p. IV, 406, Wednesday 28 September 1774.

34. In 1782, hairdresser James Stewart, *Plocacosmos,* p. 203, claimed that the very large wigs of Restoration fashion cost 100 guineas. Clearly this is a very much larger sum than the £3 that Pepys paid.

35. Smith, *Nollekens and his Times,* p. 237. This method of stealing wigs is also mentioned in Book III of John Gay's mock georgic poem, 'Trivia, or the Art of Walking the Streets of London': 'Nor is thy flaxen wig with safety worn; / High on the shoulder in a basket borne / Lurks the sly boy, whose hand, to rapine bred, / Plucks off the curling honours of thy head'; Martin Price, ed., *The Restoration and the Eighteenth Century,* The Oxford Anthology of English Literature (New York and London: Oxford University Press, 1973), p. 479.

36. For example, Jane Ashelford, *The Art of Dress: Clothes and Society 1500–1914* (London: National Trust, 1996), p. 94, who also quotes from John Gay's satirical poem 'Trivia, or the art of walking the streets of London' (1716), which describes the same trick. Also Liza Picard, *Dr Johnson's London: Everyday Life in London 1740–1770* (London: Phoenix, 2003; orig. pub. 2000), pp. 133–4.

37. *Old Common Sense; or, the Englishman's Journal,* No. 51 (Saturday 21 January 1738).

38. *The London Journal,* No. 161 (25 August 1722).

39. In August 1789. Cited in Pointon, *Hanging the Head,* p. 120.

40. *The London Journal* (Saturday 10 June 1721), p. 5.

41. Mary K. Gayne, 'Illicit Wigmaking in Eighteenth-Century Paris', *Eighteenth-Century Studies* 38/1 (2004), p. 121. My thanks to Dr Mark Jenner for drawing my attention to this *Eighteenth-Century Studies* special issue.

42. Tho. Barker, *At the Blue Peruke in Red-Lion-street, White-Chappel, liveth Tho. Barker, peruke-maker, who maketh all sorts of new work, well and fashionable, at very low prices ...* [London, 1725?], ESTC T160623.

43. Ritchie, *A treatise,* p. 82.

44. Sydney Smith, *The Works of the Rev. Sydney Smith* (London: Longmans, Green, Reader and Dyer, 1869), p. 805.

45. *Diary,* VI, p. 89, 24 and 25 April 1665.

46. *Court and Private Life in the Time of Queen Charlotte: Being the Journals of Mrs. Papendiek, Assistant Keeper of the Wardrobe and Reader to Her Majesty,* ed. Mrs Vernon Delves Broughton, 2 vols (London: Richard Bentley, 1887), pp. I, 284, 1787.

47. *Reminiscences of Georgiana Caroling Sitwell,* p. 5.

48. John Taylor, *Records of My Life,* 2 vols (London, 1832), I, p. 49. Reddish died in 1785, aged just fifty years. He first began to display mental health problems about ten years before his death.

49. Eliza Haywood, *The Female Spectator,* 4 vols (London, 1745 [1746]), III, Bk. 13 p. 21. Boswell quoted in Pointon, *Hanging the Head,* p. 120. Papendiek, *Journals,* II, p. 218.

50. Scholars are divided over the authenticity of such writings. For example, Rhoda Zuk, 'The Courtesan's Progress in the Late 1790s: Elizabeth Gooch and Margaret Coghlan', *Women's Writing* 11/3 (2004), p. 375 at n. 18, states that Ann Sheldon and Margaret Leeson were 'obviously fictional courtesans'. By contrast, the *Oxford Dictionary of National Biography,* online edition, contains a whole entry on the latter and draws heavily on her memoirs for its content (*s.v.* 'Leeson, Margaret'). Lynda M. Thompson, *The 'Scandalous Memoirists': Constantia Phillips, Laetitia Pilkington and the Shame of 'Publick Fame'* (Manchester and New York: Manchester University Press, 2000), p. 123, discusses the relationship of such texts with fiction and reality, the emerging novel, and the contemporary use of the nom de plume. Thompson concludes that 'later careful research has generally substantiated the memoirists' version of events'. For our purposes, it is less relevant who wrote these texts; more important are the

cultural understandings and assumptions they reveal. As Thompson notes (p. 124), even while charging the authors with lying or exaggerating, contemporaries simultaneously stated that the memoirs represented 'their times with accuracy'. There is no doubt at all about the existence of Sophia Baddeley, an actress and singer of fame. The real identity of her biographer, Elizabeth Steele, is less certain.

51. *Authentic and Interesting Memoirs of Miss Ann Sheldon*, 4 vols (London, 1787–8), IV, pp. 17–18.

52. *The Life of Mrs Margaret Leeson, alias Peg Plunket* (Dublin, 1798), pp. 169–72; first published in 1795–7 as *Memoirs of Mrs. Margaret Leeson. Written by Herself*. Of added significance in this anecdote is the relatively lowly status of the wig's style—a brown bob—and also the wig's wearer.

53. Elizabeth Steele, *The Memoirs of Sophia Baddeley*, 6 vols (London, 1787), I, pp. 133–6 (my emphasis). Note that this was not the famous Holland House acquired by Henry Fox (created Lord Holland), which remained in his family and was to be of such political and social importance; rather, it was a property briefly owned by Fox, which he sold to Melbourne for £16,500 on 31 March–1 April 1771. Peniston Lamb (First Viscount Melbourne and father of William Lamb, the Prime Minister) pulled the house down and built Melbourne House on the site. See *Survey of London: Volumes 31 and 32: St James Westminster, Part 2* (1963), 'Albany', pp. 367–89, http://www.british-history.ac.uk/report.asp?compid=41481, accessed 11 May 2007.

54. On eighteenth-century polite society, see Lawrence E. Klein, *Shaftesbury and the Culture of Politeness: Moral Discourse and Cultural Politics in Early Eighteenth-Century England* (Cambridge: Cambridge University Press, 1994), esp. pp. 3–8, and Peter Borsay, 'The Culture of Improvement', in Paul Langford, ed., *The Eighteenth Century* (Oxford: Oxford University Press, 2002), pp. 183–210.

55. For a discussion of this practice, see Margaret K. Powell and Joseph Roach, 'Big Hair', *Eighteenth-Century Studies*, 38/1 (2004), pp. 79–99.

56. *The Gentleman's Magazine* 44 (1774), p. 588 (hereinafter *GM*).

57. For example, Frederick George Stephens and Mary Dorothy George, eds, *Catalogue of Personal and Political Satires Preserved in the Department of Prints and Drawings in the British Museum*, 11 vols in 16 (London: British Museum, 1870–1954), V, nos. 5370, 5371, 5373, 5436, 5442, 5448, 5449, 5462.

58. Roberts, *Memoirs of Mrs. Hannah More*, I, pp. 51–2, 1775; I, p. 65, 1776. *The Letters of Hannah More*, ed. R. Brimley Johnson (London: John Lane the Bodley Head, 1925), p. 57, 1777.

59. Roberts, *Memoirs*, I, p. 52, 1775.

60. *Recollections of the Table-Talk of Samuel Rogers*, ed. Rev. Alexander Dyce (New Southgate: H. A. Rogers, 1887), pp. 23–4.

61. *Letters and Journals of Lady Mary Coke*, IV, pp. 333–4, 1Monday 8 April 1774 (my emphasis).

62. Ibid., IV, p. 30, Thursday 20 February 1772; IV, p. 37, Monday 2 March 1772.

63. *Journals of Mrs. Papendiek,* II, p. 284, 1792.

64. Ibid., I, p. 137, *c.* 1780.

65. *The Journal of Mary Frampton,* ed. Harriot Georgiana Mundy (London, 1885), pp. 2–3.

66. Stewart, *Plocacosmos,* p. 265.

67. Stated in ibid., *Plocacosmos,* pp. 265–6. As well as giving minute instruction for haircare and styling in his treatise, Stewart described products that he supplied for sale, priced 'as reasonable as any shop or warehouse in London; or perhaps more so' (p. 351).

68. Ritchie, *A treatise,* p. 88. See also Alexander Ross, *A treatise on bear's grease, with observations, to prove how indispensible the use of that incomparablesubstance, to preserve the head of hair...* (London, 1795). For a discussion of the role of bear's grease, see John Barrell, *The Spirit of Despotism: Invasions of Privacy in the 1790s* (Oxford: Oxford University Press, 2006), pp. 145–7. My thanks to Dr Mark Jenner for drawing my attention to this latter text.

69. For example, see William Moore, *The art of hair-dressing* (Bath, [1780]), pp. 3, 7.

70. *The BSE Inquiry: The Report. The Inquiry into BSE and Variant CJD in the United Kingdom,* especially, http://www.bseinquiry.gov.uk/report/volume7/chapteb6.htm#415863 and http://www.bseinquiry.gov.uk/files/ws/s407.pdf, para. 4.vi)a, accessed 26 November 2008.

71. See, for example, Kim Erickson, *Drop-Dead Gorgeous: Protecting Yourself from the Hidden Dangers of Cosmetics* (Chicago: Contemporary Books, 2002).

72. For example, see the article on making starch from potatoes in *GM* 23 (1753), p. 575, and also the abstract of the Privy Council's report on grain, including the method for making starch from horse chestnuts, in *GM* 65 pt. 2 (1795), pp. 999–1006, at p. 1005. According to William Connor Sydney, *England and the English in the Eighteenth Century,* 2 vols, 2nd edn (London: Ward and Downey, 1892), I, p. 110, in 1796, Lord William Murray, son of the Duke of Athol, took out a patent for the extraction of starch from horse chestnuts.

73. Laws regulating the content of hair powder included 10 Anne, c. 19 § 33 (1711); 13 Anne, c. 18 § 20 (1713); 4 Geo. II, c. 14 § 5, 8 (1731).

74. Stewart, *Plocacosmos,* p. 266.

75. Ibid., pp. 321–2.

76. Roberts, *Memoirs,* p. 222, 17 January 1782.

77. On the corrosive nature of hair dye, see Moore, *Art of hair-dressing,* pp. 18–19; Ritchie, *A treatise,* p. 27; James Meikle, 'Shampoo 'Risk' to Unborn Babies', *The Guardian* (Monday 6 December 2004), http://www.guardian.co.uk/uk/2004/dec/06/research.science, accessed 26 November 2008; and Linda Geddes, 'Insecticides in Pet Shampoo May Trigger Autism', *New Scientist* (15 May 2008), http://www.newscientist.com/article/dn13905-insecticides-in-pet-shampoo-may-trigger-autism.html, accessed 28 November 2008.

78. *Journal of Mary Frampton,* p. 36.

79. The exact figure is 8,170,019.5 pounds. Barrell, *Spirit of Despotism,* p. 175.

80. For illustrations, see Cunnington and Cunnington, *Handbook of English Costume,* p. 259.

81. Stewart, *Plocacosmos,* p. 276.

82. Joanna McGarry, 'Dry Shampoos Do the Dirty Work for Hair', *The Sunday Times* (30 March 2008), http://women.timesonline.co.uk/tol/life_and_style/women/beauty/article3618747. ece, accessed 26 November 2008.

83. From the Nice Cream Company Web site, http://www.nicecreamcompany.com/index.php? main_page=product_info&cPath=1_6&products_id=280, accessed 22 May 2007. Bumble and bumble was established in 1977 with a single salon. It now has a chain of establishments and manufactures its own products.

84. On this cluster of meanings, see Barrell, *Spirit of Despotism,* pp. 185–94, and Georges Vigarello, *Concepts of Cleanliness: Changing Attitudes in France since the Middle Ages,* trans. Jean Birrell (Cambridge: Cambridge University Press, and Paris: Maison des Sciences de l'Homme, 1988), pp. 83–5.

85. *Journal of Mary Frampton,* p. 23, 1789.

86. *Greville's England: Selections from the Diaries of Charles Greville 1818–1860,* ed. Christopher Hibbert (London: Folio Society, 1981), p. 95, 8 September 1831.

87. A.M.W. Stirling, *The Letter-Bag of Lady Elizabeth Spencer Stanhope* (London: John Lane the Bodley Head, 1913), II, p. 100, letter dated 23 April 1825. Osbert Sitwell, *The Scarlet Tree* (London: Macmillan, 1946), p. 179.

88. On the whole notion of performance, particularly in relation to the styles of the 1770s, see Powell and Roach, 'Big Hair'.

89. Steele, *Memoirs,* IV, pp. 60–1. Presumably the actress in question is Ann Barry (bap. 1733, d. 1801).

90. *The Lady's Magazine,* 6 (1775), p. 351 (hereinafter *LM*).

91. Roberts, *Memoirs,* I, pp. 51–2, 1775.

92. Cited in Angela Rosenthal, 'Raising Hair', *Eighteenth-Century Studies,* 38/1 (2004), p. 10.

93. Stewart, *Plocacosmos,* p. 295.

94. Steele, *Memoirs,* III, p. 105.

95. *Journal of Mary Frampon,* p. 3.

96. Ritchie, *A treatise,* pp. 61–2, 80; Stewart, *Plocacosmos,* pp. 293–4, 313.

97. Stewart, *Plocacosmos,* p. 294. Ritchie, *A treatise,* pp. 49–50, says 'some months'.

98. Stewart, *Plocacosmos,* p. 294.

99. Rosenthal, 'Raising Hair', p. 10.

100. Stewart, *Plocacosmos,* pp. 258, 295–6.

101. Rosenthal, 'Raising Hair', p. 10.

102. Ritchie, *A treatise,* pp. 90–1.

103. Stewart, *Plocacosmos,* p. 292.

104. Ibid., p. 246.

105. *Journals of Mrs. Papendiek,* I, p. 173, sitting for Zoffany for her portrait (early 1783); I, p. 178, visit to court (1783); I, p. 185, a concert for the new Musical Fund (14 February 1783); I,

p. 199, christening of the Papendiek's eldest child (New Year's Day 1784); I, p. 222, attending a concert (1784); I, p. 237, attending a concert (1785); p. I, 292, attending a dance, but using the services of Mr Theilcke instead, with which she was less satisfied (1788); II, p. 171, Kead dresses Charlotte's cousin for a dance; II, p. 293, for a performance by Haydn, Kead charging 2 *s. 6d.*

106. Ibid., II, p. 5, 1788.
107. Cecil Beaton, *The Glass of Fashion* (London: Weidenfeld and Nicolson, 1954), pp. 13–14.
108. *Letters and Journals of Lady Mary Coke,* II, p. 303, Thursday 7 July 1768.
109. *Memoirs of an Eighteenth-Century Footman,* p. 113. Ritchie, *A treatise,* pp. iv, 38–9, writes his manual partly for ladies and gentlemen in 'the remotest parts of the British empire', and he includes advice on how to preserve and manage hair in different climates.
110. *Memoirs of Richard Cumberland,* II, p. 14.
111. *Memoirs of an Eighteenth-Century Footman,* pp. 53–5.
112. Steele, *Memoirs,* p. 5.179.
113. Stewart, *Plocacosmos,* p. 246.
114. For discussion that interprets eighteenth-century hair as a Veblenesque marker of conspicuous leisure and waste, see Powell and Roach, 'Big Hair'. Thorstein Veblen, *The Theory of the Leisure Class* (New York: Transaction Publishers, 1992).
115. *Journals of Mrs. Papendiek,* I, p. 137–8, *c.* 1780.
116. *Jane Austen's Letters,* collected and ed. Deirdre Le Faye, 3rd edn (Oxford: Oxford University Press, 1995), p. 24, letter to Cassandra Austen, Saturday 1–Sunday 2 December 1798. See also Penelope Byrde, 'Dress and Fashion', in J. David Grey, ed., *The Jane Austen Handbook* (London: Athelone Press, 1986), p. 133, and G. E. Mitton, *Jane Austen and Her Times* (London: Metheun, 1905), pp. 230–2.
117. *GM* 3 (1733), p. 144.
118. *Journals of Mrs. Papendiek,* I, p. 137, *c.* 1780.
119. Ellis Pratt, *The art of dressing the hair. A poem* (Bath, 1770), p. 16, ll. pp. 235–44. Also Barrell, *Spirit of Despotism,* p. 152.
120. *The Life of Mrs. Margaret Leeson,* Introduction, pp. 17–18.
121. Phillip Stubbes, *The Anatomie of Abuses* (London, 1583), sig. D7v.
122. C. Willet Cunnington and Phillis Cunnington, *The History of Underclothes* (New York: Dover, 1992; orig. pub. London: Michael Joseph, 1951), p. 102 and note.
123. On 'Darcymania', see, for example, Sarah Cardwell, 'Darcy's Escape: An Icon in the Making', in Stella Bruzzi and Pamela Church Gibson, eds, *Fashion Cultures: Theories, Explorations and Analysis* (London and New York: Routledge, 2000), pp. 239–44.
124. *The Whole Art of Dress! or the Road to elegance and fashion … by a Cavalry Officer* (London, 1830), p. 23.
125. *Pückler's Progress: The Adventures of Prince Pückler-Muskau in England, Wales and Ireland as Told in Letters to His Former Wife,* trans. Flora Brennan (London: Collins, 1987), pp. 238, 239–30.

126. 'Who Starch'd Your Collar', printed by A. Ryle and Co., London, between 1845 and 1859, Harding B 11(4171), online at Bodleian Library Broadside Ballads, http://bodley24.bod ley.ox.ac.uk/cgi-bin/acwwweng/ballads/image.pl?ref=Harding+B+11(4171)&id=05106. gif&seq=1&size=1, accessed 26 November 2008.

127. Captain Jesse, *The Life of George Brummell, Esq, Commonly Called Beau Brummell*, rev. edn 2 vols (London: John C. Nimmo, 1886), I, p. 63.

128. R. H. Gronow, *Captain Gronow's Recollections and Anecdotes of the Camp, the Court, and the Clubs, at the Close of the Last War with France* (London, 1864), p. 52.

129. Ibid., p. 52. *Reminiscences of Georgiana Caroline Sitwel*, p. 127.

130. *Correspondence of Sarah Spenser*, p. 54, 21 December 1808; p. 62, 20 March 1809.

131. T. Moore, *The Fudge Family in Paris*, ed. Thomas Brown, 3rd edn (London, 1818), p. 5.

132. *Neckclothitania; or, Tietania: Being an Essay on Starchers by One of the Cloth* (London, 1818); H. Le Blanc, *The Art of Tying the Cravat*, 2nd edn (London, 1828); *Whole Art of Dress*. For a discussion of these texts, and related titles that appeared on the Continent, see Sarah Gibbings, *The Tie: Trends and Traditions* (London: Studio Editions, 1990), pp. 47–54.

133. We may, however, be seeing recent evidence that this paradigm is shifting; see e.g. the discussion in the review by Elaine Showalter, 'Fade to Greige', *London Review of Books*, (4 January 2001), http://www.lrb.co.uk/v23/n01/show01_.html, accessed 28 November 2008, and Richard Martin's introductory essay to Gianni Versace, *Men without Ties* (New York and London: Abbeville, 1997), pp. 7–31.

134. Stubbes, *Anatomie of Abuses*, sig. D7v–D8r.

135. Walter Vaughan, *An essay, philosophical and medical, concerning modern clothing* (1792), p. 56.

136. 'Tendency of Cravats to Produce Apoplexy', *The Times* (Thursday 25 December 1823), p. 3, col. D.

137. *Neckclothitania*, pp. 35–6. On the way a ruff obliges its wearer to hold his or her head, see Jackie Marshall-Ward, 'Mode and Movement', *Costume*, 34 (2000), pp. 123–8, at 126–7.

138. Jenny Tiramani, 'Janet Arnold and the Globe Wardrobe: Handmade Clothes for Shakespeare's Actors', *Costume*, 34 (2000), pp. 118–22, at p. 121. On all aspects of making and setting ruffs, see Janet Arnold, *Patterns of Fashion 4: the Cut and Construction of Linen Shirts, Smocks, Neckwear, Headwear and Accessories for Men and Women, c.1540–1660* (London: Macmillan, 2008).

139. *Harriette Wilson's Memoirs*, selected and ed. Lesley Branch (London: Folio Society, 1964), p. 45.

140. *Pückler's Progress*, p. 121, 5 June 1827.

141. Tiramani, 'Janet Arnold and the Globe Wardrobe', p. 121.

142. Ibid., p. 121.

143. Stubbes, *Anatomie of Abuses*, sig. D8v, F4v–F5r.

144. On sumptuary legislation, see Wildred Hooper, 'The Tudor Sumptuary Laws', *English Historical Review*, 30 (1915), pp. 433–49; Frances Baldwin, *Sumptuary Legislation and Personal Regulation in England* (Baltimore: Johns Hopkins University Press, 1926); Alan Hunt, *Gov-*

ernance of the Consuming Passions: A History of Sumptuary Law (London: Macmillan, 1996); Susan Vincent, *Dressing the Elite: Clothes in Early Modern England* (Oxford and New York: Berg, 2003), pp. 117–52.

145. Paul Hughes and James Larkin, eds, *Tudor Royal Proclamations,* 3 vols (New Haven: Yale University Press, 1969), II, p. 187, proclamation 6 May 1562, no. 493; II, p. 462, proclamation 12 February 1580, no. 646 (hereinafter *TRP*).

146. *Pückler's Progress,* p. 239, 3 January 1829.

147. Joan Thirsk, *Economic Policy and Projects: The Development of a Consumer Society in Early Modern England* (Oxford: Clarendon Press, 1978), p. 85.

148. James Larkin and Paul Hughes, eds, *Stuart Royal Proclamations*, vol. 1, *Royal Proclamations of King James I, 1603–1625* (Oxford: Oxford University Press, 1973), p. 163, no. 75, 23 August 1607 (hereinafter *SRP*).

149. See Thirsk, *Economic Policy and Projects,* pp. 86, 91–2.

150. *SRP,* I, p. 238, no. 107, 10 January 1610.

151. Robert Plot, *The Natural History of Oxford-shire* (Oxford and London, 1677), pp. 280–1. Thirsk, *Economic Policy and Projects,* pp. 84–5.

152. On the fire hazard, see Thirsk, *Economic Policy and Projects,* p. 92. On health concerns see e.g. James's proclamations of 23 August 1607, *SRP,* I, p. 164, no. 75; 22 August 1610, *SRP,* p. 251, no. 112; and 5 May 1620, *SRP,* p. 473, no. 200.

153. Quoted in Thirsk, *Economic Policy and Projects,* p. 88.

154. Thomas Nash, *Pierce Pennilesse his supplication to the diuell* (London, 1592), sig. C2v. See also John Udall's attack in his sermon, *The True Remedie against Famine and Warres ... Preached in the Time of Dearth. 1586,* 2nd edn (1588), p. 27, against the vanity that lead 'thousands of quarters of the purest wheat, which God ordeined for the food of man' to be 'yearlie couuerted [converted] into that most deuelish deuice of Startch'.

155. *SRP,* I, pp. 163–4, no. 75, 23 August 1607.

156. *SRP,* I, p. 163, no. 75, 23 August 1607. For Elizabeth's proclamations, see *TRP,* III, nos. 781, 794, 812. For a summary of regulation in the Elizabethan and Jacobean periods, see Thirsk, *Economic Policy and Projects,* pp. 88–91.

157. *SRP,* I, p. 473, no. 200, 5 May 1620.

158. Ibid., I, p. 165 n. 2.

159. Barrell, *Spirit of Despotism,* p. 182.

160. Ibid., p. 175.

161. Septimus Hodson, *An address to the different classes of persons in Great Britain on the present scarcity and high price of provisions* (London, 1795), p. 26.

162. Pratt, *Art of dressing the hair,* p. 13, ll. 185–6.

163. Barrell, *Spirit of Despotism,* p. 171.

164. 35 Geo. III, c. 49 (1795). A similar measure was proposed ten years earlier, in 1785, by the Earl of Surrey, but was opposed by Pitt; see *Cobbett's Parliamentary History of England* 25, cols 814–20; also reported in the parliamentary proceedings of *GM* 55 (1785), pp. 864–6.

165. 36 Geo. III, c. 6 (1795).

166. For a detailed analysis of the hair powder tax and its political context, see Barrell, *Spirit of Despotism,* pp. 145–209.

167. *The Times* (Friday 9 September 1796), p. 3, col. B.

168. For these figures, see Barrell, *Spirit of Despotism,* pp. 206–7.

169. Sir N. William Wraxall, *Historical Memoirs of My Own Time* (London: Kegan Paul, Trench, Trubner, 1904; orig. pub. in 2 vols. in 1815), p. 84.

170. *LM* 23 (1792), p. 567.

171. Quoted in G. E. Mingay, ed., *The Agrarian History of England and Wales,* vol 6: *1750–1850* (Cambridge: Cambridge University Press, 1989), p. 399.

172. 40 Geo. III, c. 25 (1800); 52 Geo. III, c. 127 (1812); 53 Geo. III, c. 2 (1812); 53 Geo. III, c. 23 (1813).

CHAPTER 2

1. J[ohn] B[ulwer], *Anthropometamorphosis: man transform'd: or, the artificiall changling historically presented* (London, 1653), pp. 536–7.

2. Frederick George Stephens and Mary Dorothy George, eds, *Catalogue of Personal and Political Satires Preserved in the Department of Prints and Drawings in the British Museum* (British Museum, 1870–1954), VII, nos. 8569, 8570. On this print, see Amanda Vickery, *The Gentleman's Daughter: Women's Lives in Georgian England* (New Haven and London: Yale University Press, 1998), pp. 178–9.

3. *LM* 49 (1818), p. 570. The humpback impression was probably strengthened by the high bustle or rolls worn underneath short-waisted dresses. The trope was common and recurred in different satirical contexts; see for example the 1801 song 'The Prevailing Fashions', in Frederick W. Fairholt, ed., *Satirical Songs and Poems on Costume from the 13th to the 19th Century* (London: Percy Society, 1849), p. 266, and *LM*, ns. 1 (1820), p. 100.

4. Both quoted in Norah Waugh, *Corsets and Crinolines* (London: Batsford, 1954), pp. 115, 117.

5. *The Times* (Thursday 19 September 1929), p. 16, col. E; (Wednesday 2 October 1929), p. 17, col. F.

6. Valerie Steele, *The Corset: A Cultural History* (New Haven: Yale University Press, 2001), pp. 152, 162.

7. Ibid., pp. 27, 48. Also Anne Hollander, *Sex and Suits* (New York: Alfred A. Knopf, 1994), p. 140; Leigh Summers, 'Yes, They Did Wear Them: Working-Class Women and Corsetry in the Nineteenth Century', *Costume,* 36 (2002), pp. 65–74; and on corsetry and plebeian women of the eighteenth century, John Styles, *The Dress of the People: Everyday Fashion in Eighteenth-Century England* (New Haven: Yale University Press, 2007), pp. 35–8, 42–3, 65, 72, 75, 283–4.

8. George More, *A true discourse concerning the certaine possession and dispossessio[n] of 7 persons in one familie in Lancashire* (1600), pp. 26–7.

9. Janet Arnold, *Queen Elizabeth's Wardrobe Unlock'd* (Leeds: Maney, 1988), p. 146. Sarcenet was a fine silk.

10. Pierre Erondelle, *The French garden: for English ladyes and gentlewomen to walke In,* 2nd edn (London, 1605), sig. [D8v]. Selections from the text have also been printed in M. St. Clare Byrne, ed., *The Elizabethan Home* (London: Methuen, 1949); see pp. 37–8 for this quote.

11. Elizabeth Stern, 'Peckover and Gallyard, Two Sixteenth-Century Norfolk Tailors', *Costume,* 15 (1981), pp. 13–23. The Bacons were a leading East Anglian Puritan family. Nathanial was son of Lord Keeper Sir Nicholas and half-brother to the eminent Francis.

12. On the pearl tied below Elizabeth's stomacher in the Armada Portrait, see Andrew Belsey and Catherine Belsey, 'Icons of Divinity: Portraits of Elizabeth I', in Lucy Gent and Nigel Llewellyn, eds, *Renaissance Bodies: the Human Figure in English Culture c. 1540–1660* (London: Reaktion, 1990), pp. 11–35, at p. 13.

13. Although there was a brief period (*c.* 1794–*c.*1800) in which some women wore lighter corsets, bust bodices or no corsets, many women in England continued to use long, boned stays throughout. See Steele, *The Corset,* pp. 30–3; Norah Waugh, *Corsets and Crinolines* (London: Batsford, 1954), pp. 45, 75; C. Willet Cunnington and Phillis Cunnington, *The History of Underclothes* (New York: Dover, 1992), p. 115.

14. *LM* 42 (1811), p. 367.

15. For example, *LM* 42 (1811), pp. 304–6.

16. *LM* 42 (1811), p. 304; Sir N. William Wraxall, *Historical Memoirs of My Own Time* (London: Kegan Paul, Trench, Trubner, 1904), p. 84.

17. *Jane Austen's Letters,* collected and ed. Deirdre Le Faye, 3rd edn (Oxford: Oxford University Press, 1995), p. 86, 12–13 May 1801; pp. 156–7, 9 December 1808; p. 220, 15–16 September 1813.

18. *LM* 20 (1789), p. 372; *LM* 29 (1798), p. 119.

19. Quoted in Waugh, *Corsets and Crinolines,* p. 71.

20. However, in Janet Arnold, *Patterns of Fashion: the Cut and Construction of Clothes for Men and Women c1560–1620* (London: Macmillan, 1985), p. 46, Fig. 328; pp. 112–13, no. 46, Janet Arnold includes detailed photographs and drawings of a sixteenth-century German bodice in which the lace holes are reinforced inside and out with metal rings. Cunnington and Cunnington, *History of Underclothes,* give the date of metal eyelets as 1828 (p. 132); Lucy Johnston, *Nineteenth-Century Fashion in Detail* (London: Victoria and Albert Museum, 2005), p. 142, puts it at 1823.

21. Steele, *The Corset,* p. 43.

22. Waugh, *Corsets and Crinolines,* p. 83.

23. Johnston, *Nineteenth-Century Fashion,* p. 144.

24. This information, drawn from trade directories, has been compiled at http://homepage.ntl world.com/stephen.pomeroy/local/loccom.pdf, accessed November 2007.

25. Steele, *The Corset,* p. 46.

26. *Official descriptive and illustrated catalogue: Great Exhibition of the Works of Industry of All Nations, 1851* (London: Spicer Brothers, [1851]), II, p. 579, no. 40A George Roberts; II, p. 586, no. 162, Hurst and Reynolds; II, p. 584, no. 119, Charlotte Smith; II, p. 579, no. 42, Emma and Elizabeth H. Martin; II, p. 580, no. 49, Nicholas Geary; II, p. 579, no. 43, Mary Sykes. On the number of competitors—particularly the female entrants, and Sykes's medal—see Summers, 'Yes, They Did Wear Them', p. 70.
27. B[ulwer], *Anthropometamorphosis,* pp. 338–9.
28. *GM* 13 (August 1743), pp. 430–2, at p. 431.
29. *The Journal of Mary Frampton,* ed. Harriot Georgiana Mundy (London, 1885), p. 3. The Duchess is Mary Isabella Manners (née Somerset, 1756–1831), who married the Marquess of Granby in 1775. He became the fourth Duke of Rutland four years later.
30. On the vast subject, see particularly Steele, *The Corset,* pp. 35–66, 87–111, and David Kunzle, *Fashion and Fetishism: A Social History of the Corset, Tight-Lacing and Other Forms of Body-Sculpture in the West* (Totowa, NJ: Rowman and Littlefield, 1982).
31. Quoted in Steele, *The Corset,* p. 100. On the status of the infamous 'tight-lacing correspondence' that appeared in *The Englishwoman's Domestic Magazine* from 1867–74, see ibid., p. 90.
32. For this and the following data, see Steele, *The Corset,* pp. 2, 44, 100–2. For more on the Symington Collection of Corsetry, Foundation and Swimwear, see http://museums.leics.gov.uk/collections-on-line/GetSingleCollection.do?collectionKey=68, accessed November 2007.
33. Philip Treleaven, 'How to Fit into Your Clothes: Busts, Waists, Hips and the UK National Sizing Survey', *Significance,* 4/3 (2007), pp. 113–17, at pp. 114, 115. Summarized results of the survey can be found via downloads at the London College of Fashion's Web archive, http://www.fashion.arts.ac.uk/sizeuk.htm, accessed 2 December 2008.
34. Steele, *The Corset,* p. 102.
35. *The Ladies' Pocket Magazine,* Part 2 (1829), pp. 27–8.
36. Summers, 'Yes, They Did Wear Them', p. 67. Harriet Waterhouse, 'A Fashionable Confinement: Whaleboned Stays and the Pregnant Woman', *Costume,* 41 (2007), pp. 53–65, at p. 61.
37. Quoted in Stella Mary Newton, *Health, Art and Reason: Dress Reformers of the Nineteenth Century* (London: John Murray, 1974), p. 117.
38. Steele, *The Corset,* p. 54.
39. Waugh, *Corsets and Crinolines,* p. 92. I have used Waugh's phrase for the section heading.
40. This perfect description is Steele's.
41. Waterhouse, 'A Fashionable Confinement', p. 56.
42. Wetenhall Wilkes, *A letter of genteel and moral advice to a young lady* (London, 1744), p. 95.
43. *Laugh and be Fat: Or, an Antidote against Melancholy,* 9th edn (London: 1724), p. 122. *Wallop* is perhaps 'a bubbling motion' or a 'violent, heavy, clumsy, noisy movement of the body; a plunging, floundering, lurching' (Oxford English Dictionary).

44. *Letters and Journals of Lady Mary Coke*, III, p. 100, Thursday 29 June 1769.

45. Jane Ashelford, *The Art of Dress: Clothes and Society 1500–1914* (London: National Trust, 1996), pp. 229, 231. See also Elizabeth Wilson and Lou Taylor, *Through the Looking Glass: a History of Dress from 1860 to the Present Day* (London: BBC Books, 1989), pp. 30–1.

46. Lady Lucy Duff-Gordon, *Discretions and Indiscretions* (London: Jarrolds, 1932), p. 260, photo facing p. 28.

47. Elizabeth von Arnim, *The Solitary Summer* (London: Virago Press, 2000; orig. pub. New York: Macmillan, 1899), pp. 122, 124.

48. In collaboration with cardiologist Lynn Kutsche, Valerie Steele set out to find the medical truth—as we understand it today—behind corsetry, including the practice of tight lacing. What follows is drawn from this discussion. For more detail, see *The Corset*, pp. 67–85.

49. *Court and Private Life in the Time of Queen Charlotte: Being the Journals of Mrs. Papendiek, Assistant Keeper of the Wardrobe and Reader to Her Majesty*, ed. Mrs Vernon Delves Broughton (London: Richard Bentley, 1887), I, p. 224.

50. *The Private Letters of Princess Lieven to Prince Metternich 1820–1826*, ed. Peter Quennell, trans. Dilys Powell (London: John Murray, 1937), p. 61, Thursday 17 August 1820.

51. Waugh, *Corsets and Crinolines*, p. 169. I have drawn heavily on Waugh's work for this section. For more detail, see ibid., pp. 167–9.

52. Quoted in ibid., p. 168.

53. Ibid., p. 169.

54. The figure is confirmed by an article on the whaling industry, appearing in *The Times* (Monday 4 September 1911), p. 13, col. D.

55. Hollander, *Sex and Suits*, p. 44.

56. Phillip Stubbes, *The Anatomie of Abuses* (London, 1583), sig. E2r, E2v.

57. For doublet patterns showing the shaping of the arms, see Arnold, *Patterns of Fashion*. For further dress patterns and construction detail, see Ninya Mikhaila and Jane Malcolm-Davies, *The Tudor Tailor: Reconstructing Sixteenth-Century Dress* (London: Batsford, 2006). For more on the Renaissance elbow, see Joaneath Spicer, 'The Renaissance Elbow', in Jan Bremmer and Herman Roodenburg, eds, *A Cultural History of Gesture: From Antiquity to the Present Day* (Oxford: Polity, 1991), pp. 84–128.

58. Elizabeth Steele, *The Memoirs of Sophia Baddeley* (London, 1787), III, pp. 201–4. Count Haslang arrived at the English court in 1739. He was well known in London, partly for selling protections from arrest—the reason that Sophia Baddeley had enlisted his help. He died in 1783.

59. Walter Vaughan, *An essay, philosophical and medical, concerning modern clothing* (1792), pp. 66–7.

60. Steele, *The Corset*, p. 36.

61. *The Creevey Papers*, ed. Sir Herbert Maxwell (London: John Murray, 1905), p. 264, *c.* 1817–18. On the inclusion of corset belts in the Prince's wardrobe accounts, see Aileen Ribeiro,

The Art of Dress: Fashion in England and France 1750 to 1820 (New Haven and London: Yale University Press, 1995), p. 100.

62. 'The Dandy, O', reprinted frequently, this version by T. Wood, Birmingham, between 1806 and 1827, Johnson Ballads 1481, online at Bodleian Library Broadside Ballads, http://bodley24.bodley.ox.ac.uk/cgi-bin/acwwweng/ballads/image.pl?ref=Johnson+Ballads+1481&id=21227.gif&seq=1&size=0, accessed 3 December 2008.

63. T. Moore, *The Fudge Family in Paris,* ed. Thomas Brown, 3rd edn (London, 1818), pp. 79–80. The text glosses 'Donaldson' as an English tailor in Paris; glosses 'Schneider' as a dandy term for a tailor; and says 'a ship is said to miss stays, when she does not obey the helm in tacking'.

64. *The Times* (Saturday 24 October 1818), p. 3, col. D.

65. Alymra Gray, *Papers and Diaries of a York Family 1764–1839,* ed. Mrs Edwin Gray (London: Sheldon Press, 1927), p. 119.

66. Hollander, *Sex and Suits,* p. 139.

67. *The Whole Art of Dress! or the Road to Elegance and Fashion … by a Cavalry Officer* (London, 1830), p. 83.

68. Steele, *The Corset,* p. 38.

69. Ibid., p. 38.

70. For example, advertisements in *The Age* (Sunday 26 July 1835), p. 234, and *The Satirist* (Sunday 18 September 1836), p. 298.

71. *John Bull and Britannia* (Saturday 6 August 1859), p. 512.

72. *The County Gentleman: Sporting Gazette, Agricultural Journal, and 'the Man about Town'* (Saturday 16 March 1889), p. 368. *John Bull* (Saturday 31 December 1842), p. 626.

73. For example, *Myra's Journal of Dress and Fashion* (Thrusday 1 September 1887), p. 484, and *The Licensed Victualler's Mirror* [Tuesday 28 January 1890], issue 105.

74. *Official descriptive and illustrated catalogue,* II, p. 579, no. 39.

75. Letter from 'M. C.' in 'The Englishwoman's Conversazione', *The Englishwoman's Domestic Magazine* [Saturday 1 August 1868], p. 112. For an example of contemporary uncertainty over the status of the tight-lacing correspondence, see the letter from 'An Irishwoman', same page. For differing opinion today, see n. 29.

76. John Mollo, *The Prince's Dolls,* cited in Steven Parissien, *George IV: the Grand Entertainment* (London: John Murray, 2001), p. 110.

77. See Parissien, *George IV,* pp. 94–115.

78. Elisabeth Hackspiel-Mikosch, 'Beauty in Uniform: the Creation of Ideal Masculinity during the Nineteenth Century', in Regine Falkenberg, Adelheid Rasche and Christine Waidenschlager, eds, *On Men: Masculine Dress Code from Ancient Greeks to Cowboys,* ICOM Costume Committee, 57th Annual General Meeting, Berlin, 13–17 June 2005 (Berlin: DHM, 2005), pp. 63–70, at p. 63.

79. See ibid. and Johnston, *Nineteenth-Century Fashion,* pp. 12–21.

80. Jane Austen, *Pride and Prejudice* (1813; repr. London: Oxford University Press, 1970), vol. 1, chap. 7, p. 25.

81. Hollander, *Sex and Suits,* pp. 84–88. See also Hackspiel-Mikosch, 'Beauty in Uniform', p. 64, and Ian Kelly, *Beau Brummell: the Ultimate Dandy* (London: Hodder and Stoughton, 2005), pp. 169–71.

82. Hackspiel-Mikosch, 'Beauty in Uniform', p. 65; Kelly, *Beau Brummell,* p. 175.

83. Johnson, *Nineteenth-Century Fashion,* p. 158.

84. Sarah Levitt, *Victorians Unbuttoned: Registered Designs for Clothing, Their Makers and Wearers, 1839–1900,* cited in Christopher Breward, *The Culture of Fashion: a New History of Fashionable Dress* (Manchester: Manchester University Press, 1995), p. 172.

85. Christopher Breward, *The Hidden Consumer: Masculinities, Fashion and City Life 1860–1914* (Manchester: Manchester University Press, 1999), p. 160.

86. See passages from *The Tailor and Cutter,* quoted in ibid., pp. 160–1.

87. Kelly, *Beau Brummell,* pp. 197–8.

88. Ibid., p. 199.

89. For an analysis of a suit with all these features and the implications for its wearer, see Hackspiel-Mikosch, 'Beauty in Uniform'.

90. William Power, *The Tailor's Scientific Instructor, or Foreman's Unerring Guide in the Art of Cutting,* quoted in Johnson, *Nineteenth-Century Fashion,* p. 138; see ibid., pp. 138–9 for construction details of this innovative style. Also, on the importance of collar and lapel, see Hollander, *Sex and Suits,* p. 90, and Kelly, *Beau Brummell,* p. 196.

91. Edward Bulwer Lytton, *Pelham: or, Adventures of a Gentleman* (London: George Routledge, 1895; orig. pub. 1828), chap. 44, p. 171.

92. Kelly, *Beau Brummell,* p. 199.

93. See C. Willett Cunnington and Phillis Cunnington, *Handbook of English Costume in the Nineteenth Century* (London: Faber, 1959), pp. 39–43; Johnson, *Nineteenth-Century Fashion,* pp. 142–3; Kelly, *Beau Brummell,* p. 204.

94. Hackspiel-Mikosch, 'Beauty in Uniform', pp. 68–9; Kelly, *Beau Brummell,* p. 175; Cunnington and Cunnington, *Handbook of English Costume,* pp. 45–7, 49.

95. See Kelly, *Beau Brummell,* pp. 207–8. This sort of accounting system has a long history, however. For example, one of the Norfolk tailors who supplied the Bacon family in the sixteenth century seems to have sent in his bills on an annual basis; see Stern, 'Peckover and Gallyard', p. 15.

96. Kelly, *Beau Brummell,* p. 193.

97. R. H. Gronow, *Recollections and Anecdotes: Being a Second Series of Reminiscences* (London: Smith, Elder, 1863), pp. 271–3.

98. For a brief summary of the so-called corset controversy, see Joanne Entwhistle, *The Fashioned Body: Fashion, Dress and Modern Social Theory* (Cambridge: Polity, 2000), pp. 195–200. The most influential revisionist analyses are Kunzle, *Fashion and Fetishism,* and Steele, *The Corset.*

99. Gwen Raverat, *Period Piece* (1952), quoted in Waugh, *Corsets and Crinolines,* p. 146.

100. Jackie Marshall-Ward, 'Mode and Movement', *Costume,* 34 (2000), p. 125.

101. See Georges Vigarello, 'The Upward Training of the Body from the Age of Chivalry to Courtly Civility', in Michel Feher, ed., with Ramona Naddaff and Nadia Tazi, *Fragments for a History of the Human Body* (New York: Zone, 1989), II, pp. 148–99.

102. Wilkes, *A letter of genteel and moral advice,* p. 96.

103. John Essex, *The young ladies conduct* (London, 1722), p. 81.

104. M. Lawrence, *The School of Femininity,* quoted in Aileen Ribeiro, *Dress and Morality* (New York: Holmes and Meier, 1986), pp. 154–5; also see Angela J. Latham, *Posing a Threat: Flappers, Chorus Girls, and Other Brazen Performers of the American 1920s* (Hanover, NH and London: University Press of New England for Wesleyan University Press, 2000), pp. 20–1, 23.

105. Hollander, *Sex and Suits,* pp. 138–42, at pp. 140, 141. Herbert Blau, *Nothing in Itself: Complexions of Fashion* (Bloomington and Indianapolis: Indiana University Press, 1999), p. 232, says something similar.

106. Anne Fogarty, *Wife Dressing* (1959), quoted in Kunzle, *Fashion and Fetishism,* p. 335.

107. Hollander, *Sex and Suits,* p. 140.

108. Wilkes, *A letter of genteel and moral advice,* p. 95.

109. Steele, *The Corset,* p. 132.

110. Fogarty, *Wife Dressing,* quoted in Kunzle, *Fashion and Fetishism,* p. 336.

111. A.L. Kennedy, 'The Basque', in Kirsty Dunseath, ed., *A Second Skin: Women Write about Clothes* (London: Women's Press, 1998), pp. 17–20, at pp. 18–19.

112. Beatrice Faust, *Women, Sex, and Pornography* (London: Melbourne House, 1980), p. 49.

CHAPTER 3

1. George More, *A true discourse concerning the certaine possession and dispossessio[n] of 7 persons in one familie in Lancashire* (1600), p. 27.

2. William Warner, *Albions England a continued historie of the same kingdome* (1597), p. 220.

3. William Curtis, *The botanical magazine; or, flower-garden displayed,* 18 vols (London, 1793–1803), III, p. 88, 'Narcissus Bulbocodium. Hoop-Petticoat Narcissus'.

4. Elizabeth Wilson and Lou Taylor, *Through the Looking Glass: a History of Dress from 1860 to the Present Day* (London: BBC Books, 1989), p. 22.

5. The article in which this appeared, 'Levities in Fashion', was printed in both the *General Advertiser (1784)* (Saturday 20 August 1785) and the *London Chronicle* (Tuesday 6 September 1785).

6. This was reported in the news section of the *General Evening Post* on Saturday 27 June 1778 and reprinted, also as news, in the *St. James's Chronicle or the British Evening Post* three days later (Tuesday 30 June).

7. See for example, *LM* 49 (1818), p. 570; *LM,* ns. 1 (1820), p. 100.

8. J[ohn] B[ulwer], *Anthropometamorphosis: Man Transform'd: or, the Artificiall Changling Historically Presented* (London, 1653), pp. 541–2.

9. *TRP,* II, pp. 189–90, proclamation 6 May 1562, no. 493.

10. *Journals of the House of Commons,* I, pp. 68, 70, 89, 90.

11. Wildred Hooper, 'The Tudor Sumptuary Laws', *English Historical Review*, 30 (1915), pp. 440–1.

12. Ibid., pp. 440–1.

13. F. G. Emmison, *Elizabethan Life I: Disorder* (Chelmsford: Essex County Council, 1970), pp. 30, 33.

14. Anne Hollander, *Sex and Suits* (New York: Alfred A. Knopf, 1994), p. 83.

15. Alexandra Shepard, *Meanings of Manhood in Early Modern England* (Oxford: Oxford University Press, 2003), explores the varied constructs of masculinity in this period, including that of youth, a category particularly informed by intemperance, flamboyant dress and swaggering gesture. Also on sixteenth- and seventeenth-century masculinity, see Anthony Fletcher, *Gender, Sex and Subordination in England 1500–1800* (New Haven: Yale University Press, 1995); Elizabeth A. Foyster, *Manhood in Early Modern England: Honour, Sex and Marriage* (New York: Longman, 1999); Mark Breitenberg, *Anxious Masculinity in Early Modern England* (Cambridge: Cambridge University Press, 1996).

16. On Chesterfield's advice to present an 'unruffled' countenance, see Dallett Hemphill, *Bowing to Necessities: a History of Manners in America, 1620–1860* (Oxford: Oxford University Press, 1999), p. 80. On the development of bourgeois morality, economics and politics, and its effect on men's dress, see David Kuchta, *The Three-Piece Suit and Modern Masculinity: England 1550–1850* (Berkeley: University of California Press, 2002). On eighteenth-century masculinity, see George Mosse, *The Image of Man: the Creation of Modern Masculinity* (New York: Oxford University Press, 1996).

17. Philip Dormer Stanhope, Earl of Chesterfield, *Principles of Politeness, and of Knowing the World,* 2nd edn (London, 1775), p. 2. On Chesterfield's enormous influence and his emphasis on reserve and bodily control, see Hemphill, *Bowing to Necessities,* pp. 70–1, 76–9, 81, 91–2, 101.

18. Janet Arnold, *Patterns of Fashion: the Cut and Construction of Clothes for Men and Women c1560–1620* (Costume and Fashion Press, 1985), pp. 7 and 10, for the lack of survival of farthingales; ibid., p. 7, for quoted instructions for their construction and the estimation of a handspan.

19. M. Channing Linthicum, *Costume in the Drama of Shakespeare and His Contemporaries* (Oxford: Clarendon Press, 1936), p. 181. This measure is also used by Jane Ashelford, *Dress in the Age of Elizabeth I* (London: Batsford, 1988), p. 36.

20. Quoted in Norah Waugh, *Corsets and Crinolines* (London: Batsford, 1954), p. 33.

21. Quoted in C. Willet Cunnington and Phillis Cunnington, *The History of Underclothes* (New York: Dover, 1992), p. 90.

22. *Purefoy Letters 1735–1753,* G. Eland, ed., (London: Sidgwick and Jackson, 1931), II, p. 308.

23. *Fashion: A History from the 18th to the 20th Century* (Taschen, 2006), p. 276, Inv. AC1064 78-30-75; pp. 276–7, Inv. AC2227 79-9-32; pp. 234–5, Inv. AC9380 96-27-1AE.

24. *GM* 17 (1747), p. 374. The article in which this appears is a reprint of a piece that appeared at least once previously; see *Weekly Journal or British Gazetteer* (Saturday 13 September 1718), pp. 1147–8.

25. *The Spectator,* II, p. 7, no. 127 (Thursday 26 July 1711).

26. Fidelis Morgan, ed., *The Female Tatler* (London: Dent, 1992), p. 166, no. 82, 11–13 Wednesday 11 to Friday 13 January 1710.

27. Donald Bond, ed., *The Tatler* (Oxford: Clarendon Press, 1987), II, p. 180, no. 113, Thursday 29 December 1709.

28. Ibid., pp. 191–5, no. 116, Thursday 5 January 1710.

29. Eliza Haywood, *The Female Spectator,* ed. Gabrielle M. Firmager (London: Bristol Classical Press, 1993), III, Book XV, pp. 184–6. On the history of the periodical and its various reprintings, see ibid., pp. 8–14.

30. A. W., *The enormous abomination of the hoop-petticoat* (London, 1745), pp. 11–15. In the petticoat's defence, see Jack Lovelace, *The hoop-petticoat vindicated* (London, 1745).

31. A. W., *Enormous abomination,* pp. 10–11.

32. *LM* 13 (1782), pp. 432–3.

33. *The Ladies Cabinet* [Monday 1 August 1853], p. 109.

34. Ibid., [Monday 1 October 1855], pp. 218–19. Like so many of the complaints against big skirts, the theme of wearers incurring additional charges echoed earlier sentiments. A 'Woman in six Yards of Hoop', it was pointed out in 1746 in regard to public entertainments, 'is dishonest if she doth not pay for three or four Places'; *True Patriot: and History of Our Own Times* (Tuesday 4 February 1746).

35. 'Crinoline: or What a Ridiculous Fashion', without place, year or name of publication, Harding B 14(147), online at Bodleian Ballad Catalogue http://bodley24.bodley.ox.ac.uk/cgi-bin/acwwweng/ballads/image.pl?ref=Harding+B+14(147)&id=06097.gif&seq=1&size=1, accessed 8 December 2008.

36. David Kunzle, *Fashion and Fetishism: a Social History of the Corset, Tight-Lacing and Other Forms of Body-Sculpture in the West* (The History Press, Ltd, 1982), p. 136.

37. 'The Wrongs of Crinoline', *Punch* (Saturday 20 September 1856), p. 117; 'Luggage Trains for Ladies', *Punch* (Saturday 30 October 1858), p. 173; 'Church and Crinoline', *Punch* (Saturday 24 July 1858), p. 40; 'Crinoline', *Punch* (Saturday 14 January 1893), p. 22.

38. *The Letters of John Chamberlain,* ed. by Norman Egbert McClure, 2 vols (Philadelphia, American Philosophical Society, 1939), I, p. 426, 18 February 1612 (old style).

39. *The Letters and Journals of Lady Mary Coke,* ed. J. A. Home (Kingsmead Reprints, 1970), III, p. 37, Wednesday 8 March 1769; p. 38, Thursday 9 March 1769.

40. Dorothy Nevill, *Under Five Reigns,* 2nd edn (London: Methuen, 1910), pp. 336, 337.

41. George Augustus Sala, *Twice Round the Clock or the Hours of the Day and Night in London* (pub. in serial form 1858; pub. in book form 1859; repr. Leicester: Leicester University Press, 1971), p. 199.

42. Hippolyte Taine, *Taine's Notes on England*, trans. Edward Hyams (New York: Thames and Hudson, 1957), p. 19.

43. *The Times* (12 June 1860), p. 5, col. E; *The Times* (18 October 1861), p. 7, col. F; *The Times* (8 Oct. 1862), p. 4, col. A.

44. Erin Mackie, *Market à la Mode: Fashion, Commodity, and Gender in the Tatler and the Spectator* (Baltimore: Johns Hopkins University Press, 1997), sees the threatening assertiveness of the hoop petticoat as the cause of much early-eighteenth-century satire, an assertiveness that she also suggests contemporaries linked with sexual independence. For further discussion of the hoop petticoat, see also Kimberly Chrisman, 'Unhoop the Fair Sex: the Campaign against the Hoop Petticoat in Eighteenth-Century England', *Eighteenth-Century Studies,* 30 (1996), pp. 5–23.

45. On monarchs' political and personal uses of dress from 1660, see Philip Mansel, *Dressed to Rule: Royal and Court Costume from Louis XIV to Elizabeth II* (New Haven and London: Yale University Press, 2005).

46. *The Spectator,* II, p. 6, no. 127, (Thursday 26 July 1711). *Universal Spectator and Weekly Journal* (Saturday 31 January 1741). *True Patriot: and History of Our Own Times* (Tuesday 4 February 1746). Lovelace, *Hoop-petticoat vindicated,* p. 12. *GM* 17 (1747), p. 375. *The Ladies' Monthly Magazine, Le Monde Élégant, or the World of Fashion* [Wednesday 1 June 1859].

47. Nevill, *Under Five Reigns,* p. 336.

48. *Leaves from the Notebooks of Lady Dorothy Nevill,* ed. Ralph Nevill (Macmillan, 1907), p. 156.

49. *Recollections of the Table-Talk of Samuel Rogers,* ed. Rev. Alexander Dyce (H. A. Rogers, 1887), p. 11.

50. 'Woman's Rights', *The Lady's Newspaper* (Saturday 16 May 1863).

51. *Punch* (Saturday 17 December 1859), p. 244. The Oxford English Dictionary glosses *vis-à-vis* as a carriage for two persons sitting face to face. See also Figure 4.

52. Jackie Marshall-Ward, 'Mode and Movement', *Costume,* 34 (2000), pp. 125–6.

53. More, *A true discourse,* p. 27.

54. *The Spectator,* II, p. 6, no. 127, (Thursday 26 July 1711).

55. *Whitehall Evening Post or London Intelligencer* (Thursday 13 August 1747).

56. Haywood, *Female Spectator,* I, Book V, p. 298.

57. Ibid., III, Book XV, pp. 185–6.

58. *Weekly Journal or British Gazeteer* (Saturday 13 September 1718).

59. *True Patriot: and History of Our Own Times* (Tuesday 4 February 1746). *Universal Spectator and Weekly Journal* (Saturday 31 January 1741). *Weekly Journal or Saturday's Post* (Saturday 2 November 1717).

60. *GM* 23 (1753), p. 11.

61. *Weekly Journal or British Gazetteer* (13 September 1718), pp. 1148; repr. *GM* 17 (1747), p. 376.

62. *GM* 3 (1733), p. 131.

63. See Anne Hollander, *Seeing through Clothes* (Berkeley: University of California Press, 1993), p. 218.

64. 'Crinoline at Church', *The Times* (12 June 1860), p. 5, col. E.

65. Quoted in Cunnington and Cunnington, *History of Underclothes,* pp. 155–6.

66. Maria Edgeworth, *Belinda* (orig. pub. 1801; London: J. M. Dent, 1993), p. 66.

67. Here I have drawn on the work of Mimi Hellman, 'Furniture, Sociability and the Work of Leisure in Eighteenth-Century France', *Eighteenth-Century Studies,* 32 (1999), pp. 414–45, esp. here p. 423, who argues that eighteenth-century furniture required skilful negotiation, the performance of which helped configure elite bodies and social personae.

68. *Letters and Journals of Lady Mary Coke,* IV, p. 234, Monday 6 September 1773; p. 81, Saturday 6 June 1772; p. 224, Saturday 21 August 1773; p. 171, Saturday 5 June 1773.

69. *Court and Private Life in the Time of Queen Charlotte: Being the Journals of Mrs. Papendiek, Assistant Keeper of the Wardrobe and Reader to Her Majesty,* ed. Mrs Vernon Delves Broughton (Richard Bentley, 1887), II, p. 283.

70. Erving Goffman, *The Presentation of Self in Everyday Life* (orig. pub. 1959; repr. Harmondsworth: Penguin, 1984), esp. pp. 109–40.

71. Advertisement for Sansflectum crinolines, appearing in *The Ladies' Monthly Magazine, Le Monde Élégant, or the World of Fashion* [Sunday 1 April 1866].

72. Goffman, *Presentation of Self in Everyday Life,* pp. 116, 114.

73. See Arnold, *Patterns of Fashion c. 1560–1620,* pp. 7, 10–11, and Ninya Mikhaila and Jane Malcolm-Davies, *The Tudor Tailor: Reconstructing Sixteenth-Century Dress* (London: Batsford, 2006), pp. 120–5.

74. See Cunnington and Cunnington, *History of Underclothes,* pp. 88–91

75. See ibid., pp. 163–6; Lucy Johnston, *Nineteenth-Century Fashion in Detail* (London: Victoria and Albert Museum, 2005), pp. 128–9, 132–3; Nevill, *Under Five Reigns,* pp. 336–7.

76. See n. 35.

77. Nevill, *Reminisences,* pp. 96–7.

78. *The Times* (28 January 1860), p. 7, col. C.

79. *The Times* (7 June 1860), p. 9, col. F.

80. *The Times* (1 August 1863), p. 12, col. B.

81. *The Times* (1 April 1864), p. 10, col. F.

82. For example, 28 January 1860, p. 35; 6 April 1861, p. 143; 23 August 1862, p. 79; 22 December 1866, p. 251; 4 June 1870, p. 230.

83. *The Times* (Tuesday 27 April 1858), p. 12, col. E.

84. *The Times* (Thursday 9 July 1865), p. 5, col. A. Also in this report, a salesman from Bradford whose foot caught in crinoline was paid compensation of £10. This column had earlier appeared on Monday 30 December 1867, p. 4, col. A.

85. *The Times* (Monday 18 September 1865), p. 10, col. D.

86. *General Evening Post* (Saturday 13 December 1735).

87. *Daily Journal* (Friday 7 April 1721), no. 65.

88. *The Times* (Tuesday 12 January 1858), p. 4, col. E.

89. *The Times* (Thursday 28 August 1862), p. 11, col. B.

90. *The Times* (Monday 25 July 1864), p. 9, col. A, reported from the *Western Morning News.*

91. Nevill, *Under Five Reigns,* p. 340.

92. *Letters and Journals of Lady Mary Coke,* IV, p. 178, September 20 June 1773.

93. Ibid., III, p. 343, Friday 28 December 1770; III, pp. 457–8, Saturday 28 September 1771; III, p. 472, Friday 1 November 1771; IV, p. 1, Wednesday 1 January 1772; IV, p. 95, Wednesday 8 July 1772; IV, p. 178, Monday 21 June 1773.

94. 'The Victorian Age', *The Times* (Saturday 25 October 1930), p. 14, col. A.

95. Gwen Raverat, *Period Piece* (1952), quoted in Waugh, *Corsets and Crinolines,* p. 146.

96. *The Times* (Saturday 19 October 1861), p. 9, col. C.

97. *Parker's London News or the Impartial Intelligencer* (Wednesday 23 December 1724), p. 4.

98. On the second-hand market, see Wilson and Taylor, *Through the Looking Glass,* pp. 38–41; and for the complex relationship between clothing trades, the second-hand market and theft, see Beverly Lemire, *Dress, Culture and Commerce: the English Clothing Trade before the Factory, 1660–1800* (Houndmills: Macmillan, 1997), esp. p. 125 for statistics on theft. Also, on the frequency of theft of clothing and textiles, see John Styles, *The Dress of the People: Everyday Fashion in Eighteenth-Century England* (New Haven: Yale University Press, 2007), p. 327.

99. *The Public Advertiser,* no. 15176 (Saturday 18 January 1783).

100. *London Evening Post* (Tuesday 28 March 1738); *The Times* (Tuesday 13 June 1786), p. 3, col. B.

101. *Old England or the National Gazette,* no. 37 (Saturday 14 December 1751); also reported in *The Westminster Journal or New Weekly Miscellany* (Saturday 14 December 1751).

102. *GM* 20 (1750), p. 129; *Punch* (21 January 1860), p. 32.

103. *The Times* (Monday 2 June 1862), p. 11, col. F.

104. *The Times* (Wednesday 1 March 1865), p. 11, col. F.

105. *The Times* (Monday 27 August 1866), p. 11, col. F.

CHAPTER 4

1. John Doran, *Habits and Men* (London: Richard Bentley, 1855), p. 197.

2. On riding dress, see Janet Arnold, 'Dashing Amazons: The Development of Women's Riding Dress, *c.* 1500–1900', in Amy de la Haye and Elizabeth Wilson, eds, *Defining Dress: Dress as Object, Meaning and Identity* (Manchester: Manchester University Press, 1999), pp. 10–29.

3. The fairly extensive historiography on female cross-dressing includes Rudolf Dekker and Lotte van de Pol, *The Tradition of Female Transvestism in Early Modern Europe* (Basingstoke: Macmillan, 1989); Valerie R. Hotchkiss, *Clothes Make the Man: Female Cross-Dressing in Medieval Europe* (New York: Garland, 1996); Vern L. Bullough and Bonnie Bullough, *Cross Dressing,*

Sex, and Gender (Philadelphia: University of Pennsylvania Press, 1993); Lesley Ferris, ed., *Cross the Stage: Controversies on Cross-Dressing* (London and New York: Routledge, 1993); David Cressy, 'Gender Trouble and Cross-Dressing in Early Modern England', *Journal of British Studies,* 35 (1996), pp. 438–65; Patricia Crawford and Sara Mendelson, 'Sexual Identities in Early Modern England', *Gender and History,* 7 (1995), pp. 363–77; Julie Wheelwright, *Amazons and Military Maids: Women Who Dressed as Men in the Pursuit of Life, Liberty and Happiness* (London: Pandora, 1989); Anne Laurence, *Women in England 1500–1760: a Social History* (London: Phoenix Press, 1996), pp. 250–2. Michael Shapiro, *Gender in Play on the Shakespearean Stage: Boy Heroines and Female Pages* (Ann Arbor, MI: University of Michigan Press, 1994), Appendix C, is a transcription of thirteen cross-dressing cases documented in the Repertories of the Alderman's Court and the Minute Books of Bridewell Hospital. F. G. Emmison, *Elizabethan Life II: Morals and Church Courts* (Chelmsford: Essex County Council, 1999), p. 8, lists a few cases that came before local church courts.

4. *The Memoirs of Robert Carey,* ed. F. H. Mares (Oxford: Clarendon Press, 1972), p. 70.

5. John Harington, *Nugae Antiquae: Being a Miscellaneous Collection of Original Papers*, ed. Thomas Park, 2 vols (London, 1804), I, pp. 391–2.

6. When applied to the body or limbs, the *Oxford English Dictionary* dates the phrase to 1619.

7. See Ellen Chirelstein, 'Emblem and Reckless Presence: the Drury Portrait at Yale', in Lucy Gent, ed., *Albion's Classicism: the Visual Arts in Britain, 1550–1650* (New Haven and London: Yale University Press, 1995), pp. 287–312, at p. 295.

8. See Joan Wildeblood and Peter Brinson, *The Polite World: a Guide to English Manners and Deportment from the Thirteenth to the Nineteenth Century* (London: Oxford University Press, 1965), pp. 133, 165, 261–3. Quote from John Cleland, *The Institution of a Young Nobleman* (Oxford, 1607), p. 178.

9. Ben Jonson, *Every Man Out of His Humour* (1599), quoted in Wildeblood and Brinson, *Polite World,* p. 165.

10. Cleland, *Institution of a Young Nobleman*, p. 225.

11. *The Life of Edward, First Lord Herbert of Cherbury,* ed. J. M. Shuttleworth (London: Oxford University Press, 1976), pp. 31–2.

12. *Memoirs of John Reresby,* ed. Andrew Browning (Glasgow: Jackson, 1936), pp. 2, 1.

13. *Memoirs of Sir James Melville of Halhill 1535–1617,* ed. A. Francis Steuart (London: Routledge, 1929), p. 26.

14. *Memoirs of John Reresby,* pp. 7, 17, 20.

15. William Brenchley Rye, ed., *England as Seen by Foreigners in the Days of Elizabeth and James the First* (London: John Russell Smith, 1865), p. 110.

16. For example, see André Hurault, Sieur de Maisse, *A Journal of All That Was Accomplished by Monsieur de Maisse Ambassador in England,* trans. and ed. G. B. Harrison (Nonesuch Press, 1931), p. 95.

17. *The Letters of John Chamberlain,* ed. Norman Egbert McClure (American Philosophical Society, 1939), I, p. 428.

18. Jackie Marshall-Ward, 'Mode and Movement', *Costume*, 34 (2000), p. 126. On the importance of courtly dancing to elite self-fashioning, see Skiles Howard, *The Politics of Courtly Dancing in Early Modern England* (Amherst: University of Massachusetts Press, 1998).

19. Howard, *Politics of Courtly Dancing*, p. 126.

20. Brenchley Rye, *England as Seen by Foreigners*, p. 123.

21. Online Oxford Dictionary of National Biography, *s.v.* 'Henry Frederick, prince of Wales'.

22. *Letters of John Chamberlain*, I, p. 497.

23. *Dudley Carleton to John Chamberlain 1603–1624: Jacobean Letters*, ed. Maurice Lee Jr (New Brunswick: Rutgers University Press, 1972), p. 67.

24. On the relationship between duelling, manliness and civility, see Markku Peltonen, *The Duel in Early Modern England: Civility, Politeness and Honour* (Cambridge: Cambridge University Press, 2003).

25. Vincento Sauiolo, *Vincentio Sauiolo his practice in two bookes. The first intreating of the vse of the rapier and dagger. The second, of honor and honorable quarrels* (London, 1595), sig. 8v, illustration at sig. 8r.

26. Lucy Hutchinson, *Memoirs of the Life of Colonel Hutchinson*, ed. N. H. Keeble (London: Dent, 1995), p. 19.

27. *Memoirs of John Reresby*, p. xliii.

28. *Life of Lord Herbert of Cherbury*, p. 35.

29. William Shakespeare, *Romeo and Juliet* (1597), quoted in Liza Picard, *Eliabeth's London: Everyday Life in Elizabethan London* (London: Weidenfeld and Nicolson, 2003), p. 126.

30. Ben Jonson, *Every Man in His Humour* (first acted 1598, pub. 1601), 1.iii.31–41.

31. For example, Anne Hollander, *Seeing through Clothes* (Berkeley: University of California Press, 1993), pp. 208, 228, 234; Claudia Brush Kidwell and Valerie Steele, eds, *Men and Women: Dressing the Part* (Washington, DC: Smithsonian Institute Press, 1989), Plate 16. Penelope Byrde, *The Male Image: Men's Fashion in England 1300–1970* (London: Batsford, 1979), pp. 61, 63, says even less, merely noting the codpiece's presence. By contrast, Grace Q. Vicary, 'Visual Art as Social Data: the Renaissance Codpiece', *Cultural Anthropology*, 4 (1989), pp. 3–25, offers an anthropological reading in which she posits the codpiece as a functional and symbolic response to the syphilis epidemic that swept Europe at the same time. Literary historian Will Fisher, *Materializing Gender in Early Modern English Literature and Culture* (Cambridge: Cambridge University Press, 2006), pp. 59–82, reads the codpiece as a prosthetic item, whose presence, or absence, helped fashion ideologies of manhood.

32. Edmund Gayton, *Pleasant notes upon Don Quixot* (1654). The *Oxford English Dictionary* glosses *umbonically* as 'in the manner of an umbo or sheild-boss', *s.v.* 'umbonically' and 'umbo'.

33. This seems to be the explanation favoured by Picard, *Elizabeth's London*, p. 130.

34. *Montaigne'e Essays: John Florio's Translation*, ed. J.I.M. Stewart, 2 vols (London, 1931), II, p. 254.

35. The third volume appeared in 1693. Pierre Motteux completed the translation with the publication of Books 4 and 5 in 1694 and 1708, respectively.

36. Using the online resource Lexicons of Early Modern English, it is possible to word search for *codpiece* and its variants through a corpus of over 10,000 early English printed books. Instances occur in only a handful of pre-1600 texts; most usage occurs in books printed between 1600 and 1700. See http://leme.library.utoronto.ca/, search 'codpiece' under Period Word List, accessed July 2008.

37. *Purefoy Letters 1735–1753* (Sidgwick and Jackson, 1931), II, p. 301; see also a similar use at II, p. 297.

38. Poor Robin. *Poor Robins Character of France* (London, 1666), p. 21.

39. Barnabe Rich, *Greenes newes both from heauen and hell* (London, 1593), sig. D4v.

40. Thomas Nash, *Haue vvith you to Saffron-wwaldon* (London, 1596), sig. R2r.

41. Well-Willer, *The women's petition against coffee representing to publick consideration the grand inconveniences accruing to their sex from the excessive use of that drying, enfeebling liquor* (London, 1674), p. 2. On the petition specifically, see Markman Ellis, *The Coffee House: a Cultural History* (London: Weidenfeld and Nicolson, 2004), pp. 136–8.

42. Randle Holme, *The academy of armory* (Chester, 1688), Book 3, chap. 3, p. 94.

43. Valerie Steele, *The Corset: a Cultural History* (New Haven: Yale University Press, 2001), p. 10.

44. Quoted in Steele, *The Corset*, p. 11.

45. Samuel Rowlands, *Doctor Merrie-man, or Nothing but mirth written by S.R.* (London, 1609), sig. C2v.

46. I.C., *Alcilia Philoparthens louing folly. To which is added pigmalions image* (London, 1613), sig. I4v.

47. Edward Phillips, *The mysteries of love & eloquence, or, The arts of wooing and complementing as they are manag'd in the Spring Garden, Hide Park, the New Exchange, and other eminent places* (London, 1685), pp. 14–15.

48. Nicolas Andry de Bois-Regard, *Orthopædia: or, the art of correcting and preventing deformities in children* (London, 1743), I, p. 68.

49. François Nivelon, *Rudiments of genteel behavior by F. Nivelon* ([London], 1737), sig. Av.

50. Ibid., sig. Er (emphasis mine).

51. Ibid.

52. Ibid., sig. Ev.

53. *The polite academy, or school of behaviour for young gentlemen and ladies* (London, 1762), p. 36.

54. For example, see Pierre Rameau, *The dancing-master: or, the whole art and mystery of dancing explained,* 2nd edn (London, 1731). On the importance of ballet to elite self-fashioning, see Norman R. Gabriel, 'An "Informalizing Spurt" in Clothing Regimes: Court Ballet and the Civilizing Process', in William J. F. Keenan, ed., *Dressed to Impress: Looking the Part* (Oxford and New York: Berg, 2001), pp. 69–84.

55. Rameau, *The dancing-master,* p. 3.

56. *Reflections upon theatrical expression in tragedy. With proper instruction, and appendix* (London, 1755), p. 31.

57. Rameau, *The dancing-master*, p. 4.

58. Alex Kuczynski, *Beauty Junkies: Under the Skin of the Cosmetic Surgery Industry* (London: Random House, 2007), p. 253.

59. Rameau, *The dancing-master*, pp. 17–21, quote at p. 18.

60. Nivelon, *Rudiments of genteel behavior*, sig. [E3r]–[G2r]; quote from sig. [F3r].

61. See Wildeblood and Brinson, *Polite World*, p. 196, for the development of this bow in the seventeenth century; pp. 227 and 267–70 on the different types of bow. Note that in the 'bow backwards', the feet were placed side by side, with no step forwards. This is closest to the modern bow.

62. For example, *The dancing-master. A Satyr. Canto I* (London, 1722).

63. *The Memoirs of Richard Cumberland*, ed. Richard J. Dircks (New York: AMS Press, 2002), I, p. 122.

64. *The Life of Mrs Margaret Leeson, alias Peg Plunket* (Dublin: 1798), Introduction, p. 23.

65. Ann Sheldon, *Authentic and Interesting Memoirs of Miss Ann Sheldon* (London, 1787–8), III, pp. 116–18.

66. See for example, *The delicate jester; or wit and humour divested of ribaldry* (London, [1780]), pp. 55, 66; *Laugh and be fat: Or, an antidote against melancholy*, 9th edn (London, 1724), pp. 140–1; *Joke upon joke. Or the last packet from the land of festivity and mirth* (London, 1800), pp. 37–8, 51, 141, 260.

67. *Life of Mrs Margaret Leeson*, pp. 177–8.

68. *The Midwife, or the Old Woman's Magazine* (London, 1751), vol. 1, no. 1, p. 8.

69. Quoted in C. Willet Cunnington and Phillis Cunnington, *The History of Underclothes* (New York: Dover, 1992), p. 80. The play appeared under three titles: *The Relapse*; a version of which was reworked by Sheridan in 1777 as *A Trip to Scarborough*; and *The Man of Quality*, a reworking by John Lee.

70. For example, in the advertisement section of *London Daily Post and General Advertiser*, Saturday 24 October 1741; *Morning Chronicle and London Advertiser*, Friday 26 April 1776; *Morning Post and Daily Advertiser*, Tuesday 30 April 1776; *Morning Post and Daily Advertiser*, Saturday 4 May 1776; *Morning Post and Daily Advertiser*, Tuesday 14 May 1776; *Morning Post and Fashionable World*, Wednesday 17 December 1794; *Morning Post and Fashionable World*, Tuesday 10 November 1795; *Morning Post and Fashionable World*, Thursday 24 December 1795; *Star*, Friday 25 December 1795; *Morning Post and Fashionable World*, Saturday 26 December 1795; *Star*, Friday 4 March 1796; *Star*, Thursday 31 March 1796.

71. For example, in the advertisement section of the *Oracle and Public Advertiser*, Wednesday 7 February 1798, Saturday 10 February 1798, Saturday 10 March 1798; *Observer*, Sunday 3 February 1799; *True Briton (1793)*, Thursday 4 April 1799, Tuesday 9 April 1799, Monday 22 April 1799, Friday 17 January 1800.

72. *The Whole Art of Dress! or the Road to Elegance and Fashion … by a Cavalry Officer* (London, 1830), p. 18.

73. 'The Emperor Napoleon's "Sour Grapes"', *Lloyd's Weekly Newspaper* (Sunday 30 January 1853), p. [1].

74. 'Fashionable Rumours', *The Age* (Sunday 16 March 1828), p. 86. R. H. Gronow, *Captain Gronow's Recollections and Anecdotes of the Camp, the Court, and the Clubs, at the Close of the Last War with France* (London, 1864), p. 32, describes Wellington being refused entry at Almack's in 1814. He also describes the disapproval he encountered in 1816 when attending a party for the purpose of meeting the Prince Regent dressed in black trousers, rather than knee breeches (pp. 267–8).

75. For information on Arthur Wellesley, Duke of Wellington; Henry John Temple, Third Viscount Palmerston; Henry Brougham, First Baron Brougham and Vaux; John Russell, First Earl Russell; and Harriette Wilson, see the relevant entries in the *Oxford Dictionary National Biography*, online edition.

76. *Oxford English Dictionary, s.v.* 'calf'. 'Miscellaneous', *The Bristol Mercury* (Saturday 21 January 1865), p. 6.

77. *The Satirist, and the Censor of the Time* (Sunday 13 July 1834), p. 221.

78. 'Chit-Chat', *The Satirist: The Censor of the Times* (Sunday 27 May 1838), p. 165. Note that the title of this publication changes slightly in different issues. Lady Cowper was widowed in 1837, and two years later, she and Palmerston married, around thirty years after their relationship first began. After the marriage, Palmerston's affairs continued.

79. *The Satirist; or, the Censor of the Times* (Sunday 3 June 1838), p. 174.

80. 'Terrific Hubbub Among the Ministers', *The Age* (Sunday 11 November 1838), p. 355.

81. *The Age* (Sunday 16 September 1838), p. 293.

82. *Memoirs of Harriette Wilson, Written by Herself,* 4 vols (1825); the most recent edition is available as *Harriette Wilson's Memoirs,* selected and ed. Lesley Branch (London: Phoenix, 2003; originally pub. *c.* 1957).

83. 'Matrimonial Agency', *Punch* (Saturday 14 August 1841), p. 59.

84. 'To the Right Hon. Lord Palmerston', *Reynold's Newspaper* (Sunday 24 April 1853), p. 4.

85. *Punch* (Saturday 15 January 1848), p. 93.

86. 'Club and Social Gossip', *The Ipswich Journal* (Tuesday 25 June 1872), p. 2.

87. Christopher Breward, 'The Dandy Laid Bare: Embodying Practices and Fashion for Men', in Stella Bruzzi and Pamela Church Gibson, eds, *Fashion Cultures: Theories, Explorations and Analysis* (London and New York: Routledge, 2000), pp. 221–38, at p. 223; Karen Baclawski, *The Guide to Historic Costume* (London: Batsford, 1995), pp. 157–8; Hollander, *Seeing through Clothes,* pp. 225–9; Lucy Johnston, *Nineteenth-Century Fashion in Detail* (London: Victoria and Albert Museum, 2005), pp. 14–15; C. Willet Cunnington and Phillis Cunnington, *Handbook of English Costume in the Nineteenth Century* (London: Faber, 1959), p. 49.

88. *The Taylor's Complete Guide* (London, [1796]), p. 24. *Albion and Evening Advertiser* (Wednesday 3 December 1800).

89. Walter Vaughan, *An Essay, Philosophical and Medical, Concerning Modern Clothing* (1792), p. 69.

90. *Morning Chronicle* (Saturday 24 August 1799).

91. Hollander, *Seeing through Clothes*, p. 228.

92. *Taylor's Complete Guide*, p. 29. Wider 'whole falls' (as opposed to the narrower small or half falls) were also used, though they were less fashionable; see Cunnington and Cunnington, *Handbook Nineteenth Century*, pp. 45, 49.

93. Gronow, *Recollections*, pp. 32, 124, 267–8, for example, illustrates the changing conventions with regard to the social occasions at which each of these garments was acceptable.

94. 'Parisian Fashions', *Morning Post and Gazetteer* (Friday 24 August 1798).

95. *Taylor's Complete Guide*, p. 150.

96. For braces and trouser straps, see Johnston, *Nineteenth-Century Fashion in Detail*, pp. 140–1. Brummell's biographers insist that the trouser strap was his, or his tailor's, invention, and put its origin in 1799–1800; see Ian Kelly, *Beau Brummell: the Ultimate Dandy* (Hodder and Stoughton, 2005), pp. 200–1, 205. Kelly also quotes Captain Jesse (Brummell's original biographer), who is of the same opinion. Johnston, however, puts the date of the trouser strap after Brummell's departure from England, at the much later date of 1820. Cunnington and Cunnington, *Handbook Nineteenth Century*, p. 82, date strapped pantaloons to 1819. The evidence of trouser straps in a satirical print of 1818, however (Figure 18), would indicate that both Johnston and the Cunningtons are mistaken on this point.

97. Vaughan, *An essay*, pp. 45–6.

98. *Leaves from theNotebooks of Lady Dorothy Nevill*, ed. Ralph Nevill (London: Macmillan, 1907), pp. 169–70.

99. Kelly, *Beau Brummell*, p. 203.

100. *The Tailor and Cutter* (1880), quoted in Christopher Breward, *The Hidden Consumer: Masculinities, Fashion and City Life 1860–1914* (Manchester: Manchester University Press, 1999), pp. 160–1. Although this text comes from later in the century, the issues with which it deals date from this earlier period; see Kelly, *Beau Brummell*, pp. 198–9, 203.

101. 'Poetry', *Trewman's Exeter Flying Post and Cornish Advertiser* (Thursday 17 December 1818). In this instance, *amateur* is used in its sense of one who loves something. The mention of wide inexpressibles refers to a minor fashion for Cossacks: very full trousers that were inspired by the dress of the Russian soldiers brought to London for peace celebrations in 1814; see Cunnington and Cunnington, *Handbook Nineteenth Century*, pp. 49–50, 84–5.

102. A.M.W. Stirling, *The Letter-Bag of Lady Elizabeth Spencer Stanhope* (London: John Lane the Bodley Head, 1913), II, pp. 49–50.

103. On fascistic tendency at the heart of the dandy ethic, see Christopher Breward, 'The Dandy Laid Bare: Embodying Practices and Fashion for Men', in Stella Bruzzi and Pamela Church Gibson, eds, *Fashion Cultures: Theories, Explorations and Analysis* (New York and London: Routledge, 2000), and Elizabeth Wilson, *Adorned in Dreams: Fashion and Modernity* (London: Virago, 1985), p. 204.

104. Gronow, *Recollections,* pp. 160–1.

105. *The Autobiography of the Hon. Roger North,* ed. Augustus Jessopp (London, 1887), letters dated 10 October 1679 and 12 October 1679, pp. 215–16.

106. *The Diary of Sir Henry Slingsby,* entry dated 1641, quoted in Phillis Cunnington and Anne Buck, *Children's Costume in England from the Fourteenth to the End of the Nineteenth Century* (London: Adam and Charles Black, 1965), p. 71.

107. *Court and Private Life in the Time of Queen Charlotte: Being the Journals of Mrs. Papendiek, Assistant Keeper of the Wardrobe and Reader to Her Majesty,* ed. Mrs Vernon Delves Broughton (London: Richard Bentley, 1887), I, p. 78; II, 230–1.

108. 'Tom's First Knickerbockers', *Good Words for the Young* (Saturday 1 May 1869), pp. 343–4.

109. 'Only and Old Maid', *The Monthly Packet* (December 1890), p. 81.

110. Jo Paoletti and Carol Kregloh, 'The Children's Department', in Brush Kidwell and Steele, *Dressing the Part,* pp. 22–41, at p. 33.

111. 'Dress', *Myra's Journal of Dress and Fashion* (Wednesday 1 November 1876), p. 2231.

112. 'Paris and London Fashions', *The Lady's Newspaper* (Saturday 23 October 1852), p. 244 and Figures 2 and 3.

113. *Taylor's Complete Guide,* pp. 134–5.

114. *Jane Austen's Letters,* collected and ed. Deirdre Le Faye, 3rd edn (Oxford: Oxford University Press, 1995), p. 76, letter to Cassandra Austen, Wednesday 21–Thursday 22 January 1801.

115. *Jane Austen's Letters,* p. 8, letter to Cassandra Austen, Monday 5 September 1796.

116. 'The Fitz-Chizzle Papers.—No. 4', *The Satirist; or, the Censor of the Times* (Sunday 8 September 1844), p. 283.

117. On the early modern definition of normative manhood as strong and reasoning compared with the weak instability of women, see for example Alexandra Shepard, *Meanings of Manhood in Early Modern England* (Oxford: Oxford University Press, 2003), p. 8. On the position of women under law, see Laurence, *Women in England 1500–1760,* pp. 227–35.

118. *The Diary of Bulstrode Whitelocke 1605–1675,* ed. Ruth Spalding, Records of Social and Economic History, n.s. 13 (The British Academy, 1990), pp. 45, 47. Whitelocke has an authorial habit of referring to himself in the third person.

119. John Fletcher, *Monsieur Thomas* (1639), I.i.6–7.

120. Thomas Middleton and Thomas Dekker, *The Roaring Girl* (1611), II.ii.77–78.

121. Cunnington and Cunnington, *History of Underclothes,* p. 114.

122. *Oracle and Public Advertiser* (Friday 25 May 1798).

123. For example, 'Female Fashions', *Star* (Monday 22 October 1798); 'Parisian Fashions', *Jackson's Oxford Journal* (Saturday 7 July 1804).

124. 'Foreign Intelligence', *London Packet or New Lloyd's Evening Post* (Monday 25 June 1798).

125. 'Incompatibility of Disposition', *True Briton (1793)* (Wednesday 1 February 1797).

126. 'Fashions for June, 1806', *La Belle Assemblée; or, Bell's Court and Fashionable Magazine* [Thursday 1 May 1806], [p. 279].

127. *The Glenbervie Journals,* Walter Sichel, ed. (London: Constable, 1910), p. 153.

128. On acceptance of drawers, see Cunnington and Cunnington, *History of Underclothes,* p. 130. For an example of modest resistance, see *The Times* (Friday 17 October 1851), p. 8, col. F.

129. Aileen Ribeiro, *Dress and Morality* (New York: Holmes and Meier, 1986), p. 148.

130. *Punch,* vol. 20, p. 200 [1851, no date]. *Pottus* perhaps relates to *potulent,* which the *Oxford English Dictionary* glosses as 'drunken; given to or characterized by drinking'.

131. 'The Bloomer Ball', *The Times* (Friday 31 October 1851), p. 4, col. F.

132. 'Bloomerism at the Crystal Palace', *The Times* (Saturday 27 September 1851), p. 8, col. C.

133. For example, *The Aberdeen Journal,* Wednesday 10 September 1851, Wednesday 17 September 1851, Wednesday 1 October 1851, Wednesday 29 October 1851, Wednesday 5 November 1851, Wednesday 12 November 1851, Wednesday 19 November 1851, Wednesday 26 November 1851.

134. 'Woman and her Master, and the Bloomers', *The Lady's Newspaper* (Saturday 18 October 1851), p. 209.

135. See Stella Mary Newton, *Health, Art and Reason: Dress Reformers of the Nineteenth Century* (London: John Murray, 1974), p. 3.

136. Ibid., p. 3.

137. *The Times* (Thursday 23 October 1851), p. 4, cols D–E.

138. 'Election Intelligence', *The Times* (Saturday 3 July 1852), p. 5, col. B.

139. *The Times* (Thursday 30 September 1852), p. 4, col. F.; p. 5, col. A.

140. Quoted in 'Miss Nightingale', *The Lady's Newspaper* (Saturday 7 April 1855), p. 217.

141. *The Times* (3 July 1856), p. 8, col. C.

142. 'The Higher Education of Women', *The Englishwoman's Review* [1 January 1869], p. 127, quoting *Pall Mall Gazette* (16 December 1868). Women were denied full membership of the University of Cambridge until 6 December 1947.

143. 'Parliamentary Intelligence', *The Times* (8 April 1875), p. 6, col. E.

144. Quoted in *Pall Mall Gazette* (Thursday 16 May 1881), p. 6; also *Myra's Journal of Dress and Fashion* (Friday 1 July 1881), p. 337.

145. *The Liverpool Mercury* (Wednesday 3 August 1881), p. 5.

146. 'Rational Dress', *Punch* (Saturday 25 June 1881), p. 293.

147. Newton, *Health, Art and Reason,* p. 94.

148. For a highly condemnatory report, see 'Cycling by Ladies', *Pall Mall Gazette* (Tuesday 19 September 1893), p. 10.

149. 'Rationals *v.* Skirts Competition', *Hearth and Home* (Thursday 5 December 1895), p. 163. A very similar competition was being run at the same time by a Cardiff paper, the *Western Mail*; see 'Shall Bloomers be Worn or Not?', which ran Saturday 9 November 1895; Saturday 16 November 1895; Saturday 24 November 1895; Saturday 30 November 1895; Saturday 7 December 1895.

150. 'Through the Air on Wheels', *The Woman's Signal* (Thursday 3 September 1894), p. 168.

151. 'Rational Dress', *Cycling: an Illustrated Weekly* (Saturday 4 November 1893), p. 248.

152. See *The Woman's Signal* (Thursday 16 May 1898), p. 327.

153. The case is reported in detail in 'Innkeepers and Rational Dress', *The Times* (Thursday 6 April 1899), p. 8, cols E–F.

154. 'Lady Harberton and the Hotel-Keeper', *Pall Mall Gazette* (Wednesday 5 April 1899), p. 7.

155. Katina Bill, 'Attitudes towards Women's Trousers: Britain in the 1930s', *Journal of Design History*, 6.1 (1993), pp. 45–54, at p. 53.

156. M-OA: TC Personal appearance and clothes, 1/I, Trouser Count, 1941.

157. 'Pyjamas on Parade', *The Times* (Saturday 10 July 1948), p. 5, col. D.

158. See Elizabeth Wilson and Lou Taylor, *Through the Looking Glass: a History of Dress from 1860 to the Present Day* (London: BBC Books, 1989), p. 113; Catherine Horwood, *Keeping up Appearances: Fashion and Class between the Wars* (Stroud: Sutton, 2005), p. 79.

159. 'Cold for Sedentary Work', *The Times* (Friday 23 November 1962) p. 13, col. G.

160. 'Trouser ban on teacher', *The Times* (Thursday 2 October 1969), p. 3, col. E.

161. Wilson and Taylor, *Through the Looking Glass,* p. 170.

162. 'Trouser suit upsets judge', *The Times* (Tuesday 24 February 1970), p. 2, col. E.

163. 'NUS fears of Police "spies" at debate', *The Times* (Monday 2 December 1974), p. 2, col. F.

164. 'Teachers claim victory in trouser dispute', *The Times* (Wednesday 14 June 1978), p. 6, col. A.

165. 'Woman in trousers loses claim to job', *The Times* (Tuesday 9 August 1983), p. 3, col. H.

166. Nicholas Pyke, 'Girls in Trousers an Issue for EOC', *The Guardian* (Thursday 4 July 2002), http://www.guardian.co.uk/uk/2002/jul/04/schools.education1, accessed 10 December 2008.

167. 'PM's pants prove problematic', http://tvnz.co.nz/view/page/423466/83922, accessed September 2008. My thanks to Rev. B. M. Vincent for this reference.

CHAPTER 5

1. Desiderius Erasmus, *De Civilitate Morum Puerilium* (1530), trans. Brian McGregor, in *Literary and Educational Writings 3, Collected Works of Erasmus* (Toronto: University of Toronto Press, 1974–2008), XXV, p. 278.

2. John Chamberlain, *The Letters of John Chamberlain,* ed. Norman Egbert McClure (Philadelphia: American Philosophical Society, 1939), II, p. 416, 22 December 1621.

3. Emanuel van Meteren, *Nederlandtsche Historie,* translated excerpts in William Brenchley Rye, ed., *England as Seen by Foreigners in the Days of Elizabeth and James the First* (London: John Russell Smith, 1865), pp. 69–70.

4. *Court and Private Life in the Time of Queen Charlotte: Being the Journals of Mrs. Papendiek, Assistant Keeper of the Wardrobe and Reader to Her Majesty,* ed. Mrs Vernon Delves Broughton (London: Richard Bentley, 1887), I pp. 221, 314; II, 2, 207.

5. *Letters of the Lady Brilliana Harley, Wife of Sir Robert Harley of Brampton Bryan,* ed. Thomas Taylor Lewis (Camden Society, o.s. 58, 1854), p. 20, letter dated 14 January 1638/9.

6. *The Memoirs of Anne, Lady Halkett and Ann, Lady Fanshawe,* ed. John Loftis (Oxford: Clarendon Press, 1979), p. 188.

7. *The Diary of Bulstrode Whitelocke 1605–1675,* ed. Ruth Spalding, Records of Social and Economic History, n.s. 13 (British Academy, 1990), pp. 332–3 n. 1. Whitelocke has an authorial habit of referring to himself in the third person. On Christina's relationship with the Countess, see p. 333 n. 1.

8. *A Journal of All That Was Accomplished by Monsieur de Maisse Ambassador in England,* trans. and ed. G. B. Harrison (London: Nonesuch Press, 1931), p. 59. Janet Arnold, *Queen Elizabeth's Wardrobe Unlock'd* (Leeds: Maney, 1988), pp. 9–10.

9. Chamberlain, *Letters,* II, p. 157, 20 April 1618.

10. See Ralph Houlbrooke, ' "Public" and "Private" in the Funerals of the Later Stuart Gentry: Some Somerset Examples', *Mortality,* 1 (1996), pp. 163–76.

11. Ralph Josselin, *The Diary of Ralph Josselin 1616–1683,* ed. Alan Macfarlane, Records of Social and Economic History, n.s. 3 (London, 1976), p. 635, 26 October 1681. For mourning clothes in general, see Lou Taylor, *Mourning Dress: a Costume and Social History* (George Allen and Unwin, 1983).

12. *The Diary of Henry Machyn,* ed. John Gough Nichols, Camden Society, o.s. 42 (1847), p. 219. *Diary of Ralph Josselin,* p. 290, December 1652. Chamberlain, *Letters of John Chamberlain,* I, p. 217, 12 March 1606.

13. Thomas Jordan [1612–85], 'The Epilogue, on New-Years-Day at Night', in *A Nursery of Novelties* ([1665]).

14. *Diary of Henry Machyn,* II, p. 40, 22 February 1661; IV, p. 68, 7 March 1663; IX, p. 449, 15 February 1669. *Loves garland: or posies for rings, hand-kerchers, & gloves: and such pretty tokens that lovers send their loves* (London, 1674).

15. William Strode (1600/1601–45), 'A Pair of Gloves', in *The Poetical Works* (1907).

16. *Barrington Family Letters 1628–1632,* ed. Arthur Searle, Camden 4th ser. 28 (London, 1983), p. 119, letter dated [30 December 1629]. *Diary of Bulstrode Whitelock,* p. 366 and note, May 1654.

17. In the transcript of the 1584 gift roll, in J. L. Nevinson, 'New Year's Gifts to Queen Elizabeth I, 1584', *Costume,* 9 (1975), pp. 27–31, at p. 30.

18. *Greville's England: Selections from the Diaries of Charles Greville 1818–1860,* ed. Christopher Hibbert (London: Folio Society, 1981), p. 95.

19. *Journals of Mrs. Papendiek,* I, pp. 313–14.

20. For Pitt's proposals, see *Cobbett's Parliamentary History of England,* vol. 25, col. 555; for Fox's reply, and his figure of eight million for the total British population, see col. 558. For the debate in general, see also *The Times* (Tuesday 10 May 1785), p. 2, col. C (at that point, published under the paper's first title, *The Daily Universal Register*). It passed into law as 25 Geo. III c. 55 and was summarised in *Ridgeway's Abstract of the Budget; or Ways and Means for the Year 1785,* 2nd edn (London, [1785?]), pp. 18–20.

21. *Reports from Committees of the House of Commons* 11, § 7, p. 44. See also *The Times* [*The Daily Universal Register*] (Friday 5 May 1786), p. 1, col. D.

22. *The Times* [*The Daily Universal Register*] (Saturday 27 Oct. 1787), p. 3, col. A. The law was repealed in 1794; see Valerie Cumming, *Gloves,* Costume Accessory Series (London: Batsford, 1982), p. 54.

23. For example, 6 Geo. III, c. 19, made the importation of foreign-made gloves illegal. For the debate, see *The Times* (1 February 1832), p. 2, cols B–D, quote at col. D, comment by Mr Hume.

24. Cumming, *Gloves,* p. 58.

25. *The Times* (1 February 1832), p. 2, col. D.

26. *The Whole Art of Dress! or the Road to Elegance and Fashion … by a Cavalry Officer* (London, 1830), p. 39.

27. Cumming, *Gloves,* p. 58.

28. Ibid., p. 55.

29. Such 'rules' were echoed and repeated in numerous etiquette manuals. These appear in *Etiquette; or, the perfect gentleman* (London: Milner, n.d.), on pp. 14, 24, 29, 91, 104, 149, 152, 154, 163, 180–1; quotes at pp. 154, 152, 163, 29, 91.

30. *The Bristol Mercury and Daily Post* (Thursday 30 December 1886), p. 6.

31. Penelope Byrde, *The Male Image: Men's Fashion in England 1300–1970* (London: Batsford, 1979), p. 210.

32. Osbert Sitwell, *The Scarlet Tree* (London: Macmillan, 1946), p. 193.

33. *The Times* (12 September 1928), p. 15, col. F.

34. Quoted in Cumming, *Gloves,* p. 78.

35. *The Times* (3 December 1928), p. 16, col. D.

36. Katherine Horwood, *Keeping up Appearances: Fashion and Class between the Wars* (Stroud: Sutton, 2005), p. 130.

37. M-OA: TC Personal Appearance and Clothes, 1/C.

38. Phillip Stubbes, *The Anatomie of Abuses* (London, 1583), sig. G2r.

39. Emanuel van Meteren, *Nederlandtsche Historie,* translated excerpts in Brenchley Rye, *England as Seen by Foreigners,* pp. 69–70, 73.

40. *The Private Diary of Dr John Dee,* ed. James Orchard Halliwell, Camden Society, o.s. 19 (1842), p. 37, 4 December 1590.

41. Quoted in Arnold, *Queen Elizabeth's Wardrobe,* p. 12.

42. *Dudley Carleton to John Chamberlain 1603–1624: Jacobean Letters,* ed. Maurice Lee Jr (New Brunswick: Rutgers University Press, 1972), pp. 34–5, 4 July 1603.

43. Pierre Erondelle, *The French garden: for English ladyes and gentlewomen to walke in,* 2nd edn (London, 1605), sig. [E4v]; also repr. in M. St Clare Byrne (ed.), *The Elizabethan Home* (London: Methuen, 1949), p. 40.

44. British Library, Salisbury MSS, microfilm 485, no. 126, Box H. 'Mundis muliebris: or the ladies dressing room unlocked, and her toilet spread' (1690), in Frederick W. Fairholt, ed.,

Satirical Songs and Poems on Costume from the 13th to the 19th Century, Early English Poetry, Ballads, and Popular Literature of the Middle Ages, vol. 27 (Percy Society, 1849), p. 194.

45. *Diary of Henry Machyn,* II, pp. 90–1, 30 April 1661; V, p. 28, 27 January 1664; VIII, p. 423, 6 September 1667; IV, p. 181, 12 June 1663.

46. Quoted in Arnold, *Queen Elizabeth's Wardrobe,* p. 12.

47. *Diary of Henry Machyn,* VIII, pp. 71–2, 18 February 1667. For a similar report of masked women at Vauxhall, see IX, p. 220, 1 June 1668.

48. Ibid., IV, p. 181, 12 June 1663.

49. The order was given on 17 January 1704, and a copy was printed in the *Daily Courant* on 24 January. The song is referred to by John Doran, *Habits and Men* (Richard Bentley, 1855), p. 210.

50. Karl Ludwig von Pöllnitz, *The memoirs of Charles-Lewis, Baron de Pollnitz. Being the observations he made in his late travels ... In letters to his friend,* 2 vols (London, 1737), II, p. 461. I found the source for this quotation in Christoph Heyl, 'When They Are Veyl'd on Purpose to Be Seene: the Metamorphosis of the Mask in Seventeenth- and Eighteenth-Century London', in Joanne Entwhistle and Elizabeth Wilson, eds, *Body Dressing* (Oxford: Berg, 2001), pp. 121–42.

51. In *Asylum for fugitive pieces, in prose and verse, not in any other collection,* 3 vols (London, 1789), III, p. 254.

52. Fanny Burney, *Cecilia, or Memoirs of an Heiress* (1782), ed. Peter Sabor and Margaret Anne Doody (Oxford: Oxford University Press, 1988), p. 106. On the masquerades of this period, see Terry Castle, *Masquerade and Civilisation: The Carnivalesque in Eighteenth-Century English Culture and Fiction* (London: Methuen, 1986), and Aileen Ribeiro, *The Dress Worn at Masquerades in England, 1730 to 1790, and Its Relation to Fancy Dress in Portraiture* (New York and London: Garland, 1984). Hayl, 'When They are Veyl'd', maintains that over the course of the seventeenth century, the purpose of masks changed from a cosmetic to a disguise function, which allowed the wearer a degree of anonymity. This, he says, culminated in the eighteenth-century practice of masquerade.

53. Thomas Marriott, *Female conduct: being an essay on the art of pleasing* (London, 1759), p. 178.

54. See C. Willet Cunnington and Phillis Cunnington, *Handbook of English Costume in the Eighteenth Century,* rev. edn (London: Faber, 1972), pp. 365–6; C. Willet Cunnington and Phillis Cunnington, *Handbook of English Costume in the Nineteenth Century* (London: Faber, 1959), pp. 365, 415, 436, 459, 511, 564–5. On the cultural practice of wearing veils in Second Empire Paris, see Marni Reva Kessler, *Sheer Presence: the Veil in Manet's Paris* (Minneapolis: University of Minnesota Press, 2006).

55. 'The Veil', in *The whim of the day, (for 1793) Containing an entertaining selection of the choisest and most approved songs,* 2nd edn (London, 1793), p. 79. James Smith Barr, *Lost since Sunday evening 7 o'clock, from Curzon street, May Fair, a Brussels lace veil...* ([London], [1800]).

56. L. E. Craig, *True politeness: OR, Etiquette for ladies and gentlemen* (Philadelphia, 1848), p. 19.

57. Juan Luis Vives, *A very fruteful and pleasant booke called the instruction of a Christen woman,* trans. Richard Hyrde (London, 1567), Book II, c. ix, fol. Cc2r–v. This was first published in 1528 or 1529 and was reprinted in nine known editions between then and 1592: see William St Clair and Irmgard Maassen, eds, *Conduct Literature for Women, 1500–1640* (London: Pickering and Chatto, 2000), I, pp. 17–20.

58. *Journal of De Masse,* p. 59.

59. 'Extracts from Paul Hentzner's Travels in England, 1598', translated excerpts in Brenchley Rye, *England as Seen by Foreigners,* p. 105.

60. Quoted in Arnold, *Queen Elizabeth's Wardrobe,* p. 11: 'dans chaque Audience qu'il eut, elle se déganta plus de cent fois pour luy faire voir ses mains qui êtoient tres-belles & tres-blanches'.

61. Cumming, *Gloves,* p. 24.

62. *A manual of politeness, comprising the principles of etiquette and rules of behavior in genteel society* (Philadelphia: J. B. Lippincott, 1856), p. 160. *Etiquette; or the perfect gentleman,* p. 104.

63. *LM* 42 (1811), p. 306. Claudia Brush Kidwell and Valerie Steele, eds, *Men and Women: Dressing the Part* (Washington, DC: Smithsonian Institute Press, 1989), p. 50, also remind us of the importance of context to bodily revelation.

64. *The Works of Joseph Hall* (Oxford: D. A. Talboys, 1837), V, p. 470.

65. *Dudley Carleton to John Chamberlain,* p. 68.

66. J. S., *A brief anatomie of women* (London, 1653), p. 2. Jacques Boileau, *A just and seasonable reprehension of naked breasts and shoulder written by a grave and learned papist,* translate by Edward Cooke, Esquire (1678). Robert Codrington, *The Second Part of Youths Behaviour,* 2nd edn (London, 1672), p. 77.

67. *The Guardian,* ed. John Calhoun Stephens (Lexington: University Press of Kentucky, 1982), pp. 353–5, at p. 354.

68. *GM* 1 (1731), p. 388; *GM* 23 (1753), p. 10; see also, for example, *GM* 58, Pt 2 (1788), p. 788; *GM* 74, Pt 1 (1804), pp. 427–9; *GM* 74, Pt 2 (1804), p. 1013; see also *GM* 74, Pt 2 (1804), p. 1017 and *GM* 86, Pt 2 (1816), p. 316.

69. *Journal of DeMaisse,* p. 25.

70. *Diary of Henry Machyn,* VII, p. 379, 22 November 1666.

71. *Jane Austen's Letters,* collected and ed. Deirdre Le Faye, 3rd edn (Oxford: Oxford University Press, 1995), p. 86, letter to Cassandra, Tuesday 12–Wednesday 13 May 1801; pp. 156–7, Friday 9 December 1808; pp. 261, 262, Wednesday 9 March 1814.

72. *Leaves from the Notebooks of Lady Dorothy Nevill,* ed. Ralph Nevill (London: Macmillan, 1907), pp. 268–9.

73. Jane Austen, *Pride and Prejudice* (Oxford: Oxford University Press, 1970), vol. 3, chap. 3, p. 238.

74. *Journal of De Masse,* pp. 25, 29. Gerschow is quoted in Arnold, *Queen Elizabeth's Wardrobe,* p. 12.

75. *Memoirs of Sir James Melville of Halhill 1535–1617,* ed. A. Francis Steuart (London: Routledge, 1929), pp. 95–6.

76. *Taine's Notes on England,* trans. Edward Hyams (London: Thames and Hudson, 1957), p. 20. *LM* 42 (1811), pp. 305–6.

77. Quoted in Jane Ashelford, *The Art of Dress: Clothes and Society 1500–1914* (London: National Trust, 1996), p. 16. Lucy Hutchinson, *Memoirs of the Life of Colonel Hutchinson,* ed. N. H. Keeble (London:Dent, 1995), pp. 18–19. Captain R. H. Gronow, *Recollections and Anecdotes: Being a Second Series of Reminiscences* (London: Smith, Elder, 1863), p. 146. *A manual of politeness,* pp. 159–60.

78. *LM* 42 (1811), p. 305.

79. Michael Drayton, 'Edward the Fourth of Mistres Shore', in *The Works of Michael Drayton,* ed. J. William Hebel, 5 vols (Shakespeare Head Press by Basil Blackwell, 1961), II, p. 249.

80. A.M.W. Stirling, *The Letter-Bag of Lady Elizabeth Spencer Stanhope* (London: John Lane the Bodley Head, 1913), I, p. 116.

81. *GM* 74, Pt 2 (1804), p. 1013.

82. See for example, the collection of patch boxes at Lotherton Hall, Yorkshire.

83. *Diary of Henry Machyn,* VIII, pp. 186–7, 26 April 1667.

84. Robert Codrington, *The Second Part of Youths Behaviour,* 2nd edn (London, 1672), p. 22. Hannah Woolley, *The Gentlewomans Companion* (London, 1673), pp. 57, 59; note that this text may be an unauthorised, compiled work.

85. J.S., *A brief anatomie of women,* p. 2.

86. *The British Apollo,* vol. 2, no. 5 (Friday 8–Wednesday 13 April 1709).

87. *Diary of Henry Machyn,* I, p. 283, 4 November 1660; I, p. 234, 30 August 1660; I, p. 269, 20 October 1660; I, p. 299, 22 November 1660. For other mentions, see I, p. 138, 14 May 1660; III, p. 239, 27 October 1662; VI, p. 9, 13 January 1665; VIII, pp. 196–7, 1 May 1667.

88. *Spectator,* I, (Saturday 2 June 1711).

89. On differences in temperature, see Ninya Mikhaila and Jane Malcolm-Davies, *The Tudor Tailor: Reconstructing Sixteenth-Century Dress* (London: Batsford, 2006), pp. 9–10.

90. *Diary of Henry Machyn,* VIII, p. 105, 9 March 1667. Pepys calls it 'snow', but presumably, he means that moisture had condensed and then frozen.

91. *Journals of Mrs. Papendiek,* II, p. 34.

92. *Correspondence of Sarah Spencer, Lady Lyttelton 1787–1870,* ed. Hon. Mrs Hugh Wyndham (London: John Murray, 1912), p. 53.

93. *Diary of Ralph Josselin,* p. 170, 22 June 1649.

94. *The Autobiography of Mrs. Alice Thornton,* Surtees Society 62 (1875), p. 166.

95. *Diary of Henry Machyn,* V, p. 277, 22 September 1664; VI, p. 89, 24 April 1665.

96. *Letters of Brilliana Harley,* p. 12.

97. *Letters of John Chamberlain,* I, p. 497, 30 December 1613.

98. Stirling, *Letter-Bag of Lady Spencer Stanhope,* p. 355, 12 May 1821.

99. British Library, Lansdowne MSS, vol. 6, no. 77, fol. 182. My thanks to Dr Caroline Bowden for this letter.

100. *Diary of Henry Machyn*, V, p. 222, 26 July 1664.

101. Charles Allen, *The Polite Lady: or, a course of female education* (London, 1760), pp. 99–101.

102. *The Ladies' Pocket Magazine*, Pt 2 (London: Joseph Robin, 1829), p. 24.

103. *GM* 58, Pt 2 (1788), p. 989.

104. A.L.M. Cardigan and Lancastre, *My Recollections* (London: Eveleigh Nash, 1909), p. 4.

105. For example, see Paul Slack, *The Impact of Plague in Tudor and Stuart England* (London: Routledge and Kegan Paul, 1985), pp. 207 ff.

106. John Davies, 'The triumph of death: or, the picture of the plague; according to the life, as it was in Anno Domini. 1603', in *Humours Heau'n on Earth* (London: 1609), p. 240.

107. Andrew Wear, *Knowledge and Practice in English Medicine, 1550–1680* (Cambridge: Cambridge University Press, 2000), p. 329.

108. York City Archives, City of York House Books, B 35, fol. 146r, 12 December 1631.

109. *GM* 73, Pt 2 (1803), p. 885; 74, Pt 1 (1804), p. 186; 73, Pt 1 (1803), p. 274; 74, Pt 1 (1804), p. 190.

110. William Roberts, *Memoirs of the Life and Correspondence of Mrs. Hannah More* (London, 1834), IV, pp. 413, 416–17.

111. *GM* 73, Pt 1 (1803), pp. 233–4.

112. *LM* 30 (1799), pp. 150–1; 39 (1808), pp. 479–80; 42 (1811), p. 9.

113. *The Times* (Friday 20 December 1844), p. 5, col. C, for the coroner's inquest; Wednesday 25 December 1844, p. 6, col. F.

114. For the display at the International Exhibition, see *The Times* (Friday 28 June 1872), p. 3, col. F, and *The Times* (Thursday 1 August 1872), p. 1 col. C. For *The Lancet* report (of 22 June 1872), see *The Times* (Wednesday 13 November 1872), p. 13, col. C.

115. See *The Times* (11 November 1872), p. 6, col. A, and *The Times* (Wednesday 13 November 1872), p. 13, col. C.

EPILOGUE

1. Osbert Sitwell, *The Scarlet Tree* (London: Macmillan, 1946), p. 161. The Society for the Protection of Birds was formed in 1891 in response to the threatened extinction of the great crested grebe, whose feathers were used in fashionable millinery. In 1904, the society was incorporated by Royal Charter, becoming the RSPB.

2. For example, see Christopher Breward, *The Culture of Fashion: A New History of Fashionable Dress* (Manchester: Manchester University Press, 1995), p. 228.

3. Cecil Beaton, *The Glass of Fashion* (London: Weidenfeld and Nicolson, 1954), p. 160.

4. Kate Cann, 'Free Dressing', in Kirsty Dunseath, ed., *A Second Skin: Women Write about Clothes* (London: Women's Press, 1998), pp. 84–7, at p. 84. Another text that explores the importance of dress, again, to its female wearers, is Ali Guy, Eileen Green and Maura Banim, eds, *Through the Wardrobe: Women's Relationships with Their Clothes* (Oxford: Berg, 2001).

5. See the comment by Sarah Evans of Discovery Recruitment and Training, in Anne Wollenberg, 'Public Image Limited', *The Guardian* (Saturday 4 October 2008), Features section, pp. 17–18, at p. 17.

6. Ibid., p. 18.

7. Quote from Helen Williamson, ibid., p. 17.

8. Lady Lucy Duff-Gordon, *Discretions and Indiscretions* (London: Jarrolds, 1932), p. 80.

9. *The Letters and Journals of Lady Mary Coke,* ed. J. A. Home (Bath: Kingsmead Reprints, 1970), IV, p. 178, Sunday 20 June 1773.

10. Ibid., II, pp. 197–8, Sunday 21 February 1768; II, pp. 217–18, Sunday 20 March 1768.

11. Ibid., III, p. 481, Monday 18 November 1771; see also III, p. 477, Saturday 9 November 1771, and III, p. 478, Tuesday 12 November 1771.

12. Blacks, Catalogue Spring/Summer 2005, excerpts from 'Buyers Guide' inserted between pp. 82 and 83.

13. Elizabeth Wilson, *Adorned in Dreams: Fashion and Modernity* (London: Virago, 1985), p. 131.

14. 'Curative Power of the Sun', *The Times* (Friday 23 May 1924), p. 16, col. B.

15. See, for example, 'Bathing in the Parks: Mr. Lansbury's Plans', *The Times* (Tuesday 17 September 1929), p. 7, col. C; 'Sun-Bathing in Parks', *The Times* (Saturday 21 September 1929), p. 10, col. F; 'Use of Public Parks: Mr Lansbury's Plans and Hopes', *The Times* (Wednesday 3 September 1930), p. 9, col. E.

16. On the development of seaside leisure, see John K. Watson, *The British Seaside: Holidays and Resorts in the Twentieth Century* (Manchester: Manchester University Press, 2000); John Hassan, *The Seaside, Health and the Environment in England and Wales since 1800* (Aldershot: Ashgate, 2003); Fred Gray, *Designing the Seaside: Architecture, Society and Nature* (London: Reaktion Books, 2006); Steven Braggs and Diane Harris, *Sun, Sea and Sand: the Great British Seaside Holiday* (Stroud: Tempest, 2006).

17. Robert Graves and Alan Hodge, *The Long Week-End: A Social History of Great Britain 1918–1939* (London: Faber and Faber, 1940), p. 278.

18. Both statistics quoted in Catherine Horwood, *Keeping up Appearances: Fashion and Class between the Wars* (Stroud: Sutton, 2005), p. 68.

19. Graves and Hodge, *Long Week-End,* p. 278.

20. Beaton, *Glass of Fashion,* p. 135.

21. Duff-Gordon, *Discretions and Indiscretions,* p. 78.

22. Beaton, *Glass of Fashion,* p. 66.

23. Ibid., p. 163.

24. See Graves and Hodges, *Long Week-End,* chap. 7, and Lesley A. Hall, *Sex, Gender, and Social Change in Britain since 1880* (Houndmills and London: Macmillan, 2000).

25. Duff-Gordon, *Discretions and Indiscretions,* p. 80.

26. Beaton, *Glass of Fashion,* p. 162.

27. The increasing body of literature on this topic includes Margo DeMello, *Bodies of Inscription: a Cultural History of the Modern Tattoo Community* (Durham, NC: Duke University Press,

2000); Jane Caplan, *Written on the Body: the Tattoo in European and American History* (London: Reaktion, 2000); Margot Mifflin, *Bodies of Subversion: a Secret History of Women and Tattoo*, rev. edn (New York: Juno Books, 2001); Nicholas Thomas, Anna Cole and Bronwen Douglas, eds, *Tattoo: Bodies, Art and Exchange in the Pacific and the West* (London: Reaktion, 2005); Mindy Fenske, *Tattoos in American Visual Culture* (New York and Basingstoke: Palgrave Macmillan, 2007). Ted Polhemus, *Hot Bodies, Cool Styles: New Techniques in Self-Adornment* (London: Thames and Hudson, 2004), includes piercings and other stylistic interventions.

28. On the history of cosmetic surgery, see, though principally in the American context, Elizabeth Haiken, *Venus Envy: a History of Cosmetic Surgery* (Baltimore and London: Johns Hopkins University Press, 1997), and Sander L. Gilman, *Making the Body Beautiful: a Cultural History of Aesthetic Surgery* (Princeton: Princeton University Press, 1999).

29. See http://www.consultingroom.com/Statistics/Display.asp?Statistics_ID=26&Title=2007:%20BAAPS:%20Over%2032,400%20Cosmetic%20Surgery%20Procedures%20in%20The%20UK%20in%202007, accessed November 2008.

30. In 2007 the number was 32,453, as opposed to 10,700 in 2002. For the latter figure, see http://www.consultingroom.com/Statistics/Display.asp?Statistics_ID=5&Title=2003%20BAAPS:%20Over%2010,700%20Plastic%20Surgery%20Procedures%20in%20UK%20in%202003, accessed November 2008.

31. See British Association of Aesthetic Plastic Surgeons, 'Surgeons Reveal UK's Largest-Ever Breast Augmentation Survey', http://www.baaps.org.uk/content/view/404/62/, accessed November 2008.

32. See http://www.consultingroom.com/Statistics/Display.asp?Statistics_ID=26&Title=2007:%20BAAPS:%20Over%2032,400%20Cosmetic%20Surgery%20Procedures%20in%20The%20UK%20in%202007, accessed November 2008.

33. See 'The Rise of the Mummy Tuck: How New Mothers Are Spending Thousands on Cosmetic Surgery', *Mail Online* (13 May 2008), http://www.dailymail.co.uk/health/article-563799/The-rise-mummy-tuck-How-new-mothers-spending-thousands-cosmetic-surgery.html, accessed November 2008.

34. Graham Lawton, 'Extreme Surgery', in Linda Welters and Abby Lillethun, eds, *The Fashion Reader* (Oxford and New York: Berg, 2007), pp. 248–9, at p. 249.

35. 'Body Transformations', in a special issue magazine 'The Body Uncovered', *The Observer (1791–2003)* (26 October 2003), available from http://proquest.umi.com/, accessed 20 December 2008.

36. On Botox, see Alex Kuczynski, *Beauty Junkies: Under the Skin of the Cosmetic Surgery Industry* (London: Random House, 2007), pp. 33–60.

37. Hadley Freeman, *The Meaning of Sunglasses: a Guide to (Almost) All Things Fashionable* (London: Viking, 2008), pp. 166–7.

38. On the impossibility of the natural, see Suzanne Fraser, *Cosmetic Surgery, Gender and Culture* (Houndmills: Palgrave Macmillan, 2003); also see Wilson, *Adorned in Dreams,* p. 234.

39. Examples at Haiken, *Venus Envy,* p. 14, and Deborah A. Sullivan, *Cosmetic Surgery: The Cutting Edge of Commercial Medicine in America* (New Brunswick, NJ and London: Rutgers University Press, 2001), cover image.

40. For example, see the Web sites for the cosmetic surgery providers Transform (http://www.transforminglives.co.uk/) and the Hospital Group (http://www.thehospitalgroup.org/), both accessed November 2008.

41. 'Kerry Katona Reveals Her New Body!', *OK* (28 October 2008), pp. 44–57, at pp. 45, 49, 51.

42. 'My New Body Ruined My Marriage', *Daily Mirror* (Tuesday 30 October 2007), pp. 30–1.

43. Kuczynski, *Beauty Junkies,* p. 252.

44. *LM* 42 (1811), p. 367.

45. *LM,* n.s. 1 (1820), p. 100.

46. *The farthingale reviv'd: or, more work for the cooper* ([London], 1711), cols 3–4.

47. William Vaughan, *The golden-groue moralized in three books* (1600), sig. G6r.

48. 'My New Body', pp. 30–1.

49. Screened in the United Kingdom in October 2008.

50. 'Diary of a Boob Job', *Daily Mirror* (Tuesday 22 October 2002), pp. 23–25, at pp. 23, 25.

51. Kuczynski, *Beauty Junkies,* p. 260.

52. See Debra L. Gilman, *Body Work: Beauty and Self-Image in American Culture* (University of California Press, 2002), pp. 104–9.

53. Quoted in Lawton, 'Extreme Surgery', p. 249.

54. Freeman, *Meaning of Sunglasses,* p. 167.

55. Kathy Davis, *Dubious Equalities and Embodied Differences: Cultural Studies on Cosmetic Surgery* (Lanham and Oxford: Rowman and Littlefield, 2003), pp. 95, 118, 128.

56. 'Kerry Katona Reveals Her New Body!', p. 51.

57. 'India Knight: Nip, Tuck and Nuttiness', *Times Online* (30 January 2005), http://www.timesonline.co.uk/tol/news/article508110.ece, accessed November 2008.

58. On the redefinition of the normal, see Deborah Caslav Covino, *Amending the Abject Body: Aesthetic Makeovers in Medicine and Culture* (Albany: State University of New York Press, 2004), and Davis, *Dubious Equalities.* Specifically, on eyelid surgery for Asian Americans and the erasure of the signs of ethnicity in general, see Davis, *Dubious Equalities,* pp. 87–103; and on cosmetic surgery to remove the physical characteristics of Down's syndrome, see ibid., pp. 134–44.

59. On these and other artificialities of the surgically constituted breast, see Kuczynski, *Beauty Junkies,* pp. 246–64.

60. Anne Hollander, *Seeing through Clothes* (Berkeley: University of California Press, 1993), p. 447.

BIBLIOGRAPHY

MANUSCRIPTS

British Library, Lansdowne MSS, vol. 6, no. 77.

British Library, Salisbury MSS, microfilm 485, no. 126, Box H.

Mass-Observation Archive, M-OA: TC Personal Appearance and Clothes, 1/C.

Mass-Observation Archive, M-OA: TC Personal Appearance and Clothes, 1/I, Trouser Count, 1941.

York City Archives, City of York House Books, B 35.

WEB SITES

17th–18th Century Burney Collection Newspapers, http://www.gale.cengage.com/

19th Century British Library Newspapers, http://www.gale.cengage.com/

19th Century UK Periodicals, http://www.gale.cengage.com/

Bodleian Library Broadside Ballads, http://www.bodley.ox.ac.uk/ballads/ballads.htm

British Association of Aesthetic Plastic Surgeons, http://www.baaps.org.uk/

British History Online, http://www.british-history.ac.uk/

BSE Inquiry, http://www.bseinquiry.gov.uk/

Consulting Room, http://www.consultingroom.com/

Early English Books Online (EEBO), http://eebo.chadwyck.com/home

Eighteenth Century Collections Online (ECCO), http://www.gale.cengage.com/

English Poetry Full-Text Database, http://collections.chadwyck.co.uk/

Hospital Group, http://www.thehospitalgroup.org/

Lexicons of Early Modern English (LEME), http://leme.library.utoronto.ca/

London College of Fashion, http://www.fashion.arts.ac.uk/

London Review of Books, http://www.lrb.co.uk/

Mail Online, http://www.dailymail.co.uk/home/index.html

Nexis UK, http://www.lexisnexis.com/uk/nexis/

Nice Cream Company, http://www.nicecreamcompany.com/

Oxford Dictionary of National Biography, http://www.oxforddnb.com/

Portsmouth Local History, http://homepage.ntlworld.com/stephen.pomeroy/local/local.htm

Symington Collection of Corsetry, Foundation and Swimwear, http://museums.leics.gov.uk/collec tions-on-line/HomePage.jsp

Television New Zealand, http://tvnz.co.nz/

Transform, http://www.transforminglives.co.uk/

Times Digital Archive, 1785–1985, http://www.gale.cengage.com/

Times Online, http://www.timesonline.co.uk/

NEWSPAPERS AND PERIODICALS

The Aberdeen Journal
The Age
Albion and Evening Advertiser
The Bristol Mercury
The Bristol Mercury and Daily Post
The British Apollo
The County Gentleman: Sporting Gazette, Agricultural Journal, and 'the Man about Town'
Cycling: an Illustrated Weekly
Daily Courant
Daily Journal
Daily Mirror
The Englishwoman's Domestic Magazine
The Englishwoman's Review
The Female Spectator
The Female Tatler
General Advertiser (1784)
General Evening Post
The Gentleman's Magazine
Good Words for the Young
The Guardian
Hearth and Home
The Ipswich Journal
Jackson's Oxford Journal
John Bull and Britannia
La Belle Assemblée; or, Bell's Court and Fashionable Magazine
The Ladies Cabinet
The Lady's Magazine
The Ladies' Monthly Magazine, Le Monde Élégant, or the World of Fashion
The Ladies' Pocket Magazine
The Lady's Newspaper
The Licensed Victualler's Mirror
The Liverpool Mercury
Lloyd's Weekly Newspaper
London Chronicle
London Daily Post and General Advertiser
London Evening Post
The London Journal
London Packet or New Lloyd's Evening Post
The Midwife, or the Old Woman's Magazine
The Monthly Packet
Morning Chronicle
Morning Chronicle and London Advertiser

Morning Post and Daily Advertiser
Morning Post and Fashionable World
Morning Post and Gazetteer
Myra's Journal of Dress and Fashion
New Scientist
Observer
OK
Old Common Sense; or, the Englishman's Journal
Old England or the National Gazette
Oracle and Public Advertiser
Pall Mall Gazette
Parker's London News or the Impartial Intelligencer
The Public Advertiser
Punch
Reveal
Reynold's Newspaper
The Satirist
The Spectator
Star
St. James's Chronicle or the British Evening Post
The Sunday Times
The Tatler
The Times
Trewman's Exeter Flying Post and Cornish Advertiser
True Briton (1793)
True Patriot: and History of Our Own Times
Universal Spectator and Weekly Journal
Weekly Journal or British Gazetteer
Weekly Journal or Saturday's Post
Western Mail
The Westminster Journal or New Weekly Miscellany
Whitehall Evening Post or London Intelligencer
The Woman's Signal

PRINTED PRIMARY SOURCES

Allen, Charles, *The Polite Lady: or, a course of female education*, London, 1760.

The annual register or a vew of the history, politics, and literature, for the year 1765, 4th edn, London, 1784.

Arnim, Elizabeth von, *The Solitary Summer*, London: Virago Press, 2000; orig. pub. Macmillan, 1899.

Asylum for fugitive pieces, in prose and verse, not in any other collection, 3 vols, London, 1789.

Austen, Jane, *Jane Austen's Letters*, collected and ed. Deirdre Le Faye, 3rd edn, Oxford: Oxford University Press, 1995.

Austen, Jane, *Pride and Prejudice*, 1813; repr. London: Oxford University Press, 1970.

Barker, Tho., *At the Blue Peruke in Red-Lion-street, White-Chappel, liveth Tho. Barker, peruke-maker, who maketh all sorts of new work, well and fashionable, at very low prices. . .*, London, [1725].

Barr, James Smith, *Lost since Sunday evening 7 o'clock, from Curzon street, May Fair, a Brussels lace veil. . .*, [London, 1800].

Barrington Family Letters 1628–1632, ed., Arthur Searle, Camden 4th ser. 28, London, 1983, p. 119.

Beaton, Cecil, *The Glass of Fashion*, London: Weidenfeld and Nicolson, 1954.

Blacks Catalogue, Spring/Summer 2005

Boileau, Jacques, *A just and seasonable reprehension of naked breasts and shoulder written by a grave and learned papist*, trans. Edward Cooke, Esquire, 1678.

Bois-Regard, Nicolas Andry de, *Orthopædia: or, the art of correcting and preventing deformities in children,* vol. 1, London, 1743.

Brenchley Rye, William, ed., *England as Seen by Foreigners in the Days of Elizabeth and James the First*, London: John Russell Smith, 1865.

B[ulwer]., J[ohn]., *Anthropometamorphosis: man transform'd: or, the artificiall changling historically presented*, London, 1653.

Bulwer Lytton, Edward, *Pelham: or, Adventures of a Gentleman*, London: George Routledge and Sons, 1895; orig. pub. 1828.

Burney, Fanny, *Cecilia, or Memoirs of an Heiress*, ed. Peter Sabor and Margaret Anne Doody, Oxford: Oxford University Press, 1988; orig. pub. 1782.

Byrne, M. St. Clare, ed., *The Elizabethan Home*, London: Methuen, 1949.

C., I., *Alcilia Philoparthens louing folly. To which is added Pigmalions image*, London, 1613.

Cardigan and Lancastre, A.L.M., *My Recollections*, London: Eveleigh Nash, 1909.

Campbell, R., *The London tradesman. Being a compendious view of all the trades, professions, arts, both liberal and mechanic, now practised in the cities of London and Westminster*, London, 1747.

Cann, Kate, 'Free Dressing', in Kirsty Dunseath, ed., *A Second Skin: Women Write about Clothes*, London: Women's Press, 1998, pp. 84–7.

Carey, Robert, *The Memoirs of Robert Carey*, ed. F. H. Mares, Oxford: Clarendon Press, 1972.

Carleton, Dudley, *Dudley Carleton to John Chamberlain 1603–1624: Jacobean Letters,* ed. Maurice Lee Jr, New Brunswick: Rutgers University Press, 1972.

Catalogue of Personal and Political Satires Preserved in the Department of Prints and Drawings in the British Museum, eds., George Frederick Stephens and Mary Dorothy Stephens, 11 vols in 16, London: British Museum, 1870–1954.

Chamberlain, John, *The Letters of John Chamberlain,* ed. Norman Egbert McClure, 2 vols, Philadelphia: American Philosophical Society, 1939.

Cleland, John, *The Institution of a Young Nobleman*, Oxford, 1607.

Cobbett's Parliamentary History of England, 36 vols, London, 1806–20.

Codrington, Robert, *The Second Part of Youths Behaviour,* 2nd edn, London, 1672.

Coke, Mary, *The Letters and Journals of Lady Mary Coke,* ed. J. A. Home, 4 vols, 1889–96; facs. repr. Bath: Kingsmead Reprints, 1970.

Craig, L. E., *True politeness: or, Etiquette for ladies and gentlemen*, Philadelphia, 1848.

Creevey, T., *The Creevey Papers,* ed. Sir Herbert Maxwell, London: John Murray, 1905.

Cumberland, Richard, *The Memoirs of Richard Cumberland,* ed. Richard J. Dircks, 2 vols in 1, New York: AMS Press, 2002.

Curtis, William, *The botanical magazine; or, flower-garden displayed*, 18 vols, London, 1793–1803.

The dancing-master. A satyr. Canto I, London, 1722.

Davies, John, 'The triumph of death: or, the picture of the plague; according to the life, as it was in Anno Domini. 1603', in *Humours Heau'n on Earth*, London: 1609.

Dee, John, *The Private Diary of Dr John Dee,* ed. James Orchard Halliwell, Camden Society, o.s. 19, 1842.

The delicate jester; or wit and humour divested of ribaldry, London, [1780].

Drayton, Michael, 'Edward the Fourth of Mistres Shore', in *The Works of Michael Drayton,* ed. J. William Hebel, 5 vols, Oxford: Shakespeare Head Press by Basil Blackwell, 1961.

Duff-Gordon, Lady Lucy, *Discretions and Indiscretions*, London: Jarrolds, 1932.

Dunseath, Kirsty, ed., *A Second Skin: Women Write about Clothes*, London: Women's Press, 1998.

Edgeworth, Maria, *Belinda*, London: J. M. Dent, 1993; orig. pub. 1801.

Erasmus, Desiderius, *De Civilitate Morum Puerilium,* 1530, trans. by Brian McGregor, in *Literary and Educational Writings 3, Collected Works of Erasmus,* Toronto, 1974–97, XXV.

Erondelle, Pierre, *The French garden: for English ladyes and gentlewomen to walke in,* 2nd edn, London, 1605.

Essex, John, *The young ladies conduct*, London, 1722.

Etiquette; or, the Perfect Gentleman, London: Milner, n.d.

Fairholt, Frederick W., ed., *Satirical Songs and Poems on Costume from the 13th to the 19th Century,* Early English Poetry, Ballads, and Popular Literature of the Middle Ages 27, London: Percy Society, 1849.

Fanshawe, Ann, *The Memoirs of Anne, Lady Halkett and Ann, Lady Fanshawe,* ed. John Loftis, Oxford: Clarendon Press, 1979.

The farthingale reviv'd: or, more work for the cooper, [London], 1711.

The Female Spectator, 4 vols, London, 1745 [1746].

The Female Tatler, ed., Fidelis Morgan, London: Dent, 1992.

Fletcher, John, *Monsieur Thomas*, 1639.

Frampton, Mary, *The Journal of Mary Frampton,* ed. Harriot Georgiana Mundy, London, 1885.

Gayton, Edmund, *Pleasant notes upon Don Quixot*, 1654.

The Glenbervie Journals, ed., Walter Sichel, London: Constable, 1910.

Gray, Almyra, *Papers and Diaries of a York Family 1764–1839,* ed. Mrs Edwin Gray, London: Sheldon Press, 1927.

Greville, Charles, *Greville's England: Selections from the Diaries of Charles Greville 1818–1860,* ed. Christopher Hibbert, London: Folio Society, 1981.

Gronow, R. H., *Captain Gronow's Recollections and Anecdotes of the Camp, the Court, and the Clubs, at the Close of the Last War with France*, London, 1864.

Gronow, R. H., *Recollections and Anecdotes: Being a Second Series of Reminiscences*, London: Smith, Elder, 1863.

The Guardian, ed., John Calhoun Stephens, Lexington: University Press of Kentucky, 1982.

Hall, Joseph, *The Works of Joseph Hall*, 12 vols, Oxford: D. A. Talboys, 1837.

Harington, John, *Nugae Antiquae: Being a Miscellaneous Collection of Original Papers,* ed. Thomas Park, 2 vols, London, 1804, I, pp. 391–2.

Harley, Brilliana, *Letters of the Lady Brilliana Harley, Wife of Sir Robert Harley of Brampton Bryan,* ed. Thomas Taylor Lewis, Camden Society, o.s. 58, 1854.

Hayood, Eliza, *The Female Spectator,* 4 vols, London, 1745 [1746].

Haywood, Eliza, *The Female Spectator,* ed. Gabrielle M. Firmager, London: Bristol Classical Press, 1993.

Herbert, Edward, *The Life of Edward, First Lord Herbert of Cherbury,* ed. J.M. Shuttleworth, London: Oxford University Press, 1976.

Hodson, Septimus, *An address to the different classes of persons in Great Britain on the present scarcity and high price of provisions,* London, 1795.

Holme, Randle, *The academy of armory,* Chester, 1688.

Hurault, André, Sieur de Maisse, *A Journal of all that was accomplished by Monsieur de Maisse Ambassador in England,* trans. and ed. G.B. Harrison, London: Nonesuch Press, 1931.

Hutchinson, Lucy, *Memoirs of the Life of Colonel Hutchinson,* ed. N.H. Keeble, London: Dent, 1995.

Jesse, Captain, *The Life of George Brummell, Esq, Commonly Called Beau Brummell,* rev. edn, 2 vols, London: John C. Nimmo, 1886.

Joke upon joke. Or the last packet from the land of festivity and mirth, London, 1800.

Jonson, Ben, *Every Man in His Humour,* first acted 1598, pub. 1601.

Jordan, Thomas, 'The Epilogue, on New-Years-Day at Night', in *A Nursery of Novelties,* [1665?].

Josselin, Ralph, *The Diary of Ralph Josselin 1616–1683,* ed. Alan Macfarlane, Records of Social and Economic History, n.s. 3, London, 1976.

Journals of the House of Commons

Kennedy, A.L., 'The Basque', in Kirsty Dunseath, ed., *A Second Skin: Women Write about Clothes,* London: Women's Press, 1998, pp. 17–20.

Laugh and Be Fat: Or, an Antidote against Melancholy, 9th edn, London: 1724.

Le Blanc, H., *The Art of Tying the Cravat,* 2nd edn, London, 1828.

Leeson, Margaret, *The Life of Mrs Margaret Leeson, alias Peg Plunket,* Dublin, 1798; orig. pub. *Memoirs of Mrs Margaret Leeson. Written by Herself,* 1795–7.

Lieven, Dorothea, *The Private Letters of Princess Lieven to Prince Metternich 1820–1826,* ed. Peter Quennell, assisted in translation by Dilys Powell, London: John Murray, 1937.

Lovelace, Jack, *The hoop-petticoat vindicated,* London, 1745.

Loves garland: or posies for rings, hand-kerchers, & gloves: and such pretty tokens that lovers send their loves, London, 1674.

Macdonald, John, *Memoirs of an Eighteenth-Century Footman: John Macdonald Travels (1745–1779),* ed. John Beresford, London: George Routledge, 1927; facs. repr. Routledge Curzon, 2005; orig. pub. 1790.

Machyn, Henry, *The Diary of Henry Machyn,* ed. John Gough Nichols, Camden Society, o.s. 42, 1847.

A manual of politeness, comprising the principles of etiquette and rules of behavior in genteel society, Philadelphia: J.B. Lippincott, 1856.

Marriott, Thomas, *Female conduct: being an essay on the art of pleasing,* London, 1759.

McGarry, Joanna, 'Dry Shampoos Do the Dirty Work for Hair', *The Sunday Times* (30 March 2008).

Melville, James, *Memoirs of Sir James Melville of Halhill 1535–1617,* ed. A. Francis Steuart, London: Routledge, 1929.

Middleton, Thomas, and Dekker, Thomas, *The Roaring Girl,* 1611.

Montaigne, Michel de, *Montaigne's Essays: John Florio's Translation,* ed. J.I.M. Stewart, 2 vols, London, 1931.

Moore, T., *The Fudge Family in Paris; ed. by Thomas Brown,* 3rd edn, London, 1818.

Moore, William, *The art of hair-dessing,* Bath, [1780].

More, George, *A true discourse concerning the certaine possession and dispossessio[n] of 7 persons in one familie in Lancashire,* 1600.

More, Hannah, *The Letters of Hannah More,* ed. R. Brimley Johnson, London: John Lane the Bodley Head, 1925.

Nash, Thomas, *Haue vvith you to Saffron-wwaldon,* London, 1596.

Nash, Thomas, *Pierce Pennilesse his supplication to the diuell,* London, 1592.

Neckclothitania; or, Tietania: Being an Essay on Starchers by One of the Cloth, London, 1818.

Nevill, Dorothy, *Leaves from the Notebooks of Lady Dorothy Nevill,* ed. Ralph Nevill, London: Macmillan, 1907.

Nevill, Dorothy, *The Reminiscences of Lady Dorothy Nevill,* ed. Ralph Nevill, London: Thomas Nelson, 1906.

Nevill, Dorothy, *Under Five Reigns,* 2nd edn, London: Methuen, 1910.

Nevinson, J. L., 'New Year's Gifts to Queen Elizabeth I, 1584', *Costume,* 9 (1975), pp. 27–31.

Nivelon, François, *Rudiments of Genteel Behavior by F. Nivelon,* [London], 1737.

North, Roger, *The Autobiography of the Hon. Roger North,* ed. Augustus Jessopp, London, 1887.

Official Descriptive and Illustrated Catalogue: Great Exhibition of the Works of Industry of All Nations, 1851, 3 vols, London: Spicer Brothers, [1851].

Papendiek, Charlotte, *Court and Private Life in the Time of Queen Charlotte: Being the Journals of Mrs. Papendiek, Assistant Keeper of the Wardrobe and Reader to Her Majesty,* ed. Mrs Vernon Delves Broughton, 2 vols, London: Richard Bentley, 1887.

Pepys, Samuel, *The Diary of Samuel Pepys,* ed. Robert Latham and William Matthews, 11 vols, London: G. Bell, 1970–83.

Phillips, Edward, *The mysteries of love & eloquence, or, the arts of wooing and complementing as they are manag'd in the Spring Garden, Hide Park, the New Exchange, and other eminent places,* London, 1685.

Plot, Robert, *The Natural History of Oxford-shire,* Oxford and London, 1677.

The polite academy, or school of behaviour for young gentlemen and ladies, London, 1762.

Pöllnitz, Karl Ludwig von, *The memoirs of Charles-Lewis, Baron de Pollnitz. Being the observations he made in his late travels . . . In letters to his friend,* 2 vols, London, 1737.

Pratt, Ellis, *The art of dressing the hair. A poem,* Bath, 1770.

Pückler-Muskau, Hermann, *Pückler's Progress: The Adventures of Prince Pückler-Muskau in England, Wales and Ireland as Told in Letters to His Former Wife,* trans. Flora Brennan, London: Collins, 1987.

Purefoy Letters 1735–1753, ed., G. Eland, 2 vols, London: Sidgwick and Jackson, 1931.

Rameau, Pierre, *The dancing-master: or, the whole art and mystery of dancing explained,* 2nd edn, London, 1731.

Reflections upon theatrical expression in tragedy. With proper instruction, and appendix, London, 1755.

Reports from Committees of the House of Commons, 16 vols, 1803–6.

Reresby, John, *Memoirs of John Reresby,* ed. Andrew Browning, Glasgow: Jackson, 1936.

The Restoration and the Eighteenth Century, ed., Martin Price, The Oxford Anthology of English Literature, London: Oxford University Press, 1973.

Rich, Barnabe, *Greenes newes both from heauen and hell*, London, 1593.

Ridgeway's Abstract of the Budget; or Ways and Means for the Year 1785, 2nd edn, London, [1785?].

Ritchie, David, *A treatise on the hair: . . . also a description of the most fashionable methods of dressing ladies and gentlemens hair*, London, 1770.

Roberts, William, *Memoirs of the Life and Correspondence of Mrs. Hannah More,* 4 vols, London, 1834.

Robin, Poor, *Poor Robins Character of France*, London, 1666.

Rogers, Samuel, *Recollections of the Table-Talk of Samuel Rogers,* ed. Rev. Alexander Dyce, New Southgate: H. A. Rogers, 1887.

Ross, Alexander, *A treatise on bear's grease, with observations, to prove how indispensible the use of that incomparable substance, to preserve the head of hair. . .*, London, 1795.

Rowlands, Samuel, *Doctor Merrie-man, or Nothing but mirth written by S.R.*, London, 1609.

S., J., *A Brief anatomie of women*, London, 1653.

St Clair, William, and Maassen, Irmgard, eds, *Conduct Literature for Women, 1500–1640,* 6 vols, London: Pickering and Chatto, 2000.

Sala, George Augustus, *Twice Round the Clock or the Hours of the Day and Night in London*, pub. in serial form 1858; pub. in book form 1859; repr. Leicester: Leicester University Press, 1971.

Saviolo, Vincentio, *Vincentio Sauiolo his practice in two bookes. The first intreating of the vse of the rapier and dagger. The second, of honor and honorable quarrels*, London, 1595.

Sheldon, Ann, *Authentic and Interesting Memoirs of Miss Ann Sheldon,* 4 vols, London, 1787–8.

Sitwell, Georgiana, *The Dew, It Lyes on the Wood, Reminiscences of Georgiana Caroline Sitwell,* in *Two Generations,* ed. Osbert Sitwell, London: Macmillan, 1940.

Sitwell, Osbert, *The Scarlet Tree*, London: Macmillan, 1946.

Smith, J.T., *Nollekens and his Times*, London: Turnstile Press, 1949.

Smith, Sydney, *The Works of the Rev. Sydney Smith*, London: Longmans, Green, Reader and Dyer, 1869.

The Spectator, ed., Donald F. Bond, 5 vols, Oxford: Clarendon Press, 1965.

Spencer, Sarah, *Correspondence of Sarah Spencer, Lady Lyttelton 1787–1870,* ed. Hon. Mrs Hugh Wyndham, London: John Murray, 1912.

Stanhope, Philip Dormer, Earl of Chesterfield, *Principles of Politeness, and of knowing the world,* 2nd edn, London, 1775.

Steele, Elizabeth, *The Memoirs of Sophia Baddeley,* 6 vols, London, 1787.

Stern, Elizabeth, 'Peckover and Gallyard, Two Sixteenth-Century Norfolk Tailors', *Costume,* 15 (1981), pp. 13–23.

Stewart, James, *Plocacosmos: or the whole art of hair dressing*, London, 1782.

Stirling, A.M.W., *The Letter-Bag of Lady Elizabeth Spencer Stanhope,* 2 vols, London: John Lane the Bodley Head, 1913.

Strode, William, 'A Pair of Gloves', in *The Poetical Works,* 1907.

Stuart Royal Proclamations, Vol 1: *Royal Proclamations of King James I, 1603–1625,* eds., James Larking and Paul Hughes, Oxford: Oxford University Press, 1973.

Stubbes, Phillip, *The Anatomie of Abuses*, London, 1583.

Taine, Hippolyte, *Taine's Notes on England,* trans. Edward Hyams, London: Thames and Hudson, 1957.

The Tatler, ed., Donald Bond, 3 vols, Oxford: Clarendon Press, 1987.

Taylor, John, *Records of My Life,* 2 vols, London, 1832.

The Taylor's Complete Guide, London, [1796].

Thornton, Alice, *The Autobiography of Mrs. Alice Thornton,* Surtees Society 62, 1875.

Tudor Royal Proclamations, ed., Paul Hughes and James Larkin, 3 vols, New Haven: Yale University Press, 1969.

Udall, John, *The True Remedie against Famine and Warres . . . Preached in the Time of Dearth. 1586,* 2nd edn, n.p., 1588.

Vaughan, Walter, *An essay, philosophical and medical, concerning modern clothing*, 1792.

Vaughan, William, *The golden-groue moralized in three books*, 1600.

Versace, Gianni, *Men without Ties*, New Yord and London: Abbeville, 1997.

Vives, Juan Luis, *A very fruteful and pleasant booke called the instruction of a Christen woman*, trans. Richard Hyrde, London, 1567.

W., A., *The enormous abomination of the hoop-petticoat*, London, 1745.

Warner, William, *Albions England a continued historie of the same kingdome*, 1597.

Well-Willer, *The women's petition against coffee representing to publick consideration the grand inconveniences accruing to their sex from the excessive use of that drying, enfeebling liquor*, London, 1674.

The whim of the day, (for 1793) Containing an entertaining selection of the choisest and most approved songs, 2nd edn, London, 1793.

Whitelocke, Bulstrode, *The Diary of Bulstrode Whitelocke 1605–1675,* ed. Ruth Spalding, Records of Social and Economic History, n.s. 13, British Academy, 1990.

The Whole Art of Dress! or the Road to elegance and fashion . . . by a Cavalry Officer, London, 1830.

The wig. A burlesque-satirical poem, London, 1765.

Wilkes, Wetenhall, *A letter of genteel and moral advice to a young lady*, London, 1744.

Wilson, Harriette, *Harriette Wilson's Memoirs,* selected and ed. Lesley Branch, London: Phoenix, 2003.

Wollenberg, Anne, 'Public Image Limited', *The Guardian* (Saturday 4 October 2008), Features section, pp. 17–18.

Woolley, Hannah, *The Gentlewomans Companion*, London, 1673.

Wraxall, Sir N. William, *Historical Memoirs of My Own Time*, London: Kegan Paul, Trench, Trubner, 1904; orig. pub. 1815, in 2 vols.

PRINTED SECONDARY SOURCES

The Agrarian History of England and Wales, Vol 6, 1750–1850, ed., G. E. Mingay, Cambridge: Cambridge University Press, 1989.

Arnold, Janet, 'Dashing Amazons: The Development of Women's Riding Dress, *c.* 1500–1900', in Amy de la Haye and Elizabeth Wilson, eds, *Defining Dress: Dress as Object, Meaning and Identity*, Manchester: Manchester University Press, 1999, 10–29.

Arnold, Janet, *Patterns of Fashion: The Cut and Construction of Clothes for Men and Women c1560–1620*, London: Macmillan, 1985.

Arnold, Janet, *Patterns of Fashion 4: The Cut and Construction of Linen Shirts, Smocks, Neckwear, Headwear and Accessories for Men and Women, c.1540–1660*, completed with additional material by Jenny Tiramani and Santina M. Levey, London: Macmillan, 2008.

Arnold, Janet, *Queen Elizabeth's Wardrobe Unlock'd*, Leeds: Maney, 1988.

Ashelford, Jane, *The Art of Dress: Clothes and Society 1500–1914*, London: National Trust, 1996.

Ashelford, Jane, *Dress in the Age of Elizabeth I*, London: Batsford, 1988.

Baclawski, Karen, *The Guide to Historic Costume*, London: Batsford, 1995.

Baldwin, Frances, *Sumptuary Legislation and Personal Regulation in England*, Baltimore: Johns Hopkins University Press, 1926.

Barrell, John, *The Spirit of Despotism: Invasions of Privacy in the 1790s*, Oxford: Oxford University Press, 2006.

Belsey, Andrew, and Belsey, Catherine, 'Icons of Divinity: Portraits of Elizabeth I', in Lucy Gent and Nigel Llewellyn, eds, *Renaissance Bodies: The Human Figure in English Culture c.1540–1660*, London: Reaktion, 1990, pp. 11–35.

Bill, Katina, 'Attitudes towards Women's Trousers: Britain in the 1930s', *Journal of Design History*, 6/1 (1993): pp. 45–54.

Blau, Herbert, *Nothing in Itself: Complexions of Fashion*, Bloomington: Indiana University Press, 1999.

Borsay, Peter, 'The Culture of Improvement', in Paul Langford, ed., *The Eighteenth Century*, Oxford: Oxford University Press, 2002, pp. 183–210.

Braggs, Steven, and Harris, Diane, *Sun, Sea and Sand: The Great British Seaside Holiday*, Stroud: Tempest, 2006.

Breitenberg, Mark, *Anxious Masculinity in Early Modern England*, Cambridge: Cambridge University Press, 1996.

Breward, Christopher, *The Culture of Fashion: A New History of Fashionable Dress*, Manchester: Manchester University Press, 1995.

Breward, Christopher, 'The Dandy Laid Bare: Embodying Practices and Fashion for Men', in Stella Bruzzi and Pamela Church Gibson, eds, *Fashion Cultures: Theories, Explorations and Analysis*, London: Routledge, 2000, pp. 221–38.

Breward, Christopher, *The Hidden Consumer: Masculinities, Fashion and City Life 1860–1914*, Manchester: Manchester University Press, 1999.

Brush Kidwell, Claudia, and Steele, Valerie, eds, *Men and Women: Dressing the Part*, Washington, DC: Smithsonian Institute Press, 1989.

Bryer, Robin, *The History of Hair: Fashion and Fantasy Down the Ages*, London: Philip Wilson, 2000.

Bullough, Vern L., and Bullough, Bonnie, *Cross Dressing, Sex, and Gender*, Philadelphia: University of Pennsylvania Press, *c.* 1993.

Byrde, Penelope, 'Dress and Fashion', in J. David Grey, ed., *The Jane Austen Handbook*, London: Athelone Press, 1986.

Byrde, Penelope, *The Male Image: Men's Fashion in England 1300–1970*, London: Batsford, 1979.

Caplan, Jane, *Written on the Body: The Tattoo in European and American History*, London: Reaktion, 2000.

Cardwell, Sarah, 'Darcy's Escape: An Icon in the Making', in Stella Bruzzi and Pamela Church Gibson, eds, *Fashion Cultures: Theories, Explorations and Analysis*, London: Routledge, 2000, pp. 239–44.

Chirelstein, Ellen, 'Emblem and Reckless Presence: The Drury Portrait at Yale', in Lucy Gent, ed., *Albion's Classicism: The Visual Arts in Britain, 1550–1650*, New Haven: Yale University Press, 1995 pp. 287–312.

Chrisman, Kimberly, 'Unhoop the Fair Sex: The Campaign against the Hoop Petticoat in Eighteenth-Century England', *Eighteenth-Century Studies*, 30 (1996), pp. 5–23.

Collins, Jane Lou, *Threads: Gender, Labor, and Power in the Global Apparel Industry*, London: University of Chicago Press, 2003.

Covino, Deborah Caslav, *Amending the Abject Body: Aesthetic Makeovers in Medicine and Culture*, Albany: State University of New York Press, 2004.

Crawford, Patricia, and Mendelson, Sara, 'Sexual Identities in Early Modern England', *Gender and History*, 7 (1995), pp. 363–77.

Cressy, David, 'Gender Trouble and Cross-Dressing in Early Modern England', *Journal of British Studies*, 35 (1996), pp. 438–65.

Cumming, Valerie, *Gloves,* Costume Accessory Series, London: Batsford, 1982.

Cunnington, C. Willett, and Cunnington, Phillis, *Handbook of English Costume in the Eighteenth Century,* rev. edn, London: Faber, 1972.

Cunnington, C. Willett, and Cunnington, Phillis, *Handbook of English Costume in the Nineteenth Century*, London: Faber, 1959.

Cunnington, C. Willet, and Cunnington, Phillis, *The History of Underclothes*, New York: Dover, 1992; orig. pub. London: Michael Joseph, 1951.

Cunnington, Phillis, and Buck, Anne, *Children's Costume in England from the Fourteenth to the End of the Nineteenth Century*, London: Adam and Charles Black, 1965.

Davis, Kathy, *Dubious Equalities and Embodied Differences: Cultural Studies on Cosmetic Surgery*, Lanham: Rowman and Littlefield, 2003.

Dekker, Rudolf, and Pol, Lotte van de, *The Tradition of Female Transvestism in Early Modern Europe*, Basingstoke: Macmillan, 1989.

DeMello, Margo, *Bodies of Inscription: A Cultural History of the Modern Tattoo Community*, Durham: Duke University Press, 2000.

Doran, John, *Habits and Men*, London: Richard Bentley, 1855.

Ellis, Markman, *The Coffee House: A Cultural History*, London: Weidenfeld and Nicolson, 2004.

Elton, G. R., *England under the Tudors,* 3rd edn, London: Routledge, 1991.

Emmison, F. G., *Elizabethan Life I: Disorder*, Chelmsford: Essex County Council, 1970.

Emmison, F. G., *Elizabethan Life II: Morals and Church Courts*, Chelmsford: Essex County Council, 1999.

Entwhistle, Joanne, *The Fashioned Body: Fashion, Dress and Modern Social Theory*, Cambridge: Polity, 2000.

Erickson, Kim, *Drop-Dead Gorgeous: Protecting Yourself from the Hidden Dangers of Cosmetics*, Chicago: Contemporary Books, 2002.

Fairholt, F. W., *Costume in England: A History of Dress to the Eighteenth Century,* ii: *Glossary,* 4th edn, London: George Bell, 1896.

Fashion: A History from the 18th to the 20th Century, 2 vols, *Volume I: 18th and 19th Century, Volume II: 20th Century,* Cologne: Taschen, 2006.

Faust, Beatrice, *Women, Sex, and Pornography*, London: Melbourne House, 1980.

Fenske, Mindy, *Tattoos in American Visual Culture*, Houndmills: Palgrave Macmillan, 2007.

Ferris, Lesley, ed., *Cross the Stage: Controversies on Cross-Dressing*, London: Routledge, 1993.

Festa, Lynn, 'Personal Effects: Wigs and Possessive Individualism in the Long Eighteenth Century', *Eighteenth-Century Life*, 29/2 (2005), pp. 47–90.

Fisher, Will, *Materializing Gender in Early Modern English Literature and Culture*, Cambridge: Cambridge University Press, 2006.

Fletcher, Anthony, *Gender, Sex and Subordination in England 1500–1800*, New Haven: Yale University Press, 1995.

Foyster, Elizabeth A., *Manhood in Early Modern England: Honour, Sex and Marriage*, New York: Longman, 1999.

Fraser, Suzanne, *Cosmetic Surgery, Gender and Culture*, Houndmills: Palgrave Macmillan, 2003.

Freeman, Hadley, *The Meaning of Sunglasses: A Guide to (Almost) All Things Fashionable*, London: Viking, 2008.

Gabriel, Norman R., 'An "Informalizing Spurt" in Clothing Regimes: Court Ballet and the Civilizing Process', in William J. F. Keenan, ed., *Dressed to Impress: Looking the Part*, Oxford: Berg, 2001, pp. 69–84.

Gayne, Mary K., 'Illicit Wigmaking in Eighteenth-Century Paris', *Eighteenth-Century Studies*, 38/1 (2004), pp. 119–37.

Gibbings, Sarah, *The Tie: Trends and Traditions*, London: Studio Editions, 1990.

Gilman, Debra L., *Body Work: Beauty and Self-Image in American Culture*, London: University of California Press, 2002).

Gilman, Sander L., *Making the Body Beautiful: A Cultural History of Aesthetic Surgery*, Princeton: Princeton University Press, 1999.

Goffman, Erving, *The Presentation of Self in Everyday Life* (1959; repr. Harmondsworth: Penguin, 1984).

Graves, Robert, and Hodge, Alan, *The Long Week-End: A Social History of Great Britain 1918–1939*, London: Faber and Faber, 1940.

Gray, Fred, *Designing the Seaside: Architecture, Society and Nature*, London: Reaktion Books, 2006.

Guy, Ali, Green, Eileen, and Banim, Maura, eds, *Through the Wardrobe: Women's Relationships with Their Clothes*, Oxford: Berg, 2001.

Hackspiel-Mikosch, Elisabeth, 'Beauty in Uniform: The Creation of Ideal Masculinity during the Nineteenth Century', in Regine Falkenberg, Adelheid Rasche, and Christine Waidenschlager, eds, *On Men: Masculine Dress Code from Ancient Greeks to Cowboys*, ICOM Costume Committee, 57th Annual Meeting, Berlin, 13–17 June 2005, Berlin: DHM, 2005.

Haiken, Elizabeth, *Venus Envy: A History of Cosmetic Surgery*, Baltimore: Johns Hopkins University Press, 1997.

Hall, Lesley A., *Sex, Gender, and Social Change in Britain since 1880*, Houndmills: Macmillan, 2000.

Hassan, John, *The Seaside, Health and the Environment in England and Wales since 1800*, Aldershot: Ashgate, 2003.

Hellman, Mimi, 'Furniture, Sociability and the Work of Leisure in Eighteenth-Century France', *Eighteenth-Century Studies*, 32 (1999), pp. 414–45.

Hemphill, Dallett, *Bowing to Necessities: A History of Manners in America, 1620–1860*, Oxford: Oxford University Press, 1999.

Heyl, Christoph, 'When They Are Veyl'd on Purpose to Be Seene: The Metamorphosis of the Mask in Seventeenth- and Eighteenth-Century London', in Joanne Entwistle and Elizabeth Wilson, eds, *Body Dressing*, Oxford: Berg, 2001, pp. 121–42.

Hoel, Barbro, 'Contemporary Clothing "Sweatshops", Asian Female Labour and Collective Organisation', in Jackie West, ed., *Work, Women and the Labour Market*, London: Routledge and Kegan Paul, 1982, pp. 80–98.

Hollander, Anne, *Feeding the Eye: Essays*, Berkeley: University of California Press, 1999.

Hollander, Anne, *Sex and Suits*, New York: Alfred A. Knopf, 1994 / New York, Tokyo, and London: Kodansha International, 1995.

Hooper, Wildred, 'The Tudor Sumptuary Laws', *English Historical Review*, 30 (1915), pp. 433–49.

Horwood, Catherine, *Keeping up Appearances: Fashion and Class between the Wars*, Stroud: Sutton, 2005.

Hotchkiss, Valerie R., *Clothes Make the Man: Female Cross-Dressing in Medieval Europe*, New York: Garland, 1996.

Houlbrooke, Ralph, ' "Public" and "Private" in the Funerals of the Later Stuart Gentry: Some Somerset Examples', *Mortality*, 1 (1996), pp. 163–76.

Howard, Skiles, *The Politics of Courtly Dancing in Early Modern England*, Amherst: University of Massachusetts Press, 1998.

Hunt, Alan, *Governance of the Consuming Passions: A History of Sumptuary Law*, London: Macmillan, 1996.

Johnston, Lucy, with Kite, Marion, and Persson, Helen, *Nineteenth-Century Fashion in Detail*, London: V & A Publications, 2005.

Kelly, Ian, *Beau Brummell: The Ultimate Dandy*, London: Hodder and Stoughton, 2005.

Kessler, Marni Reva, *Sheer Presence: The Veil in Manet's Paris*, Minneapolis: University of Minnesota Press, 2006.

Klein, Lawrence E., *Shaftesbury and the Culture of Politeness: Moral Discourse and Cultural Politics in Early Eighteenth-Century England*, Cambridge: Cambridge University Press, 1994.

Kuchta, David, *The Three-Piece Suit and Modern Masculinity: England 1550–1850*, Berkeley: University of California Press, 2002.

Kuczynski, Alex, *Beauty Junkies: Under the Skin of the Cosmetic Surgery Industry*, London: Random House, 2007.

Kunzle, David, *Fashion and Fetishism: A Social History of the Corset, Tight-Lacing and Other Forms of Body-Sculpture in the West*, Totowa: Rowman and Littlefield, 1982.

Latham, Angela J., *Posing a Threat: Flappers, Chorus Girls, and Other Brazen Performers of the American 1920s*, Hanover: University Press of New England for Wesleyan University Press, 2000.

Laurence, Anne, *Women in England 1500–1760: A Social History*, London: Phoenix Press, 1996; orig. pub. 1994.

Lawton, Graham, 'Extreme Surgery', in Linda Welters and Abby Lillethun, eds, *The Fashion Reader*, Oxford: Berg, 2007, pp. 248–9; orig. pub. *New Scientist* (30 October 2004), pp. 54–6.

Lemire, Beverly, *Dress, Culture and Commerce: The English Clothing Trade before the Factory, 1660–1800*, Houndmills: Macmillan, 1997.

Linthicum, M. Channing, *Costume in the Drama of Shakespeare and His Contemporaries*, Oxford: Clarendon Press, 1936.

Mackie, Erin, *Market à la Mode: Fashion, Commodity, and Gender in the Tatler and the Spectator*, Baltimore: Johns Hopkins University Press, 1997.

Mansel, Philip, *Dressed to Rule: Royal and Court Costume from Louis XIV to Elizabeth II*, New Haven: Yale University Press, 2005.

Marshall-Ward, Jackie, 'Mode and Movement', *Costume*, 34 (2000), pp. 123–8.

Martin, Richard, introductory essay in Gianni Versace, *Men without Ties*, New York: Abbeville, 1997, pp. 7–31.

Mifflin, Margot, *Bodies of Subversion: A Secret History of Women and Tattoo,* rev. edn, New York: Juno Books, 2001.

Mikhaila, Ninya, and Malcolm-Davies, Jane, *The Tudor Tailor: Reconstructing Sixteenth-Century Dress,* London: Batsford, 2006.

Mitton, G. E., *Jane Austen and Her Times,* London: Metheun, 1905.

Newton, Stella Mary, *Health, Art and Reason: Dress Reformers of the Nineteenth Century,* London: John Murray, 1974.

Paoletti, Jo, and Kregloh, Carol, 'The Children's Department', in Claudia Brush Kidwell and Valerie Steele, eds, *Men and Women: Dressing the Part,* Washington, DC: Smithsonian Institute Press, 1989, pp. 22–41.

Parissien, Steven, *George IV: The Grand Entertainment,* London: John Murray, 2001.

Peltonen, Markku, *The Duel in Early Modern England: Civility, Politeness and Honour,* Cambridge: Cambridge University Press, 2003.

Phizacklea, Annie, *Unpacking the Fashion Industry: Gender, Racism, and Class in Production,* London: Routledge, 1990.

Picard, Liza, *Dr Johnson's London: Everyday Life in London 1740–1770,* London: Phoenix, 2003; orig. pub. 2000.

Picard, Liza, *Elizabeth's London: Everyday Life in Elizabethan London,* London: Weidenfeld and Nicolson, 2003.

Pointon, Marcia, 'The Case of the Dirty Beau: Symmetry, Disorder and the Politics of Masculinity', in Kathleen Adler and Marcia Pointon, eds, *The Body Imaged: The Human Form and Visual Culture since the Renaissance,* Cambridge: Cambridge University Press, 1993, pp. 175–89.

Pointon, Marcia, *Hanging the Head: Portraiture and Social Formation in Eighteenth-Century England,* New Haven: Yale University Press, 1993.

Polhemus, Ted, *Hot Bodies, Cool Styles: New Techniques in Self-Adornment,* London: Thames and Hudson, 2004.

Powell, Margaret K., and Roach, Joseph, 'Big Hair', *Eighteenth-Century Studies,* 38/1 (2004), pp. 79–99.

The Pursuit of Beauty: Five Centuries of Body Adornment in Britain, text by Clare Gittings, London: National Portrait Gallery, 1997.

Ribeiro, Aileen, *The Art of Dress: Fashion in England and France 1750 to 1820,* Hew Haven: Yale University Press, 1995.

Ribeiro, Aileen, *Dress and Morality,* New York: Holmes and Meier, 1986.

Rosenthal, Angela, 'Raising Hair', *Eighteenth-Century Studies,* 38/1 (2004), pp. 1–16.

Ross, Andrew, ed., *No Sweat: Fashion, Free Trade, and the Rights of Garment Workers,* New York: Verso, 1997.

Shapiro, Michael, *Gender in Play on the Shakespearean Stage: Boy Heroines and Female Pages,* Ann Arbor: University of Michigan Press, 1994.

Shepard, Alexandra, *Meanings of Manhood in Early Modern England,* Oxford: Oxford University Press, 2003.

Showalter, 'Elaine, Fade to Greige', *London Review of Books* (4 January 2001).

Slack, Paul, *The Impact of Plague in Tudor and Stuart England,* London: Routledge and Kegan Paul, 1985.

Spicer, Joaneath, 'The Renaissance Elbow', in Jan Bremmer and Herman Roodenburg, eds, *A Cultural History of Gesture: From Antiquity to the Present Day*, Oxford: Polity, 1991, pp. 84, pp. 84–128.

Steele, Valerie, 'Appearance and Identity', in Claudia Brush Kidwell and Valerie Steele, eds, *Men and Women: Dressing the Part*, Washington, DC: Smithsonian Institute Press, 1989.

Steele, Valerie, *The Corset: A Cultural History*, New York: Yale University Press, 2001.

Styles, John, *The Dress of the People: Everyday Fashion in Eighteenth-Century England*, New Haven: Yale University Press, 2007.

Sullivan, Deborah A., *Cosmetic Surgery: The Cutting Edge of Commercial Medicine in America*, New Brunswick: Rutgers University Press, 2001.

Summers, Leigh, 'Yes, They Did Wear Them: Working-Class Women and Corsetry in the Nineteenth Century', *Costume*, 36 (2002), pp. 65–74.

Sydney, William Connor, *England and the English in the Eighteenth Century*, 2nd edn, 2 vols, London: Ward and Downey, 1892.

Taylor, Lou, *Mourning Dress: A Costume and Social History*, London: George Allen and Unwin, 1983.

Thirsk, Joan, *Economic Policy and Projects: The Development of a Consumer Society in Early Modern England*, Oxford: Clarendon Press, 1978.

Thomas, Nicholas, Cole, Anna, and Douglas, Bronwen, eds, *Tattoo: Bodies, Art and Exchange in the Pacific and the West*, London: Reaktion, 2005.

Thompson, Lynda M., *The 'Scandalous Memoirists': Constantia Phillips, Laetitia Pilkington and the Shame of 'Publick Fame'*, Manchester: Manchester University Press, 2000.

Tiramani, Jenny, 'Janet Arnold and the Globe Wardrobe: Handmade Clothes for Shakespeare's Actors', *Costume*, 34 (2000), pp. 118–22.

Treleaven, Philip, 'How to Fit into Your Clothes: Busts, Waists, Hips and the UK National Sizing Survey', *Significance*, 4/3 (2007), pp. 113–17.

Veblen, Thorstein, *The Theory of the Leisure Class*, New York: Macmillan, 1899; repr. New Brunswick: Transaction Publishers, 1992.

Vicary, Grace Q., 'Visual Art as Social Data: The Renaissance Codpiece', *Cultural Anthropology*, 4 (1989), pp. 3–25.

Vigarello, Georges, *Concepts of Cleanliness: Changing Attitudes in France since the Middle Ages,* trans. Jean Birrell, Cambridge: Cambridge University Press and Paris: Maison des Sciences l'Homme, 1988.

Vigarello, Georges, 'The Upward Training of the Body from the Age of Chivalry to Courtly Civility', in Michel Feher, ed., with Ramona Naddaff and Nadia Tazi, *Fragments for a History of the Human Body*, vol. 2, New York: Zone, 1989, II, pp. 148–99.

Vincent, Susan, *Dressing the Elite: Clothes in Early Modern England*, Oxford: Berg, 2003, pp. 117–52.

Waterhouse, Harriet, 'A Fashionable Confinement: Whaleboned Stays and the Pregnant Woman', *Costume*, 41 (2007), pp. 53–65.

Watson, John K., *The British Seaside: Holidays and Resorts in the Twentieth Century*, Manchester: Manchester University Press, 2000.

Waugh, Norah, *Corsets and Crinolines*, London: Batsford, 1954.

Wear, Andrew, *Knowledge and Practice in English Medicine, 1550–1680*, Cambridge: Cambridge University Press, 2000.

Wheelwright, Julie, *Amazons and Military Maids: Women Who Dressed as Men in the Pursuit of Life, Liberty and Happiness*, London: Pandora, 1989.

Wildeblood, Joan, and Brinson, Peter, *The Polite World: A Guide to English Manners and Deportment from the Thirteenth to the Nineteenth Century*, London: Oxford University Press, 1965.

Wilson, Elizabeth, *Adorned in Dreams: Fashion and Modernity*, London: Virago, 1985.

Wilson, Elizabeth, and Taylor, Lou, *Through the Looking Glass: A History of Dress from 1860 to the Present Day*, London: BBC Books, 1989.

Zuk, Rhoda, 'The Courtesan's Progress in the Late 1790s: Elizabeth Gooch and Margaret Coghlan', *Women's Writing*, 11/3 (2004), pp. 363–76.

INDEX

Bold numbers denote references to illustrations.